PRODUCING AND NEGOTIATING N[

Precarious Legal Status in Canada

Edited by Luin Goldring and Patricia Landolt

Most research on non-citizens in Canada focuses on immigrants await-ing citizenship or on specific categories of temporary workers. *Produc-ing and Negotiating Non-citizenship* goes beyond this limited scope in that it considers a wide range of people whose pathway to citizenship is uncertain or non-existent. These categories include migrant work-ers, students, refugee claimants, and people with expired permits, all of whom have limited formal rights to employment, housing, education, and health services.

The contributors to this volume present theoretically informed em-pirical studies of the regulatory, institutional, discursive, and practi-cal terms under which precarious-status non-citizens – those without permanent residence – enter and remain in Canada. They consider the historical, social, and legal production of non-citizens' precarious sta-tus in Canada, as well as everyday experiences among various migrant groups including, youth, refugee claimants, and agricultural workers. This timely volume contributes to a rethinking of non-citizenship in its multiple forms, and of the institutional policies and practices that mi-grants encounter and negotiate.

LUIN GOLDRING is an associate professor in the Department of Sociology at York University.

PATRICIA LANDOLT is an associate professor in the Department of Sociol-ogy at the University of Toronto, Scarborough.

Producing and Negotiating Non-citizenship

Precarious Legal Status in Canada

EDITED BY LUIN GOLDRING AND
PATRICIA LANDOLT

UNIVERSITY OF TORONTO PRESS
Toronto Buffalo London

© University of Toronto Press 2013
   Toronto Buffalo London
   www.utppublishing.com
   Printed in Canada

   ISBN 978-1-4426-4587-5 (cloth)
   ISBN 978-1-4426-1408-6 (paper)

Printed on acid-free, 100% post-consumer recycled paper with vegetable-based inks.

Library and Archives Canada Cataloguing in Publication

Producing and negotiating non-citizenship : precarious legal status in Canada / edited by Luin Goldring and Patricia Landolt.

Includes bibliographical references and index.
ISBN 978-1-4426-4587-5 (bound). – ISBN 978-1-4426-1408-6 (pbk.)

1. Aliens – Canada.   2. Aliens – Canada – Social conditions.   3. Canada – Emigration and immigration – Government policy.   I. Goldring, Luin.   II. Landolt, Patricia.

FC104.P75 2012   323.3'2910971   C2012-907225-7

This book has been published with the help of a grant from the Canadian Federation for the Humanities and Social Sciences, through the Aid to Scholarly Publications Program, using funds provided by the Social Sciences and Humanities Research Council of Canada.

University of Toronto Press acknowledges the financial assistance to its publishing program of the Canada Council for the Arts and the Ontario Arts Council.

ONTARIO ARTS COUNCIL
CONSEIL DES ARTS DE L'ONTARIO
50 YEARS OF ONTARIO GOVERNMENT SUPPORT OF THE ARTS
50 ANS DE SOUTIEN DU GOUVERNEMENT DE L'ONTARIO AUX ARTS

Canada Council   Conseil des Arts
for the Arts   du Canada

University of Toronto Press acknowledges the financial support for its publishing activities of the Government of Canada through the Canada Book Fund.

Contents

Figures

Tables

Acknowledgments

Working on an edited volume takes time, usually more than anticipated. Over this time, we have accumulated a growing list of people
and institutions whose support and contributions deserve thanks and
recognition. We would like to do that by identifying several of the intersecting collaborations upon which this volume builds.

One collaboration involves a working group we eventually named
the Research Alliance on Precarious Status (RAPS). RAPS was envis-
aged as a space where faculty, students, researchers in community and
service-delivery organizations, union organizers, and community activists could meet regularly to discuss various kinds of work in progress on the general topic of precarious status and migrant illegality in
Canada. The chapters assembled here were developed in the context
of the working group's meetings, which began in September 2008 and
continued every six to eight weeks, over the course of two years.

A second collaboration involves conceptualizing the concept of precarious status, which was presented in an article by Luin Goldring,
Carolina Berinstein, and Judith Bernhard published in *Citizenship Studies* in 2009.

Recognizing the specificity of the institutional production of precarious status in Canada, RAPS sought to develop empirical studies
informed by discussions of citizenship, non-citizenship, temporary migration policies, migrant illegality, and social movements. The forum
offered a stimulating space for lively and supportive dialogue on these
issues. Over the period that we met, we exchanged valuable feedback;
the comments of Cynthia Wright, Salimah Valiani, Patricia Landolt, and
Rupaleem Bhuyan stand out. Salimah Valiani and Katharine Brasch
were not always living in Toronto, yet travelled to maintain their active

involvement in our discussions. Janet McLaughlin and Jenna Hennebry also joined many of our discussions. Other people whose work does not appear in this volume made valuable contributions to RAPS discussions; these include Soheila Pashang, Christine Carrasco, Maya Buhllar, and Tracy Smith-Carrier. Others, such as Alan Li and Craig Fortier, were unable to join the discussions but contributed to the volume. As editors, we are grateful to all of the RAPS participants and volume contributors.

Third, the volume is part of a long-standing collaboration between the editors. Luin Goldring and Patricia Landolt have developed and worked on several research projects together, including a study of Latin American community organizing and political incorporation in Toronto, and a project entitled Immigrants and Precarious Employment in the Greater Toronto Area. In connection to the latter project, in 2009 we organized a workshop with other colleagues and with support from York University's Fiftieth Anniversary Fund, entitled "Migration, Work and Citizenship: Toward Decent Work and Secure Citizenship," where we presented our early work on the determinants of precarious work. That workshop confirmed the importance of pursuing the topic of precarious status in Canada.

We organized a later workshop called "Producing and Negotiating Precarious Migratory Status in Canada" (held in September 2010 at York University) to bring the volume contributors together with invited commentators who offered insightful comments on early drafts of the chapters. We are grateful to Vappu Tyyskä, Abigail Bakan, Tanya Basok, Anneke Rummens, Audrey Macklin, Cara Zwibel, Anna Korteweg, and Nancy Mandell for their valuable and detailed comments on their assigned chapters and for contributing to the overall discussion.

Two anonymous reviewers provided comments on the volume as a whole. They offered important insights, helped us sharpen our own arguments, and offered useful directions for working with contributors on revisions. Adrie Naylor and Heather Brady copy-edited the first draft of the volume, and Jessica Rayne reviewed the bibliography. We also acknowledge Linn Clark's incisive editorial assistance in the final preparation of the manuscript.

Each of us also has specific individual and institutional acknowledgments. Luin is glad that Patricia was willing to add yet another project to our collaborative "to-do" list. Working on this volume delayed other work on our agenda but opened space for fruitful conceptual discussions on non-citizenship. As a domain leader for CERIS – The Ontario Metropolis Centre, Luin had institutional backing to initiate the call for the working group. She is grateful to Valerie Preston, York's CERIS director, and Bethany Osborne, who was then the CERIS coordinator. Luz Maria Vazquez coordinated the working group meetings and expertly organized our workshop. York University's Centre for Research on Latin America and the Caribbean (CERLAC) has been a base for Luin's work and provided logistical support for the workshop "Migration, Work and Citizenship." Luin acknowledges the collegiality of her CERLAC colleagues and in particular thanks Marshall Beck, CERLAC's coordinator, for cheerful and efficient assistance.

Patricia is grateful to Luin, who confidently enlisted her to co-edit the volume at a time when institutional instability made her academic future look quite bleak. In the Department of Sociology at the University of Toronto, she thanks Jeffrey Reitz, Monica Boyd, and Michal Bodemann for their friendship. While their approaches to the study of international migration differ considerably from hers, their enthusiasm for distinctive and different kinds of research is a steady source of encouragement.

We are both grateful to the Cities Centre at the University of Toronto. Two people there deserve particular thanks: Grace Ramirez and Pat Doherty have lent many kinds of support over the years to Patricia Landolt's research and to our collaborative work. We are grateful for their collegiality, assistance, and cheer.

We also wish to acknowledge our editor at the University of Toronto Press. Douglas Hildebrand was enthusiastic about this book project from the beginning. His support throughout the process is gratefully acknowledged.

Contributors

Judith K. Bernhard is a professor in the Faculty of Community Services at Ryerson University. Her research program has focused on the impact of migration on family functioning.

Rupaleem Bhuyan is an assistant professor at the Factor-Inwentash Faculty of Social Work, University of Toronto. She has campaigned for women's rights and immigrant rights in the United States and Canada, as a women's advocate, community educator, and community-based researcher. Her current work involves participatory action research with social service providers and women from Mexico and Central America who have precarious immigration status in Canada with a focus on how their lives and migration(s) have been shaped by gendered forms of violence.

Katherine Brasch approaches the study of migration through a combination of anthropological and sociological theory, using an ethnographic approach to understand motivations and experiences of Brazilian migrants in Canada. A contract professor at universities across southern Ontario, she has held visiting scholar positions with the R.F. Harney Program in Ethnic, Immigration and Pluralism Studies and at the University of Ottawa as the Bank of Montreal Visiting Scholar in Women's Studies.

Craig Fortier is a Toronto-based researcher and organizer in Indigenous sovereignty, anti-poverty, and migrant justice struggles. He is a PhD student in sociology at York University, where he researches the intersections of decolonization theory and anarchist/autonomist practice in contemporary social movements.

Luin Goldring is an associate professor of sociology at York University. Her research is informed by interests in the precarization of citizenship and legal status, substantive citizenship, immigrant politics, and transnational engagements in the context of trans-boundary migrations. She is currently involved in research on immigrants and precarious work, and poverty and employment precarity. Recent publications address the intersections of precarious legal status and precarious work, the institutional production of precarious migratory status, Latin American community organizing in Toronto, and methodological challenges in transnational studies.

Jenna Hennebry is an associate professor in communication studies, and the Associate Director of the International Migration Research Centre (IMRC) at Wilfrid Laurier University. Her research focuses on international migration and mobility, with a specialization in labour migration in Canada and Spain. She has experience in academic, public policy, and applied research domains. Hennebry's research includes comparative studies of migration policy and foreign worker programs, migrant rights and health, the formation of migration industries, and non-state migration mediation.

Priya Kissoon is a lecturer in human geography at the University of the West Indies, St Augustine Campus, Trinidad. She comes to UWI from the University of Toronto, where she was a lecturer in urban geography. Dr Kissoon completed postdoctoral work at the University of British Columbia, and her doctorate at King's College London. Her areas of expertise are forced migration and refugee integration, and housing and homelessness.

Patricia Landolt is an associate professor of sociology at the University of Toronto at Scarborough and research associate at the Cities Centre. Her research examines the institutional production and reproduction of systems of social exclusion and inequality associated with global migrations. Areas of focus include labour market incorporation and immigrant politics and community organizing. She is currently doing research on precarious legal status migrants and the Toronto public school system.

Alan Li is a primary care physician at Regent Park Community Health Centre, which serves marginalized communities including newcomers, people living with HIV/AIDS (PHA), and people without health care coverage. In addition, Alan is a co-founder of the Committee for Accessible AIDS Treatment (CAAT), a coalition dedicated to improving service access for marginalized PHAs. Alan also works as a community research scholar at the Ontario HIV Treatment Network and has led various studies on issues affecting newcomer and racialized communities.

Janet McLaughlin is an assistant professor of health studies at Wilfrid Laurier University, and a research associate with the International Migration Research Centre (IMRC), housed in the Balsillie School of International Affairs. A social-cultural and medical anthropologist, her research explores issues of health, human rights, development, food systems, labour, citizenship, and transnational migration, with a particular focus on Latin American and Caribbean migrant farmworkers in Canada.

Delphine Nakache teaches and researches in the areas of public international law and migration and refugee law. Her current research focuses on the protection of migrant workers admitted in Canada under the general Temporary Foreign Worker Program (TFWP), and on opportunities for permanent residency from within Canada for these workers.

Samia Saad has worked as a therapist/counsellor and program coordinator at a social agency called The Lighthouse for the last 22 years. Her focus is primarily with Spanish-speaking refugees, newcomers, and non-status immigrants. Ms Saad has two master's degrees in counselling/therapy and interdisciplinary studies. In 2011 she defended her thesis "The Psychosocial Impact of Falling Out of Status" at York University. She has done advocacy work with the Rights of Non-Status Women Network and the Status Now Campaign.

Salimah Valiani is associate researcher with the Centre for the Study of Education and Work at the University of Toronto. Along with academic research in the areas of labour migration and world historical political economy, she conducts economic policy research in the trade union movement. She has worked with unions and nongovernmental organizations in Canada, the Philippines, Indonesia, India, and South Africa. Her research monograph, *Rethinking Unequal Exchange: The Global Integration of Nursing Labour Markets* was published in March 2012 by the University of Toronto Press.

Francisco J. Villegas is a doctoral student in the Department of Sociology and Equity Studies in Education at the Ontario Institute for Studies in Education, University of Toronto. His research focuses on immigration, race, and schooling. He received his MA in Mexican American Studies from San Jose State University.

Paloma E. Villegas received her PhD from the Department of Sociology and Equity Studies in Education at the Ontario Institute for Studies in Education/University of Toronto (OISE/UT). She has a masters degree in women's studies from San Francisco State University and a bachelors degree in molecular cell biology from UC Berkeley. Her dissertation, entitled "Assembling and (Re)Making Migrant Illegalization: Mexican Migrants with Precarious Status in Toronto, Canada," analyses the transitional, multiscalar, and discursive production of migrant illegalization in relation to Mexican nationals.

Cynthia Wright teaches in the School of Women's Studies, and the Departments of History and Geography at York University. Her diverse research interests include the social and historical production of migrant "illegality"; the origins of immigration controls and resistance to controls; colonialism and imperialism; Cuba; critical gender, race and sexuality studies; and social movements.

Julie Young recently completed a doctorate in geography at York University in Toronto. She has worked as a researcher in academic, public sector, and non-profit settings. Her dissertation, "Border City of Refuge: Refugee Advocacy, the Politics of Mobility, and the Reframing of the Windsor-Detroit Border," focused on collaborative advocacy across the Canada-US border in response to the Central American refugee "crisis" of the late 1980s.

PRODUCING AND NEGOTIATING NON-CITIZENSHIP

Precarious Legal Status in Canada

1 The Conditionality of Legal Status and Rights: Conceptualizing Precarious Non-citizenship in Canada

LUIN GOLDRING AND PATRICIA LANDOLT

State-defined legal status categories establish configurations of rights for people occupying these categories; this holds for political rights as well as civil, employment, and social rights. Access to public services is also based on legal status. Thus, status and rights have far-reaching effects on people's lives. Citizenship status does not necessarily correspond to citizenship practice, nor does citizenship resolve inequality – many citizens live with discrimination and poverty. However, non-citizenship, by definition, is associated with limits in terms of voice, membership, and rights in a political community, and with social exclusion and vulnerability. Despite the development of international human rights protocols, non-citizens worldwide are vulnerable precisely because of their legal status situation (Weissbrodt & Meili, 2009; Bloom & Feldman, 2011).

This collection focuses on the regulatory, institutional, discursive, and practical terms under which precarious status non-citizens – those without permanent residence – enter and remain in Canada.[1] Precarious legal status refers to authorized and unauthorized forms of non-citizenship that are institutionally produced and share a precarity rooted in the conditionality of presence and access (Goldring, 2010; Goldring, Berinstein, & Bernhard, 2009). Migrant trajectories of precarious legal status are non-linear, often lengthy, and can involve moments of irregularization, regularization, and illegalization.

Conditionality has two dimensions. It refers to the insecurity and contingency surrounding an individual's ongoing presence, and includes the formal and practical conditions that must be met in order to retain some form of legal status and/or remain present in a jurisdiction.

It also refers to the uncertainty of access: to the multi-actor negotiations required to secure resources or public goods, whether or not these are formally defined as a right of the precarious non-citizen (cf. Delgado, 1993; Lister, 1997; Stasiulis & Bakan, 2005). For people living with different forms of precarious non-citizenship, the terms of presence and access are largely beyond their control. Meeting the conditions necessary to remain present, retain status or secure rights calls for ongoing work and is based on unequal relations with a range of social actors (employers, family and friends, medical practitioners, school officials, co-workers, etc.). The conditionality of presence and access points to non-citizenship as an assemblage of legal status in which the boundaries between citizenship and non-citizenship can be contested, breached, negotiated, and altered by different combinations of actors, across a variety of institutional sites and at different scales (cf. Goldring, 2010; Sassen, 2006; Villegas, 2012; Villegas and Landolt, 2010).

Contributors to this volume analyse the production and experiences of various forms of non-citizen precarious status, the complex relationships between them, and the multi-level facets of negotiation and at times contestation of the boundaries and content of non-citizen precarious status. We use "chutes and ladders"[2] to characterize and conceptually frame trajectories and negotiations within and across legal status categories. Together, the authors reveal the dynamic policy-mediated landscape that sets the broad conditions for the policy dimension of the chutes and ladders, as well as the institutionally rooted actors and processes that propel people up ladders to secure status, down chutes to "illegality,"[3] or along horizontal bridges to other forms of precarious status. The authors also address institutional challenges that emerge when conducting research with or about people with precarious legal status. Most of the chapters focus on contemporary issues, but historical shifts in the construction and contestation of non-citizenship are also examined. Together, the authors provide a rich theoretical and empirical analysis that offers a complex portrayal of precarious non-citizenship in Canada. While the jurisdictional referent for this volume is Canada, trends in the country's immigration policy that favour temporary entry over permanent settlement make the book relevant to readers in other settings.

***

Non-citizenship, like citizenship, is not a homogeneous category of membership and social relations (Andrijasevic, 2010; Bosniak, 2000b).

At the national level, non-citizenship is usually comprised of several legal status categories, depending on the jurisdiction, including the relatively secure status of permanent residence. The non-citizen category may include native-born residents without citizenship (e.g., members of minority groups in countries with *ius sanguini*, or indigenous peoples lacking full citizenship or similar recognition). More often it consists of foreign-born individuals with temporary authorization to work and/or reside: temporary workers, refugees and people seeking asylum, students, and visitors, as well as stateless people, unauthorized entrants, and im/migrants who may have entered through legal channels but have been "illegalized" (Weissbrodt & Meili, 2009).

Linda Bosniak (2006) and other scholars (Bakan & Stasiulis, 1997; Ngai, 2004; Stasiulis & Bakan, 2005) have convincingly argued that the boundaries between citizenship and non-citizenship are not fixed in time or space, and that these boundaries are permeable and potentially blurry. Boundaries may change over time, bringing additional people into the realm of citizenship (e.g., women and racialized groups). People may cross boundaries through naturalization, regularization, and irregularization. Citizens may behave as non-citizens, and non-citizens may in some situations resemble citizens (Bosniak, 2000b, 2006; Sassen, 2006). For example, citizens do not uniformly exercise political rights: voter turnout is uneven, as is participation in parties, unions, and related organizations. Conversely, non-citizens with various forms of precarious status, including no status, may participate in community mobilizations and organizations, often with citizens – even if they cannot vote (Delgado, 1993; Pulido, 2007; Sassen, 2006).

Despite awareness about these issues, non-citizenship remains relatively under-theorized compared with citizenship, partly because non-citizenship's difference is taken for granted, and because of how boundaries and categories are understood. Non-citizenship is usually conceptualized as a residual category of citizenship, and different categories of non-citizenship are conceptualized independently. Researchers have investigated the production of particular non-citizen categories and the people in these categories, but have not developed a clear framework for identifying coherence and connections among the diverse forms of non-citizenship, and between these and citizenship. When citizenship and non-citizenship are examined together, binary models prevail and assume a sharp boundary between the categories of citizen and non-citizen. These boundaries may be crossed through naturalization, but they remain fairly rigid and otherwise impermeable. Insufficient attention has been paid to how various actors produce, uphold, contest, breach, and negotiate the boundaries between citizenship and non-citizenship, and between particular categories of non-citizenship.[4]

Clarifying the complexities of non-citizenship is important to (1) highlight the heterogeneity of, and institutional connections between, the forms of non-citizen precarious status, and between these and citizenship; (2) empirically analyse the making, negotiation, and contestation of boundaries around these diverse forms of non-citizenship; (3) reconceptualize the production, negotiation, and contestation of forms of non-citizen precarious status; and (4) consider the long-term effects of precarious status trajectories and negotiations for a range of social actors and institutions. These are the immediate goals of this volume. More broadly, the book is intended to contribute to public and academic debates about transformations in rights and citizenship and the implications of these changes. The next section outlines trends that contextualize the book. This is followed by a brief review of the research and theoretical debates that we used to develop a framework for our analyses of precarious legal status and the concept of conditionality. The final section lays out the volume's organization.

Non-citizenship in an Era of Global Migration

Changes in non-citizenship and citizenship are embedded in what Castles and Miller (2009) dubbed "the age of migration." Three trends are worth highlighting, as they offer reasons for paying attention to non-citizen precarious status. First is the seemingly unprecedented scope of contemporary migrations, which effectively creates and recreates non-citizenship. Certainly the numbers are sobering: according to the United Nations, in 2010 almost 214 million individuals lived outside their country of birth (United Nations, 2008). However, it is difficult to estimate how many people live without citizenship and without permanent residence. Relevant legal status categories include temporary workers, refugees, asylum refugees, international students, and irregular or undocumented migrants. Tourists could also be included. Global figures for formally designated temporary workers are problematic because they are collected on a country-by-country basis, usually among migrant-importing countries, and using different definitions. Variable visa and contract regulations and informal arrangements, such as those made through unregulated labour contractors and recruiters, may complicate the reliability of such data. In 2010, 15.4 million people were refugees or living in refugee-like situations (UNHCR, 2011a). International student numbers are also significant. According to UNESCO, in 2007 there were over 2.8 million tertiary mobile students[5] worldwide, a figure that was 53 percent higher than in 1999 (UNESCO 2009, p. 36). Estimates of the unauthorized migrant population involve considerable measurement challenges and error, but an estimate of the undocumented population in 2010 in the United States alone was 11.2 million (Passel & Cohn, 2011). The Clandestino Project (2009) estimated that 1.9 to 3.8 million irregular foreign residents were living in the EU's 27 member states in 2008. Clearly, it is difficult to obtain reliable figures to construct a comprehensive estimate of the total number of non-citizens worldwide or in a particular region.

In the case of Canada, estimating the total number of non-citizens poses serious challenges. Administrative data from Citizenship and Immigration Canada (CIC) on temporary residents provide annual information on entries and those still present on 1 December, but no estimate of the potential overlap between these categories.[6] Those still present in a given year may have entered in a previous year, and those entering in a given year may have left by 1 December (which would hold for most seasonal workers). Adding the number of entries to the number still present could in theory overestimate the total number of temporary residents, but the number of those still present in December excludes seasonal workers who may have spent four to eight months of the year in Canada (cf. Bhuyan, 2012, p. 4).

In spite of these challenges, the administrative data present useful information on trends in temporary migration. The number of temporary workers entering Canada increased from 63,441 in 1983 to 112,295 in 1990 (CIC, 2008b) and to 182,276 in 2010 (CIC, 2011a). The number of temporary workers still present was 34,055 in 1983 (CIC, 2008b) and consistently remained at around 40,000 below the number of entries for nearly two decades. However, the gap began to close in the early 2000s, and in 2006 the number of temporary workers still present overtook the number of entries by about 20,000. In 2010, 250,406 temporary workers were still present in December (CIC, 2011a). Adding the number of temporary entries and those still present in 2010 yields a total of 432,684 people with temporary worker status, but does not tell us how many were in fact present for most of the year. According to the UNHCR, 169,434 refugees and 61,170 asylum seekers were in Canada in 2010 (UNHCR, 2011a), though the government figure for the humanitarian population in that year was 134,894 people (CIC, 2011a). Foreign students are another piece of the puzzle: in 2010, Canada had 278,146 foreign students still present, and 96,157 entries that year (CIC, 2011a). The 2010 grand total of temporary resident entries in all categories was 383,929, and the total number still present in all categories reached 660,801. The latter probably underestimates the number of temporary residents present for most of the year, while the sum of the two figures, 981,137 people, may be an overestimate (CIC, 2011a).[7] If administrative data offer a sense of the authorized temporary population, determining the size of the unauthorized population poses even more serious challenges as there are no systematic estimates. The size of the "illegal" migrant population in Canada was estimated at 200,000–500,000 in 2006 (Jiménez 2006). This range has undoubtedly increased, but no new estimates are available.

A second trend is the proliferation of forms of "temporary" legality in the Global North as countries resurrect temporary worker programs and revamp visa and entry criteria. The increase in temporary authorized migration corresponds to efforts to manage migration in general and exert stricter controls on permanent immigration (Martin, 2006). Although Canada is known for its relatively high naturalization rates (Bloemraad, 2006), avenues of permanent immigration have narrowed, refugee admissions have declined, and the backlog of refugee claimants has grown dramatically (Collacott, 2010; Macklin, 2005; UNHCR, 2011b). There has also been a dramatic expansion of its temporary worker programs (Nakache & Kinoshita, 2010), so that in 2008 temporary admissions exceeded permanent entries (Alboim, 2009; Goldring, Hennebry, & Preibisch, 2009).[8]

Regulations about the conditions for, and employment of, temporary workers in Canada are increasingly uneven rather than following a standardized national-level framework (Nakache, in this volume). Tensions surround the federal government's transfer of certain aspects of national immigration policy (selection, employment regulations, and monitoring) to the provinces and private citizens. Temporary authorization increasingly acts as a trial or probationary period to assess people's suitability for longer-term employment and settlement, particularly for those designated as skilled workers. In some provinces, programs such as the Provincial Nominee Program and Canadian Experience Class offer a pathway to permanent status for some temporary workers who meet specific criteria ("skill" level,[9] education, and health) but not others (most workers in "unskilled" or "low-skilled" categories, and tourists) (Nakache, in this volume; Valiani, in this volume). For the state, temporary entrance categories offer a solution to the challenges of limiting citizenship and controlling migration. These policies and related processes contribute to increases in the number of individuals with precarious status, both authorized and unauthorized (Goldring, Berinstein, & Bernhard, 2009; Sharma, 2006).

The third trend is the reconfiguration of the boundaries and locations of citizenship and non-citizenship. Worldwide security concerns have resulted in militarized borders, high fences, and increasingly sophisticated surveillance along border zones (Andrijasevic, 2010; Bloch & Schuster, 2005; M.L. Cook, 2009; Mountz, 2009; Sylvan & Chetail, 2007–2011). Detention and removal have become normalized instruments in the project of immigration and border control. Migrant criminalization is intimately connected to detention and removal efforts, as it lays the groundwork for normalizing such practices (de Genova & Peutz, 2010; Rajaram & Grundy-Warr, 2004).[10] Im/migration and transit policies and politics thus reconfigure the framework of non-citizenship, and by logical extension narrow the doorways into and reduce the perimeter of citizenship.

The location, dispersion, and scale of citizenship practice is also shifting, as people engage with the affairs of their "home" communities, states, and diasporas, as well as institutional actors in their new residence (Bakker, 2011; Cheran, 2007; Fox, 2005; Landolt & Goldring, 2010; Sherrell & Hyndman, 2006). The monetary remittances of migrants (overseas citizens) are applauded by the "home" state (Hernández & Coutin, 2006). While access to citizenship for non-citizens in the Global North is narrowing, many emigrant-producing countries are expanding the rights and geography of citizenship and celebrating the multiple memberships of their nationals abroad (Bose, 2007; Fitzgerald, 2006; Itzigsohn, 2000).

To summarize, contemporary global migration patterns and migration and citizenship policies are reproducing non-citizenship, forms of temporary and conditional non-citizenship are proliferating, and avenues for citizenship in destination countries are narrowing at the same time that many people maintain formal and practical membership across borders. In Canada, these changes have led to a dramatic reorientation in the country's immigration and nation-building framework. The reduction of avenues to settlement and citizenship, the expansion of temporary migration, and the porous boundaries between categories and trajectories result in a complex, multi-entry and multi-directional set of legal status trajectories and negotiations that we refer to as the *chutes-and-ladders* model of legal status dynamics.[11] As long as these trends continue, and as long as national citizenship remains a relevant rights-mediating institution, non-citizenship will remain a widespread and relevant lived experience and institutionalized social location for a significant and growing number of people worldwide. This provides a practical and social justice rationale for analysing non-citizenship. We now turn to the conceptual arguments that inform our approach to the conditionality of non-citizen precarious status.

The Challenges of Conceptualizing Non-citizenship and "Illegality"

A post-Marshallian revival in the study of citizenship has addressed global transformations affecting legal status, membership, rights, and political community.[12] Modifiers such as *post-national, multi-level, multi-local, transnational, post-colonial,* and *neoliberal* have been attached to the term *citizenship* to capture transformations in one or more dimensions of citizenship and/or in relation to its key institutional location and arbiter, the nation-state (Kivisto & Faist, 2007; Sassen, 2006). Discussions about non-citizenship (or alienage; Bosniak, 2006) and migrant "illegality" (de Genova, 2002) emerged at the edges of these debates but are now gaining centrality. Non-citizenship is an integral but often residual component of most conceptions of citizenship, which are based on a model of political community that distinguishes those with membership, status, and rights from those without them. These conceptions hold whether citizenship is defined as a relational membership in a national community or state, or as membership and practice in other political communities or social groups, whether sub- or supra-national (Lister, 1997; Sassen, 2004). Citizenship, whatever the definition, rests on the idea of the non-citizen "other" to give it meaning (Bosniak, 2006; Gutiérrez, 2007).

We argue that non-citizenship and "illegality" must be investigated through a conceptual lens that connects citizenship with the institutional production of precarious and conditional legalities as well as illegality. This involves two conceptual steps: first, conceptualizing the construction of social boundaries related to citizenship and non-citizenship as multiple rather than binary; and second, approaching legal status boundaries from a perspective that highlights the multi-actor work that goes into producing, contesting, bridging, breaching, and negotiating these boundaries and associated rights (Brettell, 2005; de Genova 2005; Giddens, 1984; Stasiulis & Bakan, 2005).

North American scholarship on non-citizenship has been dominated by work on the undocumented.[13] This scholarship established the basis for conceptualizing legal status in binary terms, with individuals occupying a sequence of dichotomous and mutually exclusive categories. Migrants are classified as non-citizens in opposition to citizens, then as authorized or unauthorized, legal or "illegal." Categories of legal status and their boundaries are usually assumed to be given and fixed. Rules for inclusion in a category may change over time through shifts in state policies. Boundary crossing is assumed to take place mainly as individuals move from one category to another through administrative procedures (naturalization), state programs and regulatory shifts (regularization or changes in citizenship rules that open citizenship to new categories of people), or criminalization (illegalization).

Contemporary work on non-citizenship reframes earlier research on "the undocumented," inviting immigration scholars and citizenship theorists to work together (Bosniak, 2006). These analyses revolve around non-citizenship and non-citizens, expanding on important areas of research: the historical and uneven construction of citizen subjects (Ngai, 2004) and the role of institutional gatekeepers in the process of immigrant incorporation (Iacovetta, 2006; Mar, 2010); the history of the passport and other forms of state-based identification in the context of nation-building and sovereignty (Mongia, 1999; Torpey, 2000); the securitization and enforcement of national borders (Heyman & Cunningham, 2004; A. Pratt, 2005); the production and enforcement of borders internal to and beyond the national (M.L. Cook, 2009; Mountz, 2009); the politics of detention and deportation (de Genova & Peutz, 2010; Peutz, 2006); migrant rights mobilization, organizing, and advocacy (Basok, 2009; Basok, Ilcan, & Noonan, 2006; Chun, 2009; M.L. Cook, 2010); migrant irregularization and the production of illegality (Calavita, 1998; Coutin, 2005; Dauvergne, 2008; de Genova, 2002); non-binary approaches to legal status (Menjívar, 2006); and specific categories of non-citizens, such as migrant workers, and the new generation of temporary worker programs (Bakan & Stasiulis, 1997; Hennebry & Preibisch, 2010b; Nakache & Kinoshita, 2010; Preibisch, 2010; Ruhs, 2006; Sharma, 2006).

Within this body of scholarship, several branches of literature are particularly relevant to analyses of how boundaries between categories are conceptualized and crossed. One branch considers migrant agency in crossing legal status boundaries (Coutin, 2000; Hagan, 1994). A second highlights the substantive citizenship practices (or political and civic engagement) of non-citizen migrants in their countries of origin and destination, revealing inconsistencies in the presumably homogenous spaces of citizenship *and* non-citizenship (Delgado, 1993; Fox, 2005; Smith & Bakker, 2008; Wright, 2006; Zlolniski, 2008). A third and related branch emphasizes migrant agency in negotiating the constraints imposed by non-citizenship or lack of authorized status (Chavez, 1991; Coutin, 2000; Hondagneu-Sotelo, 1994; Vasta, 2011; Zlolniski, 2006). Together, this body of scholarship portrays undocumented migrants as social and political actors able to effect change through community organizing, activism, and sometimes moving from undocumented to documented status. This work challenges assumptions about what it means to be undocumented, though it shows that some of the strategies used by the undocumented have limited long-term positive effects. However, the focus is on a set of actors within a state-defined category; the boundary between documented and undocumented may be crossed and encompasses diverse actors and practices, but it remains fixed.

Other researchers have worked to understand legal status in non-binary terms. Menjívar's (2006) elaboration of "liminal" legality and Mountz et al.'s (2002) analysis of the "limbo" or "in-between" status of Central Americans with Temporary Protected Status are key examples. These researchers present a tri-partite model of legal status, with a third space of "temporary legality" situated between migrant legality and illegality. Others have highlighted boundary construction through law and the practices of a widening set of actors, including advocacy by community organizations (Coutin, 1998, 2000). These researchers recognize multi-directional boundary-crossing movement, including movement towards greater security. However, their models account for the social and legal production of an additional status category, so that a dichotomous model is replaced with a tripartite one. Legal status boundaries remain clearly defined, mutually exclusive, and fairly rigid.

At the heart of non-binary approaches to non-citizenship is a shift in orientation to emphasize social and institutional processes of boundary making. Conceptual and empirical work on migrant irregularization and "illegality" reveals how state laws, policies, and social institutions work to produce migrant illegality (Calavita, 1998; Dauvergne, 2008; de Genova, 2002; Ngai, 2004). In the United States, the criminalization of undocumented migrants and border securitization have institutionalized and normalized the production and reproduction of migrant illegality as a socially sanctioned process. Focusing on Spain in the 1990s, Calavita (1998) demonstrated how the regulations governing temporary work permits for undocumented entrants, temporary workers, and asylum seekers established a patchwork of contradictory rules that institutionalized migrant irregularization and illegalization for both authorized and unauthorized entrants (cf. Vicente, 2000). In Canada, Goldring and her colleagues mapped the many different ways in which migrants are irregularized or fall out of status through the refugee determination system and by failing to meet administrative and visa requirements (Goldring & Berinstein, 2003; Goldring, Berinstein, & Bernhard, 2009). This echoes the pathways to migrant "illegality" in other jurisdictions, including the United Kingdom and Italy (Andrijasevic, 2010; Black et al., 2006; Dauvergne, 2008).

Researchers are also expanding work on migrant illegality in several important directions. One is a push for a more nuanced and less uniform perspective on "illegality." For example, Coutin (2000) theorized the "legal non-existence" of undocumented Salvadorans. Her work added richness to the concept of illegality by highlighting transnational continuities in the spaces of non-existence and clarifying the strategies used by migrants to increase their safety by making themselves legally "non-existent" or, alternatively, by seeking legality. Another line of inquiry revealed the precarity of citizenship in North America: Peter Nyers' (2006) analysis of the unmaking of citizenship for certain kinds of naturalized citizens demonstrated that state sovereignty can unmake and criminalize citizens in ways that parallel the criminalization and illegalization of unauthorized migrants. A third follows up on the production of migrant "illegality" by analysing migrant removal and introducing the concept of deportation regimes (de Genova & Peutz, 2010; Ellermann, 2005; Peutz, 2006).

Research about migrant "illegality," "illegalization," and "irregularization" has made an important contribution to non-citizenship studies by framing the production of migrant illegality as a social, institutional, and ideological process. However, this work has limitations. First, analyses of the production of illegality, ironically, run the risk of normalizing the boundaries between legality and illegality, and in so doing, reifying a reconceptualized but nonetheless *binary* model of legal status categories. Second, the focus on illegality is so prominent that other forms of non-citizenship, such as authorized temporariness, are neglected or minimized. Third, these analyses privilege the power of nation-states in defining and constituting legal status categories, which leaves under-theorized the role and agency of other actors in contesting and changing state categories (Wright, in this volume). Fourth, relatively little attention has been paid to how boundary crossing occurs, with notable exceptions (Coutin, 1998, 2000; Hagan, 1994), leaving open questions about the porosity and rigidity of this process (Bosniak, 1994, 2006), as well as the politics of contesting and negotiating the construction of boundaries (Stasiulis & Bakan, 1997, 2005) and of granting access across or moving across boundaries as well as their possible repositioning (Villegas & Landolt, 2010). Fifth, accounts of migrant illegalization and irregularization often depict a process inexorably leading to illegality, with little attention to what may be experienced in the process, including transitions or movement among other, usually temporary, categories.[14] Complex *interconnections* between a wider range of authorized and unauthorized forms of non-citizenship require further consideration.

The Conditionality of Precarious Status as an Assemblage

To address the challenges outlined above, here we develop a framework that brings together precarious legal status and conditionality, and is consistent with repositioning non-citizenship as central to studies of citizenship and legal status. We start by presenting and refining the concept of precarious status. Next, we draw on research on social and cultural boundaries to develop the concept of conditionality in relation to non-citizen precarious status (Brettell, 2005; de Genova, 2005; Grimson, 2011; Lamont & Molnár, 2002). This allows us to conceptualize non-citizenship as an assemblage.

Goldring and her colleagues (2009) elaborated the concept of precarious legal status as an alternative to binary models of citizenship and legality. In its original formulation, precarious legal status referred to a range of contextually specific forms of temporary authorized status as well as unauthorized status, marked by the absence of any of the following elements normally associated with permanent residence (and citizenship)[15] in Canada: (1) permanent work authorization, (2) the right to remain permanently in the country (residence permit), (3) social citizenship rights available to permanent residents (e.g., post-secondary education and public health coverage), and (4) not depending on a third party for one's right to be in Canada (such as a sponsoring spouse or employer) (Goldring, Berinstein, & Bernhard, 2009: 240–1). The concept of precarious status captures the institutional production of multiple forms of "less-than-full-status" non-citizenship, including authorized and unauthorized forms. It also takes into account people's nonlinear trajectories through different categories of status. Non-citizens' moves into and out of various precarious legal status categories are thus understood as generated by state policies and shifts in these policies, changing regulations, and by migrants' own efforts to improve their situation.[16] Immigration policy is a key dimension of the chutes-and-ladders model of legal status dynamics.

We complement this framework with the concept of the conditionality of legal status. As noted earlier, conditionality denotes the contingency surrounding an individuals' ongoing presence in a legal status category and jurisdiction, as well as the uncertainty of accessing rights or exercising substantive citizenship. Specifically, our use of "conditionality" includes (1) state- and government-imposed conditions associated with a legal status category (e.g., policies, rules, regulations, and associated rights); (2) the variable capacity and ability of actors to meet formal as well as informal conditions (including, but not limited to, social and financial resources); and (3) the multiple ways that conditions are upheld, breached, or challenged in practice, at various levels and sites, by multiple institutional actors, with variable outcomes. These outcomes may include granting or closing access to services, gaining secure status, acquiring false documents, reporting someone without status, moving to another form of authorized precarious status, illegalization, and deportation.

This use of "conditionality" highlights the multi-level and multi-actor "work" that goes into organizing ongoing presence and securing formal rights or access to resources for people with precarious legal status (Goldring, 2010), and into constructing, reproducing, and enforcing legal status categories and boundaries. Conditionality thus offers a means of examining the ways in which boundaries are challenged and perhaps resituated through negotiation. The concept captures the shared precarity that defines and cuts across various legal status categories, including permanent status and citizenship (cf. Nyers, 2006). Using conditionality can clarify the specific sites, arenas, and actors involved in these processes, and the formal rules and substantive practices implicated in conditionality. This approach to conditionality also imbues the chutes-and-ladders model with power: that embedded in policies and regulations, but also that of variously positioned actors, including migrants, who may tip the balance at various points by renegotiating access to services within a legal status category or recharting the course of legal status trajectories. Through negotiated encounters precarious legal status migrants can climb up ladders towards more secure presence and rights (perhaps only momentarily) or be pushed down a chute towards more vulnerability, fewer rights or less access, and a more uncertain presence in Canada.

Theorizing the conditionality of precarious legal status allows us to analyse multiple forms of non-citizenship, both authorized and unauthorized, as elements of a systemic, multi-scalar, and multiple-actor production of variegated and unstable membership, rights, and inclusion/exclusion. Adding the concept of conditionality to social and legal analyses of the production of boundaries also opens research to questions about how boundaries are maintained by upholding formal and informal conditions, and how networks of social and institutional actors with asymmetrical resources, authority, and legal status work to control, negotiate, and contest boundary crossing. Identifying conditionality as a core element underlying legal status allows us to theorize precarious status, and non-citizenship more generally, as an assemblage (Bhuyan, 2012; Sassen 2006; Villegas, 2012). Framing non-citizenship as an assemblage invokes the complex and dynamic web of differently positioned social actors, institutions, regulations, and so on, working at various levels and scales, that together constitute non-citizenship. It also invites attention to how non-citizenship is assembled over time and across space, presenting a dynamic conceptualization of the chutes and ladders of legal status.

Legal status categories, boundaries, and the conditions associated with them tend to be established by state actors. In Canada, some temporary workers and foreign students can become permanent residents; permanent residents may become citizens; people without status may gain status on humanitarian and compassionate grounds (H&C application). However, most temporary worker categories lack a pathway or ladder to secure status (cf. Nakache, in this volume; Nakache & Kinoshita, 2010). Most legal status categories allow for perpetual or greater precarity, and loss of status: individuals on temporary visas for work, study, or tourism may remain in Canada after their visas expire, but without status (Brasch, McLaughlin & Hennebry, in this volume). Failed refugee claimants may follow a similar path or chute (Saad, Kissoon, in this volume). Undocumented entrants join the non-status population more directly. Individuals lacking status with a deportation order have no avenue to further precarity, although there might be some variation in the groups of people targeted for actual deportation.

In our view, the emerging immigration and legal status model consists of immigration policies and variously positioned actors, including but not limited to policy makers, front-line workers and their agencies, lawyers, employers, teachers and schools, doctors in their work settings, migrants, and their friends and co-workers, who together contribute to moving migrants along legal status trajectories. The trajectories follow pathways generated through policy practice, but they increasingly start from various entry points, and are also altered by the institutions and actors that may open chutes and/or ladders that can illegalize, regularize, or keep people churning through various forms of precarious status.

Moving beyond the assignment and trajectories of state regulations and their categories, contributors to this volume demonstrate the conditionality and boundary work of status and rights. People with precarious status have limited or no control over the terms regulating their entry, employment, and ongoing presence (Nakache, McLaughlin & Hennebry, Valiani, in this volume). Presence depends upon meeting work or study permit, visa, and employment-related formal conditions (e.g., temporary workers remaining with an employer when required to; SAWP workers in Ontario refraining from labour organizing; Live-In Caregivers' eligibility for citizenship: see Nakache, McLaughlin & Hennebry, Valiani, in this volume). Practical conditions related to work performance and personal conduct may also come into play. Presence may also be conditional on passing various tests (including refugee hearings and health examinations; see McLaughlin & Hennebry, Kissoon, Saad, Li, in this volume), paying fees, renewing permits, and making further applications as required (Saad, in this volume).

Concerted political action can produce shifts in the conditions and location of boundaries between citizens and non-citizens and across categories of non-citizenship (Wright, Fortier, F. Villegas, in this volume). The durability and scope of such changes may be uneven (Fortier, F. Villegas, in this volume). In addition, the enforcement of status category boundaries and attendant rights depends on actors situated in various institutional locations. Acting as petty bureaucrats or in direct contestation of state and bureaucratic authority, front-line workers and other institutional actors can work to reproduce or challenge the conditions and conditionality of boundaries – for example, by offering access to services (Bhuyan, P. Villegas, F. Villegas, in this volume). Individuals may be in a category where rights and thus access is limited, but gaining or being granted access to services – for example to education, health, and other social services (F. Villegas, P. Villegas, Bhuyan, in this volume) – signals breaching and connections made across boundaries. Whether and how repeated breaching leads to durable shifts in boundaries is not clear. Similarly, migrant rights groups, NGOs, advocacy networks, and other collectives work to claim and expand both access and rights by adjusting institutional policies and procedures to extend services to non-citizens. Boundaries and rights may not necessarily be expanded permanently, but they are breached (de Genova, 2005; Wright, P. Villegas, F. Villegas, Bhuyan, Fortier, in this volume). Thus, the quality and security of presence claimed by and granted to noncitizens usually depend on additional actors and negotiations about boundaries, which involves gaining access to social citizenship, rather than being based on formal or fixed principles of membership, rights, or entitlements (Bhuyan, F. Villegas, Fortier, in this volume; Holston, 1998; Zlolniski, 2008).

In addition to gaining practical – if not formal – access to services and seeking to expand their "social citizenship," people with precarious status, including illegality, use various strategies to remain present and improve their situation. Some strategies involve the seemingly straightforward steps of meeting conditions, from formal employment conditions to less formal ones associated with conduct. The ability to meet conditions may be circumscribed by limited resources, long hours of work, and unhealthy work environments (Landolt & Goldring; McLaughlin & Hennebry; Saad, in this volume). People also devote considerable time and resources to crossing boundaries in an effort to gain more secure status (Brasch, Landolt & Goldring, Saad, in this volume). Their efforts may be thwarted by insufficient resources, accidents and health problems, bad legal counsel, insecure housing, and other challenges (Saad, Brasch, McLaughlin & Hennebry, Landolt & Goldring, Kissoon, in this volume). Alternatively, they may gain secure status but remain stuck in precarious work (Landolt & Goldring, in this volume). Another set of strategies involves managing the complexities of situational identity and presentation of legal status by "passing" as legal and attempting to control information about one's legal status (Young, Saad, Brasch, in this volume).

The conditionality of legal status is fundamental; it establishes asymmetrical power relations for people in situations of conditional legality as well as illegality. Conditionality entrenches insecurity and loss of autonomy for precarious status migrants while situating them in subordinate social locations in relation to external actors who may attempt to regulate and exploit them. In the case of temporary workers, the state (federal and/or provincial government) and employers can exercise control at the level of labour markets, industries, occupations, worksites, and individual workers (Nakache, Valiani, in this volume). When terms are violated, the state can deport people or simply threaten removal (Saad, Brasch, McLaughlin & Hennebry, in this volume). Employment is also a key arena for highlighting conditionality and precarity for those with other forms of precarious status, such as migrants with authorized presence but no work authorization (visitors, some student permits) or refugee claimants whose social insurance number identifies their temporary status (Landolt & Goldring, in this volume). Undisrupted access to work and livelihood is contingent on employers, managers, co-workers, acquaintances, and others with the power to report, fire, harass, underpay, or extort. This underscores the non-trivial work that goes into meeting conditions in an ongoing effort to maintain presence. For those without valid work permits or without authorization to reside, conditionality may involve not being identified or reported by co-workers, acquaintances, landlords, bosses, frontline workers, school staff, or relatives (Saad, Brasch, Young, Kissoon, F. Villegas, P. Villegas, in this volume). Having a deportation order enforced becomes an extreme source of precarity and vulnerability, but it is certainly not the only one (Bhuyan, Saad, Landolt & Goldring, in this volume).

As noted earlier, conditionality is largely established externally, beyond the control of most precarious status migrants. However, various actors and institutions reproduce and enforce conditions, and play key roles in opening or closing access. These include municipal governments, police forces, school boards, health clinics, hospitals, legal clinics, shelters, and the staff that deal with migrants with precarious or no status (Bhuyan, P. Villegas, F. Villegas, in this volume). Migrants are also involved in these processes as they seek services, make efforts to regularize their status, or avoid detection (Brasch, Landolt & Goldring, Saad, P. Villegas, Young, in this volume). Highlighting the conditionality of precarious status also means recognizing the wide constellation of actors that may play a role in determining the durability, scope, and terms of access to rights (whether it is temporary or long-term; who is included; and whether it is understood as granting access as a gift, extending a right, or conferring de facto membership).[17] Acknowledging the role of multiple actors in reproducing or enforcing conditions can help clarify the ways that boundaries may be negotiated at various times and places, and brings into relief the assemblage of non-citizenship constituted by a dynamic array of actors and institutions involved in the chutes and ladders of legal status.

Because conditionality cuts across authorized and unauthorized forms of precarious status, it also provides a basis for questioning dichotomous conceptions and rigidly bounded models of citizenship and legality (cf. Bosniak 2006). Tracing multi-scalar and multi-actor conditionality under particular forms of precarious status and illegality helps clarify the porosity of boundaries and the heterogeneity of categories. Making explicit the conditionality of forms of precarious status and illegality also highlights the precarity and conditionality of the seemingly secure categories of citizenship and permanent residence. Citizenship can be "unmade" through deportation and other institutional processes (Nyers, 2006), and permanent residents wishing to naturalize must conduct themselves lawfully and meet other conditions so as not to jeopardize their transition to citizenship. Thus, a focus on conditionality can offer a response to concerns about lumping together apparentlyly disparate forms of authorized and unauthorized status. It should be possible to assess the specificity of particular status situations while recognizing continuities across them – in this case, the continuities implicated in conditionality.

To sum up, focusing on the conditionality of precarious status allows us to conceptualize non-citizenship as an assemblage constituted by practices, actors, and institutions. As policies shift, and as institutional actors negotiate access and perhaps alternative pathways across the chutes and ladders of legal status, the board game may be redrawn, the assemblage reconstituted. But that takes work. Precarious status emphasized the institutional production of variable forms of non-citizen categories and trajectories across categories, and problematized binary approaches to the location, rigidity, and porosity of boundaries. The notion of conditionality introduces the work that goes into maintaining or shifting multiple boundaries, remaining in or transitioning across categories, staying in a jurisdiction and accessing rights, services, and resources. The concept of an assemblage of non-citizenship brings these together, as it allows us to attend to institutional processes and also focus on variously situated actors' efforts to redraw boundaries – boundaries that exclude and include, and involve efforts to remain in a status or jurisdiction in the face of efforts or pressures to the contrary.

Organization of the Volume

This book is divided into three parts. The first part addresses the production of precarious status historically and through state regulations (at federal and provincial levels. The second part focuses on the everyday experiences and lived consequences of people with various forms of precarious status. The third part addresses how social actors negotiate status-related rights and status boundaries by examining practices aimed at gaining access to services and granting or limiting such access. It also considers institutional boundary regulation related to knowledge production and research ethics.

Producing Precarious Non-citizenship and Illegality

The first part of the volume considers the historical and contemporary production of non-citizen precarious status and illegality in Canada. Chapters in this section focus on a variety of institutional actors implicated in the production of precarious status and migrant illegality, showing how state policies and legal categories are produced through dialogue and contestation among many of these actors at various levels and different times. Cynthia Wright's chapter challenges a statist reading of immigration policy and state-making by showing how immigration policies and categories are not simply handed down from the state. Rather, she argues, historically, the Canadian state only expanded entry, widened citizenship, and made existing rights more effective in response to challenges and claims by activists, social movements, and rights organizations associated with various racialized groups. These processes also included negotiations with subnational governments, employers, and other social actors. Salimah Valiani offers a structural explanation for the expansion of temporary migrant worker programs and the selective devolution of national immigration policy to provinces and private sector employers. Her analysis also underscores the importance of including employers as relevant institutional actors implicated in the production of non-citizenship. Delphine Nakache examines the Temporary Foreign Worker Program to establish whether the rules relating to the legal status of temporary migrant workers admitted for employment in Canada are structured to assist eventual integration in the country of employment, or whether they discourage (or even prevent) such integration. Her analysis of the conditions regulating the presence and employment of migrant workers demonstrates how differential inclusion is structured for skilled workers, who are welcome to settle permanently, versus low-skilled workers, who are expected to leave when their work permits expire. Jurisdictional conflict and overlap between agencies and levels of government and the restrictive nature of the temporary work permit present key challenges to the potential integration of temporary migrant workers.

Each contributor to this section emphasizes the importance of state policies in structuring the regulatory parameters and social relations that organize the legal status and conditional presence for precarious status migrants. Valiani and Nakache demonstrate how employers and provincial governments contribute to producing or reproducing conditions that shape whether and on what terms certain groups of temporary migrants are able to remain in Canada, and that may also push them into greater status insecurity. This section reveals how federal policies, provincial governments, and employers produce and/or reproduce a range of social categories and boundaries, all of which structure precarity and conditionality of presence. Put differently, these chapters illustrate important aspects of the constitution of the assemblage of non-citizenship.

Precarious Status and Everyday Lives

The second section analyses everyday experiences of precarious status. Julie Young explores the constitution of social boundaries of legality and belonging in everyday practices among youth. Two chapters examine strategies for coping with the conditionality of precarious status and the effects of the transition to loss of status: Katherine Brasch does so with ethnographic research on Brazilians navigating the tensions of personal projects and legal status trajectories in transnational social contexts, while Samia Saad focuses on the psychosocial dimensions of losing status among denied refugee claimants. A third set of contributors analyse the social production, and the effects of, vulnerability structured through state policies, employer practices, or interaction with other actors (e.g., landlords) on outcomes such as work (Landolt & Goldring, McLaughlin & Hennebry), health (McLaughlin & Hennebry), and housing careers (Kissoon). Together, the chapters in this section reveal how precarious status is produced and reproduced through policies that draw boundaries and set conditions affecting presence and livelihood for specific status categories, and through precarious status migrants' interactions with other actors and institutions. The chapters identify coping strategies, but also note the long-term impacts, social costs, and difficulties of living with precarious status.

Institutional Negotiations of Status and Rights

The third section analyses the negotiation of status and rights in specific institutional arenas, by diversely situated actors. Negotiations related to access to health care (P. Villegas), violence against women (VAW) services (Bhuyan), and education (F. Villegas) provide an entry point for examining how service delivery staff, counsellors, hospital boards, school boards, municipal staff, NGOs, and social movements (Fortier) in Toronto work to improve and/or limit access. What access means in relation to rights and membership is complicated because the relationship between access to "public goods" on one hand and rights and membership on the other is unclear. Individuals and institutions (e.g., health care providers, teachers, librarians) may facilitate non-citizens' access to public goods without altering the boundaries around rights or membership. Other actors may associate facilitating access with deeper shifts aimed at redrawing rights and even the boundaries of membership. Paloma Villegas, Rupaleem Bhuyan, and Francisco Villegas point to the mixed and often contradictory negotiations surrounding access to health, VAW services, and children's education. In some cases, membership boundaries appear to be redrawn, as when school board policies became more inclusive. However, actual results are uneven. In health and VAW services, access may be temporary and partial due to the discretionary power of institutional actors, constraints imposed by funders, and variable conceptions of "public," "membership," "rights," and "access."

Craig Fortier locates questions of rights and membership within the context of migrant justice and social movement struggles. His analysis of three campaigns and associated alliances involving the No One Is Illegal collectives in Toronto and Vancouver focuses on challenges to the state's internal bordering practices that restrict rights and/or membership based on legal status, including indigeneity. He pushes the discussion of non-citizen precarious status in a critical direction that merits further work.

The final chapters in this section remain consistent with the theme of institutional negotiations, but the focus shifts to knowledge production. Alan Li discusses a community-based action research project that successfully expanded treatment access for immigrants and refugees with precarious status living with HIV/AIDS. This case of boundary and access renegotiation also offers insights into conducting research with a vulnerable population. The final chapter, by Julie Young and Judith Bernhard, examines negotiations of risk and ethics in conducting social science research involving precarious status migrants from a different perspective. Research ethics boards are identified as institutional actors with the capacity to shape research and knowledge production related to migrants' legal status. Institutional mandates to avert risk can shape research methods and limit longitudinal research. Bringing these actors into the analysis reveals a layer of conditionality that influences how we produce knowledge about non-citizenship. Fortunately, as we see throughout the volume, researchers have developed strategies to analyse precarious status non-citizenship.

Public discussion about non-citizenship in Canada has begun to change over the last decade. Migrant illegality has gained occasional visibility in the media. Temporary worker programs have garnered more consistent attention, particularly since the 2008 recession, global economic crisis, and domestic unemployment rates did not lead to a significant or lasting drop in temporary worker entries. More recently, changes to the refugee system are generating criticism from health care providers and many others concerned about refugees' access to health services (Brennan, 2012).

Where does this leave researchers and the wider public? We hope that the conceptual framework laid out here will help reduce the compartmentalization of discussions that focus on one or another category of precarious legal status. Such silos limit our understanding of how forms of non-citizenship are linked and cross-cut by racialization, gender, class, language, skill, ability, and so forth. They also leave the negotiation of rights and access to the discretion of gatekeepers. In contrast, drawing out these connections can support the agenda for change that has been taken up by migrants, advocates, and allies. Making these connections also requires further research and data collection informed by better framed questions.

NOTES

1   This does not mean that permanent residence (or citizenship) offers firmly secure status. In Canada permanent residents (the equivalent of green card

holders in the United States) and naturalized citizens may be subject to removal under certain conditions (Goldring, Berinstein, & Bernhard, 2009; Nyers, 2006).

2   This use of "chutes and ladders" to describe navigations in and across legal status categories invokes the element of chance in the popular board game. Conceptually, we draw on Katherine Newman's (2006) *Chutes and ladders: Navigating the low-wage labour market*, in which she discusses pathways or ladders out of low-wage jobs, and the chutes that often lead the working poor back into low-wage jobs or out of the labour market altogether.

3   We enclose migrant "illegality" and related terms within quotation marks to underscore the institutional and social production of migrant illegality (de Genova, 2002). However, for reasons of style, we use quotes marks sparingly. It should be understood that we intend such terms to be understood in this way throughout this text.

4   Exceptions include literature on the incompleteness and unevenness of citizenship in feminist, anti-racist, post-colonial, and other scholarship in several disciplines. However, much of this work has focused on *citizens*. We are pointing to a dearth of conceptual discussions of non-citizenship that include non-citizens or deal explicitly with non-citizenship. Research on temporary workers and the undocumented does focus on non-citizens, but tends to remain category specific and usually concentrates on the role of vulnerable non-citizen labour in relation to capital. Work on migrant illegalization and deportation tackles non-citizenship more squarely; see, e.g., de Genova's critique of the "spurious distinction that divides the *citizen* from the *non-citizen*," which he argues helps to constitute state power (2010, p. 49). Linda Bosniak, Catharine D'Auvergne, and Audrey Macklin are among the legal scholars whose work on non-citizenship is most relevant to this volume's agenda.

5   UNESCO uses "mobile students" to refer to those more commonly described as "international students." Mobile students include those studying in a country where they do not have permanent residence or citizenship (UNESCO, 2009, p. 36).

6   Data on temporary workers and other temporary residents distinguish between the number of entries (original and re-entries) and those still present in the country on 1 December (Citizenship and Immigration Canada, 2011a).

7   To put these figures in context, the population of Canada surpassed 34 million in April 2010 (Statistics Canada, 2010). The sum of temporary entries and those still present in 2010 represented 2.8 per cent of the population.

8   The number of temporary migrants admitted in 2009 dropped slightly compared to 2008, then rose again in 2010 (Citizenship and Immigration Canada, 2011a).

9   We enclose the term "skill" within quote marks to emphasize the process of skill construction, which may undervalue international training and experience. Moreover, people with high skill levels in a particular field may be unable to leverage them into entry to Canada under one category, and may choose to apply under another category requiring "lower" skill.

10 However, deportation does not operate uniformly across countries (Ellermann, 2005).

11 We use "legal status" to include state-imposed categories of citizenship and non-citizenship as well as the practices, social relations, and institutions that mediate their dynamic construction and reformulation.

12 "Citizenship debates are extensive and multidisciplinary. Key works include Soysal (1994), Kymlicka (1995), Shafir (1998), Aleinikoff and Klusmeyer (2001), Isin (2002), Benhabib (2007, 2002), Bosniak (2006), Turner (2006), Kivisto and Faist (2007), and Joppke (2007).

13 A comprehensive review of the literature on the undocumented is beyond the scope of this introduction. Early work introduced a structural perspective (Burawoy, 1976; Castles & Kosak, 1973; Portes, 1978) and generated a tradition of analysing undocumented migrants as vulnerable workers (Cf. Bloch, 2010).

14 Exceptions include Calavita's (1998) analysis of irregularization in Spain, where unauthorized migrants could obtain temporary permits, but the system worked to irregularize their status. The direction (and outcome) was overwhelmingly towards illegality, but some movement between authorized temporary and unauthorized statuses was not only possible but likely, making the trajectory to illegality somewhat complicated (Cf. McKay et al., 2009).

15 The high-profile case of Maher Arar, a Syrian-born Canadian citizen who was "rendered" to Syria and tortured there, serves as a reminder of the potential insecurity of citizenship (Cf. Nyers, 2006).

16 Precarious status can be seen as the other side of the coin of the concept of flexible citizenship (Ong, 1999). From a Foucauldian perspective, precarious status could be understood as physical presence accompanied by limited or no rights and the absence of formal political membership, with sovereign power disciplining precariously situated subjects who are differentially incorporated into the nation and economy through their non-citizenship (Goldring, Berinstein, & Bernhard, 2009; Sharma, 2006). The concept also links legal status to broader transformations in

the organization of work, the liberal welfare state, and social citizenship, which in turn are connected to neoliberal governance and the expansion of flexible labour on a global scale (Cross, 2010; Fudge and MacPhail, 2009; Hagan, 2005; Ilcan et al., 2007; Schierup, 2007; Vosko 2006).

17 People with precarious status may gain informal access to services and rights through negotiations that cast them as victims, supplicants, and claims-making activists – but not as people with formally recognized entitlements. This highlights the question of whether they are negotiating access, or membership and rights (Goldring and Landolt, 2011).

PART ONE

Producing Precarious Non-citizenship and Illegality

2 The Museum of Illegal Immigration: Historical Perspectives on the Production of Non-citizens and Challenges to Immigration Controls

CYNTHIA WRIGHT

Of course it is not simply history as history that is being obliterated by immigration controls. Living contemporary human beings are pulverized and rendered virtually non-existent, rendered unpersons, by being first defined as illegal and then being deported. Everyone removed in this way is effectively being dropped down their own memory hole ... Can we hope that the *sans-papiers* and their supporters in this country (and in all other countries) will establish a Museum of Illegal Immigration, so that the memory of those detained and deported, of those who fought and resisted with success, will not be forgotten, will not be annihilated, will not be vaporized? This could be a living memory and part of the struggle against controls.

– Steve Cohen, *Deportation Is Freedom!*
The Orwellian World of Immigration Controls

The (re)emergence of radical migrant rights campaigns in Canada and transnationally since the 1990s has challenged the existing frameworks of im/migrant and refugee rights and how the space of and for politics is conceived (Balibar, 2004). These campaigns often make a number of important intermediate demands for reform ("papers for all"/"stop the deportations"), but also challenge borders, immigration controls, and associated state practices and categories – perhaps most notably that of "illegal immigrant." Recently, international literature has tried to develop a "no borders" theoretical framework in conjunction with ongoing organizing by migrant collectives and their allies (Anderson, Sharma, & Wright 2009; Burridge 2009; Gill 2009; McDonald 2009; Moulin 2009; Stobart 2009; Varela 2009).

While the conditions for the emergence of such campaigns are often particular to the context of the 1990s (Abu-Laban & Gabriel, 2002; de Genova, 2005; Wright, 2000), their genealogy dates at least to the imposition of modern immigration controls and the documentary organization of passports and visas. Researchers have recently focused on why immigration controls were imposed in many countries of the Global North before and after the First World War (de Genova & Peutz, 2010; Mongia, 2003; Rosenberg, 2006; Torpey, 2000), as well as in the newly independent states in Africa in the 1960s (Adepoju, 2007; Fanon, 1963; Neocosmos, 2010). Other researchers have investigated the history of the state production of "illegality" and its management (Balibar, 2004; de Genova, 2005; de Genova & Peutz, 2010; Ngai, 2004). Still others have worked to reconceptualize world migration, racial hierarchies, and labour history (Feldman, 2007; Gabaccia, 1997; Gabaccia & Iacovetta, 2002; Lucassen, 2007; Lucassen and Lucassen, 1997; Mazumdar, 2007).

Together, this body of work has challenged scholars to rethink state-centred accounts of migration, categories such as "forced" and "free" labour/migration, and the practice of human migration itself (de Genova, 2005; de Genova & Peutz, 2010) – an issue long ignored in nation-centred histories that often assume, and construct, a sedentary population. Nicholas de Genova commented on the "epistemological obsession with stasis and social order" that undergirds such frameworks: "It is presumed that migration is an anomaly that must culminate in a re-establishment of 'roots' and a normative sedentariness. In other words, what might have been an inquiry into *migration* inevitably becomes an insistent affirmation of 'immigration,' foreclosing the possibility of continued movement" (de Genova, 2005, p. 83, italics in original).

This chapter draws on themes and evolving conceptual frameworks from selected international literature, especially the history of immigration controls, deportation, and the state production of "illegality," to foreground several moments in Canadian history involving questions of migrations, immigration controls, and the ever-shifting constructions of "illegality" – as well as resistance to controls and deportations. Drawing on international literature helps clarify issues that have not been asked in the Canadian context. Mainstream historians of immigration have generally developed their research questions and categories from the standpoint of the nation-state; they rarely ask, for example, how and why the control of borders and the movement of people have become so central to modern sovereignty, or why the post-WWII era of official multicultural citizenship is the same in which the category "illegal immigrant" came into being. Some excellent anti-racist, feminist scholarly analyses have addressed "race," gender, citizenship, colonialism, and nation in Canada – like the violent process of race-making through the construction of citizens, non-citizens, immigrants, refugees, "Indians," and others. We also need more dynamic, transnational, and historical accounts of agency, intimacies, and subjectivities among those produced through these processes.

Strikingly, although both mainstream historical and critical anti-racist sociological approaches converge, relatively few analyses have focused on the dynamic points of contestatory struggle, or how diverse political challenges to immigration controls have shaped, for example, resultant discourse, policy, legislation, or administrative measures – and even the broader sphere of politics. As de Genova commented in the context of a discussion of deportation and the criminalization of migrants, "the legal regimes of national states are always preconditioned by the historically specific and uneven tempos of various forms of social struggle and in fact institutionalize the political strategies designed to intervene in and ultimately contain those disruptive forces" (Peutz & de Genova, 2010, p. 17; see also Gutiérrez, 2007). This chapter will provide a preliminary historical genealogy of contemporary challenges to immigration controls in Canada, particularly with regard to "illegality." How does one write about migrant resistance, the deported, the illegalized, and the clandestine? How do contemporary debates about agency and resistance in relation to power (Scott, 2004) clash with celebratory historical approaches? When and how does the category "illegality" come into existence and what work does it do? How has "illegality" been experienced and challenged historically, especially given that pathways to "illegality," past and present, are in fact diverse? How have the terms and organization of what Luin Goldring and Patricia Landolt (in this volume) call "conditionality" changed over time?

This chapter should also stimulate further historical research and theoretical elaboration in these areas. The production of illegality and practices of deportation have only recently begun to receive sustained attention from international scholars, especially historians. Therefore, this chapter will not provide a comprehensive history of immigration controls – and the many associated practices, including border control, immigration policing, immigration bureaucracies, surveillance, deportation, and the documentary organization of identification – or the state production of illegality in Canada. Much more historical research is needed before practices in these areas can be situated, with the benefit of the international literature, in a global comparative context.

This chapter has a more modest goal. It begins with a short account of the imposition of immigration controls in Canada in the early twentieth century and the brutal deportation regime directed at – to name only a few – labour radicals, anarchists, socialists, "immoral" women, the poor, the unemployed, the disabled, and criminalized and racialized people (Molinaro, 2010; Roberts, 1988). It will show that two central axes of resistance to immigration controls throughout the twentieth century have been anti-deportation campaigns, and – crucially – various forms of clandestine and autonomous migration (organized and otherwise). Immigration controls and deportations were also strongly resisted through the courts, as well as through organizing by anti-colonial activists and labour radicals with an *internationalist* vision that recognized, as the radical syndicalist Industrial Workers of the World put it, "no alien but capital" (Avery, 1979; McKay, 2008). Crucially, their defeat (and deportations) set the terms for the campaigns that emerged in the early post-WWII period that would largely be confined to the space of the nation-state.

My discussion will begin with the historic campaign to end the "colour bar" in immigration as an aspect of the broader campaign for rights and full citizenship *within the nation-state* for all those subject to racial discrimination. Ultimately, the question of immigration cannot be contained within such a framework, because of the constitutive role racism and colonialism have played in the formation of the Canadian state (Thobani, 2007), and also because immigration was linked to *global* colour bars and a global nation-state system. As in the United States, the apparent liberalization and "de-racialization" of immigration law is linked to the production of forms of "illegality" because liberalization and de-racialization did not end the racism in the immigration system, which is one reason why "illegal immigrant" was and is a racialized category (Sharma, 2006). Clearly, forms of embryonic "illegality" existed before this period, but in the 1960s and especially the 1970s "illegal immigrants" became a key focal point of policing, hegemonic discourse, and policy formation – even as overt legal racism and exclusion based on "race" in the immigration system was ending (cf. Wicker, 2010). Some "illegal immigrants" also begin to speak in their own name in the 1970s and a new politics of anti-racism emerged.

After WWII, as historian Clifford Rosenberg argues in his account of immigration controls in France, "inequalities based on nationality and citizenship status have become pervasive, as countries around the world have increasingly found themselves compelled to provide substantial benefits to their own citizens and to recruit foreigners to satisfy their labor needs" (2006, p. xv). This ultimately forged new pathways to "illegality" and forms of precarious legal status (Goldring, Berinstein, & Bernhard, 2009; Goldring & Landolt, Nakache, Valiani, in this volume; Sharma, 2006; Valiani, 2009). These forms of precarious legal and work status have proliferated since the 1990s and intensified in recent years, as have the numbers of undocumented. By the early 1990s, the struggle by many activists to make the immigration system more "just" and "fair" – a key focus of the 1970s and 1980s – was collapsing under the weight of these various stresses, not the least of which was the apparent contradiction between liberal humanist universalism and the logics of immigration policies and their nationalist exclusions and ruthless deportation regimes.

Currently, immigration is often perceived as a transgression, a scandal, a crisis, as a story of "illegal immigrants" on one hand and "traffickers" on the other (Papadopoulos, Stephenson, & Tsianos, 2008). Detention and deportation regimes have become global (de Genova & Peutz, 2010). Anti-immigration parties and formations, as well as brutal violence directed at "foreigners," exist in many states. At the same time, transnational political associations and experiments in labour organizing are emerging among im/migrants, and "no one is illegal" and "no borders" campaigns and formations are challenging precariousness and "illegality" and realigning the boundaries of migrant politics (Fortier, P. Villegas, F. Villegas, in this volume). Such new formations also demand new histories.

The Imposition of Immigration Controls and Impossible (British) Subjects

Scholars have recently begun to investigate the origins of contemporary immigration controls, the passport system, and the historical construction of "illegality," but largely not in the Canadian historical context.[1] There is no book-length Canadian counterpart to rival, for example, Rosenberg's (2006) remarkable study of French immigration controls in the context of the French empire, *Policing Paris*, or Ngai's (2004) history of the state construction of "illegality" within the United States, *Impossible Subjects*. Scholars have explored the history of racist and other exclusionary practices within Canadian immigration history, their implications for Canadian citizenship practices and class, and "race"/ethnic and gender relations, but relatively few have addressed the fundamental issue of how and why immigration controls *as such* came into practice. Radhika Mongia argues, "It is the long process of empires that generates the nation-state as a contained entity that, significantly, is the first kind of state formation to have a monopoly over migration" (2003, p. 205), so how are immigration controls related to nation-state formation, empire, "race," class, gender/ sexuality, and Canadian "nationality"? How did they affect the colonial control of movements of indigenous people both within Canada and across imposed international borders? How did relatively recent modern immigration controls come to be so taken for granted and hegemonic that relatively few historians have seen the need to investigate their origins and organization?

Informed by international scholarship on "race," nation, empire, indenture, and anti-colonialism, important recent research about the famous *Komagata Maru* story has brought new perspectives to the imposition of controls in Canada, the dynamics of resistance to them in the context of the British Empire, and notions of Canadian nationality and sovereignty (Dua, 2003; Kazimi, 2004; Macklin, 2011; Mongia, 2003; Walker, 1997). Mongia argued that one outcome of the terrible and tragic defeat of the *Komagata Maru* challenge to racist controls and colour bars was that such controls and exclusions would be re-articulated as "national" with profound implications for Canadian nation-state formation, what it means to be a "British subject," and the evolution of categories of citizenship (Mongia, 2003).

The *Komagata Maru* was a ship carrying 376 passengers (almost all Indian Sikh men). It arrived in Vancouver in 1914 with the explicit aim of challenging limitations on the right of Indians, as British subjects, to move freely within the British Empire, including Canada. Various racially discriminatory practices, especially regarding Asian migrants (Chinese, Japanese, and Indian), were a certainly a major feature of Canadian immigration long before the *Komagata Maru* sailed in to Vancouver. Perhaps the best known and earliest is the "head tax" first imposed on Chinese migrants in 1885. The earliest Immigration Acts had few exclusions, but the 1910 Immigration Act authorized the Canadian cabinet to exclude "any race deemed unsuited to the climate or requirements of Canada." Kelley and Trebilcock summarized this development, noting that "at the core of the immigration policy that evolved during the eighteen years between 1896 and 1914 was the principle that the absolute right of the state to admit and exclude new members was an essential feature of state sovereignty" (1998, p. 113).

Within this context of ever-expanding controls with serious discretionary power placed in the hands of the executive, the *Komagata Maru* challenge was highly significant. It directly confronted racist exclusionary controls by insisting on the right of movement within the British Empire for the Empire's subjects, regardless of colour.[2] The challenge was not isolated; it built on prior legal strategies and other struggles by South Asians in Canada to contest a variety of earlier measures designed to exclude them (Dua, 2003; Walker, 1997). Thus, the *Komagata Maru* passengers were supported by radical South Asian residents of British Columbia, many of whom were under strict police surveillance. As Andrew Parnaby and Gregory Kealey documented, the *Komagata Maru* story is integrally linked to the origins of political policing in Canada, itself bound up with the attempt to destroy Irish and South Asian anti-colonial resistance in the United States and Canada, as well as the links that bound these radicals to formations such as the Socialist Party and the Industrial Workers of the World (McKay, 2008; Parnaby & Kealey, 2003).

From the standpoint of the Canadian government, the *Komagata Maru* posed at least two problems. The first was how to deal with the legal challenge raised by one of the ship's passengers, Munshi Singh, who argued that the federal government did not have control over British subjects and their movements within the British Empire (Dua, 2003, p. 55). The second was how to bar the passengers of the *Komagata Maru* – and the government was determined that they should be barred – without invoking "race" and thereby further inflaming Indian anti-colonial agitation. The British authorities were by no means anxious to see the further growth and development of global circuits of Indian anti-colonial migrants throughout the Empire. At the same time, the British had serious problems with any measures contemplated by the Canadian government that risked inflaming anti-colonial agitation in any part of the Empire, including India and South Africa. Barring *Komagata Maru* passengers on the basis of colour fell into that category. As Mongia notes, "by 1913, the situation of Indian emigrants in Canada and South Africa had become something of a political cause célèbre" (2003, p. 206). The Canadian parliamentary record (Hansard) for the period clearly reveals that the Canadian authorities were also very aware of contemporaneous agitation by Indians in South Africa, where Gandhi was then pressing their demands (Mongia, 2003, p. 201).

The outcome to this dilemma involved a lengthy legal and political process. At its core was the appeal to "the principle of the sovereignty of states based on *national* grounds" (Mongia, 2003, p. 207, italics in original). The introduction of the requirement for Indians to have a passport before leaving India was central to this new regime. Ultimately, "it would be the 'universal' category of nationality, already overlaid with culturalist racism, that could be mobilized in such a way as to tether people to geographical space" (Mongia, 2003, p. 209). It should be stressed that this process of controlling movement, of linking people to nationally defined territories, cannot be accomplished without violence. This is a central and often forgotten aspect of the tragic story of the *Komagatu Maru*: twenty-two passengers were massacred after the ship was forced to return to India. Several men in the Vancouver community who had collaborated with Canadian authorities were murdered, as was William Charles Hopkinson, formerly of the Indian police, whom the Canadian government had hired to conduct surveillance on South Asian radicals in British Columbia and the United States.

Modern deportation, which, along with violence, tethers people to nationally defined territories, is another central pillar of contemporary immigration control, as is the formation of internal immigration policing and enforcement. It is not surprising, then, that deportation has historically been a central site of struggle. William Walters (2010) locates a genealogy of deportation within related practices of expulsion including population transfers, transportation of convicts, and removal of the poor. Walters's analysis provides a ground-breaking starting point for analyses of Canadian history, which has involved forced removals of indigenous people, the expulsion of the Acadians, the transport of convicts and political exiles from Britain to Canada, and the mass deportation of Japanese-Canadians, political radicals, and the poor. Walters also argues that while deportation is centrally linked to sovereignty and "the discourse of international law" (2010, p. 83), it is also fundamentally bound up with governmentality: the early twentieth century marked the removal of those considered *socially* undesirable, individuals who were, for example, poor, unemployed, or classified as mentally ill (p. 86).

In Canada, the early deportation regime targeted individuals deemed unsuitable on the basis of "race," political radicals, the socially undesirable (including women deemed "immoral"), and "foreign" industrial workers. Deportation became legal in Canada in 1907, but "it had long been practised extra-legally" (Roberts, 1994, p. 267). As a deportation regime, Canada would become "by far the worst in the entire British Commonwealth" (Abella, in Roberts, 1988, p. ix). According to Roberts, the years from "1914 to the early 1930s saw the first deliberate and systematic deportation of agitators, activists and radicals" (Roberts, 1994, p. 267); being a naturalized citizen offered no protection (p. 273). Dennis Molinaro (2010) recently reopened inquiry into political deportation and its role in Canadian nation-building, a topic long neglected by historians since the publication of Roberts's pioneering work, *Whence They Came* (1988). As Molinaro noted (2010, p. 61), while historians of labour and the working class in Canada have long been aware of the draconian round-ups of early labour radicals, they have not always applied the findings to a wider understanding the role of deportation in nation-making. Molinaro also analysed how deportation practices and resistance to them produced a transnational geography of deported radicals. The global circulation of deported radicals reveals how many spent their lives on the move as they were hounded in country after country; these conditions often meant they became multilingual and deeply internationalist in outlook (McKay, 2008).

The links between the policing and surveillance of radicals (socialists, anarchists, and anti-colonial activists) on one hand and the formation and development of immigration policing in Canada on the other remain relatively unexplored (but see Parnaby & Kealey, 2003). As Walters comments:

> From 1914 onward we see a proliferation of schemes to document and identify the alien, including identity cards, registrations with police, employer and residence permits, and passports. The nonrenewal of these various permits by officials could henceforth operate as a means to initiate deportation. (2010, p. 87)

Another crucial aspect of immigration controls needs further attention: their relationship to welfare state formation and regulation of movements *within* "national" space. As Walters argues, "The welfare state does not fully escape the logic of the poor law. As the history of aliens policy reveals, at the same time that social policy was being nationalized, deportation was a regular instrument in the export of the 'foreign' unemployed and other undesirable groups" (2010, p. 91). Canadian municipalities and cities were extremely active in encouraging the federal deportation of immigrant radicals and the poor, so that they did not have to provide for them.

These deportations were ferociously resisted by the left, a very difficult proposition in the face of the power of the post-WWI red scare, draconian police raids, arrests, and blacklisting. Often people were deported before anyone could offer any resistance. In the 1930s, the communist Canadian Labour Defence League mounted the principal opposition to deportations of radicals and the unemployed (Roberts, 1988, p. 146). It did so through mass mobilization, as well as publicizing deportation cases and producing propaganda, including the early pamphlet *Deported!* (Roberts, 1988, pp. 146–8). The success rate of such initiatives (perhaps especially for communist deportees) was mixed, but over time the tide slowly began to turn. As Roberts noted, it was "the wholesale deportation of the unemployed," especially during the Depression, which began to trouble many people (p. 277), including liberals as well as church and labour groups – especially when such deportations involved unemployed immigrants from Britain (p. 164). Canada's deportation practices were becoming "an Imperial issue" (p. 167) and therefore difficult. Deportation practices, and opposition to them, could simultaneously engage municipal, national, and international political actors. For example, many European states wrote to the Winnipeg City Council to ask why so many of their nationals were being deported (Roberts, 1988). Left-wing councillors – as opposed to municipal bureaucrats – could therefore also act as important allies against deportation and help create municipal-level zones where the federal deportation regime was called into question.

Anti-deportation was a central axis of protest to immigration controls in this period and would continue to be so in the post-WWII context. I will conclude this section with some brief remarks about two other central routes of resistance in this period that would also reappear after WWII: legal challenges and clandestine migration. The first of these has received considerable attention from sociolegal scholars in both the United States and Canada who have found that racialized non-citizens – for example Asians, who faced significant exclusionary legal barriers to full citizenship – developed sophisticated strategies to press their claims, especially in the economic and property spheres. Gutiérrez commented: "By bringing these actions and making equity claims against the state, non-citizen denizens aggressively claimed rights in other domains, even while tacitly acknowledging the juridical disabilities and bars to civic participation that constrained them in some areas of their lives. This was a crucial, essential move" (2007, p. 107).

Second, clandestine or autonomous migration has historically been an important mode of resistance to controls. Formal exclusion from entry did not stop everyone, especially in an era when the technologies of identification were either inefficient or wholly lacking. Nor were all detained migrants necessarily deported, nor were all those ordered to be deported actually removed. It was not in the interests of the Canadian state and employers to bar everyone; then, as now, the goal was not exclusion but rather making the conditions under which people worked and lived more precarious and exploitative. Deportation centrally operated, as Roberts suggests, to make the immigrant industrial workers of the period into de facto guest workers. In theory such workers had access to naturalization, but in fact they were deported the first time they became idle, unwanted by employers, or involved in labour or radical politics (Roberts, in Tulchinsky, 1994, p. 280). Unsurprisingly, both anti-deportation campaigns and clandestine migration, as well as various kinds of legal challenges around non-citizen claims, continued after the Second World War, albeit in a radically changed context.

Contesting "Jim Crow Iron Curtain": Race, Nation, and Immigration after WWII

In the spring of 1954, a delegation of thirty-five people under the leadership of the Negro Citizenship Association (NCA) decided to take on the Canadian immigration minister, Walter Harris. Their immediate aim was to challenge racist immigration regulations that effectively barred the migration of non-white people from the British Caribbean (then British subjects); their longer-term strategy was to challenge unequal treatment of British subjects by "race" to create an opening for a wider challenge to the colour bar in immigration more generally. The NCA, a Toronto-based group of West Indians, was formed in the early 1950s to determine why people from the Caribbean were being deported from Canada or finding it impossible to gain entry in the first place. This was not the only group confronting this question. In 1951, the Toronto Labour Committee for Human Rights, an anti-discrimination project founded in 1947 by the Jewish Labour Committee of Canada, discovered that challenging discrimination meant taking on the immigration system when West Indians facing deportation came to them for aid.

The delegation to Ottawa was supported by two dozen organizations, including labour and religious groups, as well as the United Negro Improvement Association and the Brotherhood of Sleeping Car

Porters. It was armed with a brief that cited the 1948 Universal Declaration of Human Rights and the Queen's 1953 Christmas message: "To that new conception of an equal partnership of nations and races I shall give myself heart and soul, every day of my life." Leading delegation member Stanley Grizzle, then the Toronto president of the Brotherhood of Sleeping Car Porters and many years later a citizenship judge, took a tougher tone than the Queen. He assailed the immigration minister over a "Jim Crow Iron Curtain" immigration system that placed "other races in a position of subordination and inferiority. It is against this very attitude people the world over are in revolt" (quoted in Walker, 1997, p. 280; Taylor, 1994).

At one level, the NCA-led delegation was unsuccessful – the immigration minister was aghast at the idea that a non-racial admissions policy for the Caribbean would mean that British West Indians of Chinese descent would be admitted to Canada ("If I admit Chinese from the West Indies, how can I exclude Chinese from places other than the West Indies?" [quoted in Walker, 1997, p. 280]). Also unsuccessful was a Supreme Court challenge initiated on behalf of a West Indian couple, Harry and Mearl Singh, who were barred in the spring of 1954 and ordered deported from Canada despite Harry Singh's desire to join the Canadian military. Explicit anti-discrimination language was not added to the Immigration Act until years later, but the government was now on the defensive.

The long struggle to eliminate the colour bar in Canadian immigration was connected to the campaign to end racial discrimination, including anti-Semitism, through legal and legislative means. In the postwar period, a diverse and interconnected group of labour, CCF,[3] legal, media, academic, and faith (Christian and Jewish) activists worked to tackle discrimination within employment, housing, and commercial public spaces such as restaurants and hotels. This struggle expanded on 1940s efforts, including those by Jewish Canadians and allies to end restrictive covenants (Walker, 1997) and by the little-known Committee for the Repeal of the Chinese Immigration Act (CRCIA), an alliance of Chinese-Canadians and non-Chinese Canadians that formed in late 1946 to try to abolish the 1923 legislation commonly known as the Chinese Exclusion Act (Bangarth, 2003). Many anti-discrimination and human rights pioneers had first worked together to stop the deportation of Japanese Canadians after the Second World War (Bangarth, 2003; Lambertson, 2001; Miki, 2004; Patrias & Frager, 2001) or to challenge the deep anti-Semitism of the Canadian government, which turned away a boatload of Jewish refugees (the famous *St. Louis*) on the eve of the Holocaust (Abella & Troper, 1982).

Historical accounts often describe general postwar shifts in thinking about "race," but Carmela Patrias and Ruth Frager (2001) demonstrated that these campaigns were actually organized and concerted: "Widespread efforts to dispel prejudice and fight against discrimination after the Second World War were not spontaneous reactions against the horrific consequences of racism that had manifested themselves during the war, but the result of campaigns that were carefully and painstakingly orchestrated by small groups of Anglo-Canadian activists, and especially by key minority groups" (Patrias & Frager 2001, p. 2). The war and the Holocaust were certainly important to the postwar context, as were a number of other key global moments, including anti-colonial struggle and challenges to the global colour line, the US civil rights movement, the pressures exerted by the Commonwealth, and Cold War geopolitical considerations. However, clarifying how and why the state responded as it did to pressures for change requires examining the work of organizers in the postwar period.

The labour movement was a key ally for organizers working to challenge racism and discrimination. Why was the mainstream trade union movement – which had in many cases been on the frontline of racist anti-immigration politics from the late nineteenth-century onward (Goutor, 2007) – now prepared to challenge racism within the immigration system and Canadian society? More research is needed on the postwar labour movement, immigration, and racism, but clearly labour, having won some major battles and on the cusp of an unprecedented economic boom period, felt in a position to be more expansive about immigration. With regard to the struggle to end Jim Crow practices in restaurants in Dresden, Ontario, Lambertson wrote, "The trade union movement was strengthened by legal recognition of the workers' right to form unions, go on strike, and bargain collectively, as well as the adoption of the 'Rand formula' for union membership" (2001, p. 48; see also Walker, 1997, p. 267). Then as now, arguments about "population" and the need for more workers in a context of a low birth rate were used to support less restrictive immigration regulations. The labour movement did not challenge immigration controls, or citizenship as an institution of national exclusion, but its position was clearly shifting.

As in the desperate period of mass deportations during the 1930s and then the deportation of Japanese Canadians immediately after the Second World War, deportation orders were often what first mobilized people to inquire into the immigration system and – crucially – to learn about its workings. In many ways the postwar radical migrant justice campaigns were about anti-deportation. Comparatively fewer people were deported in this period than during the Depression years: from 1946 to 1961 slightly more than eight thousand people were officially deported (Kelley & Trebilcock, 1998, p. 344), but many more were deported without anyone noticing or coming to their aid. Yet, just as in the decades before the Second World War, anti-deportation organizing sometimes reverberated in the press and Parliament as CCF allies assailed the government. Sometimes, as with the case of the Singhs, deportations were challenged in the Supreme Court of Canada. Not surprisingly, straightforward victories in this arena – then as now – were rare. Yet the failures also revealed to organizers how the immigration system worked, and how social change might be effected and with whom.

In resisting individual or group deportations, those most affected and their allies encountered a number of barriers, including the wholly untransparent way in which the immigration system functioned. Many people who were issued deportation orders found it virtually impossible to figure out why they were even being deported, which made fighting it legally and politically very difficult. Much of the racism in the system was explicit but a lot was also carried out through "administrative means." As Kelley and Trebilcock noted, this strategy meant that "the Canadian government did not have to pass regulations which blatantly discriminated against non-preferred immigrants" (1998, p. 326). It also "reduced the potential for embarrassment in international relations" at a historical moment in the Cold War when the international context was vital in shaping race and immigration politics (Kelley & Trebilcock, 1998, p. 326).

The broad administrative measures for barring people also meant that the government could simultaneously liberalize immigration (Kelley & Trebilcock, 1998) while barring people of colour, among other "undesirables." Thus, while the repeal of the Chinese Exclusion Act in 1947, for example, was a vitally important victory in that the act was explicitly racist and was historically a centrepiece of immigration controls, the reality is that it would not have been repealed if the state had no other means of discriminating against Chinese migrants and Chinese Canadians. As Stephanie Bangarth noted, Chinese immigrants "did not automatically receive the same rights as other non-Chinese immigrants. Family reunification was still limited, as was the immigration of Chinese nationals" (Bangarth, 2003, p. 1).

Major differences between white and non-white immigrants and citizens were evident at the level of rights to family reunification, and not just for Chinese. Struggles over admission of family members were a critical part of postwar campaigns by immigrant communities and their allies, just as they were in the early twentieth century after the imposition of exclusions on Asians. As James Walker commented, "Family reunification became the primary campaign theme and the chief moral argument for South Asian organizations over the next several decades" (1997, p. 256; see also Dua, 2000). Conservative commentators such as Freda Hawkins have shown that the eventual expansion of the family class caused no end of trouble for immigration authorities. Issues included the definitions of "family," the desire of many immigrants to sponsor what were seen as "more distant relatives" (Hawkins, 1989, p. 85), the large proportion of family class compared to other categories of immigrants, and the fact that, as Hawkins put it, a "difficult aspect of family reunion is that the demand for it is so uneven among national groups" (1989, p. 85). Recent scholarship in the history of sexuality, anti-"miscegenation" discourses, population, and immigration (Camiscioli, 2009) has also suggested new lines of inquiry. However uneasy states were about the migration of wives, they were in many cases even more uneasy about so-called miscegenation. If populations and nations were to be built – especially in countries like Canada where demography and population always figured heavily in debates about the number of immigrants and the "right mix" of immigrants – wives would have to be admitted. Before and after the Second World War, one of the meanings of family reunification was the migration of wives for male immigrants in Canada. Women's independent right and capacity to migrate other than as "wives" was not the issue here, so one of the principal demands made by immigrant women's groups in the 1980s was to end the construction of women as "dependents" within immigration policy and practice (Bhuyan, in this volume). While an emerging lesbian and gay movement campaigned in the early 1970s against the formal exclusion of "homosexuals" in the Immigration Act, it was not until the 1990s that LGBT groups would begin to develop a critique of the heteronormativity of the immigration system; indeed, the assumed uniform heterosexuality of immigrants of colour is not "natural" but, as recent analyses have established, built deeply into the logic of the family class system in both the United States and Canada (Reddy, 2005).

Considerable migrant justice work in the decades after the Second World War turned on legal and other challenges to the system's administrative operations because so much discrimination was embedded in these practices. Much of Ninette Kelley and Michael Trebilcock's (1998) extensively researched standard, *The Making of the Mosaic: A History of Canadian Immigration Policy*, is devoted to chronicling both the arbitrary character of the system and the very long struggle for due process guarantees and other measures to limit official and ministerial discretion. While the fight for democratic legal processes should not be discounted, because for some prospective immigrants they would make a huge difference, the reality is that it was obvious to others that the immigration system could not be made more "just" and "humane" simply through such measures. Nor did it tackle the racism at its roots. As the immigration system became apparently less exclusionary in the postwar years, analyses of the system's fundamentally undemocratic character would need to become increasingly more sophisticated.

A number of historians of the early human rights and anti-discrimination movement have noted that this work was itself often limited in its frameworks and not devoid of problems that reinforced the issues of racism they were trying to address. Patrias and Frager noted, "Many human rights activists ... continued to believe there were inherent differences among people based on 'race.' In effect, this meant that they sometimes endorsed discriminatory policies, especially concerning immigration" (2001, p. 3). So, for example, the largely white Committee for the Repeal of the Chinese Immigration Act did not frontally challenge racist assumptions about Chinese and Asian migration, much less immigration controls as such. While the CRCIA called for the repeal of the Chinese Exclusion Act, it also made statements such as, "We are not asking you to open wide the gates for Chinese immigration" (cited in Bangarth, 2003). In other words, much of the liberal reformism in this era sought to challenge some exclusions but not others: to reform immigration without fundamentally challenging nationalist assumptions linking peoples to territories.

A number of issues were involved here. One was the role of the state itself in the production and reproduction of racism. As Alana Lentin commented in her excellent book, *Racism and Anti-Racism in Europe*, "western states in the aftermath of the Holocaust and colonialism treated racism as an external force, coming to divert the course of democracy. It was proposed, therefore, that with a return to the principles upon which modern nation-states are founded that racism would, naturally, disappear" (2004, p. 19). For this reason, more mainstream approaches to racism sometimes emphasized its aberrant character, for example its affront to notions of British "fair play." Second, it is not surprising that the acute limitations of some early postwar reform campaigning were particularly sharp in relation to immigration (Patrias & Frager, 2001). Some reformers, while prepared to challenge racism within the space of the nation-state, and aspects of the colour bar within immigration, still believed that states had the right to control migration for the cause of "the nation," and therefore territorialized people according to where they "naturally" belonged in a nationalized geography of "separate but equal." Some of these assumptions were blown open in the 1970s in the context of both the repoliticization of racism and the growth of "illegal immigration" as a policing and state category.

As some struggled with the political work of challenging the postwar immigration regime, others were challenging immigration controls by living and working underground – as people had done since the imposition of immigration controls. Unsurprisingly, given the long history of racism directed against them within the immigration system, many of these were Chinese people denied citizenship, denied the right to family formation, denied entry to Canada. They found their own way to the country and made their own families through the practice of "paper sons." After the Second World War, they would be joined by many others from many historically "non-preferred," often colonized, regions of the world.

Clandestine and Autonomous Migration: From "Paper Sons" to the "Illegal Immigration" Raids of the 1960s

In 2002, an elderly man – apparently named On Wong – died in a Toronto homeless shelter. For forty-seven years he had lived and worked hard in Canada, mainly as a cook. At the time of his death, he was without a home, a family, money – and Canadian citizenship. He had no legal status in Canada at all; there was no record of him even entering the country. Shortly before his death, a Toronto lawyer had tried to secure him citizenship so that he could access social benefits, including a pension. In January 2002, his application for citizenship was rejected and he died not long after of a massive heart attack. A dignified funeral service and burial were organized for him by Toronto community activists.

People have always found ways to migrate, regardless of immigration control regimes. For example, Chinese migrants in both the United States and Canada resisted explicitly racist immigration legislation, and regulations that limited family reunification, through what became known as the "paper sons" system. On Wong – whose real name was Shui Jim Wong – entered Canada in 1955 (note that this was *after* the repeal of the Chinese Exclusion Act) using someone else's papers. He claimed to be the son of a man who was actually his uncle (Go, 2002, p. 5; Keung, 2002). Some twelve thousand or more people entered Canada this way, a testament to the inability of state regimes to control their borders and to the creativity of migrants who managed to use the documentary organization of immigration and citizenship to their advantage (Ngai, 2004, pp. 204–6).

Chinese migrants were really the first modern "illegal immigrants" in Canada. Mae Ngai's observations about the United States hold equally true for Canada: "The Chinese exclusion laws, which barred all Chinese laborers from entry and prohibited Chinese from acquiring naturalized citizenship, generated the nation's first illegal aliens as well as the first alien citizens" (2004, p. 202).[4] The Cold War period provided a new context for movement, "when unsettled conditions created by civil war and revolution in China prompted many Chinese to emigrate" (Ngai, 2004, p. 206). In 1960, there were dozens of "illegal immigration" raids within Chinese Canadian communities across Canada (Anderson, 1991; Kelley & Trebilcock, 1998). These may be the first example in Canadian context of what has become a feature of so many societies today: the high-profile "immigration raid" designed not just to terrorize those directly affected and to drive others further underground so that they might be further exploited by employers and landlords, but also to show that the borders are being defended and the population is secured against foreign "Others" and nefarious smugglers and traffickers.

Finally, the Canadian state responded with the Chinese Adjustment of Status Program, after the first Chinese Canadian Member of Parliament, Douglas Jung, introduced a private member's bill in the House and after a delegation composed of people from various Chinese Canadian communities met with the prime minister and the immigration minister. The program was designed to close the door on the problem of illegal immigration by granting legal status to "paper sons"; it also made people identifiable by the state and therefore subject to control. In this sense, regularization/adjustment of status programs have a mixed character: they may be a response to organizing from below but they also are an attempt to control and contain migration and may also serve to further reproduce states of illegality (McDonald, 2009). In the specific case of the Chinese status program, thousands were regularized through this process by 1973. Yet the story of Shui Jim Wong reveals that an unknown number of others were not. The United States introduced a comparable program, and Ngai's research has revealed that, while some were deemed ineligible for regularization, they were not deported; this was "a mixed blessing, since they were left with no status at all" (Ngai, 2004, p. 221). Some – often Chinese American leftists – were deported rather than regularized (Ngai, 2004, p. 221). In other words, the United States used *both* deportation and regularization in tandem based on both "race" and Cold War considerations. Further historical research in Canada may establish how many Chinese Canadian leftists were deported in this period, as well as the broader patterns of who was regularized, who was deported, and how this shaped the configurations of "conditionality" (Goldring & Landolt, in this volume). Ngai's analysis suggests that recent calls by scholars for more work on deportation (de Genova & Peutz, 2010) need to be supplemented by work on the alternating state practices of regularization and deportation, carried out at the same historical moment but in relation to different categories of people.

If clandestine and autonomous migration has always existed in Canada, it was arguably first defined as a public "problem" in the 1960s and especially the 1970s through a whole set of media, legal, institutional, and other practices including dramatic "illegal immigration" sweeps. This phenomenon was also evident in much of western Europe, where constructions of "illegality" were linked to the decline of foreign worker programs in the 1970s. As Wicker wrote of Germany, "despite the creation of nationalist laws that, developed between the two world wars, specifically targeted foreigners, undocumented migrants were not a matter for public discussion until the late 1960s" (2010, p. 228). Crucially, as a "problem," "illegal immigration" was both racialized from the start and thoroughly shaped by Cold War politics (Iacovetta, 2006). The ongoing racialization of the category "illegal immigrant" suggests that it worked to exclude people of colour in a context in which the language of explicit racist exclusion was no longer available (i.e., through the Chinese Exclusion Act). It also seems clear that the ongoing refusal of people to be stopped by immigration controls meant that the state had to elaborate new responses to control people's movements. While the Chinese Adjustment of Status Program was designed to deal with the long legacy of Chinese exclusion, there were others whose presence in Canada was also shaped by lack of access to full status and citizenship. The "problem" of "illegal immigration" would not go away, but would begin to involve an expanding number of people. The program was by no means the last of its kind – and those without status, "the illegals," would also speak in their own names.

The 1970s and Early 1980s: "Cry of the Illegal Immigrants"

In many mainstream accounts of Canadian immigration and immigration policy, the 1970s emerge as a decisive turning point. This was the decade of the 1976 Immigration Act, often judged as "an innovative, liberal and effective piece of legislation and a vast improvement on its 1952 predecessor" (Hawkins, 1989, p. 70; see also Kelley & Trebilcock, 1998, p. 385). From another standpoint, however, things looked very different. If the 1950s and 1960s had largely been about the slow widening of the category "European" to include immigrants (mainly southern and eastern European) who had earlier been seen as not quite the best class of material for Canadian nation-building (Iacovetta, 2006), then the 1970s proved to be about the terms of entry into the white Canadian nation for Third World migrants of colour (Sharma, 2006) and left-wing Latin American political exiles. In the period leading up to the new Immigration Act, the federal government released the Green Paper to stimulate discussion about immigration policy options as part of an attempt to build consensus for a new act through public consultations. The Green Paper was an explosive document: it caused a storm of controversy and was widely seen by critics as blaming the immigrants of the 1960s and 1970s for a host of urban problems and "racial" tensions. It included a proposal for quotas according to region and continent (Kelley & Trebilcock, 1998, pp.372, 374). Notably, the Green Paper was occasioned by what the state perceived as a massive crisis in "illegal immigration" (Hawkins, 1989, p. 46).

From the standpoint of administration and ruling, the crisis had two causes: a provision introduced in the regulations in the late 1960s that allowed people to apply for landed immigrant status from within the country, and the introduction of an appeals process for those ordered deported. Thousands of people on visitors' permits began arriving and applying for landed status, and by 1973 there was "a backlog of more than 17,000 cases" before the Immigration Appeal Board (Kelley & Trebilcock, 1998, p. 371). The state responded with another adjustment-of-status program and some thirty-nine thousand people were landed (Kelley & Trebilcock, 1998). Many who were regularized had their origins in the United States as well as parts of the world long disadvantaged by exclusionary regulations: Hong Kong, the Caribbean, India, and southern Europe (see Table 1 in Hawkins, 1989, p. 49). Castañeda's comments on Germany also apply to Canada in this period:

> During the 1950s and 1960s, "illegal" migration was considered the "third way" to immigrate – the first being via guest worker programs and the second via individual work visas. In this framework, many people entered the country under tourist visas, found work, and were eventually given official residency and work permits – a form of de facto legalization (2010, p. 247).

Entry via visitors' visas was also gendered, as in Switzerland women often did not have the same access as men to work permits and were more likely to come as visitors (Wicker, 2010, pp. 230–1).

Such was the case for an "illegalized" woman who had come to Canada from Guyana on a visitor's permit and who published *Cry of the Illegal Immigrants* (1979), a forty-one-page testimony originally circulated under a name she had chosen for herself: Haile Telatra Edoney. The fact that her text was published suggests that a space was finally being made to challenge the official category of "illegality" from the standpoints of those outside its official production and regulation. Those who had been illegalized by the state were beginning to write themselves into existence and speak in their own name. The text was also clearly influenced by black liberation discourses that were circulating in the period. In her account of racisms and anti-racisms in postwar Europe, Alana Lentin noted that the anti-colonialist critique that was developed in the 1950s and 1960s and progressed through the United States was by the 1970s making its way to Europe's cities and challenging "depoliticised explanations of racism" (2004, p. 11). Similar processes were at work in Canada (Austin, 2007; Mills, 2010).

Cry of the Illegal Immigrants suggested that migrants, including "illegals," had a clear right to stay given the history of slavery and exploitation in Africa and the Caribbean. The text elaborated a labour-based critique of the immigration system that emphasized the intersections of a racist immigration system with class and gender exploitation. For example, Edoney wrote about the sexual coercion of black women from the Caribbean by immigration officers and how women took jobs as domestic workers in part because they feared immigration raids in factories. An outstanding feature of the system today – the vast expansion of temporary workers' permits and programs that serve to create a largely non-white working class that does not have access in most cases to permanent residency – became institutionalized in large part by the mid-1970s (Sharma, 2006). If the 1980s would be shaped by the figure of the "refugee" (and the growing problem of failed refugee claimants), then the 1970s radical critiques were all about the immigrant worker (later the "immigrant woman worker"), as texts of the period such as the Law Union's *The Immigrant's Handbook: A Critical Guide* (1981) make clear. In emphasizing the exploitation and oppression of the migrant as *labourer* and linking that condition with histories of slavery and colonialism, discourses such as these also sought to locate the basis for a right of migrants to stay.

The streams of left-wing political exiles who came in or after the 1970s revealed and challenged the Cold War construction of the category "refugee"; the battles over the admission of Chileans, for example, contrasted sharply with the reception accorded others, such as the Hungarians of the 1950s, who were seen to be escaping the Iron Curtain and the evils of Communism and thus understood as refugees (Iacovetta, 2006). "Refugee" was a useful category at the height of the Cold War, when relatively few actual refugees came from Eastern Europe and the Soviet Union (Hungarians were an important exception). When refugees began to come from elsewhere in large numbers in the 1980s and 1990s, the refugee system was tightened considerably in response to this "crisis"; the result was more failed claimants, and the figure of the "illegal" began to be identified with that of "the refugee" – often one who was allegedly "criminally trafficked." Decades after the "illegal worker" made her appearance in *Cry of the Illegal Immigrant*, non-status refugees would begin to organize in their own names with the 2002 formation of the Montreal-based Action Committee of Non-Status Algerians (McDonald, 2009; Nyers, 2003; Wright, 2003).

Conclusion

> It may be that illegal immigration will persist as long as the world remains divided into sovereign nation-states and as long as there remains an unequal distribution of wealth among them.
>
> – Mae M. Ngai, Impossible Subjects

In recent decades, migration regimes have increasingly deployed the concept of "illegal," have "illegalized" more people, and have devoted more resources to draconian detention and deportation practices that are now internationalized (de Genova & Peutz, 2010). These moves are also being accompanied in many contexts by renewed nationalisms and racisms, "new fantasies of whiteness" (Hage, 1998), linked to shifts in the organization of "State, sovereignty and citizenship" (Mezzadra, 2010). This chapter has suggested some ways to think about the historical construction of "illegality" in the Canadian context, a difficult proposition given that "illegality is an exceptionally fluid and often transitory category, produced by shifting practices of inclusion and exclusion" (Castañeda, 2010, 245). Understanding "illegality" historically means situating it within broader histories of inclusion and exclusion. For example, although the construction of "illegality" is largely a post–Second World War development – as it was also across western Europe – it also builds on prior histories of racial, labour, and gender subordination, as well as a host of legal and extra-legal developments in the interwar period, including deportation, identification, and policing practices and the exclusion of migrants and racialized people from emerging social welfare provisions.

It is also important to understand *how modes of inclusion and exclusion themselves* have changed over time and in relation to the complex regulation within labour regimes of the "mobility and immobility of bodies" (Goldring & Landolt, in this volume; Mezzadra, 2010). This has structured how various social actors and movements have historically worked for inclusion and integration, how they have understood racisms, and how they have pushed against the limits of the nation and nationally bounded citizenship in the post–Second World War context. With *Cry of the Illegal Immigrants*, one Afro-Caribbean "illegal" woman sought to mobilize the anti-racist discourses of the period for positioning "illegals" as wealth creators, as workers – but within a global analysis of exploitation. After all, the "unequal distribution of wealth" is connected to long histories of colonialism, racism, slavery, and indenture. Similarly, the evolution of a system of "sovereign nation-states," a central feature of which is the control of migration and people's movements, is also connected to the end of slavery and indenture, and with empires, as exemplified by tragic story of the *Komagata Maru*.

Throughout this chapter, I have argued that migrants have always challenged regimes of control over their movements. They have done so through legal challenges of various kinds, including those aimed at narrowing the gap between the rights enjoyed by citizens and non-citizens, anti-deportation campaigns, labour strikes, and clandestine migrations (including the "paper sons"). They have mobilized direct confrontations – what else was the *Komagata Maru* moment? But they have also resisted by imagining (and living) both geographies and people's relationship to one another differently. Following recent arguments in the literature on autonomous migration (Papadopoulos, Stephenson, & Tsianos, 2008), I want to suggest that migrants did not just respond to regimes of control over movement but that their movements frequently initiated particular measures to recapture control. The increasing "illegalization" of millions of people today, in a context of massive legal migration, surely falls into this category, as does the further criminalization of movement itself and the ongoing representation of migrants as either victims of traffickers or criminals themselves (Kempadoo et al., 2011). We are living in a complex moment in which the regulation of bodies, territories, and movement is shifting profoundly: "current configurations of racism in Italy and Europe do not aim at assigning different populations to different territories, *they aim rather to regulate, to 'manage' as European rhetoric wants it, the intersection of their bodies … within a single territory*" (Mezzadra, 2010, italics in original). Moreover, the migrants located within this regime have diverse and heterogeneous pathways to, and experiences of, precarious labour, precarious legal status, and "illegalization." Given their diverse trajectories and lives, there can be no common "migrant experience." But the challenges that migrant lives pose for contemporary regimes of national citizenship, as well as for an international system of sovereignties, states, and territories constituted through labour and mobility control, mean that migrant politics will continue to be central for imagining and practising liberatory futures.

NOTES

1   But see Sean Mills's (2011) work on deportation and Haitians in Quebec.
2   Notably, there is no history of challenge to the Chinese "head tax" during the period it was first imposed (Macklin, 2011).
3   The CCF became the New Democratic Party.
4   Aboriginal people in Canada were legally in a similar situation when it came to citizenship, and much work remains to be done to excavate these citizenship regime histories (Bohaker & Iacovetta, 2009; Fortier, in this volume).

3 The Shifting Landscape of Contemporary Canadian Immigration Policy: The Rise of Temporary Migration and Employer-Driven Immigration

SALIMAH VALIANI

One decade ago, taking a long view of Canadian immigration policy, policy analyst Ravi Pendakur underlined that "permanent migration has constituted the cornerstone of Canadian immigration policy since Confederation" (2000, p. 3). Not so long afterward, political economist Nandita Sharma argued that with the introduction of the Non-Immigrant Employment Authorization Program (NIEAP) in 1973, the Canadian state shifted immigration policy "away from a policy of permanent immigrant settlement towards an increasing reliance on temporary migrant workers" (2006, p. 20). Using the latest official statistical data available, this chapter maps the shift from permanent to temporary migration in Canada that began in the twentieth century, and links it to another shift in the early twenty-first century. Though the legal framework for temporary migration was introduced in the early 1970s, I argue that a material shift did not occur until the mid-1980s, when the number of workers entering Canada on temporary work permits of longer than one year began outpacing the number of workers entering as permanent residents. A new policy shift occurred in the early twenty-first century, when primary decision making around access to permanent residency was transferred by the Canadian state to Canadian employers. Using data from the Live-in Caregiver Program, the longest-standing Canadian immigration program in which employers hold primary decision-making power, I argue that an employer-driven immigration system does not bode well for the long-term needs of building an inclusive society and stable labour supply in Canada.

Permanent Migration and Family Reunification: 1940–1970

In his study of the intersection of post–World War II labour market formation and immigration policy in Canada, Ravi Pendakur (2000) traces
two waves of permanent migration in the post–World War II period.
The first wave, occurring in the 1940s and 1950s, was based on family
reunification and immigration from Europe. Reflecting international
discussions around human rights and principles of anti-racism, and
perhaps more importantly, the diminishing number of applications for
immigration from Europe, discriminatory selection criteria were removed from Canadian immigration legislation beginning in 1962. The
second wave of permanent migration was thus based on family reunification and labour force requirements, leading to increasing numbers
of Asian, African, and Latin American immigrants settling in Canada
in the 1960s and 1970s. Family reunification was key in both waves of
migration following World War II. Due to the socially accepted notion
that workers should migrate along with their families, workers were
able to settle with the crucial support of spouses and other immediate
family members. Society as a whole was seen to benefit via immediate
population growth and future labour force expansion.

As shown in Table 3.1, workers migrating to Canada were likely accompanied by at least one family member in most of the years between
1966 and 1979.

Along with family reunification, permanent migration and the accompanying legal status of permanent residency consists of several
other rights and entitlements that have come to be known as the basic
starting point for inclusion in Canadian society. Most important among
these are rights of protection under municipal, provincial, and federal
legislation; mobility rights, or the right to choose one's place(s) of work
and residence; and eventual access to citizenship and hence participation in political decision making.

Material Shift, 1980s: From Permanent Migration to Temporary Labour Migration

From around the mid-1980s, the number of workers in Canada with
temporary employment authorizations of more than one year began
outpacing the number of workers permitted entry on a permanent basis
(see Tables 3.2 and 3.3 below).[1] Through the 1980s, workers in the teaching, services, clerical, and fabricating/assembly/repair sectors figured in

Table 3.1. Permanent Migration and Family Reunification, 1966–1979

	Immigrant Workers*	Immigrant Non-workers**
1966	99,210	95,533
1967	119,539	103,337
1968	95,446	88,528
1969	84,349	77,182
1970	77,723	69,990
1971	61,282	60,618
1972	59,432	62,574
1973	92,228	91,972
1974	106,083	112,382
1975	81,189	106,692
1976	61,461	87,968
1977	47,625	67,289
1978	35,211	51,102
1979	48,234	63,862

Source: Department of Manpower and Immigration Canada (2005);
Employment and Immigration Canada (2005)

*Counted by "intended occupational groups."
**Includes spouses, children, students, and others.

the top five sectors for which temporary work authorizations of more than one year were issued (Employment and Immigration Canada, 2005). For the most part, workers on temporary employment authorizations do not enjoy the basic rights and entitlements accorded to permanent residents: family reunification, rights protection under various levels of legislation, mobility rights, and eventual access to citizenship. The absence of these basic rights is encompassed in the notion of "precarious legal status" elaborated throughout this volume (cf. Goldring, Berinstein, & Bernhard, 2009). The specificities of precarious status as experienced by temporary migrant workers in Canada are explored in chapters 4 and 9 of this volume.

The increased use of temporary migrant workers was part and parcel of growing employer preference for what is known today as a flexible labour force, the major driver of labour market restructuring occurring

Table 3.2. The Rise of Temporary Migration: Immigrant Workers and Temporary Migrant Workers Compared, 1980–1989

	Immigrant Workers*	Employment Authorizations, Long-Term**
1980	63,745	29,181
1981	56,969	44,990
1982	55,472	n/a***
1983	37,109	n/a
1984	38,500	n/a
1985	38,453	69,953
1986	48,200	78,244
1987	76,712	97,624
1988	76,350	126,313
1989	98,227	n/a****

Source: Employment and Immigration Canada (2005)

*Counted by "intended occupational groups."
**Includes workers employed in Canada on temporary work authorizations for more than one year (as defined in Immigration Regulations, 1978 and Immigration Act, Government of Canada, 1976, cited in Employment and Immigration Canada, 2005).
***For the years 1982–1984, only aggregated figures are available: long-term and short-term employment authorizations combined. They are excluded here due to the extremely high number of short-term (i.e., less than one year) work authorizations.
****Without explanation, from 1989 to 1996, data on temporary residents cease to be included in immigration statistic archives.

in Canada from the late 1970s onward. Two key aspects of labour market restructuring are legislative changes and changing employment forms. Beginning with legislative changes, the federal Anti-Inflation Program of 1975–78 limited the increase of salaries of employees of federal and crown corporations, federal and some provincial public-sector employees, and employees of large private-sector firms. Following from this, several provinces instituted wage restraint programs through the 1980s and 1990s. Combined with back-to-work legislation introduced by the federal and provincial governments through the 1970s and 1980s, wage restraint programs severely affected the collective bargaining power of unionized workers, rendering them more "flexible" to the plans and needs of employers (McBride & Shields, 1997, pp. 67–69). Another

Table 3.3. Skilled Workers and Temporary Migrant Workers Compared, 1999–2009*

	Skilled Workers, Principal Applicants	Employment Authorizations, Short and Long Term**
1999	41,544	107,139
2000	52,123	116,565
2001	58,911	119,714
2002	52,974	110,915
2003	45,377	103,239
2004	47,894	112,553
2005	52,269	122,723
2006	44,161	139,103
2007	41,251	164,905
2008	43,360	192,519
2009	40,729	178,640

Source: Citizenship and Immigration Canada (CIC) (2009b, 2010d)

*In the most recent official statistical compilations available, for the years 1984–1998, skilled workers are counted as part of the "economic immigrant" category rather than as a distinct category. In order to maintain a consistent pattern of comparison with the earlier period featured in Table 3.2, Table 3.3 begins with the year 1999, from which time disaggregated figures for skilled workers as principal applicants are available.
**Unlike in the earlier period, disaggregated figures are unavailable for short- and long-term temporary work authorizations. The figures included here represent initial entries and re-entries of temporary migrant workers on both long- and short-term employment authorizations. Given the lack of disaggregation, these numbers risk overstating, to a certain extent, the proportion of temporary migrant workers employed in Canada for one year or more.

major element of labour market restructuring via legislative change is the easing of state regulation of workplaces, including decreased state monitoring of employers and enforcement of employment contracts – a process that began unfolding in the 1980s and continues today in some provinces.

The abandoning of full employment policies in most rich countries in the early 1980s went hand in hand with the rise of non-standard employment forms. In Canada, between 1975 and 1985, the number of part-time employment positions (i.e., thirty hours per week or less) increased by 78 per cent while the number of full-time positions increased by a mere 15 per cent (Shields & Russell, 1994, p. 330). Taking into account the broad range of non-standard employment beyond part-time work, including temporary-help agency work, short-term work, and self-employment, non-standard employment represented one half of all new jobs created between 1981 and 1986 (Economic Council of Canada, cited by Shields & Russell 1994, p. 330). The use of non-standard employment forms allows employers to shift the risk of business downturns to workers and persisted following the end of the 1982–1984 recession. Non-standard employment forms also allow employers to reduce labour costs. In 1984, for instance, the average hourly wage of a part-time worker was two-thirds that of an average full-time worker performing the same work (Burke, 1986, cited by Shields & Russell, 1994, p. 335). Similarly, in the same year, temporary and casual workers – many of whom were likely temporary migrant workers – earned 43 per cent less than full-time, permanent workers in equivalent positions (Shields & Russell, 1994, p. 335).

The increasing number of workers entering Canada on employment authorizations also reflects the various bilateral and multilateral trade agreements of the 1990s onward, permitting labour mobility for highly skilled workers (Fudge & MacPhail, 2009). Also driven by the interests of employers, temporary migration of highly skilled workers is seen to increase the competitiveness of Canadian industries in the global context. Though Fudge and MacPhail (2009, p. 13) underline the lower number of entry requirements imposed on highly skilled temporary migrant workers than on lesser skilled temporary migrants, as Sharma (2006, p. 125) points out, both groups are unfree in that their mobility is restricted within Canada.

More specifically, unlike workers with permanent resident status, under the 1973 Non-Immigrant Employment Authorization Program (NIEAP) and the subsequent Temporary Foreign Worker Program, both sets of temporary migrants are bound to particular employers and hence particular geographic locations. Given that the legal status of temporary migrant workers is tied to employers, employers of those workers hold yet more power in the already unequal employer-employee relationship, and temporary migrant workers are thus more vulnerable to coercion, abuse, and differential treatment in the workplace.

One example of such differential treatment is in the area of remuneration. A Statistics Canada study of remuneration of temporary migrant workers reports that though temporary migrant workers in Canada are more likely than Canadian-born workers to have university degrees, returns on education are lower for temporary migrant workers than for Canadian-born workers. In greater detail, a Canadian-born worker with a university degree earns about $674 more per week than a Canadian-born worker without a degree, while for a temporary migrant worker with a degree, earnings are about $512 per week, or 24 per cent less. For a temporary migrant worker from a country with Gross Domestic Product amounting to less than half that of Canada, earnings are about $175 per week, or 74 per cent less (Thomas, 2010, p. 44).[2] In 2006, 63 per cent of temporary migrant workers in Canada were from such lower-income countries, and 62 per cent were racialized workers (Thomas, 2010, p. 37).

From 2001, following the pattern of the NIEAP and increased temporary labour migration through trade agreements, the Immigration and Refugee Protection Act (IRPA) allowed employers the possibility of further access to temporary migrant workers through an array of different mechanisms (Fudge & MacPhail, 2009, p. 11). This was in spite of projections of economists and some government policy analysts that net labour force growth, as well as net population growth, would occur solely through permanent migration by 2011 and 2031 respectively (Denton et al., 1997; Gluszyski & Dhawan-Biswal, 2008).

In the early twenty-first century, rather than reverting to the longer history of permanent migration and family reunification in light of long-term needs to build an inclusive society and stable labour force, the Canadian state moved to deepen the shift to temporary migration. The federal government created the Low Skilled Pilot Project in 2002, primarily in response to claims of shortages by employers having neglected to invest in apprenticeship training in the skilled trades sectors from the 1990s (Canadian Labour Congress, 2006). In 2006, in consultation with employers and provincial governments, the federal government created the Occupations Under Pressure Lists (Valiani, 2007a). This program reduced from six weeks to one week the time employers in particular sectors were required to advertise job openings within Canada before being able to claim a labour shortage and become eligible to recruit temporary migrant workers. In 2007 and 2008, the Expedited Labour Market Opinion guaranteed expedited government assessment of employer applications to recruit temporary migrant workers in certain categories previously listed as "occupations under pressure." Through these various streams of the Temporary Foreign Worker Program, Canadian employers gained accelerated access to temporary migrant workers in a range of occupations and skill levels, while being required to provide less evidence of efforts to recruit and train workers within Canada.

The Early-Twenty-First-Century Policy Shift: From Public to Private Decision Making around Permanent Residency

In August 2008, the federal government announced the creation of a new immigration program, the Canadian Experience Class (CEC). The CEC offers the "carrot" of permanent residency to international students and internationally trained workers of various skilled categories following the completion of, respectively, twelve or twenty-four months of work in Canada, on the basis of a temporary work authorization. The CEC thus further entrenches the "stick" held by Canadian employers to whom the legal status of temporary migrant workers is bound through the temporary work authorization. Within the context of weakened and poorly enforced employment standards legislation in most Canadian provinces, migrant workers hoping to remain permanently in Canada and eventually sponsor their families are thus rendered yet more dependent and exploitable by employers well aware of their employees' precarious legal and economic status.

In addition, the CEC follows the 2006 recommendation of the Citizenship and Immigration Law Section of the Canadian Bar Association that some temporary migrant workers be retained permanently in Canada where there is employer support (Canadian Bar Association, 2006, p. 9). In other words, applications of temporary migrant workers and international students to remain in Canada as permanent residents are dependent or conditional upon employer approval. Only after the completion of twelve to twenty-four months of full-time employment, during which employers can test workers for their suitability, are applicants accepted as worthy of remaining in Canada permanently. The language in Canada's 2007 federal budget elaborates further on this shared employer-state vision, rationalizing a $33.6 million budgetary allocation for the establishment of a new immigration program based on temporary migration as a path to permanent residency:

> To ensure that Canada retains the best and brightest with the talents, skills and knowledge to meet rapidly evolving labour market demands, the Government will introduce a new avenue to immigration by permitting, under certain conditions, foreign students with a Canadian credential and skilled work experience, and skilled temporary foreign workers who are already in Canada, to apply for permanent residence without leaving the country. Recent international graduates from Canadian post-secondary

institutions with experience and temporary foreign workers *with signifi-cant skilled work experience* have *shown that they can succeed in Canada, that they have overcome many of the traditional barriers to integration,* and that they *have formed attachments to their* communities and *jobs.* (Department of Finance Canada, 2007, p. 218, emphasis added)

The CEC is the federal corollary to immigration programs in several provinces and territories of Canada in which employers recommend permanent resident status for certain internationally trained workers. In turn, provincial governments, under these Provincial and Territorial Nominee Programs, "nominate" the employer-selected workers for permanent resident status to the federal government. As shown in Table 3.4, the number of internationally trained workers obtaining permanent resident status through Provincial and Territorial Nominee Programs increased significantly starting in 2000 (Alboim, 2009; Valiani, 2007b).

Amendments to the Immigration and Refugee Protection Act (IRPA) quietly passed in June 2008, through the Budget Implementation Bill (C-38), and sealed the shift of primary decision-making power around permanent residency from the state to employers. The amendments gave the power to the minister of citizenship and immigration to issue periodically changing instructions regarding the processing of applications for permanent residency, thereby replacing the first-come, first-serve system of application processing previously enshrined in IRPA. By way of example, these instructions may include limiting the number of permanent residency applications to be processed, prioritizing the processing of applications of workers in certain occupations, or capping the number of permanent residency applications accepted by category.

The first set of instructions published by Citizenship and Immigration Canada (CIC) in November 2008 specified that new permanent residents to Canada under the Federal Skilled Worker category would be selected according to a list of thirty-eight occupations. These occupations – mainly in the health, construction, and other skilled trades sectors – were quite similar to those appearing in the employer-driven lists of "occupations under pressure" published in 2006, and additionally were all drawn from the same skill levels included in the Canadian Experience Class[3] (Valiani, 2009). The criteria accompanying the November 2008 list of thirty-eight occupations stated that people already working in Canada on temporary work permits and people able to

Table 3.4. Permanent Residents Nominated through Provincial and Territorial Nominee Programs, 1997–2009

Year	Provincial/Territorial Nominees (Principal Applicants)
1997	23
1998	0
1999	151
2000	368
2001	411
2002	680
2003	1, 417
2004	2, 086
2005	2, 643
2006	4, 672
2007	6, 329
2008	8,343
2009	11,801

Source: CIC (2008b, 2010d).

secure employment contracts prior to arrival would be given priority in being considered for permanent residency. In June 2010, CIC released a revised list of twenty-nine occupations prioritized for permanent residency drawn from the same skill levels as the previous list but reflecting slight changes in the labour demand of Canadian employers.

Unheeded Lessons of Canada's First Employer-Driven Immigration Program

The shift to employers of primary decision-making power over access to permanent residency follows logically from the pattern of increased temporary labour migration driven by employers. But how well does it serve the long-term needs of Canadian society as a whole, particularly given a low birth rate and decreasing labour supply due to retirement? An examination of the federal Live-in Caregiver Program (LCP) is useful in answering this question, given that, prior to the Canadian Experience Class and Provincial/Territorial Nominee programs, the LCP was the only employer-driven immigration program in Canada offering temporary migrant workers a path to permanent resident status.

Formerly known as the Foreign Domestic Movement, the LCP is a program enabling individuals in Canada to employ live-in caregivers from other countries on the basis of temporary work authorizations. A few dates and program changes are important to highlight in order to understand the characteristics of the LCP as it is known today.

Due to the historic undervaluing of carework inside the home – and the poor wages and working conditions flowing from it – retention rates of workers in the occupation of domestic care have historically been low in Canada. Prior to 1973, workers admitted to Canada to perform carework inside the home sought other employment not long after arriving. This happened because these workers had the employment and geographic freedom associated with permanent residency (Arat-Koc, 1992). In 1973, the introduction of mobility restrictions – allowing careworkers to enter Canada only on a temporary basis and obliging them to live with employers – solved the retention issue for employers, leaving the real problem of undervaluing untouched. In 1982, due to political pressure from live-in caregivers and their allies, the program was amended, allowing live-in caregivers to apply for permanent residency upon completion of twenty-four months of live-in care work in Canada. At the time, live-in caregivers and advocates viewed the amendment as a victory. In hindsight, it is clear that a return to the pre-1973 policy of permanent residency for domestic workers upon arrival would have been a far superior policy gain given the far-reaching experiences of abuse LCP workers face because of the live-in requirement and precarious migration status. These abuses have been documented by various researchers, including in government publications (Arat-Koc, 1992, 2001; Langevin & Belleau, 2000; Pratt, 1999; Stasiulis & Bakan, 2005). What follows is an analysis of LCP data to answer the question alluded to above: how well did the LCP serve as a means of recruiting workers to eventually remain in Canada as permanent residents, as the CEC is ostensibly designed to do?

Calculating on the basis of CIC data for the sample period, 2003–2007, and taking into account the LCP requirement that workers complete twenty-four months of live-in work in Canada to qualify for permanent residency, the overall estimated retention rate for the period is 53 per cent (Valiani, 2009).[4] In other words, of the 19,072 live-in caregivers entering Canada from 2003 to 2005, only 10,043 attained permanent resident status by 2007 (see Table 3.5).[5]

Table 3.5. Initial Entry and Permanent Residency of Live-in Caregivers, 2003–2007 (Raw Data)

Year	Initial Entry, Live-in Caregivers (all Canada)	Permanent Residency, Live-in Caregivers, Principal Applicants (all Canada)
2003	5,110	2,230
2004	6,741	2,496
2005	7,221	3,063
2006	9,387	3,547
2007	13,840	3,433

Source: CIC (2008b). Reproduced from Valiani (2009, p. 11)

Complicating matters further is the well-documented fact that many live-in caregivers are not able to complete the twenty-four-month requirement within a period of two years of employment in Canada.[6] For this reason, LCP requirements for permanent residency were changed twice, requiring workers to complete twenty-four months of live-in work within a period of three and then four years, rather than two. It is therefore useful to examine estimated retention rates (ERR) over time, or the ability of the program to retain migrant live-in caregivers as permanent residents by year, over a period of time (Valiani, 2009). Table 3.6 provides an estimation of the dynamics caused by discrepancies between official expectations underlying the LCP design, and the lived reality of workers having to change employers at least once prior to being able to fulfil the twenty-four-month live-in requirement. What must be underlined is that each time a temporary migrant worker changes employers, s/he is required to leave the workforce and obtain a new temporary work permit, which decreases the time available to complete the twenty-four-month requirement.

Though growing numbers of migrant workers were granted entry to Canada under the LCP from 2003 to 2007, the estimated retention rate of the program fell as low as 28 per cent, despite ongoing demand for labour in this occupational category (Valiani, 2009). For the 2003–2007 period, the decreasing ERRs indicate that each year the LCP was less successful in retaining temporary migrant workers as permanent residents. The ERR diminishes over time because, though more migrant caregivers are drawn in due to high demand and the LCP promise of

Table 3.6. Estimated Retention Rates (ERR) over Time, Live-in
Caregiver Program, 2003–2007

ERR 2003*	60%
ERR 2004**	40%
ERR 2005***	28%

Source: Reproduced from Valiani (2009, p. 12)

* This ratio is based on the assumption that all live-in caregivers entering in
2003 attained permanent resident status in 2005, as per the official expectations
underlying the LCP design. Given the weaknesses of this assumption, this ratio is an
overestimation.
** This ratio allows for the widely known fact that not all live-in caregivers are able to
fulfil the twenty-four-month requirement within two years.
*** This ratio allows for the possibility that some live-in caregivers complete the twenty-
four-month requirement over a period of three to four years.

permanent residency, the number of permanent residencies granted
remained fairly stable as workers could not fulfil program requirements and were obliged to extend their temporary status for periods
up to four years. All of this suggests that the LCP, and the model of employer-driven, temporary migration as a path to permanent residency,
are unsuccessful in terms of building labour supply.

Adding a longer-term dimension are the figures tracking the number
of live-in caregivers' spouses and dependents attaining permanent residency between 2003 and 2007. The numbers are low in comparison to
the number of spouses and dependents obtaining permanent residency
under principal applicants of the Federal Skilled Worker and Self-Employed Worker categories in the same period (see Figures 3.1 and 3.2).
This confirms that with regard to the long-term needs of Canadian society – labour force expansion and social inclusion – the historical model
of permanent migration and family reunification offers far more promise than the employer-driven model of temporary migration as a path
to permanent residency.

With regard to the ability of the Canadian Experience Class to retain temporary migrants as permanent residents, evaluation is difficult given the relatively recent introduction of the program. Thus far
the figures reflect the pattern traced for the LCP. In 2009, 1,774 primary

Figure 3.1. Family Reunification, Labour Force Expansion, Live-in Caregivers

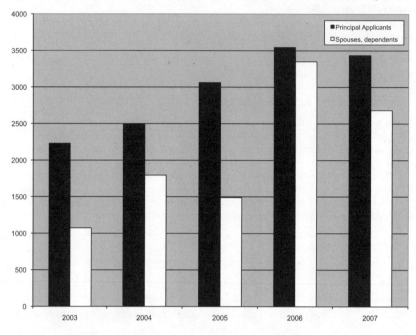

Source: CIC (2008b)

applicants and 770 dependents were admitted to Canada under the CEC, amounting to a total of 2,544 (CIC, 2010d). This is far below the 25,500 permanent residents the federal government expected to retain through the CEC program in 2009 (Mamann, 2010).

Conclusion

This chapter traces two major, interrelated shifts in Canadian immigration policy: from permanent to temporary migration and from a publicly determined immigration system to one driven by private interests. As part of labour force restructuring reflecting the changing preferences of employers from the late 1970s, employer-driven temporary migration replaced permanent migration as the principal

Figure 3.2. Family Reunification, Labour Force Expansion, Skilled and Self-Employed Workers

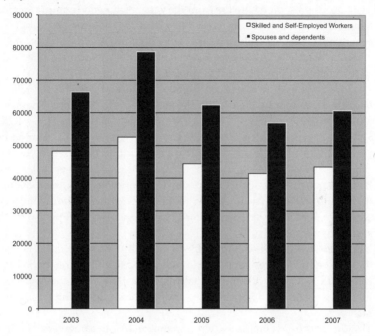

Source: CIC (2009b)

means of entry of internationally trained workers to Canada in the mid-1980s. In turn, in the early twenty-first century, the Canadian state transferred primary decision-making over access to permanent residency of internationally trained workers to employers. Drawing from retention data calculated for one sample period of the Live-in Caregiver Program – the longest-standing immigration program in Canada based on employer-driven determination of entry and access to permanent residency – I have offered evidence to support the argument that an employer-driven immigration system is unlikely to provide for the long-terms needs of building a stable labour force and socially inclusive society in Canada.

NOTES

1   The figures presented here are from the Citizenship and Immigration Statistics Archives (1966–1996), dated 12 April 2005. These are the most recent official data available and differ considerably from those presented in Nandita Sharma's (2006) *Home Economics*. The discrepancies are likely due to changes and improvements in counting methods.

2   Weekly remuneration of temporary migrant workers cited here is calculated by the author on the basis of the percentages provided in Thomas (2010).

3   Skilled workers included in both the Canadian Experience Class and the permanent residency priority lists to date fall within managerial, professional, technical, and skilled trades occupations (i.e., Skill Types 0, A, and B of the Canadian National Occupation Categories list). For more details on the minister's instructions, refer to the Citizenship and Immigration web page, http://www.cic.gc.ca/English/immigrate/skilled/apply-who-instructions.asp#list.

4   Due to privacy laws, it is impossible to match initial entry figures with those of permanent residents by individual applicant. The retention rates calculated here must therefore be taken as an estimate. See the Appendix in Valiani (2009) for the calculations and rationale underlying these estimated rates.

5   This figure is based on the assumption that all live-in caregivers entering in this period applied for permanent residency. In December 2009, as part of an announcement of changes to the LCP, CIC stated, without providing any data, that over 90 per cent of LCP workers apply for permanent residency (Citizenship and Immigration Canada [2009d], http://www.cic.gc.ca/English/department/media/releases/2009/2009-12-12.asp, accessed 13 December 2009.

6   For a government-funded study on this subject, see Louise Langevin and Marie-Claire Belleau (2000). For an academic treatment of the subject, see Stasiulis and Bakan (2003).

4   The Canadian Temporary Foreign Worker Program: Regulations, Practices, and Protection Gaps

DELPHINE NAKACHE

More people are entering Canada on a temporary basis, to the point that in 2008 Canada admitted more temporary than permanent residents (Goldring & Landolt, in this volume). In 2010, 45 per cent more international students entered the country than in 2004 (partly because Canada's post-secondary educational institutions are making a concerted effort to attract them), but the highest increase was in the number of temporary migrant workers[1] (TMWs). Between 2002 and 2010, the number of TMWs present in Canada (on 1 December) rose by 179 per cent, from 101,259 to 283,096, while total entries of these workers (i.e., the sum of initial entries and re-entries) in the same period rose by 64 per cent, from 110,915 to 182, 322 (Citizenship & Immigration Canada [CIC], 2009b, pp. 62–4; CIC, 2011b).[2] Canada's two main temporary labour migration programs, the Seasonal Agricultural Worker Program and the Live-in Caregiver Program, have remained relatively stable over the years, but the Temporary Foreign Worker Program (TFWP) has undergone significant changes in its purpose, size, and target populations. To date, the TFWP has operated largely below the radar of public debate; this chapter will address this gap. First, I will show that major shifts within the TFWP have led to increased concern about the employment-related rights of all TMWs. Second, I will demonstrate that while Canada wants TFWs to fill jobs on an ongoing basis, in fact

This chapter is a condensed and updated version of a paper by Nakache and Kinoshita (2010). I am grateful to Sarah D'Aoust for her research assistance.

only skilled workers are permitted to settle permanently. My objective throughout the chapter is to highlight the exclusionary dimension of immigration law, which is committed to preserving the so-called "identity" of the Canadian nation-state at the expense of low-skilled TMWs.

The TFWP was implemented in January 1973 (Department of Manpower and Immigration Canada, 1975, p.186). It was initially targeted at specific groups of people with highly specialized skills, including academics, business executives, and engineers. However, employer demand for workers to perform jobs requiring lower skill levels prompted the federal government to introduce in July 2002 the Pilot Project for Hiring Foreign Workers in Occupations that Require Lower Levels of Formal Training (hereafter the Low-Skill Pilot Project). A higher proportion of low-skilled workers have entered Canada since this pilot project began. In 2002, only 26.3 per cent of all TMWs were in occupations designated as low-skilled (National Occupational Classification C and D Occupations); in 2008, the proportion had shifted to 34.2 per cent (CIC, 2009b, p. 66). By far the largest increase was in National Occupational Classification D occupations, which accounted for only 1 per cent of the workforce in 2002 but rose to 8.8 per cent in 2008 (CIC, 2009b, p. 66; Nakache & Kinoshita, 2010, pp . 4–5).[3]

Despite the need for temporary migrant workers to fill jobs on an ongoing basis, in both "skilled" and "low-skilled" occupations (Alboim, 2009; Canadian Bar Association, 2006; Preibisch, 2007; Sharma, 2006), temporary labour migration remains structured in Canadian immigration law as a "temporary" phenomenon. For example, the rationale behind the restrictive nature of the temporary migrant work permit (i.e., temporary migrant workers are tied to one job, one employer, and one location) keeps migrant workers in a precarious legal status, in that temporary labour migration programs serve as a tool to fill specific shortages in the labour market, and are therefore designed to respond to immediate employer needs (Bauder, 2006; Nakache & Kinoshita, 2010, p. 3). Canadian immigration law expects migrant workers to leave the country once their work permits expire. To ensure the "temporary" nature of the TFWP, the government implemented regulatory changes in April 2011, limiting the stay of migrant workers for a maximum of four years, followed by a period of six years during which they are not allowed to work in Canada (CIC, 2011b). The government noted that "this provision would signal clearly to both workers and employers that the purpose of the TFWP is to address temporary labour shortages," thereby reinforcing the temporary nature of labour migration programs

(Government of Canada, 2009). However, if we move away from the specific regulatory framework governing the entry and stay of TMWs in Canada, and instead locate existing labour migration programs in the more general context of the changing face of economic immigration to Canada (Nakache & Kinoshita, 2010, pp. 9–11), it is apparent that immigration law has actually been modified to enable highly skilled TMWs to transition to permanent residency from within Canada. In contrast, low-skilled TMWs, with a few rare exceptions, have not been given the same opportunity. These modifications highlight the tension and contradiction at the heart of Canadian immigration law.[4] I argue that although immigration law contributes to the creation of precarious status for all temporary migrant workers in the arena of employment, immigration law also acts as a gatekeeper, allowing for the inclusion of skilled migrant workers but excluding low-skilled migrant workers as "outsiders."[5]

To clarify how immigration law is structured for skilled versus low-skilled workers, it is important to examine the rules relating to the legal status of TMWs admitted for employment in Canada, both on paper and in practice, and to establish whether these rules are structured so as to assist eventual integration in the country of employment, or whether they discourage or even prevent such integration. Cholewinski (2004, p. 6) identified three policy perspectives on the legal status of TMWs: (1) the temporary migrant is offered the opportunity to remain and integrate in the country of employment; (2) the official scheme is indifferent to the temporary migrant's future position in society; it is left to the worker or the employer whether or not to encourage integration or participation in the social or political life of the country; and (3) the aim of the official rules is to prevent the integration of the temporary migrant, who is admitted for employment in the country only for a designated period of time. A key aspect of integration, and the focus of this chapter, concerns the employment-related rights for TMWs. My research questions can be summarized as: First, what rights do workers have to change their job, employer, or employment sector? Second, do TMWs have a right to claim unemployment benefits and, if so, under what conditions? Is there a period for which unemployment benefits will be paid, and is there a period of unemployment after which TMWs may face expulsion from the country? Third, what protections do TMWs have at work in terms of the enforcement of employment standards and the ability to claim workers' compensation? I will also briefly discuss issues surrounding family accompaniment and access to permanent residency from within Canada, to clarify, first, whether family members of low-skilled TMWs are permitted to join them, and second, whether and how such workers can acquire permanent residency after a period of time.

Method and Sample

The findings presented here are based on an analysis of documents as well as on eleven interviews conducted in spring 2009 with individuals involved in the TFWP. The interviews were necessary to clarify and confirm the research findings, but most importantly to help me learn more about the growing disconnect between what is stated in law and what happens in practice. The main difficulty that I encountered during the research process was clarifying TMWs' rights in both law and practice. There are three reasons for this. First, the administration of the TFWP is complex and confusing. According to the 1867 Constitution Act, immigration is under shared federal-provincial jurisdiction. The Parliament of Canada can enact laws with respect to "aliens," "unemployment insurance," and "criminal law," whereas provincial legislatures are responsible for "civil rights" such as employment rights, health care, education, and housing.[6] Thus, while the federal government regulates the entry and stay of TMWs, many of their protections, with the exception of employment insurance, are covered by provincial laws. Given the shared federal-provincial jurisdiction of the TFWP, each level of government is somewhat restricted in its ability to resolve various challenges within the program. Second, even if there is no apparent distinction on paper between, for instance, the employment rights of TMWs and those of Canadian citizens or permanent residents, these rights do not always transfer well into practice. TMWs may experience additional hurdles: inexperience with the Canadian legal and social systems, limited opportunities for permanent immigration, language barriers, misleading employer-provided information, and self-censorship to protect their jobs and avoid possible deportation, to name only a few. Furthermore, the rights presented as "protection for all" may be of little value to TMWs due to their unique employment status as well as restrictions placed on their work permits. Third, a number of policy changes to the TFWP have been implemented recently, making an up-to-date analysis of the relevant law and policy extremely difficult. As a result, some discrepancies appear between legislation, jurisprudence, and internal, unpublished policy regarding employment insurance for TMWs, as I will discuss below.

I begin by describing the administration of the TFWP, including restrictions imposed on TMWs by their work permits and issues related to protection for TMWs during periods of unemployment. The following section focuses on the rights of TMWs in the workplace. Together, these sections will reveal the precarious nature of all TMWs rooted in the conditionality of their presence and in their employment-related conditions. A third section discusses the multiple barriers faced by low-skilled workers trying to obtain permanent residency from within Canada; specifically, it focuses on the exclusionary nature of immigration law with regard to this particular category of workers.

Protection Gaps within the Administration of the Temporary Foreign Worker Program

Evaluating the TFWP requires clarifying the legal regime that regulates the entry and stay of temporary migrant workers admitted into Canada. The large variety of players and policies involved in the program leads to the potential for communication and protection gaps within day-to-day program administration. Another administrative issue is the restrictive nature of the work permit, which limits workers' ability to change employers or to receive benefits such as federal employment insurance.

Overlapping Jurisdictions and Policies

Under the legal framework of the Immigration and Refugee Protection Act and the Immigration and Refugee Protection Regulations,[7] three federal departments administer the TFWP. Human Resources and Skills Development Canada administers the "employment validation" (also referred to as "employment confirmation" or "labour market opinion") and deals exclusively with employers; Citizenship and Immigration Canada deals with workers' immigration documents and matters pertaining to admissibility requirements; and the Canada Border Services Agency is responsible for immigration processing at the port of entry and has the final say about whether a worker can enter Canada.

To illustrate how these three players operate, let's turn to the extensive process by which a TMW enters Canada. First, an employer must apply to Human Resources and Skills Development Canada to get a labour market opinion regarding the impact the entry of a TMW will have on the Canadian labour market. Human Resources and Skills Development Canada considers the terms and conditions of the recruitment (such as the wages and working conditions offered), and ensures that the TMW will not be taking a job that a Canadian could perform (Human Resources and Skills Development Canada, 2009d; Immigration and Refugee Protection Regulations, sec. 203).[8] Human Resources and Skills Development Canada also requires that all applications under the Low-Skill Pilot Project have a specific contract, signed by both the employer and prospective TMW, that outlines the employer's obligations towards the worker, including wages, working conditions, round-trip transportation costs, medical coverage, assistance in finding suitable accommodation, and payment of all costs related to hiring the worker (Citizenship and Immigration Canada [CIC], 2010e, p. 34; Human Resources and Skills Development Canada, 2009c). Second, once the employer obtains a positive labour market opinion from Human Resources and Skills Development Canada, the prospective employee must apply to Citizenship and Immigration Canada for a work permit. Applications for work permits are generally made outside Canada, but in some cases a work permit may be obtained at the port of entry or within Canada. The immigration officer will not issue a work permit unless satisfied that the applicant is able to perform the work (this may include the ability to communicate in English or French) and will leave Canada at the end of the authorized period.[9] Citizenship and Immigration Canada immigration officials are expected to exercise discretionary judgment in making "well-informed decisions" when assessing work permit applications (CIC, 2010e, p. 35). The decision to issue a work permit, therefore, is made on a case-by-case basis. Finally, the Canada Border Services Agency officer at the port of entry has the final say on whether an individual can enter Canada, and the prospective worker must also satisfy the officer that he or she has the ability and willingness to leave. Thus, a positive labour market opinion and permission to work in Canada are not determinative of admission, because the Canada Border Services Agency officer must review all immigration, identity, and work-related documents before printing off the actual work permit and letting the person enter the country.

Citizenship and Immigration Canada (2010e) admitted that some cases may fall into an "apparent grey area," and recommended better communication between Human Resources and Skills Development Canada and Citizenship and Immigration Canada/Canada Border Services Agency:

> Officers are encouraged to contact HRSDC in cases where, for example, a bit more detail regarding the job offer would assist the decision, and likewise are encouraged to respond to HRSDC queries in a timely manner. Ultimately, closer communication will result in quicker, more efficient service which benefits the clients (Canadian employers and the foreign workers) and the two departments. (p. 36)

Certainly, communication between Human Resources and Skills Development Canada and Citizenship and Immigration Canada/Canada Border Services Agency is critical to clarify some of the grey areas unique to the TFWP. It is particularly important in an immigration law context, where wide discretionary powers are granted to Citizenship and Immigration Canada and Canada Border Services Agency officers, resulting in an increased risk of mistakes that could have detrimental consequences for the prospective worker. Interestingly, several interviewees indicated that communication between Citizenship and Immigration Canada and Human Resources and Skills Development Canada has increased over the years. However, they also stressed the continued communication gaps between Citizenship and Immigration Canada and Canada Border Services Agency, as officers of the two agencies have very different perspectives and take different approaches to their immigration work.

The Restrictive Nature of the Work Permit

Work permits issued under the TFWP tie each TMW to a single employer. However, individual conditions imposed on the work permit (such as the location where the applicant can work, the particular occupation, and the duration) vary. The restrictive nature of the work, which is employer specific, limits rights that workers might otherwise exercise to change employers. TMWs also might be ineligible for employment insurance because they are legally restricted from taking new employment (although they may be physically able and willing to be employed).

Temporary migrant workers who wish to renew their work permit before it expires or who want to change any of its conditions must apply to Citizenship and Immigration Canada.[10] TMWs with an expired work permit may apply from within Canada to restore their status within ninety days of the expiration of the permit, but there is no guarantee that Citizenship and Immigration Canada will restore their status.[11] Since November 2008, two application streams have been possible from within Canada (CIC, 2008c): one for renewal of a work permit with the same employer (in December 2011, the current processing time was forty days) and one for changing conditions to a new employer (in December 2011, the current processing time was thirty-two days). Workers who have applied to extend a work permit with the same employer before the expiry of their existing permit have implied status from the date on which the application is received and can continue to work at their existing place of employment as long as their application is in process and they remain in Canada (CIC, 2009f). However, workers who have applied for a work permit with a new employer are not authorized to work for the new employer until they receive the permit.[12]

Although the processing time for a new work permit with a new employer has been reduced significantly since November 2008, the overall wait time for finding a new job, obtaining a new labour market opinion, and getting a new work permit is at least three to six months (Nakache & Kinoshita, 2010, pp. 17–18). Human Resources and Skills Development Canada's job banks are available to TMWs who are looking for a new job, but federal and provincial governments have not developed any special initiative to match these workers with employers who already have an approved labour market opinion, or to assist them in finding a new job if they become unemployed or discover that there is no job waiting for them upon arrival in Canada. Legally, TMWs who have been laid off are allowed to stay in Canada for the duration of their work permit, but those who are not self-supporting are expected to return home, even if their permit has not expired, so as not to be in violation of their visa.[13] In reality, TMWs often face financial difficulty during their sometimes lengthy period of unemployment, especially if they cannot access government benefits. In response, they might resort to unauthorized employment and be at risk of exploitation by unscrupulous employers (House of Commons, Canada, 2009, p. 25).

Confusion about the Right of TFWs to Receive Employment Insurance

The federal employment insurance program temporarily compensates workers who have become unemployed through no fault of their own and who are making an effort to get back into the workforce. Along with the regular benefits program, employment insurance also includes sickness, compassionate care, and maternity/parental benefits. TMWs and their employers pay into employment insurance, just like Canadian workers. According to some recent estimates, in 2008 alone TMWs and their employers contributed as much as $303 million in employment insurance premiums (MacLaren & Lapointe, 2010). However, unemployed TMWs are not entitled to benefits merely because they have paid into the plan; all claimants, including Canadians, must have worked a certain number of hours within the last fifty-two weeks or since the last employment insurance claim. This is the "qualifying period"; the number of hours depends on the regional rate of unemployment. In addition, claimants must prove that they are "capable of and available for work and unable to obtain suitable employment."[14] TMWs face several problems when trying to access employment insurance. The first is obvious: unless the worker has been employed for the qualifying period, he or she is not entitled to benefits. Second, and more importantly, TMWs may not be entitled to receive employment insurance because their "employer-specific" work permit restricts them from being "available for work" for other employers.

Within the jurisprudence, being "available for work" is interpreted to mean both a claimant's self-imposed restrictions and state-imposed restrictions (such as restrictions on a work permit). Justice Linden of the Federal Court of Appeal wrote, "availability for work is a statutory requirement and cannot be ignored by Umpires, whatever the extenuating circumstances may be."[15] According to case law, TMWs with restricted work permits are not "available for work." The following example illustrates the consequence of this interpretation. In 1997, Josephine Simmons, a foreign national from Ghana on a restricted work permit, was laid off from her job because of a shortage of work. She applied for employment insurance but was denied. The umpire, Justice Jerome, affirmed the decision of the board, writing:

> The Board recognizes that to satisfy the requirement of availability under the Act a person has to be available for work without restrictions.

Although we sympathize with the claimant, here we find according to the evidence she is restricted involuntarily because of Employment Authorization which limits her to be employed by one employer only. As a result, when the employer laid off the claimant, she was restricted from finding other employment. Accordingly, she was not available for other work. The fact that the employer supports the claimant with a letter stating he will hire her back in April 1997 is irrelevant to this issue.[16]

The subsequent jurisprudence gives a fairly clear message: TMWs with restricted work permits are not "available for work" as defined by the Act.[17] This message puts TMWs in a legal and financial bind: on one hand, they cannot get employment insurance because they are not legally available for work; on the other, once they are legally available for work – having found new employment and having applied for changes to their work permit – they are no longer eligible for employment insurance. Thus, according to the jurisprudence, TMWs are entitled to benefits, but only when they no longer need them (Nakache & Kinoshita, 2010, pp. 19–20).[18]

The Human Resources and Skills Development Canada (2009b) website indicates that TMWs are, in fact, eligible for employment insurance: "Temporary foreign workers are eligible to receive regular and sickness Employment Insurance benefits if they are unemployed, have a valid work permit and meet eligibility criteria, including having worked a sufficient number of hours." However, the department's employment insurance policy manual, *Digest of Benefit Entitlement Principles* (Human Resources and Skills Development Canada, 2009a) is confusing and uses doublespeak as it grapples with the issue of the TMW. The guide states that a person whose work permit expires or is limited to one employer cannot demonstrate availability, even if the worker is willing and able to seek work. However, it also states that the referee must consider the specific facts of the case, asking such questions as: "Is the individual permitted to seek work with other Canadian employers? Is their work permit renewable? Has the work permit expired permanently?" The guide goes on to say that a claimant who does not currently have a work permit is not necessarily barred from working, because the claimant may be able to secure a work permit as soon as employment is secured due to the type of work he or she performs. This section has been indicated as "currently under review," since September 2003. The contradictory information provided is problematic because it is impossible to know clearly whether and under which conditions TMWs are eligible for employment insurance.

In some provinces, reports from lawyers and nongovernmental workers tell a different story than the jurisprudence. In Alberta, for instance, applications for employment insurance are usually accepted initially, so no appeal is necessary.[19] The change is good news for TMWs in Alberta, because there is a growing recognition that they are eligible for employment insurance benefits while their permits are still valid and they are actively looking for work.[20] Yet, employment insurance officers in other provinces are still routinely refusing benefits to migrant workers in the belief that such workers simply are not entitled to them. As a result, unions representing TMWs assert that less than one per cent of TMWs are actually able to claim regular employment insurance benefits in Canada (MacLaren & Lapointe, 2010). Given the troubling discrepancies among legislation, jurisprudence, and internal, unpublished policies, it has become crucial that Human Resources and Skills Development Canada communicate its employment insurance policy in a more coherent manner and that it ensure consistency between the official position and the decisions rendered on specific cases.

The overall administration of the TFWP involves a number of key players who do not always take full responsibility for the protection and well-being of TMWs. In addition, the restrictive nature of the work permit is contentious: strict conditions on work permits dissuade TMWs from changing employers and lead them to believe, mistakenly, that employment insurance benefits are not available to them. Consequently, TMWs who are laid off and cannot find alternative employment, cannot access employment insurance, and cannot otherwise afford to stay in Canada, are expected to leave. As the following will demonstrate, the ability of TMWs to access the full employment-related rights package also depends on the kind of work permit that was first issued to them.

The Challenge of Providing the Same Employment Rights to TMWs

Although the federal government has jurisdiction over "aliens," provinces are responsible for protecting workplace rights for TMWs. In theory, TMWs are afforded the same legal protections in the workplace as other workers in the same province, but these rights, which are complaint-driven, do not transfer well into practice. The following section explores how the employment contract, the Alberta *Employment*

Standards Code, and Alberta's workers' compensation limit the protections for TMWs in Alberta.

The Employment Contract

A key requirement under the TFWP is that the employer must sign an employment contract before initiating the Human Resources and Skills Development Canada labour market opinion process, and Human Resources and Skills Development Canada must approve the contract before it will issue a labour market opinion. The contract is a detailed job description that stipulates the terms and conditions of employment, including the minimum and maximum number of hours of work per week and the rate of pay. The employer must forward to the employee a signed copy of the contract, which the employee must then sign and present, with other required documents, at the mission abroad or at a port of entry (Human Resources and Skills Development Canada, 2009e). On paper, these layers of protection may appear satisfactory; in practice, however, protection gaps exist for the TMW. The best example of a protection gap is the worker's right to return airfare under the low-skill pilot project. As noted above, employers of TMWs in National Occupational Classification C and D occupations are required, under the low-skill pilot project, to have a specific contract, signed by both the employer and the employee, that outlines the employer's obligation towards the foreign worker (CIC, 2010e, p. 34; Human Resources and Skills Development Canada, 2009c). Among the specific contract provisions, employers are required to pay for an employee's flight to and from Canada. If a worker has had more than one employer throughout the duration of his or her work permit, the final employer is responsible for paying for the airfare. What remedies are available to a worker whose employer refuses to pay for the flight home? Although the employment contract contains mandatory provisions, the federal government cannot use it to enforce the employment rights of TMWs:

> The Government of Canada is not a party to the contract. [HRSDC] has no authority to intervene in the employer/employee relationship or to enforce the terms and conditions of employment. It is the responsibility of each party to the contract to know the laws that apply to them and to look after their own interests. (Human Resources and Skills Development Canada, 2009e)

Thus, even if Human Resources and Skills Development Canada officers use the contract to assist them in formulating their labour market opinion, the department has no regulatory authority to monitor employer compliance with the employment contract (Fudge & MacPhail, 2009, p. 30). This is so precisely because TMWs' employment rights fall under provincial jurisdiction.

In Alberta, the Employment Standards Code has only limited authority to address contractual violations. An Employment Standards officer can intervene only when an employer has violated the code, for example, when an employee complains that the employer has not paid "earnings" to which the employee is entitled. However, the officer cannot enforce the contractual right to return airfare because "this is considered an expense, required under Service Canada's Labour Market Opinion but which is outside of the scope of Employment Standards."[21] Representatives of Service Canada in Alberta recently confirmed that they would not enforce remuneration for airfare in the province.[22]

A TMW might find redress by contesting a contractual violation (such as return airfare) through court proceedings, but the time constraints of a temporary work visa might present a practical barrier to successful litigation. It takes nine to twelve months for a case to be heard in a provincial court, and it is reasonable to assume that a worker who has been denied return airfare is nearing the expiration date of his or her work permit. Moreover, litigating from abroad is an onerous proposition for a worker in the low-skill pilot project. What other options are available? The worker might pay for the flight out of his or her own pocket, or report to the Canada Border Service Agency for a removal order (but this will usually bar the worker from returning to Canada; see Immigration and Refugee Protection Act, secs. 47, 48, 52), or remain in Canada without authorization. So, although protection exists, it might be inaccessible – especially for low-skilled workers. Both levels of government offer protections to TMWs, but each is limited in its ability to enforce these rights, which is especially troubling given that protections were implemented to mitigate the "risks of similar abuse and poor working conditions" with the expected growth of the TFWP (Office of the Auditor General of Canada, 2009, p. 33).

Practical and Legal Hurdles for TMWs: A Complaint-Driven Process

Another barrier to the protection of TMWs in the workplace is the fact that a complaint-driven process is regularly used to address violations of TMWs' employment rights. If a worker faces a violation of his or her employment rights, the onus is placed on that worker to initiate a complaint against the employer. Initiating a complaint against one's employer can be both difficult and intimidating, and can often lead to "self-censorship" as TMWs may fear losing their job if they file a complaint.

In Alberta, a worker whose employment rights have been breached under the Employment Standards Code can launch a complaint through the province's Employment Standards office. Although the complaint process involves no cost to the complainant, TMWs find it intimidating. In a 2007 newspaper report, a spokeswoman for the Ministry of Employment, Immigration and Industry recognized that there was a "real disincentive" for TMWs to lodge complaints, and noted that only eighteen of the four thousand complaints being investigated came from people who self-identified as TMWs (Harding & Walton, 2007). Moreover, the bureaucratic nature of the complaint process might seem overwhelming to a TMW. Before making a complaint to an Employment Standards officer, the worker must fill out and submit a "self-help kit" to the employer as a first attempt to resolve the situation. This step is not a formal requirement of the code, but an officer has the authority to refuse to accept or investigate a claim if the worker has not first explored other means of resolving the dispute (Government of Alberta, 2009; Employment Standards Code, sec. 83(3)). Also, it is not easy to determine a foreign worker's entitlements under provincial legislation. Alberta Employment and Immigration provides documents that inform workers of their rights, but these documents are in English only, as are the complaint forms and the instructions that accompany it. Thus, the complaint process itself could prove a barrier to TMWs who may struggle to fill out the forms, adequately explain the breach, and calculate the compensation due them.

Not only is the complaint process challenging for TMWs; the protections the Employment Standards Code offers workers may not be worth the risk, because the code was not designed to consider the unique situations of these workers. For example, termination pay is an important aspect of the code, as a provision to bridge the financial gap between prior and new employment, but no termination pay is required if an employee has worked less than three months, and only one week of termination pay is required if the employee has worked less than two years.[23] Because a TMW's work permit is typically no longer than two years, this minimal institutional protection may be of little value to these workers. The length of time it takes for an employer to get a labour market opinion and for the restrictions on a work permit to be changed means that a single week of termination pay or notice will usually be insufficient to fill the gap between old and new jobs. Furthermore, termination pay is not required for certain occupations and in certain situations. While these exceptions are not unique to TMWs, only these workers are legally barred from finding immediate alternate employment.

Workers' Compensation

Temporary migrant workers are also protected under workers' compensation legislation, but few report claims to Alberta's Workers' Compensation Board, and those who do may find that the protection, although "the same" as that offered every other Albertan, is quite different due to work permit restrictions and their temporary status. A central goal of the Workers' Compensation Board is to bring a worker back to a state of "pre-accident employability" (Workers' Compensation Board - Alberta, 2004a, p. 2). Thus, entitlement to compensation lasts until the worker is physically fit to work in a job of at least equivalent pay. Ideally, after recovery, the employee returns to the same job with the same employer for the same pay. If this is not possible, and the worker is physically capable of working in a different occupation, the Workers' Compensation Board will provide wage-loss supplement benefits, that is, it will "top up" the wages of the worker to match what he or she was making before the injury or illness.[24] The Workers' Compensation Board is concerned only with "physical impediments to work," not with legal impediments such as restrictions on the work permit. Therefore, if the Workers' Compensation Board considers the worker to be physically fit to work but in a different occupation, it will ignore the work permit restrictions and treat the worker as employable. This means the Workers' Compensation Board assesses which job in Alberta the worker might be suited for and calculates wage-loss supplement benefits accordingly (Workers' Compensation Board - Alberta, 2008). This policy is extremely unfair to TMWs: although they may be physically able and willing to work in a different job for comparable pay, they are legally barred from doing so – and because of the restrictions on their work permit, they are no longer entitled to compensation under the Workers' Compensation Act.[25]

Barriers in Transitioning to Permanent Residency for TMWs

One reason for the increased number of temporary migrants arriving in Canada is that temporary migrants have discovered that it is "administratively simpler" to apply for and obtain permanent residence if they have already been admitted as a "temporary" skilled worker than to do so from abroad (Papademetriou & O'Neil, 2004, p. 8). However, this may have considerable effects on the rights of all TMWs and their prospects for full integration. For example, the risk of being exploited through inferior wages or working conditions "can be quite substantial in the case of temporary admissions, where the [m]igrants may have to leave the country if they lose their job" (Papademetriou & O'Neil, 2004, p. 11). In contrast, this risk is considerably lower for immigrants who are granted permanent work and residency rights from the beginning, because they are free to change jobs. Moreover, those "who ultimately achieve permanent residence may not make a successful transition because they did not have access to settlement or language services when they arrived ... Because two-step immigration extends the amount of time people must live in Canada before being eligible for permanent residence and then citizenship, it will also have implications on their long-term relationship to Canada" (Alboim, 2009, pp. 49, 52). An additional problem with the transition-to-permanence admission is that it is mainly directed at educated and skilled workers, offering little hope of permanent settlement and few opportunities for lower-skilled TMWs.

Legally, all TMWs, except seasonal workers admitted under the Seasonal Agricultural Worker Program,[26] may apply for permanent residence. While TMWs are expected to leave Canada after their authorized period of stay, intent to become a permanent resident does not preclude them from being admitted temporarily, as long as the immigration officer "is satisfied that they will leave Canada by the end of the period authorized for their stay."[27] Migrant workers can transition from temporary to permanent resident status from within Canada in four ways: (1) the Live-in Caregiver Program, (2) the Federal Skilled Worker Program, (3) the Canadian Experience Class, and (4) Provincial and Territorial Nominee Programs. All of these programs are subcategories of the economic class, which also includes Quebec-Selected Skilled Workers and Business Immigrants. Among the existing temporary work programs, the Live-in Caregiver Program has a unique provision: live-in caregivers may apply for permanent residency after having completed two years of authorized full-time employment within three years of their entry into Canada under the program.[28] The Federal Skilled Worker Program and Canadian Experience Class are the almost exclusive preserve of skilled TMWs, while Provincial and Territorial Nominee Programs apply to both skilled and low-skilled workers. To clarify how this difference affects skilled and low-skilled TMWs, the following section begins with an exploration of how existing federal programs for permanent residence actually prevent low-skilled workers from shifting from temporary to permanent resident status.

Barriers to Permanent Residency for Low-Skilled TFWs

Both the Federal Skilled Worker Program and the Canadian Experience Class exclude low-skilled TMWs as potential applicants for permanent residence. For a long time, the Federal Skilled Worker Program had admitted workers from all skilled occupations. Applications were assessed on the basis of "available funds" and needed to amass sufficient points from six selection factors (education, language ability, work experience including type of occupation and years worked, age, arrangements for employment in Canada, and adaptability).[29] This approach was criticized for being insufficiently responsive to short-term labour market demands (Nakache & Kinoshita, 2010). New eligibility rules were introduced in 2008 (Government of Canada, 2008), and amended in 2010, to remedy this weakness. Currently, eligibility under the skilled worker class is limited to: (1) applicants with an offer of arranged employment, or (2) applicants with one year of full-time work experience in one of twenty-nine listed occupations. Any application that does not fall within one of these two categories is not processed.[30] In addition, these two categories include only skilled occupations (i.e., Skill type 0 [managerial occupations], Skill Level A [professional occupations] or B [technical occupations and skilled trades] on the Canadian National Occupational Classification list). Therefore, low-skilled workers hoping to earn admission to Canada through the Federal Skilled Worker Program must try to fit within one of these two categories that are aimed specifically at skilled workers.

While the federal government was working to limit eligibility under the skilled worker class, it also expanded immigration opportunities for those already residing in Canada as students or temporary skilled workers. The Canadian Experience Class was implemented in

September 2008; its stated objective was "to make the immigration system more attractive and accessible to individuals with diverse skills
from around the world and more responsive to Canada's labour market needs" (CIC, 2008a). This program allows skilled TMWs with at
least two years of full-time skilled work experience in Canada, and
foreign graduates from a Canadian post-secondary institution with at
least one year of full-time skilled work experience in Canada, to apply
for permanent residence from within the country. Applicants must
also demonstrate proficiency in either English or French and their intention to reside in any part of Canada other than Quebec.[31] This new
immigration stream permits skilled workers under the TFWP to apply
for permanent residency from within Canada, but individuals in National Occupational Classification C and D occupations (those requiring lower levels of formal training, like truck drivers [C occupation] or
cleaners [D occupation]) are not eligible.

Another impediment to low-skilled workers' obtaining permanent
residency is the conditions related to family accompaniment. Immigration legislation does not bar TMWs from having family members accompany them to Canada, but low-skilled workers are less likely than
skilled workers to bring their families. The onus is on potential employees to demonstrate to the immigration officer that they are capable of
supporting their dependents while in Canada. A key issue here is the
employment situation of the applicant's spouse. Although the spouse
of a skilled worker is entitled to enter Canada with an open work permit – one with no restrictions on the employer – the spouse of a worker
hired under the low-skill pilot project is not eligible for an open permit
and requires a labour market opinion to apply for a work permit. This,
combined with the fact that workers with lower levels of formal training generally earn less (House of Commons, Canada, 2009, p. 14), raises
"very legitimate concerns regarding the applicant's bona fides and
ability to support their dependents while in Canada."[32] Furthermore,
low-skilled TMWs must demonstrate that they can meet the expenses
associated with bringing their family to Canada (travel expenses,
health care, school-related costs, and lodging [CIC, 2010e]). Low-skilled
TMWs "are less likely to be able to demonstrate adequate financial support and therefore less likely to be accompanied by family members"
(House of Commons, Canada, 2009, p. 14).[33] In summary, Canada wants
low-skilled workers to leave the country after a certain period of time
and offers skilled workers a pathway to settle permanently.

Provincial and Territorial Nominee Programs: An Interesting Avenue to Permanent Residency for Low-Skilled TMWs?

For most low-skilled workers, the only viable option for accessing permanent residency is through a Provincial and Territorial Nominee Program, which is a federal-provincial/territorial agreement under which a province or territory determines its own criteria for the selection of potential immigrants, based on its demographic and labour market needs and priorities.[34] Once selected by a province or territory, applicants are granted permanent residency if they meet federal health and security requirements.[35] Provincial and territorial nominees are not subject to the requirements of the points system used in the Federal Skilled Worker Program, nor does Citizenship and Immigration Canada impose a minimum selection threshold for these candidates. To date, all provinces (with the exception of Quebec) and territories (except for Nunavut) have negotiated Provincial and Territorial Nominee Program agreements with the federal government. Although they are relatively new (the first Provincial and Territorial Nominee Program was introduced in 1998 in Manitoba), admissions under these programs have grown quickly: from approximately 500 (or 0.9 per cent of admissions under the economic stream) in 1999 to 36,419 (or 19.5 per cent of admissions under the economic stream) in 2010 (CIC, 2011a, p. 6). In 2009, Citizenship and Immigration Canada anticipated admitting as many as 40,000 provincial and territorial nominees annually between 2010 and 2012 (CIC, 2009a, pp. 9–10, 15; CIC, 2009f, p. 10; Office of the Auditor General of Canada, 2009, p. 12).

Provincial and Territorial Nominee Programs offer a promising solution for low-skilled migrant workers in an immigration context where federal avenues for transitioning from temporary to permanent status are almost the exclusive preserve of skilled TMWs. However, these programs come with their own limitations. First, most Provincial and Territorial Nominee Programs are "employer driven," meaning that migrant workers must have a full-time permanent job offer with a local employer to be eligible for nomination. This requirement could create a power imbalance between the employer and the TMW. Second, although several Provincial and Territorial Nominee Programs have outlined specific categories for low-skilled MWs, these categories often limit eligibility to a narrow range of occupations or industries (especially in British Columbia, Alberta, Saskatchewan,

Prince Edward Island, the Yukon, and the Northwest Territories). Low-skilled MWs must fit within narrow categories based on occupations or industries that differ by a province or territory's unique labour market needs. Also, several categories were established as pilot projects of limited duration. These facts suggest that these programs are designed to attract low-skilled workers to a specific province or territory permanently, but are a "limited time offer" until a labour shortage is filled (Nakache & D'Aoust, 2012).[36] Finally, although some provinces do not have specific categories for low-skilled MWs, Newfoundland and Labrador and New Brunswick allow low-skilled MWs to apply under the program's skilled worker categories. This means that if low-skilled MWs meet locally defined needs, their applications will be considered on a case-by-case basis. This case-by-case determination exemplifies the lack of transparency in the recruitment process and reinforces the message that these programs target more overtly skilled migrant workers.

In many ways, low-skilled TMWs are systematically barred from applying for permanent residency through the existing federal immigration streams (the Federal Skilled Worker program and the Canadian Experience Class). In addition, TMWs face many challenges when having their family members accompany them to Canada, making it unlikely that low-skilled migrant workers will settle permanently.

Conclusion

The legal treatment TMWs receive in Canada and their chances of integration depend to a great extent on their employment-related rights and their concrete opportunities to achieve a more secure immigration status (through permanent residency). This chapter has shown that although all TMWs have a limited ability to take full advantage of participation, integration, and protection because of the practical and legal parameters placed around their employment-related rights, skilled workers have more opportunities than low-skilled workers to access permanent residency from within Canada. Temporary Migrant Worker Programs produce precarious status for non-citizens, but they do so unevenly. They also offer some skilled TMWs an avenue to secure status. I now turn to policy recommendations that might mitigate the external conditionality of presence and improve the potential and conditions surrounding settlement for migrant workers in all skill and entrance subcategories.

The significant increase in the number of TMWs has led to a growing concern about their employment-related rights. On paper, these workers have the same workplace rights as any other workers in Canada, but in reality they do not. The strict employer-specific conditions imposed on work permits limit not only the rights a TMW might otherwise exercise; they also limit the ability of federal and provincial governments to protect workers from exploitation. Because TMWs lack employment mobility, they are more likely to endure abusive employer practices rather than risk being unemployed. To reduce the power imbalance between employers and TMWs, and to enable greater labour mobility amongst TMWs, it is essential that the employer-tied work permit be replaced by a sector- or province-specific work permit; this recommendation has already been made by the Standing Committee on Citizenship and Immigration (House of Commons, Canada, 2009, p. 25).

Another problem is the lack of effective mechanisms to protect the rights of migrant workers at work. A complaint-based mechanism to enforce basic provincial labour standards is insufficient for the unique vulnerabilities of TMWs, who might report employment law issues – but need to understand what their rights are, who they should talk to, and what steps they should take. Perhaps most importantly, they need to see that the benefits of speaking out outweigh the inherent risks.

Finally, despite official claims that the TFWP is temporary, employers are using both skilled and low-skilled TMWs to fill long-term and even permanent vacancies. This highlights the need to reconsider the increasingly short-term focus of Canada's labour migration policies, for such a focus is unrealistic and will not help Canada achieve its long-term goals of promoting population and labour force growth. Focusing on the short term is also unfair to the vast majority of TMWs, who are expected to spend years in Canada without contributing to our society in the long run. It sends a message that Canada wants low-skilled individuals only as workers but skilled individuals as future citizens.

Alberta's employment and immigration minister, Thomas Lukaszuk, recently addressed problems with the "temporary" nature of the TFWP: "In my opinion, it was a program that had fulfilled its mandate, [by] suddenly providing a large number of workers to an economy that suddenly had a massive shortage of workers .... It's not working well now. It's a temporary solution to a permanent problem" (in Audette, 2010, paras. 2, 3). Minister Lukaszuk also maintained that permanent solutions for the temporary foreign workforce should be taken into consideration (Audette, 2010, pára. 12). The fundamental question, therefore, is whether it is really in Canada's best interest to have policies that do not support the low-skilled temporary foreign worker and do not give such workers the option to become permanent residents. There is a need for wider public debate about these federal policies, which could transform the landscape of economic immigration to Canada for years to come.

NOTES

1 TMWs enter under the Temporary Foreign Worker Program. Along with others, I use *TMWs* when referring to people, and reserve *TFWP* for the Program.
2 Between 2008 and 2009 there was a drop in the number of TMW entries to Canada (from 192,373 to 178,271) and an increase in the number of TMWs present in Canada (from 250,492 to 282,771). The decrease in entries is due to the 2008/2009 economic downturn and subsequent pressure from Human Resources and Skills Development Canada (HRSDC) on employers to hire Canadian workers (due to rising unemployment). However, with the recent economic recovery and job creation, the number of temporary migrant worker entries increased to 182,322 in 2010 (CIC, 2011a).
3 The National Occupational Classification (NOC) is a standard created by Human Resources and Skills Development Canada (HRSDC) that classifies and describes all occupations in the Canadian labour market according to skill types O, A, B, C, and D. Occupations coded "O" are senior and middle-management occupations; "A" are professional occupations; "B" are technical and skilled trade occupations; and "C" and "D" are occupations requiring lower levels of formal training. Throughout this chapter, when using the term "low-skilled workers," I am referring to workers performing jobs in NOC C and D occupations.
4 In 1973, the idea of "temporary foreign worker" was introduced to legislation, with the underlying assumption that they would perform work that unemployed Canadians were unwilling to perform (Sharma, 2006, p. 97). Today, Canada relies heavily on TMWs to fill jobs on an ongoing basis. Decisions about exclusion now involve the distinction between "high-skilled" versus "low-skilled" migrant workers, a dichotomy that makes it possible to determine who can ultimately be included or excluded from the spatial and symbolic boundaries of the Canadian nation. Skilled MWs, who perform jobs that Canadians are willing to perform, are seen as deserving a permanent resident status; in contrast, low-skilled MWs, who perform

the "dirty jobs" that Canadians are unwilling to perform, are expected to spend years in Canada as workers, but not as future citizens.

5 Undergirding my analysis is the argument that Canadian immigration law preserves the assumed identity of the Canadian nation by excluding low-skilled TMWs by positioning them as "outsiders" or "Others" (see, e.g., Derrida, 1968, 1992, 2002; Fitzpatrick, 1995, 2001; Honig, 2001; Kyambi, 2004). Law is an essential agent in the nation's relationship to the "Other." As Fitzpatrick notes, "Nation cannot be encompassed in an originary correspondence to some thing(s) which would tell us what it positively 'is.' On the contrary ... identity is formed in terms of what it is not" (1995, p. 10). The need for boundaries and the need to have an "Other" are common to national identity and law. Honig (2001) also shows how, historically, the "foreignness" of outsiders has been used to establish the self-identity of "insiders" and, more importantly, how certain foreigners are used to "re-invigorate" democracy, as myths about foreign founders are central to the stories many nations tell about themselves.

6 *The Constitution Act*, 1867 (UK), 30 & 31 Victoria, c. 3, secs. 91, 92, and 95.

7 *Immigration and Refugee Protection Regulations*, SOR/2002-227.

8 Concerns have been raised about the rate-setting process. The House of Commons Standing Committee on Citizenship and Immigration has called for more transparency and stakeholder input in calculating prevailing wage rates (Fudge & MacPhail, 2009, pp. 9–10; House of Commons, Canada, 2009, p. 24). In response, HRSDC issued revised instructions to provide clear and consistent evaluation criteria. While acknowledging the progress made, the auditor general recommended that HRSDC also provide clear directives, tools, and training to officers engaged in issuing labour market opinions, and implement a framework to ensure the quality and consistency of opinions across Canada (Office of the Auditor General of Canada, 2009, p. 31).

9 *Immigration and Refugee Protection Regulations*, secs. 179, 200. A TMW may intend to apply for permanent residence or may have an application in process, but the officer must be satisfied that the applicant will leave Canada at the end of the temporary period authorized, regardless of a future decision with respect to permanent status (*IRPA*, sec. 22[2]; *Immigration and Refugee Protection Regulations*, sec. 183; CIC, 2009b, p. 51).

10 *Immigration and Refugee Protection Regulations*, sec. 201.1. TMWs are allowed to apply to change or extend their work permit from within Canada before it expires by mailing their application to the Vegreville, Alberta, Case Processing Centre (*Immigration and Refugee Protection Regulations*, sec. 201.1). Although a worker can submit his or her application on the last day

of the work permit (section 201[1]), a CIC form stipulates: "If your current temporary resident status is still valid you can apply for an extension of your stay providing you apply at least 30 days before the expiry date of your current status" (CIC, 2010a, p. 3). In practice, however, a TMW can mail his or her application (with a tracking number) on the last date of expiry to Vegreville (Susan Wood, Edmonton Community Legal Centre, Edmonton, 5 February 2010, email communication).

11 *Immigration and Refugee Protection Regulations*, sec. 182

12 *Immigration and Refugee Protection Regulations*, sec. 186(u); sec. 124(1)(b) and (c).

13 Interview with officials from Alberta Employment and Immigration, Edmonton, 12 June 2009; interview with Randy Gurlock, Citizenship and Immigration Canada, Ottawa, 8 June 2009.

14 *Employment Insurance Act*, secs. 7(1), (2), (3), and 18(a) (Government of Canada, 1996). Qualifying periods range from 420 hours if the rate of unemployment is more than 13 per cent to 700 hours if the rate of unemployment is 6 per cent or less. For a new entrant to the workforce, the number of qualifying hours is 910 hours (*Employment Insurance Act*, 1996, sec. 7[3]).

15 *The Attorney General of Canada v. Cornelissen-O-Neill*, (A-652- 93), Federal C.A. at para. 1.

16 CUB 43501, Simmons (Jerome, J.), 21 December 1998.

17 For a complete list of all case law in that field, see Service Canada, "The Index of Jurisprudence: A Supplement to the Digest of Benefit Entitlement Principles," http://srv130.services.gc.ca/indexjurisprudence. Accessed 1 November 2009.

18 For additional examples related to EI, see Nakache and Kinoshita (2010), pp. 19–20).

19 Anonymous interview, Catholic Social Services, Edmonton, 12 June2009; interview with Susan Wood and Sarah Eadie, Edmonton Community Legal Centre, Edmonton, 9 June 2009.

20 For more details on the EI process in Alberta, see Nakache and Kinoshita (2010, p. 21).

21 Letter received from the Edmonton Community Legal Centre, 2008, in response to a claim for unpaid airfare.

22 Susan Wood, Edmonton Community Legal Centre, Edmonton, 5 February 2010, email communication.

23 *Employment Standards Code*, sec. 56.

24 *Workers' Compensation Act*, secs. 56(8), (9); sec. 63; also Workers' Compensation Board - Alberta (2004b).

25 Anonymous interview, Workers' Compensation Board, Edmonton, 4 June 2009; interview with Douglas Sackney, Workers' Compensation Board, Edmonton, 8 June 2009.

26 It is technically impossible for seasonal workers admitted to Canada under this program to access permanent residency from within Canada: the work permit is valid for one period of eight months, is non-renewable, and workers must leave the country after the expiration of this period.

27 *IRPA*, sec. 22(2); *Immigration and Refugee Protection Regulations*, sec. 183.

28 *IRPA*, secs. 110 to 115.

29 *IRPA*, sec. 12(2); *Immigration and Refugee Protection Regulations*, sec. 76(2).

30 In June 2010, Citizenship and Immigration Canada (CIC) published revised Ministerial Instructions that affect the Federal Skilled Worker Program. For more on this topic, see http://www.cic.gc.ca/English/immigrate/skilled/apply-who-instructions.asp.

31 *Immigration and Refugee Protection Regulations*, sec. 87.1.

32 Section 5.25 ("Work Permits requiring HRSDC confirmation R 203") of CIC (2010b) was revised in July 2009, September 2009, and February 2010. I am quoting here from an earlier version (May 2009, 32, hard copy on file with author).

33 Spouses of work permit holders who have been nominated for permanent residence under a Provincial and Territorial Nominee Program are entitled to open work permits for the duration of the principal applicant's work permit, irrespective of the applicant's skill level (CIC, 2010b, p. 67). For details on Provincial and Territorial Nominee Programs, see Nakache and Kinoshita (2010, pp. 33–4).

34 This section is based on the results of documentary analysis, as well as on research questionnaires completed in May–June 2010 by key governmental actors in the administration of Provincial and Territorial Nominee Programs. For a more comprehensive analysis of Provincial and Territorial Nominee Programs, see Nakache & D'Aoust (forthcoming).

35 *Immigration and Refugee Protection Regulations*, sec. 87

36 Of the provinces and territories that offer opportunities for low-skilled workers to obtain nomination through their Provincial and Territorial Nominee Programs (British Columbia, Alberta, Saskatchewan, Manitoba, the Yukon, and the Northwest Territories), only the Yukon and Manitoba do not restrict low-skilled applicants to specific occupations. For more on this topic, see Nakache & D'Aoust (2012).

PART TWO

Precarious Status and Everyday Lives

5 "This Is My Life": Youth Negotiating Legality and Belonging in Toronto

JULIE YOUNG

When I think about it, like I'm not going to be like, oh it's not my problem, obviously, because it's my family. But the thing is, it's not like I had a choice in what was happening because the thing is I was born into it so it's like I've had this with me since [*pause*] forever. Like, ever since I existed so besides that like. This is my life, so I've gotta cope with whatever.

– Ibrahim, 16-year-old awaiting decision on a Pre-Removal Risk Assessment

The migration process reverberates through everyday spaces and relationships. Precarious legal status in particular must be negotiated in relation to people and contexts in a range of interactions from health clinics, to recreation programs, to schools. I examine the everyday experiences of six youth living with precarious status in Toronto, focusing on spaces of school and family.[1] Their narratives reveal that belonging is multidimensional and negotiated. It is negotiated in the encounter with moments of uncertainty or tension when their identities might be revealed or must be reconciled with their contested presence. For these youth, age and immigration trajectory – including their status on entry and changes to their status over time – are key elements that affect their sense of belonging.

Two key insights emerge from the youths' narratives that relate to the spaces of school and family. School was an important place of belonging, but it was complicated by their precarious status: at times their status was not relevant, while at other times it was starkly highlighted. Moreover, the youth expressed trust in school authorities but also indicated that school officials were not aware of their status. Family dynamics were also affected as the youth negotiated their precarious status. The youth learned about or confronted their status in crucial moments as their family's immigration case made its way through the legal system. One child found out about his family's situation just as the case came before the refugee tribunal and another learned only once her family had been issued a deportation order. The youths' narratives highlight issues that arose as they navigated various spaces and moments in their lives where they were confronted with their legal status. Their precarious legal status influenced how they thought of themselves in relation to other students and the extent to which they felt able to make legitimate claims to the streets, neighbourhoods, and life opportunities that comprised their daily lives.

Negotiating Belonging: The Everyday Lives of Youth with Precarious Status

In focusing on the notion of "belonging," I draw from the work of Marco Antonsich (2010), who argues that belonging is a process, a negotiation – not a status. He identifies two key aspects that are simultaneously at work in the negotiation of belonging: "place-belongingness" and the "politics of belonging." The former refers to "a personal, intimate, feeling of being 'at home' in a place" while the latter underscores "belonging as a discursive resource which constructs, claims, justifies, or resists forms of socio-spatial inclusion/exclusion" (p. 645). Antonsich argues that both the personal and the discursive dimensions are necessary to understand what is at stake in claims of "belonging." An individual's attachment to and identification with a place cannot be separated from the context in which these feelings are negotiated and how that individual is positioned within that social context. In this sense, the politics of belonging "involves two opposite sides: the side that claims belonging and the side that has the power of 'granting' belonging. This means that a process of negotiation ... is always in place" (p. 650).

Antonsich indicates that legal status is a crucial mediating factor in relation to belonging, citing several US-based studies that find a "negative correlation between an individual's insecure legal status and her/ his sense of place-belongingness" (p. 648). Similarly, Caitlin Cahill (2010) talks about the "contradictory positioning" of a group of undocumented youth in Utah "between hope and despair," where the burden of their status and the negative stereotypes it engendered "made these young people lose hope and want to give up" (p. 158). However,

Cahill explains "that many of these young people found the strength to go on because they wanted to break the stereotypes that were laid on them" (p. 158). Moreover, Roberto Gonzales (2008) argues that despite the constraints of their legal status in the United States, "unauthorized students are not without the ability to take willing and purposive action in the face of social restraints" (p. 221).

Antonsich's (2010) identification of "personal" and "discursive" aspects of belonging is similar to the distinction drawn between formal and substantive citizenship: while attaining formal citizenship status may provide access to the rights and responsibilities of full membership in a given society, in practice – that is, substantively – not all citizens are treated or protected equally (G. Pratt, 2005; Ramos-Zayas, 2004). Indeed, Landolt and Goldring (in this volume) argue that attaining "regularized" status after having lived with precarious status does not automatically lead to improved economic security. While legal status may formally be the precondition for full participation in society, its absence is not always a barrier and achieving full legal status does not ensure full participation. People who do not have the status of citizenship participate in meaningful ways in their communities, and some researchers suggest that residence in a place ought to be sufficient to be recognized as a member of that place (Varsanyi, 2006; Watt, 2006; Young, 2011). And yet for residents whose legal status is precarious, their claims to membership and belonging are constantly eroded and discounted.

Pierre Bourdieu's (1979) discussion of "distinction" is helpful in examining this entrenched understanding that equates citizenship status with belonging. He argues that processes of distinction classify identities and naturalize perceived differences within societies. Inequitable experiences and practices are "misrecognized" as the natural order of things and remain hidden because they are understood to be justified (p. 172). We can see this process of distinction in the practice of immigration policy and its classification of diverse identities and mobilities into a limited set of legal categories. For example, children whose parents do not qualify for childcare subsidies on the basis of their parents' legal status are excluded from the benefits that this program provides to families with permanent status. The differential treatment of children is justified on the basis of differing forms of citizenship status and is viewed by state officials and the general public as acceptable on this basis. Goldring, Berinstein, and Bernhard (2009) argue that the legal framework of the Canadian immigration system sanctions a gradation of rights and entitlements on the basis of immigration status.

This power of distinction is implicated in everyday practices that normalize the boundaries of who belongs and who does not. Based on extensive, longitudinal research they have carried out in the United States with children of immigrant parents, Suarez-Orozco and Suarez-Orozco (2001) argue the "legal status of an immigrant child influences – perhaps more so than national origins and socio-economic background of the parents – his or her experiences and life chances" (p. 33). Children's immigration status is inseparable from that of their parents, as the legal status of a parent influences children's experiences and outcomes regardless of their status – even children who have citizenship by birth (Bernhard et al., 2007; Fix & Zimmermann, 1999; Gonzales, 2008). For example, parents may be hesitant to register them with authorities: some children do not have identification (e.g., a birth certificate) that proves their status and may as a result not be registered for provincial health care insurance (Bernhard et al., 2007). Parents may not enrol their children in school or participate in their education due to a concern that teachers and administrators may be in a position to reveal their status to immigration authorities (Bernhard et al., 2005; Bernhard & Freire, 1997; Yau, 1995). Parents also have less time to spend with children due to the need to support the family's survival, which may entail working multiple jobs, travelling around the city to access services, and dealing with the family's immigration process (Bernhard & Freire, 1997; Fantino & Colak, 2001; Yau, 1995). When a family is living with precarious status, the struggle to survive and avoid detection has serious impacts on the mental health of all family members (Saad, in this volume).

Children and youth face many challenges associated with the migration process, including loss of extended family, friends, community, and familiarity with institutions, as well as a range of issues throughout the settlement process, including potential language barriers, possible tension with their parents, uncertain financial situations, social isolation, and alienation (Fantino & Colak, 2001; Kilbride et al., 2000). Emigration does not sever all ties with the country of origin; family ties are maintained across borders, and notions of identity and belonging are better understood as transnational and multiple (Bailey et al., 2002; Levitt & Glick Schiller, 2004). The effects of such ties may be contradictory: Fantino and Colak (2001) suggest that individuals with transnational connections face "not the stress of belonging to two cultures but the stress of belonging to none" (p. 589). That being said, growing up and going to school in a particular place creates strong identifications with that place (Gonzales, 2008; Suarez-Orozco & Suarez-Orozco, 2001).

In his research with undocumented youth in southern California, Gonzales (2008) asks, "What are the consequences of growing up 'American,' yet living with only partial access to the mechanisms that promote social mobility" (p. 224)?

Legal status is worked out in an ongoing fashion in the everyday spaces and relationships that people negotiate. Key among these spaces for the youth in this study were the school and the family. In both spaces, "the state" intervenes and influences its character; the state and its borders are never far away. In speaking of the space of the state, I refer not only to the legal framework through which immigration status is determined, but also to the individuals who implement it at border crossings, immigration offices, hospitals, and schools. Discourses on legality and belonging are diffused throughout the social body, meaning that legal status must constantly be negotiated in "official" and "unofficial" interactions. People living with precarious status are confronted with their status through the practices of individuals interpreting state policies in a variety of spaces (Mountz, 2003; Sharma, 2006). Thus it is through socio-spatial practices of classification, and not through the legal framework alone, that legal status is defined, assigned, legitimated – and importantly, contested (Isin & Wood, 1999; Ong, 2003; Secor, 2004). Belonging is negotiated in the tensions between and within these classifications. Anna Secor (2004) argues the ascription of immigration status "never completely succeeds in its administration of citizens and strangers" (p. 353). Tensions that arise in the day-to-day negotiation of legal status point out alternatives to the state's powerful and insistent narratives of citizenship and belonging (Ong, 2003; Secor, 2004; Watt, 2006; Young, 2011).

The youths' own narratives underscore the complex ways in which legal status influences their experiences of belonging. For the youth in this study, belonging is negotiated in the encounter with moments of uncertainty that require them to confront their precarious status. These moments arise in everyday spaces, from the family home to the school.

Methods

The key questions motivating my research were: How do youth living with precarious status negotiate belonging? In what ways do people and contexts mediate their experiences? These questions were addressed through research examining the situations of six youth ages twelve to eighteen living with precarious status in Toronto with their families. This age range was selected in order to consider a range of issues faced by youth at various stages of their interactions with the education system. I anticipated that youth of different ages would face different challenges. In addition to age differences, the youth involved in the study were also living with different kinds of immigration status (outlined in detail below). This diversity of experiences reveals multiple ways and places in which youth struggle to belong as they negotiate their status.

I used a purposive and snowball approach to find participants, relying on community-based researchers, service providers, and activists who were in contact with youth living with precarious status. Berk and Schur (2001) and Cornelius (1982) used the snowball method to seek participants in their research with undocumented individuals in the United States. For this study, rather than having the youth point me to subsequent participants, it was service providers who directed me to other service providers that were more in touch with youth. In order to protect the confidentiality of potential participants and not place service providers in the position of knowing who participated in the project, I used a double-blind recruiting process (Bernhard & Young, 2009).[2]

I carried out individual interviews in English with the six youth who agreed to participate; their parents had also given informed consent, as the youth were all under age eighteen. The interviews took place in an informal atmosphere, in a location suggested by the youth so that that they felt comfortable and safe, and were semi-structured, with open-ended questions about the youths' experiences living in Toronto with precarious status. Using a qualitative approach allowed me to respond to issues that arose during the course of the research; the strength of a semi-structured interview is that it leaves openings to clarify and discuss issues raised by the participants (Cornelius, 1982; Longhurst, 2010; Reinharz, 1992). My aim was to learn what it is like to live in Toronto with precarious legal status and to uncover the youth's negotiations of belonging in multiple spaces and relationships. A qualitative research approach was crucial given these goals.

The small number of youth who agreed to participate in this study is a limitation. Beyond the challenges inherent in the structure of the recruiting process, there were deeper barriers to overcome in terms of trust. I attempted to recruit participants through individuals who work with youth whose status is precarious, hoping that the youth's positive and helpful interactions with these people would add to the confidence they felt in agreeing to participate. Unfortunately these connections were not sufficient to encourage many youth to contact me. This is understandable given that the existing research on people living with precarious status points to fear as an important factor influencing their decisions to access services (Berinstein et al., 2006; Bernhard et al., 2007). Moreover, I recognize that it is difficult to speak to an individual who is a stranger about experiences that are very personal. In addition, the specifics of a youth's immigration status may have increased hesitance to participate. It is possible that a refugee claimant or recently regularized person would be more willing to participate than a failed refugee claimant or someone whose visa had expired, as the latter may feel his or her situation to be more precarious. Beyond this, some youth may not realize they are considered to have precarious legal status or they may not understand what this means (Lowry & Nyers, 2003): self-conceptualization may also have been a factor in recruiting participants.

Introducing the Youth

The six youth I interviewed had different forms of precarious legal status. Their immigration status ranged from holding a temporary student visa to having a deportation order; their experiences living with precarious status also varied. Here I provide sketches of their situations.

Hector[3] was seventeen years old at the time of the interview and had lived in Toronto for almost two years. He was born in New Zealand but lived most of his life in Argentina; his first language is Spanish. His father was in Canada on a work permit that allowed Hector to attend school without having to pay fees. Although he was uncertain as to which documents he had, he knew that his permission to study had to be renewed each year. Hector did not have health insurance.

Isabel moved with her parents to Toronto two years before I met her; her older brother remained in Guatemala, and she had not seen him since moving to Canada but tried to stay in touch via email. She was fifteen years old and was awaiting an appeal of her family's refugee claim that was initially denied. She had a "brown paper"[4] that gave her access to health care and education. Isabel's first language is Spanish.

About five years prior to the interview, Sandra had moved to Toronto with her parents and her twin sister; she was twelve years old when we spoke. She missed her grandmother and other relatives who still lived in Chile and wished she could visit them. Her first language is Spanish. Sandra was not aware of her immigration status in Canada; her father indicated that the family's refugee claim had been denied and that they had no health insurance.

Gabriel had moved from Venezuela to Toronto five years before I met him; his first language is Spanish. For the first several months that he and his family were in Canada, they lived in a motel with other immigrants and refugees. It took two years for the family's refugee claim to be decided in their favour, and they had been waiting three years for permanent resident status. Gabriel was seventeen years old at the time of the interview.

Ibrahim's family left Paraguay when he was six months old and entered Canada undetected. Since that time, they had been living without status in Toronto. He was sixteen years old at the time of the interview and considers his first language to be English. A few years prior to our meeting, his parents began the process to "regularize" the family's immigration status. When I met him they were awaiting a decision on a Pre-Removal Risk Assessment that would determine whether they could remain in Canada.

Elena was born in Romania but had lived in Toronto for four and a half years at the time of the interview; her first language is not English. She had recently found out that her family's refugee appeal had been denied and that she would have to leave the friends she had made in Toronto. The family, including her Canadian-born sister, was scheduled to be deported soon after I met her. Elena was twelve years old at the time of the interview.

These brief biographical sketches of the youth who participated in the research show that each of them was living with a different kind of immigration status and that most of them had lived with various types of status during their time in Canada. Some of them even had documented or legally recognized status: Hector had a student permit that he renewed each year and Gabriel's family's refugee claim had been accepted but they had yet to receive permanent residency. Nevertheless, a sense that emerged from speaking with each of the youth was of the various ways in which one's status can be precarious. Despite the differences in their status, the youth all experienced a complicated sense of belonging. The school and the family were key spaces where the youth negotiated their status and struggled to belong.

School as a Site of Belonging

The uncertainty of their immigration status, and therefore of their tenure in Canada, influenced the youths' experiences and had particular connections to their experiences at school. Beyond education being one of the key areas in which the youth were actively engaged, schools are also an important site of belonging (Dennis, 2002; Kilbride et al., 2000; Suarez-Orozco & Suarez-Orozco, 2001). The school is an important social space where the youth negotiated relationships with school officials, friends, and classmates. The school is also, as a public institution, implicated in relations of power and governance (Basu, 2004, 2007; F. Villegas, in this volume). The youths' participation in the academic and social aspects of school was a significant element in their lives, especially in terms of feeling a sense of belonging. In moments and at particular stages in relation to their immigration trajectory, the youths' precarious status affected their experiences at school.

All six of the youth were attending public schools in Toronto, meaning their parents had managed to negotiate the registration process. School administrators, teachers, and friends were often not aware of their status. The youth were able to trust close friends with knowledge of their situations, but beyond this were willing to disclose their status only to people they felt were in a position to help them, particularly when they encountered barriers to participating on sports teams or field trips. In these instances, the youth viewed disclosure of their status as part of the necessary terms of participation; however, on most occasions, the youth could get by without having to acknowledge their status in their daily interactions at school. For some of the youth, it was their lack of health insurance in the form of an OHIP[5] card that presented a challenge:

Well, I have some problems with the health card. Like when I have a field trip or something like that, my father has to do like a note saying like he's responsible for me. And anything he has to pay, anything happens to me. (Hector)

Ibrahim indicated that he faced limitations "everywhere" yet in terms of access to services, he spoke about the "hassle" of having to go through extra steps or a more complicated process than his peers would:

Yeah, but you have to go through a little more, and you know, a little longer process than anybody else would, right? But, yeah – it's pretty much the same. As long as it's within the country and within the boundaries of what I can do, seeing my status, then yeah. It's just, they ask for it [health card] every time, right, so that's all. I just have to talk to them or if it's somebody new, I gotta tell them blah, blah, blah – the whole story and all that, and why. But yeah, and it's weird because after you tell them, usually they'll look at you different.

While the youth may have viewed the extra steps they had to go through to participate as a hassle or a "little longer process," this position of having to explain one's situation beyond what other students are asked to do is a barrier to participation and a mechanism through which state boundaries around membership are reproduced.

At times, friends from school helped them to feel like they belonged. However, they also pointed to ways in which they felt like "outsiders." These feelings were related to their immigration trajectory: when aware of the process their family was going through, the youth expressed feelings of being different. Gabriel spoke about his dislike of the label "refugee" and revealed that

I don't know, I didn't really see it as something that good. Like everybody was citizen, right, at the school so and I'm like refugee. I don't know, I didn't really like it. Probably the feeling that everybody there had been born there and then I just came, I don't know probably it was the whole situation, right? Yeah so everybody knew each other and everything, so I was like an outsider, right?

He also revealed that when he first arrived in Toronto and began school, he had a difficult time because he was unable to communicate with the other students in his class:

So, I only had like just one person that was, that I hung out with. He came from Argentina so we were like in the same situation, right. We had just come, we didn't speak the language, so yeah, it was nice being with him because I couldn't be with anybody else, right. I couldn't even understand them or anything. So I used be with him and then, then he moved so those few days there was nobody, I felt really bad you know. I mean it was tough, right?

While his limited English skills contributed to Gabriel's feelings of isolation when he first arrived in Toronto, Isabel seemed to encounter a different response from the students at her school: "People – they're nice. They don't treat me like you don't speak English or something. They treat you because of the way you are." Similarly, Hector pointed to the importance of friends he had made in Toronto, indicating they helped him with English and provided information about school and sports teams.

Elena found awaiting the decision on whether or not her family would be allowed to stay in Canada tough: she thought about it "at night when I am alone, or in the morning." Going to school was helpful because there she could play with her friends and "forget about" her family's uncertain situation. Interacting with her friends at school provided a break from having to worry about her family's situation. However, Elena also spoke of how at times she felt "different" from her friends at school, and she did not tell them about her status until she knew her family would have to leave the country because they had received a deportation order.

In the case of Ibrahim, school was alternately a place where he could do something to make his parents happy by getting good grades and a place where he felt he would have nothing to show for his time in Canada because in the end his time there benefited only himself. Ibrahim pointed out that if he worked he could at least make money to support his family. Understanding that the decision on his family's case could go either way made him feel that his efforts at school would have been for nothing:

> But the thing is, I don't want to be in school and then all of a sudden we gotta go, and then like I don't have anything. Like I haven't done anything, basically, like I'm gonna lose everything I have and I've pretty much accomplished nothing. So I'd rather be working towards something and let's say everything does work out, then I'll start school, and if it doesn't work out, good thing I was working. Any money I make I can help my parents out.

Ibrahim's assessment of his situation is interesting: on the one hand he speaks of how the decision by immigration authorities can turn what he has accomplished at school into "nothing," while on the other hand he attempts to counteract this possibility by choosing to work to help support his family while they await the decision on their case. School was also a place where the uncertainty of his status made it difficult to focus:

> As soon as the case started getting, like I'm not going to blame it on the case, because obviously teenagers are lazy, but besides that point, like. As soon

as it started getting bigger and bigger and like it started affecting my life more and more, my grades like, like I was always like thinking about it, like especially when – that's when we actually started going to court a lot and like, it's just a different transition, like doing all these different things. And it, in a way, it affected me really bad. I couldn't concentrate, like at school I'd just be sitting down and be thinking about it and be like, what am I doing here? Like just so much questions in my head and I couldn't concentrate on school and I couldn't do this and then I wouldn't get good grades and then my mum would get mad at me so it was just one big problem.

The precariousness of his family's situation meant that his head was just not in school: he did not want to go to school, he skipped class, he did poorly on assignments, and he was failing classes. His immigration status had a significant impact on his daily life, but Ibrahim did not feel that it was important to explain to the school what was happening with his family. He did not feel the school would be interested in his situation and explained why he did not tell the school about his status:

But I didn't really want to talk about it because it's not like, like, my parents have said it many times, like, if you're going to tell somebody, tell them if either you really want to tell them or tell them because they're going to help you. Obviously if I just tell like the school, it's not like they're going to do anything about it, they're just going to be, okay. And then they'll just be like whatever, next thing. You know, they got to deal with a lot of people, right.

According to the youth, the schools were not aware of their immigration status. This was a result of both the youth and their parents not telling and the schools and teachers not asking except when joining a sports team or going on a field trip, for which students had to explain that they did not have health insurance. Isabel revealed her reasons for not telling people, apart from close friends, about her status:

Because it's private I think. Well because, they're going to be asking what's my case, why am I like refugee claimant, they'd want me to tell our situation, why we're here. It's really private, we can't tell anyone. That's what they [immigration] said.

The lack of awareness on the part of schools of the challenges faced by students with precarious status emerged in particular when Gabriel revealed that his teachers and other people at the school "never even asked" about his status, and his tone suggested that he felt they did not care enough to understand his situation. Although he was aware of his status, his classmates assumed he was a citizen; when other students would make comments about immigrants, he did not let them know that he had come as a refugee:

> It's like ... they don't even know, right? I mean up to now, I mean everybody thinks we're all residents, right ... I mean, citizens, right. So like at school everybody would talk about immigrants sometimes but they wouldn't see me as one. They just think I'm already a citizen.

This differentiation by immigration status that took place within the space of the school was not directed personally at Gabriel, but it was hurtful given his family's situation.

The idea that nobody at the school took the time to ask about his situation seems to have had a lasting impact on Gabriel as he mentioned it six times through the course of the interview. He also spoke in different ways about how there was nothing anyone could have done to improve his situation or to help: "So like the days I was alone, yeah it was really bad. I mean, I don't think they could have helped me in the situation I was in, right." Despite Gabriel's conviction that his situation was beyond help, the fact that no one at the school attempted to find out what was going on in order to understand how they might support him is telling. The experiences of the youth in this study point to the need for further discussion concerning the extent to which individuals in the education system are aware of how students' immigration status may mediate their experiences.

Interestingly, not one of the youth felt that teachers, hospital staff, or coaches could be in a position to influence their status: Ibrahim expressed his trust that teachers are "taught to be confidential." The youth seemed to trust in the systems and individuals who to some extent helped to determine their experiences. For instance, Ibrahim claimed, "the government isn't going to leave you without medical coverage," whereas in reality there is a significant number of people living in Canada without health insurance and who may be unable or unwilling to access health care (Access Alliance Multicultural Community Health Centre, 2005; Bannerman, Hoa, & Male, 2003; Committee for Accessible AIDS Treatment, 2001). For some of the youth, teachers and coaches were helpful in working through issues that arose with having to show documentation to participate in field trips and on sports teams; these helpful interactions could have contributed to their trust in school authorities. Hector initially had some trouble signing up for his school's soccer team: "I had some problems with the health card, but there was a Spanish guy who was the coach and he helped me a lot." However, despite the apparent confidence the youth in this study had in school authorities, they also indicated that teachers and school administrators were generally not aware of their status. This lack of awareness could speak to the level of trust the youth had in these individuals and institutions. Subsequent to my research, which took place in the summer of 2005, the spring 2006 detention of several children in public schools in Toronto likely affected the degree of trust students living with precarious status placed in school officials and spaces (Jiménez & Alphonso, 2006; Keung, 2006).

Family Dynamics and Immigration Status

Several of the youth connected their experiences at school to their family situations. While for some going to school allowed them to be like their friends and forget about their precarious status, for others it reminded them that they were "different." Their status was intimately tied into their home spaces, not only because they shared the precarious status of their parents but also because their parents had expectations of them, at school in particular, regardless of the family's status. The parents likely made decisions with the hope that their children would benefit once the family's status was determined.[6] One choice made by some of the parents was to shelter their children from knowledge of the family's situation until they were older or until events forced them to disclose it.

Despite their status, the youth were able to develop and sustain a network of support persons both within and outside of Canada. The support of family, friends, and neighbours in Canada helped the youth as they attempted to negotiate the settlement process. This assistance included gaining access to services and programs, as well as helping their parents to find and keep employment in order to support their families and participate in the work of the community. For instance, Hector's cousin was already living in Toronto when his family arrived, and his father found work with this cousin. When Sandra's parents both had to work on the same schedule, they relied on a friend's daughter to look after their children: "There is this girl [in] my neighbourhood, she's like, her mum is my mum's best friend. So she takes care of me." When

Elena and her family arrived in Toronto, some of their relatives were already living in the city and helped her father to find work.

The migration process presents challenges to family dynamics and authority structures, as children are often not involved in these decisions. Suarez-Orozco and Suarez-Orozco (2001) found that "children in particular often have only a vague understanding of why the family is migrating" (p. 84); yet parents' decisions have an impact on the whole family. Although the youth were not necessarily involved in decisions around the migration process, they had to negotiate the ongoing consequences of being in Canada. While their parents attempted to shelter them, most of the youth were aware of the stresses involved in the process; however, age and immigration trajectory mattered here. The youths' parents took care of the details associated with the migration process. Both Ibrahim and Gabriel understood to a certain extent the strain experienced by their parents, describing the amount of time they spent completing paperwork, meeting with lawyers, and preparing for various stages of the determination of status process.

Some of the youth were not aware of the extent to which their immigration status mediated their experiences. In some cases this resulted from their parents protecting the youth from knowledge of the family's situation. There appeared to be different levels of awareness of immigration status amongst younger and older participants. For instance, Sandra, who was twelve years old, was unaware of her status ("my parents never told me"). This lack of awareness of her situation was clear from the beginning of the interview, so I modified the questions and we discussed her experiences at school and outside of school more generally. Although she was not aware of her status, a question Sandra asked at the end of the interview was interesting: "But is it true that like, is it sometimes for college you might not enter? Is that true?" While there was no indication that she connected the idea of not being able to go to college with precarious status, it is possible that this was a first inkling that some people in Canada face limitations.[7]

Although Ibrahim seemed to be the most aware of his status at the time of the interview, he revealed that he did not find out until he was about thirteen that he had been living in Canada with precarious status since he was six months old. His parents gradually revealed the situation to him, but he indicated that there had been hints of the family's situation:

But when I was younger, thing is, I didn't see much of what was going on because my parents had a good way of kind of covering it up. Like they didn't really want me to know, like they wanted me to be like enjoying my youth years and all that but like, as I got older, I started noticing things. And then after a while they just, you know, you just hear about it because then they started going through the whole case thing and I heard about the whole story, it was like, wow, it's really shocking. Like when I heard that, I was like, wow. I'm in this, like, this is happening to me.

Once Ibrahim found out about his status, he was forced to confront what it meant. He was faced with the complexity of his family's situation and the sense that although they had lived in Toronto for more than fifteen years, immigration officials could decide against them and they would have to leave.

The youths' identities were also negotiated in transnational spaces: they all spoke of connections to relatives outside of Canada, and these spaces were tied into their sense of belonging. Due to their precarious status, they were unable to visit these relatives, but through telephone and email they could maintain these connections. Their notions of "home" were comprised of multiple and complex connections to both where they were now and where they had been. When telling stories of the country in which she was born, Isabel used the phrase "in my country," which may suggest that Canada did not yet feel like "her" country. In fact, due to the uncertainty over whether or not her family would be able to stay, she indicated that Canada felt "like we're just visiting, actually." In addition, she pointed to the importance of family in feeling connected to a place: "Because like I have family in my homeland but you have opportunities here too. But I have my family there. So it's kind of balanced." In response to the question whether Canada feels like home, Sandra replied: "I want to go back ... Because I want to be with my grandma." To a certain extent, Elena considered both Canada and the country where she was born home since she had friends and family members in both places. The ongoing ties through family to their countries of emigration underscore that the youths' conceptions of home and belonging cross borders.

Ibrahim pointed to the complexity of his situation and of notions of belonging: Toronto was the only home he had ever known, yet he sensed that when officials or other people found out about his family's status, they saw him differently and questioned why he was here. He had no knowledge or experience of the country in which he was born; in a sense, he had the strongest identification with Canada of the six youth, yet he spoke in the most direct terms about his status and of the perception that he did not belong here. Ibrahim's comments reflected great awareness of his precarious status and revealed a sense of turmoil and incredulity at his situation:

> Like I said, I feel like this is my home because this is everything I know, like, and I feel at home here because I can walk around and feel safe, I know the area, I know the people that live around here. Like I know a lot of what's around me. But, you know, as long as the government, like, they can say, okay no, you're not accepted, and go. So, technically we really don't have like, you know, we can't really say that this is home to us.

Despite the evidence his life offered of the fact that Canada was his home, his status – and the reaction it elicited from government officials – told him that he did not have the right to claim it as home. This raises a key question in relation to notions of belonging and citizenship: how does one make sense of the fact that one's daily existence points to "integration" and "settlement" while one's status at times denies one's claims to belonging?

Conclusion

This study captures several dimensions of the lived experiences of youth with precarious legal status. It highlights the role of families' communication strategies around immigration status and how youth understand and confront their status, as well as the extent to which people in the Canadian education system understand the challenges faced by these youth. It also shows the importance of contextualizing specific identities and experiences – age and immigration trajectory were key factors in the youths' experiences of their status. As they got older or as their cases became more difficult, questions of status became more present in their negotiations of belonging. It was in the moment of encountering barriers, from attempting to access a sports team without health insurance to learning that one's family was about to be deported, that questions of belonging had to be confronted. The youth were asked – at times explicitly – to define and defend their presence through their interactions with various institutions and individuals, from the immigration office and the school sports field where disclosure of their status was necessary to playgrounds, classrooms, and sidewalks where they negotiated their status in more subtle and dynamic ways.

The youth experienced the uncertainty of their tenure in Canada in different ways. School in particular was an important site in which they negotiated questions of belonging. For some of the youth, school was a place where they could be with friends and forget about their situations, while for others their time at school was a reminder of their status and fostered a sense that their time spent in Canada was meaningless. School-based friendships had mixed effects: at times they helped the youth feel like they belonged, but at other times they brought out the ways in which they felt like "outsiders." The tremendous financial, emotional, social, and familial pressures of living with precarious legal status make it difficult for youth to focus on or be motivated by school; some may choose or feel forced to drop out. This was the case with Ibrahim, who felt that he could better support his family by taking time off from school to work while they awaited the decision on their status.

In order to protect young children in particular from the challenges associated with living with precarious status, parents may delay making their children fully aware of the family's precarious situation until it is necessary that they have an understanding of it (e.g., if a negative decision means they may face deportation). Suarez-Orozco and Suarez-Orozco (2001) encountered some undocumented youth in the United States who did not learn about their family's immigration status until they were applying to university and "their parents [were] forced to tell them" (p. 35). This suggests that parents communicate around status in different ways and on different timelines. In a sense this may allow children to have a "normal" childhood. In seeking to shelter their children from full knowledge of the family's status, parents bear the weight of the precariousness of their situation; however, in doing so, they claim a space in which their children can participate along with their peers.[8] To a certain extent, they assert the legitimacy of their family's presence in the community. This raises a host of questions for further research. In the case of families in which children may not yet be aware of their status, how do parents manage the barriers they face in order to protect their children from fully experiencing these same barriers? To what extent and in what ways does the fact that there are different levels of awareness of the family's legal status influence family dynamics and relationships?

The youth in this study evoke a sense of belonging that is multidimensional and complex. It is mediated by age and immigration trajectory and negotiated simultaneously at "personal" and "discursive" levels as the youth navigate the spaces and relationships of their everyday lives

(Antonsich, 2010). All children and youth living with precarious status will eventually become aware of what it means to have such status in Canada. Whether it is a student in grade 12 contemplating university and realizing that his family cannot afford to pay international student fees or a twelve-year-old girl whose family is about to be deported, the significance of immigration status becomes blatantly clear. Barriers and limitations can come in many forms, and the boundaries around belonging materialize in a range of encounters. For individuals who live part of their lives secure in the knowledge that they are "just like everybody else" and then over time, or perhaps all in one day, discover that they are not, in fact, like all of their friends, the reality of immigration status may be a confusing and overwhelming adjustment. Inevitably young people will come to know and confront their status and will have to make sense of what it means for their claims to belonging.

NOTES

1 The research project received funding support from the Ontario Graduate Scholarship and the Joint Centre of Excellence for Research on Immigration and Settlement (CERIS).
2 For a detailed examination of the ethics review process and risk mitigation methods employed, see Bernhard and Young (2009).
3 All names used are pseudonyms and countries of origin have been changed.
4 Montgomery (2002) refers to the "brown paper syndrome" experienced by unaccompanied and separated minors she interviewed in Montreal: the document they were given to designate their status as refugee claimants was both a material and symbolic reminder of their marginalized status, and a visible marker of their distinction from other individuals (p. 56).
5 Ontario Health Insurance Plan.
6 Note that I did not interview parents; references to the parents' decisions or actions are based on what was reported by the youth.
7 Her father mentioned to me before the interview that the child of a friend of theirs is not able to go to university due to their status and the high cost of tuition (since students who are neither citizens nor permanent residents must pay international fees in Ontario). It is possible that Sandra had overheard conversations about this.
8 I explore the youth's (and their parents') contestations of membership at length in Young (2011).

6 Constructing Coping Strategies: Migrants Seeking Stability in Social Networks

KATHERINE BRASCH

It is not easy to live an undocumented life. Just ask Renato the construction worker or Carolina the house cleaner. These are two Brazilians living in Toronto who have faced challenges because of their precarious status, yet remain in Canada because they are seeking better lives and better opportunities, whether for themselves or for their children. Living a precarious life means living every day with instability; it means not knowing if the life one is trying to build will come to an abrupt end. For some, their vulnerability becomes evident when state regulations influence their lives, usually constricting their choices out of fear of being identified. Other migrants enter crises when restrictions are imposed through threats to reveal their precariousness to the state.

This chapter seeks to outline experiences of precarious migrants during the course of everyday life in Toronto. Through the study of migrant networks it is possible to gain an understanding of how precariousness influences and is influenced by structures of the state and the agency of the migrant, drawing examples from work and family ties. The goal is to understand both the social costs of living without permanent status as well as the strategies those with precarious status employ to build a life in Canada. The latter includes strategies to cope with moments of precariousness that threaten the lives they are building, and strategies to regularize migrant status and become permanent residents.

I thank all of my research participants for their dedication to this research project. All names are pseudonyms to protect their identities. Certain details of their lives and experiences have been left vague to ensure their security.

Brazilian Migration to Toronto

Migration from Brazil is a relatively recent development. The country was historically a destination country for immigrants until the 1930s. Early emigration began in the 1930s and consisted primarily of return migration to countries of origin or to other Latin American countries. The early movement to the United States began in the 1960s, but only in the 1980s did the numbers grow significantly and begin to be considered as a potential reaction to the social unrest as well as political and economic instability that plagued the country (Barbosa-Nunes, 2002; Citizenship and Immigration Canada, n.d.; Sales, 1999; Vidal, 2000).[1] The three major destinations were Paraguay, the United States, and Japan. However, as American visas became increasingly difficult to obtain, and no visa was required to enter Canada, going further north became a more viable option (Barbosa-Nunes, 2002; Goza, 2003). Canada's international reputation as a "safe" and economically stable country[2] attracted Brazilians, and Toronto became one of the top five preferred North American destinations in the late 1980s along with Boston, New York, Miami, and *"Cidade Congelada"*[3] (Goza, 2003). There is now a relatively small, but growing, "Little Brazil" located at the southern end of "Little Portugal" in the west end of Toronto.

Given the small population – too small to be divided out of the Canadian census in any published documents – and the many undocumented migrants,[4] only an educated estimate can be offered of the number of Brazilians living in Toronto. Using data based on earlier work by Goza (1994), Barbosa-Nunes (2002), and information gleaned from discussion with the Brazilian Consulate in 2004, I estimate the Toronto population to be ten to twelve thousand. This number is based on an estimate that 50 per cent (or five to six thousand individuals) of the total Brazilian population living in the city are undocumented migrants. While this number must remain an estimate, there should be no question that this is a relatively small migrant population compared to other ethnic groups in the city, yet approximately half of them are living precarious everyday lives.

My work distinguishes between two primary types of migrants without permanent status entering Canada: those who wish to come for a short period of time (usually three years or less) to make money before returning to Brazil and those who wish to settle permanently. People who fall into the first category are often target earners, planning to return to their country of origin after saving a certain sum of money

(Goza, 1994). These migrants have various motivations for their economically focused goal, which may include saving to set up businesses or build rental properties, or simply making money. Others have more family-oriented goals, ensuring a higher standard of living for those family members left in Brazil by sending remittances regularly. One man told me he was in Toronto to make money so his six-year-old daughter would be able to move out of a *favela* (shanty town) in Rio de Janeiro.[5] My work focuses on the second group, those looking to build new lives in Canada, despite their precarious status.

Study Participants

The data presented for discussion were collected during two years of qualitative research from 2004 to 2006. During this time I interviewed 129 individuals, both in Canada and Brazil, to explore the role of transnational migrant networks of both documented and undocumented Brazilians, as well as those who had transitioned either from undocumented to documented (e.g., gaining refugee or immigrant status) or from documented to undocumented (e.g., falling out of status when a visa expires). The examples presented are drawn from the lives of primary participants living in Toronto, each of whom I followed for at least a year.

Most of the research participants discussed in this article had a university education but little or no professional success in Brazil. Most would consider themselves from the middle or lower-middle class in Brazil. They were visibly racialized by their various combinations of European, African, and indigenous ancestries. Most fell towards the European end of the racializing spectrum, but their skin tone, along with their accents in English, sometimes resulted in categorizations outside the Brazilian population as "Latin," "Spanish," or simply "other" within the Canadian context.

Since the research participants are undocumented migrants who are "invisible" to the state because their visas have expired, they fall under the rubric of "precarious status" (Goldring, Berinstein, & Bernhard, 2009). This distinctive categorization offers a framework to address migrants whose circumstances result in "a combination of ongoing risk and uncertainty" as they build lives in Canada (Goldring & Landolt, in this volume). Those people who live in a precarious state – never knowing if they will have to leave – include refugee claimants as well as individuals who have lapsed visitor visas or have come into the country through other means.[6] In particular I draw on interviews with three participants: Carolina, Madeleine, and Renato. For these precarious migrants, their "conditionality of presence" (Goldring & Landolt, in this volume) is based on working to meet state-imposed legal requirements for gaining permanent status (e.g., through marriage to a Canadian citizen) or on remaining undetected or invisible to the state.

Carolina came in 2001 from a very dangerous neighbourhood in the city of São Paulo. A forty-four-year-old single mother, she arrived with her nine-year-old daughter and her ninety-one-year-old mother. Her primary reason for migrating was the violence in Brazil. In addition to ongoing problems with prostitutes and muggers in the streets, a man living in their building was beaten to death in his own apartment. When Carolina left Brazil, she resolved never to return.

Madeleine came from São Luís, Maranhão, in Brazil's northeast. She was the only research participant without a university education and the only participant who did not have a firm plan to stay in Canada. She arrived in Toronto in 1997 as a single mother (age thirty-four), bringing her daughter (age thirteen) but leaving her teenage son in Brazil. Her reason for migrating was her accumulated debt from raising her children without financial support from the father. Her sister had immigrated and was able to help her settle and find work. By the time I met her, she had obtained immigrant status, but her many years of precariousness offer valuable insights for this chapter.

Renato came to Canada from Belo Horizonte, the capital of Minas Gerais, in 2002 at the age of thirty-six. Prior to arrival in Canada, he had been cheated out of money owed to him on two occasions, once by a major corporation and once by a family friend (over twenty thousand dollars in total). He had also been robbed in the street while others looked on, too afraid to intervene. He came to Canada on a business visa, but after purchasing the computer equipment for his sister's company in Brazil, he stayed in Canada to build a better life for himself.

The relationship to the state restricts work options available to these migrants; when I met them, both women were cleaning houses and Renato was working in construction. The state also influences their social networks, in particular their family relations and the resources available to them for strategic use. In turn, the resulting networks can influence decisions about status, and whether to stay or return home. In some cases, a migrant can access certain network resources and strategically use them to alter migrant status, obtaining permanent status and stability in everyday life through their actions. While not all will be successful in meeting the necessary conditions to gain state-approved immigration status, network resources can also be incorporated into discursive strategies to better position precarious status migrants and help them find further justification for remaining in Canada. This paper examines how such network and discursive resources are specifically influenced by precarious status and strategically used by these three migrants to cope with precariousness in everyday life, including the ongoing construction of "illegality" by the state.

Constructions of "Illegality"

Discrepancies between definitions of illegality have entered broader debate within the political arena and have been reproduced by the media, redrawing the border between "legal" and "illegal." On 21 March 2006, the *Toronto Star* ran a front-page story about a federal "immigration crackdown" in Canada launched by the newly elected Conservative government.[7] The first sentence of a follow-up article the next day read: "A prominent GTA developer has condemned the federal government for wanting to toss 'honest, hard-working' illegal immigrants from Portugal and other countries out of Canada" (Brennan & Wong, 2006). This statement reflects the conflicted context in which precarious status migrants live. How can one be "honest" and "illegal" at the same time? How can "hard-working" people be deported, especially when the article proceeded to outline the shortage of skilled labour in the construction industry where many of these individuals work? Research participants develop discursive strategies for coping with these broader frames that negatively affect their sense of personhood and self-worth.

Succinctly stated in another follow-up article, the state's action and responsibilities are clear: people are removed under the Immigration Act for any number of reasons, including breaking the law, working illegally, studying illegally, foreign convictions abroad, and being members of organized crime networks (Campion-Smith, 2006). For those who believe that upholding the letter of the law is the only relevant factor in discussions of migration, the issue of deportation is non-negotiable, an impermeable border between right and wrong regardless of extenuating circumstances.

These labels of "illegal" and "criminal" – even used occasionally by precarious status migrants themselves – build on the underlying assumptions that these people are acting outside of the law, and justify the ongoing threat of deportation should such individuals be identified by the federal authorities. However, migrants use counter-discourses as part of coping strategies to address these negative constructions. As shall be demonstrated, positive positioning statements are often drawn from connections within their migrant networks.

Strategic Use of Migrant Resources

Migrant networks link multiple countries and individuals. Each relationship is a "link" or a "tie" in a migrant's social network, formed and reinforced during everyday practices. Granovetter (1973) considered family members and close friends "strong" network ties while other acquaintances or people who might periodically offer access to other resources would be seen as "weak" ties.

Building and relying on small-scale, informal social ties (both strong and weak) between families or individuals is a key strategy for everyday life for many precarious status migrants. It is these individual ties that form the basis of the transnational social networks that facilitate the movement of migrants and that might provide access to resources that can assist them in difficult moments.

In the country of destination, network ties can offer settlement assistance as migrants access the resources available from or through network members. This has been shown to include initial travel funds and job and housing information as well as emotional support. Such ties are effective regardless of the physical proximity of actors at the time of interaction (Castles & Miller, 1998; Faist, 2000; Goza, 2003; Hannerz, 1996).

Migrant networks are also gendered, with certain ties more accessible to men or women. Previous work has shown how Mexican migrant women built gender-specific networks to assist them when access to male-dominated networks was denied (Hondagneu-Sotelo, 1994). Other examples show how women have sought support for gendered challenges through specific network ties as shown by Parreñas (2001) in her study of Filipina domestics and by Zentella's (1997) study of Puerto Rican women seeking assistance with child rearing.

Finally, it is important to note that migrant networks can also grow through "local transnationalism" (Ang, 2000), which encourages ethnic border-crossing interaction. For example, ties into the more established Portuguese community broaden local network ties for many Brazilians. However, the complicated colonial history and cultural differences may require negotiation before connections between members of the two ethnic communities solidify (Veronis, 2006; Vidal, 2000).

In the case of precarious status Brazilian migrants, networks are vital. Networks enable research participants to build their lives and find assistance for everything from renting an apartment to locating religious centres and learning about certain state-sponsored programs that they may be able to access, such as health care clinics and schools for their children. Of course, building work-related ties is a vital area of network construction for precarious status migrants. These newcomers need to find work where state-designated permission to work is not required, where employers are willing to hire individuals without work authorization, or they need to subvert the problem by creating or purchasing a false identity. The resources accessible through networks can also offer emotional support for the various challenges that these migrants face, and further enable them to formulate strategies in order to address threats to the lives they are building.

Sometimes these multifaceted new network ties take on characteristics of family ties, especially in the absence of other family members close by and the restrictions on travel that result from precariousness. "Fictive kin" gather to celebrate holidays, take weekend outings or even vacations together, and offer support in times of crisis (Ebaugh & Curry, 2000). When work ties can become "family" ties, overlaps between different areas of network growth occur. To demonstrate the complicated overlaps of network use, case studies will focus on how individuals grow their networks and access resources in specific ways.

Unfortunately, as shall be demonstrated, not all ties are positive. Precariousness in everyday life means that social ties can easily collapse or turn toxic (Menjívar, 2000), as Carolina's story will demonstrate. It should also be noted that not all local ties into the Brazilian community are positive. Immigration status and social class differences can further complicate a migrant's network.

Family: Shaking Seemingly Strong Ties

Family is often considered a source of strong network ties for migrants. Newcomers benefit from the experiences of those who migrated earlier, using their networks to facilitate entry into everyday life and to have ongoing support. However, family presence does not always guarantee strong network ties because sometimes blood ties are not strong enough to withstand challenges that result from precarious status.

Carolina, her daughter Elizabeth, and her mother migrated with the assistance of her brother, who had married a woman born in Canada to migrant Brazilians. The couple met in Brazil, but given the uncertain economic climate, had moved to Mississauga (a city near Toronto), and were able to offer assistance to the three women so they could come north.

Despite all of her brother's encouragement to come, once the three women arrived, Carolina's brother's attitude changed completely. When she had a tourist visa, Carolina took English classes for six months; when her visa expired, she wanted to continue the classes on the weekends and work during the week as an undocumented cleaner. Her brother, however, would not allow it. He was very nervous and especially did not want Carolina or Elizabeth to leave the house. He was especially afraid that his niece would be noticed if she was outside during school hours and told them to stay inside. For a woman who was always independent in Brazil, this was a very difficult situation for Carolina. She talked of this time as a period of isolation where she felt like a prisoner in her brother's home: "I left one prison and entered another." During this period, she felt her Canadian life was no better than the Brazilian one she left behind. Her references to "prison" again reflect the constraints that were imposed on her life: first by violence in Brazil and later by her brother, who feared the Canadian state.

The stress point was clearly focused on documentation issues, since her brother tried to impose further constraints on Carolina's actions when her tourist visa expired. She explained the situation during one of our interviews:

> My brother was nervous. "You must hear no one! You must listen to no one! You must hear me, your brother!" And I, you know, I stopped like this, I said, "Wait a minute, I came here, right? To have freedom, to feel good. I'm feeling imprisoned ... it seems like I am a criminal here."[8]

This sense of criminality mirrors experiences by the precarious status migrants in Samia Saad's research (in this volume); Carolina was similarly confused by her brother's behaviour because she had done nothing "bad." He intensified the state's control over her actions even though she was only looking after her daughter and mother, usually considered a noble cause, especially by other family members. As a result, Carolina felt the same sense of imprisonment and lack of rights that is expressed in Saad's research.

After a year of living with her brother's restrictions and feeling like a "prisoner," Carolina and her brother had a final fight and he threw her and Elizabeth out of the house. Unfortunately, she had lost her original network, which was a cost of migration she had not expected. Her brother's home became a space where the Canadian state disrupted Brazilian family relations, controlling interactions within private as well as public spaces. The brother and sister were unable to find a balance where Carolina's need for "freedom" from Brazil could co-exist with her brother's concerns about the vigilance of the Canadian state.

Carolina almost returned to Brazil, disillusioned with her brother and the migration trajectory she had planned. However, she visited a community centre that helped her locate housing, register her daughter for school, and find work. It was only after her daughter was enrolled in school that Carolina's long-term plans were resolidified. In this case, concerns about her daughter's well-being had to be addressed before she decided to stay in Canada permanently. She has since built a new network as well as a group of fictive kin that offers her support in many aspects of her difficult life, but her family ties have been served a great blow. She lost that source of network resources and support, which she had expected to have in Canada.

This case also raises issues of identity within the community, since Carolina (and her brother) initially labelled herself as "illegal" when living without a valid visa. Carolina had to cope with concerns of identification and deportation, her brother's restrictive discourses, and the public perceptions of legality, all of which led to the collapse of her family network. State ideologies destroyed seemingly strong network ties, demonstrating how substantial the influence of the state can be on precarious lives. However, the following examples drawn from migrant work networks show that there are ways to successfully circumvent state restrictions.

Finding Work through Gendered Networks

Work networks are a vital component of a precarious migrant's ability to migrate and settle in their country of destination. The type of work available for those without authorization is extremely limited. As a result, many middle-class, precarious status migrants find themselves in labour-intensive jobs in construction or cleaning. This area of network growth is gendered, with men and women usually taking different paths to find work and build related networks, gaining associated resources.

Renato found work in construction through an acquaintance he met at a barbeque. The Brazilian man first introduced Renato to the landscaper he was working for (he was about to quit because of back problems) and later, as winter approached and landscaping work was waning, introduced him to a contractor in construction for whom Renato worked throughout most of my fieldwork.

Madeleine, another precarious status migrant, also found her first job cleaning houses through a weak network tie, a Portuguese woman who overheard her say at a beauty salon that she was in need of work. The woman was going on an extended vacation and needed to find someone to clean for her clients while she was gone. This is a relatively common practice in the house-cleaning business and enables the replacement woman to obtain references from her temporary clients. By the time the Portuguese woman returned and took back her clients, Madeleina had a number of referrals and was growing her own business, which provided her with significant ties into Canadian homes. As a result of these Canadian ties, women who clean houses gain greater independence from the weak ties found in Brazilian and Portuguese work networks of precarious status migrants, and the potential for exploitation is significantly reduced.

While men tend to have an easier time finding work given the number of job openings in construction, they do not have the same access to Canadian homes, nor the resulting network ties. They find work through weak ties, as Renato did, but it rarely leads to network growth or the development of more extensive ties as it does for women. Men also tend to have problems concerning social insurance numbers (SINs). Some construction companies require paperwork; therefore, precarious status migrants sometimes borrow or buy a SIN number. My participant, Renato, at one time used his housemate's SIN in order to work when his housemate returned to Brazil and another time purchased a SIN. There are several challenges to using someone else's SIN. First, there are monetary consequences (paying the people to use their SIN, plus Renato had to pay back taxes on one number as a condition of using it). There is also occasionally the challenge that the person who lent the SIN number returns to work; then the man must give up the number, which usually means giving up his current job since changing numbers would highlight his precarious status in the job market. Women working in the informal economy, cleaning private homes, do not require a SIN number, so this common state-imposed challenge for men is not a concern for many women. While it is harder for women to find inroads into the homes – since they must know someone willing (or needing) to lend their houses – once the opportunity presents itself, their work in Canadian homes creates stronger ties with Canadians who offer the women access to valuable resources.

Strategies for Coping with Precarious Status: Network Resources and Related Migrant Discourses

Women's work networks enable precarious migrants to obtain work without having permission to work from the state (i.e., without a SIN number). However, women gain another important benefit: access to networks and social capital through their clients, who are primarily upper-middle- and upper-class Canadian women. As the ties solidify, the Canadian women try to help the Brazilian women. For example, Carolina went through a period of depression, and the flexibility her clients gave her helped her deal with her mental health issues and maintain her business. Madeleina was preparing to submit her application for permanent residency through the sponsorship of her husband when she received monetary assistance from one of her clients, who knew how hard she was working to raise funds for the trip back to Brazil (necessary for the sponsorship process at that time). This was an invaluable act of generosity that assisted in removing Madeleina's precarious status, as she ultimately received her permanent resident status. Whether migrants receive monetary assistance or help to access resources they need to remain in the country, Canadian ties gained through work networks are extremely valuable and important for their success in staying in Canada.

While there are significant benefits connected to these new networks for women, they have to clean houses to gain this access. This raises the issue of the stigma attached to becoming "the maid," which must be addressed. This situation is not only a personal issue, but can be judged harshly by family and friends back in Brazil, where domestic help is considered work for the uneducated lower class, especially when juxtaposed with the middle-class professions most of these women left. They try to justify their change of profession as a positive move.

Carolina, who has a university degree and had a job in technical support prior to migration, came with the knowledge that her work option would likely be in cleaning. However, she tried out the profession for a day during a pre-migration trip to Canada, to make sure she could adjust to this work. She now calls it "noble work," reframing cleaning in a positive light as a worthwhile job. Many women frame their work as "their business," referring to the homeowners as "clients." This gives a sense of professionalism to the job despite the menial labour involved. This discursive shift seeks to rationalize the change of profession made necessary by their precarious status in Canada.

Madeleina, who does not have a post-secondary degree and sold cars prior to migration, also cleans homes. As she explains, part of her strategy is to be very particular about her clients:

> I only clean houses of people with whom I identify ... With whom I am in tune, with whom I, I feel good. I already left various homes only because I didn't like the person. I didn't like them, no ... I didn't identify with the person.

Madeleina explained that if a client is constantly reminding her how or what to clean – suggesting that Madeleina will not remember her job – or if she simply "does not relate" with someone, she passes the house to another cleaner; she has set limits on how she will be treated. When she passes the house on, she makes sure that the client is content with the new cleaner, thus not completely severing her tie with the client and strengthening the tie with another Brazilian woman who is appreciative of the work.

Renato does not work for himself, as the women do, nor does he gain the benefits women find in their work networks. Instead, using a false SIN card causes him significant stress because it means that he is unable to be recognized for his contributions to building Canadian homes.

The following excerpt is from an email he sent me to follow up on an earlier conversation about gaining permanent status. He later explained to me that there were many grammatical errors because it had been written like a *desabafo* (confession) and he had sent it without rereading it at the time. This suggests it reflects his true, unedited frustrations:

> [only one thing still profoundly bothers me,] that I have to use the name of another to work, to not be able to be myself, because I know that in certain situations and places we have to have almost two personalities, to survive in this place in the condition of not being legal, many times we are obligated to have to lie to protect ourself, depending on the situation, but in all these happenings, we never have to conceal our name, and in this case, when you yourself can't use your name, as a result you no longer exist, and you become a [ghost] ... you produce, receive, pay your bills of rent,

shopping, entertain yourself, and in general live in this country. In summary, you do all of this thanks to your work, but the person who receives the salary, for your work, has another name; you are not called by your name.

Renato wants to be seen as a hard worker, but without the use of his own name he does not "exist" in certain spaces and feels unjustly erased from the workforce. Renato has called himself a "shadow," reflecting his unease with the person he must become to continue working. Referring to himself as "disposable," he also suggests the high cost of being invisible from the state, as no authority would know if he disappeared. These are utterances from days when he is afraid or concerned about his marginal position, which is how he interprets the limitations imposed by the Canadian government, and abused in the construction industry. During an acute crisis at work, he was literally afraid he would disappear, and being "invisible" to the state he realized the real danger to himself: who would know if an invisible person disappeared?

Renato's comments echo the frustration of non-citizenship and the sense of not belonging to Canada addressed by Julie Young (in this volume). Renato's hard work gives him a sense of building and contributing to Canada, yet he could be deported at any moment. Despite Renato's hard work, he does not "belong."

Renato does not have access to the Canadian network ties that Carolina and Madeleina have established, but he uses resources from his network to justify remaining in Canada as a precarious status migrant. He speaks of his hard work and his contributions to building homes for Canadians to live in. This hard work and assistance to others is part of his justification, which comes primarily from discourses associated with his religion, a spirit-focused group that performs rituals similar to aura cleansings. For example, Renato talks about "cleansing" his workplace of negative energies and influences:

> It's as if I'm a cleaner. I'm here to clean up. As if I were a garbage truck collecting garbage. Maybe I'm not here like that to like – physically I'm not collecting garbage, but spiritually when I am or when I go someplace, I'm cleaning. I am almost certain of this.

He goes on to discuss his boss (referring to him as "garbage") and larger problems in the construction business, including use of alcohol and drugs. He tries to show Brazilian newcomers that they do not have to go down these paths and that there are others available. In doing this religious work for the broader community, he positions himself as someone cleansing and helping others.

Renato's religion not only helps him cope with these stresses, he also considers his religious group part of his Canadian "family," gathering for festive days (e.g., Christmas and Easter) as well as personal celebrations such as birthdays. His fictive kin network ties grow stronger through ongoing contact to address religious, celebratory, and supportive needs. However, during the crisis at work when he thought he might disappear, he did not turn to the strongest ties, such as the mother figure in his local network. He felt she had her own challenges at the time and did not want to burden her. Therefore, this source of "family" can be precarious as well (Menjívar, 2000). Other migrants, such as Carolina, have blood relatives here, but as already discussed, these family ties do not guarantee a smooth migration path either.

Carolina has also confronted the "illegal" label outside her family. When she had a job cleaning offices, she addressed a potential threat made by another cleaner by speaking directly to her boss:

> I went to my boss and said, "If she turns me in, okay? I will make the biggest noise, because I'm not – am not doing anything wrong here. I am not any kind of a criminal – I just don't have the papers."

While she did risk angering the people associated with the perceived threat and being fired, her actions were successful and she was able to remain at her place of work. However, some migrants do not feel their boss will be sympathetic, and they do not want to take chances.

Carolina did occasionally label herself "illegal" – especially in times of crisis – but she directed attention elsewhere, often towards her hard work. For example, during our conversations Carolina repeatedly reinforced that while she may be "illegal" in the eyes of some, she was not a criminal:

> After nine months had passed, I wasn't a tourist here anymore. What was I? Illegal. Okay? ... I am not 100 per cent right, because I am doing something that is not legal, right? ... [but] I'm not any kind of criminal, understand? ... So it's better to say: "I am without status" rather than "illegal" that it looks like "illegal" is committing some – you know? I don't steal, I work honestly, you know? I am not involved in drugs, so I am not illegal, right? I am without status, I learned much about this.

She learned this approach to distinguishing herself at the community centre where she sought assistance after leaving her brother's home. This strategy separates "status" issues from "criminal acts." She still uses the term "illegal" during our discussions, but mixes it with other terms she uses to reinforce her behaviour as a good person. She includes a number of negative formulations, emphasizing what she is "not." While she knows that she is not entirely legal, she reinforces that she is "*not* a criminal" but instead is "*without* status." As we talked, it was clear that she is still struggling to distinguish herself within all of these discourses that both sides of the "legal" equation use to describe her situation, struggling to justify remaining precarious.

"Legal" continued to pepper Carolina's discourse in other ways to accentuate her practices as proper – above board and legitimate. For example, she resolved that she would only stay in Toronto if she had "legal work," which she clarified was "not outside of the laws," using examples of drugs and prostitution as being "outside." Carolina explains that she works "honestly or properly," and *that* is her definition of what is important when defining "legal" work. That she does not have the legal right to work according to the state is seen as a separate, almost irrelevant issue. Hard, honest work echoes her working-class values and is the focus of her justification.

Her contestation of "criminality" – the state's categorization that is dominant – invokes an alternate "illegal" discourse. This approach articulates a distinct definition of criminal and illegal acts, challenging state discourses that try to construct her and other undocumented migrants as dangerous and needing to be removed. In such instances, the participants dismiss the authority of the state to construct "illegality"; they construct their own definition of criminality that does not include their activities, especially their hard work. Carolina further explains that she is working to support her daughter and mother, which becomes a justification for remaining in Canada despite her precarious legal status.

Discussion and Conclusion: Precariousness of the Everyday

The examples of Carolina, Madeleina, and Renato all highlight the role of the state in precarious status migrants' lives. While the government in the country of origin played a role in "pushing" migrants to migrate, Canada's immigration restrictions have resulted in many individuals living their lives with undocumented immigration status. These migrants, determined to build a new life, are left in situations of precarious status where permanency is desired but very difficult to achieve. The case studies that have been presented make the costs of this precariousness especially clear.

Renato's experience highlights the lengths to which precariousness may be taken, living in a dangerous situation rather than risking identification by government authorities. However, Renato's biggest struggle involves his invisibility at work. His desire to be seen and appreciated for the hard work he values is denied, his disappointment accentuated each day as he works under another name. He finds justification for remaining in Canada through the resources obtained through other activities, primarily his religious and volunteer work. While his volunteerism is mostly informal assistance to other migrants as well as work within his religious group, he is seen and appreciated for his time and effort, strengthening his local community as well as his local network.

In Carolina's case, she found a coping strategy through community support and a new network without her brother. Now she has "siblings," other migrants whom she met after her brother cut ties rather than risk being found harbouring undocumented migrants. Although Carolina did not qualify to be sponsored by her brother, this family network collapse contributes to questions about the focus Canadian immigration policy places on family ties. Her case clearly shows that family does not always provide the best source of support for a migrant (regardless of status) and also offers a strong argument for re-evaluating the family sponsorship program.

Through these examples we see the common theme of fear created by the state. This fear is realized in the potential threat of identification and return to Brazil. This chapter has outlined some of the strategies used to build networks that do not involve the state and do provide resources to cope with precarious situations and times of vulnerability. Migrants like Carolina draw on their network resources to redefine "legality" and justify remaining in Canada; however, the power of the state can be found in both public and private spaces. Fear is easily invoked and precariousness remains dominant, contributing to "non-status stress" (Saad, in this volume), which in turn influences most aspects of migrants' everyday lives.

Despite the ongoing stress, both Renato and Carolina dismiss the state's control over hard work. Whether building homes for Canadians or looking after family, it is the work that matters and not any related paperwork. Living everyday with precarious status is justified by their good, hard work, an important part of the working-class values with which they were raised.

Some precarious status migrants try to stabilize their lives by meeting state-imposed conditions for obtaining permanent status; neither Carolina nor Renato have attempted to submit applications. While Madeleina accessed resources within her network – both in Canada and Brazil – to assist with her transition through the family sponsorship program, she married for love and sponsorship plans developed later. More strategic marriages do occur, and both Renato and Carolina have joked about finding a spouse, but have not taken steps in this direction. Renato explicitly states his disapproval of this approach, given the falsehood that is required and his strong belief in the institution of marriage.

Neither Renato nor Carolina has the points necessary to obtain a skilled worker visa. Occasionally there is talk about the "humanitarian and compassionate" application, but both of these precarious migrants are too afraid they would be sent home following the submission and evaluation of such a request. Applying for status would give them visibility, but their contributions to Canada over the last eight and nine years respectively would not be recognized since the work was done without a government-issued visa. Instead, this new visibility could focus attention on them through the discourses of "illegality" and "criminality" used by the state. If they do not qualify on humanitarian and compassionate grounds, deportation would be the end result and they would be forced to leave the lives they have built in Canada, including the close ties to fictive family that have developed over time.

Carolina's resolve to stay rarely wavers; she makes it clear that there is nothing left in Brazil for her either professionally or personally. She rationalizes her change in profession as an opportunity to work hard and support her family. Once her daughter was in school, she became focused on a long-term migration and settlement plan, bringing family priorities to the forefront over considerations of "legality" and profession. Her only question concerns what path to take to become a citizen.

Renato only talks of applying for status when threats of deportation are imminent, usually due to a crisis at work. He continues to face problems at work due to his precariousness, but with no concrete plan to transition, his frustration with his "invisibility" and non-recognition only grow. Currently, he remains hidden from the state, with his hard work and contributions to Canada remaining dominant in his discursive reasoning to remain, regardless of his status.

Madeleina never had a "plan" when she arrived in Canada, but she was able to gain permanent status through the family sponsorship program. She was on a "wait-and-see" trajectory when she began dating Jason, a Brazilian migrant with legal status. She began to consider remaining permanently in Canada; however, her plan to remain had to include a way to legalize her children. Ultimately, she married Jason, who was able to sponsor both her and her children on one application. As a result her migration goals shifted, but only when family considerations were taken into account. This example demonstrates the overlaps between different areas of network growth. Despite the reality that precarious status influences everyday life, if changes occur in other areas – in this case in the area of family (marriage) and work (financial aid from her Canadian client) – there can be a change in legal status. Therefore, while the state is a dominant influence on migrant action, precariousness does not predetermine all migrant activity, decisions, and trajectories. Strategies for coping with precarious status as well as remaining in Canada can draw on network resources and prevail.

This discussion has focused on examples of status precariousness in migrant lives in the areas of work and family, examining strategies used to combat the precariousness of everyday life, to build a life in Canada and to cope with instabilities within that life. The case studies raise questions about the costs of this precariousness to the migrants, the social ramifications of living without recognition, and living every day with uncertainty and often fear. Despite strategies to cope, moments of crisis still occur and shake the resolve of these migrants to remain and continue their hard work. This situation also raises concerns about the costs to Canada of denying permanent status to migrants who come undetected or overstay, build lives, contribute to the community by helping other migrants (including those with migration visas), and work hard in jobs that the skilled worker migrant class resists. This population fills a niche in the job market and community that should not be dismissed. Ironically, their greatest visibility might come from the holes that would be left if they are forced to return to Brazil.

NOTES

1 For further details on Brazil's emigration history, see Patarra and
   Baeninger (1996).

2 Given the extreme violence in major Brazilian cities and the hyperinflation of the 1980s, Brazilians label Canada comparatively "safe," although there are other challenges and different kinds of violence to face upon arrival (e.g., prejudicial and racial).

3 *Cidade Congelada* (Frozen City) is the pseudonym for a small city in the northeastern United States that Goza used in order to protect the many undocumented Brazilians who live there.

4 I use the term "undocumented" to refer to migrants who do not have legal status in Canada (i.e., a visa); therefore, they are undocumented by the state.

5 When I last saw this man, he had not seen his daughter in four years. She was living with her mother in Bomsuccesso, a lower-middle-class neighbourhood in Rio de Janeiro.

6 There are many ways to enter Canada as a Brazilian migrant. National border-crossing strategies include gaining visas, seeking refugee status, undetected travel, and using false documents.

7 The "crackdown" appears to have been the result of an increase in resources (primarily more staff) from the federal government, which sped up the appeals process so the paperwork does not sit for as long. Before this change, one couple in my research returned to Brazil after their last appeal was denied a year after its submission. During March 2006, another individual received the same news, but it was only a few months after her similar submission. Therefore, it was not the appeal process that changed, only the length of time to address individual appeals cases. As a result, the number of deportations rose significantly as the process was streamlined.

8 These are my translations from the original Portuguese.

7 The Cost of Invisibility: The Psychosocial Impact of Falling Out of Status

SAMIA SAAD

Little is known about the effects of precarious status on psychosocial health (Simich et al., 2007) and family well-being (Bernhard et al., 2007). In this chapter I clarify how the production of precariousness and illegality via the refugee determination system affects the psychosocial health of unsuccessful refugee claimants and their families. Drawing on the social-determinants-of-health approach, I argue that immigration legal status should be considered a key determinant of health. After introducing my research and reviewing the relationship between legal status and health, I discuss the particular pathway that leads refugee claimants to fall out of status, noting how this process is gendered. Next, I address how the illegalization process, produced by exclusionary immigration policies, limits and denies access to the determinants of health. The last part of the chapter shows how falling out of status affected the lives of the study participants, compromising their psychosocial health and family well-being.

Method and Sample

This chapter is based on semi-structured in-depth interviews I conducted[1] in Spanish with ten individuals (five women and five men), document analysis, and a journal of my work experiences with twenty-one people who had similar profiles to those I interviewed.[2] Inclusion criteria were: overstaying a deportation order following the final denial of a refugee claim; living with at least one family member; and identifying as Latin American. Participants were recruited through community agencies, community health centres, a labour union, and

Spanish-speaking churches. Study participants' countries of origin were Argentina (two), Mexico (three), Costa Rica (two), and El Salvador (one). Eight of the interviewees lived with a partner, eight had children living with them, and one had children living in the country of origin. Two of the men were single parents, and two couples were trying to have children. I will refer to the ten interviewees as such, and "study participants" will be used to refer to them plus the cases from my journal.

Migration, Irregularization, and Health

The "social determinants of health" are the social conditions and processes that determine health. A society's organization, including policy choices, determines how health resources are distributed (Health Canada, 2002; Raphael, 2009). Although status is crucial to accessing health resources (Bernhard et al., 2007; Oxman-Martinez et al., 2005; Saad, 2011; Simich et al., 2007), immigration legal status tends to be excluded as a determinant of health. This status is, however, crucial for health and well-being, especially among immigrants who possess little human capital. This often holds among people with temporary migratory status, including asylum seekers (Li, 2008). Those making refugee claims enter the refugee determination system; status is precarious, and many fall out of status after their claim is denied. After falling out of status, their human rights are severely curtailed as they become subject to the sovereign power of the nation-state that limits their international migrant rights (WHO, 2003). To justify their exclusion, the state employs a securitization agenda whereby threats to the state are associated with the image of the migrant (Bacon, 2008; Crépeau & Nakache, 2006). The criminalization of migrants justifies limiting and denying them access to the determinants of health. This production of illegality and denial of migrant's rights has become prevalent in immigration law and public policy (de Genova, 2002).

The Refugee Claimant's Pathway to "Illegality"

Canada has taken steps to reduce the number of people allowed to make refugee claims by deterring them from entering the country. After the Safe Third Country Agreement was implemented in December 2004, the number of refugee claims dropped by 40 per cent (Boyd and Grieco, 2003; Girzu, 2010; Pullenayegem, 2007; Toronto Refugee

Affairs Council, 2005). In spite of these changes, people deemed "undesirable" as immigrants or permanent settlers do enter Canada, some on temporary visas, others as refugee claimants. While refugee claimants await the outcome of their claim, many encounter procedures and policies that keep them on a pathway marked by legal status precarity and perhaps illegality (de Genova, 2002; Goldring, Berinstein, & Bernhard, 2009).

Many obstacles await those who do manage to make a refugee claim. Some challenges are created by the Immigration and Refugee Board's lack of sensitivity to cultural difference and insufficient understanding of the trauma that claimants have experienced. The fact that claimants tend to be from racialized groups contributes to power asymmetries, which may disadvantage them. Gender also intersects with social location and the claim process. These factors may disadvantage people as they confront the refugee system. Two stages define the refugee determination process, the first of which lasts until claimants have their refugee hearing. My research focuses on a subsequent stage, which involves attempting to overturn a negative decision.

The Initial Stage

In this initial stage people make a refugee claim. First they tell their story to an immigration officer. They are then required to fill out the Personal Information Form (PIF) in which they provide reasons for seeking protection in Canada.[3] Most claimants have access to legal aid, so they can hire a lawyer or a consultant to develop their legal case. They are entitled to an oral hearing to determine their claim.

The complexity of this initial process works to irregularize claimants and make them fall out of status in several ways. First, while it is essential to have good legal representation, there is inadequate funding for legal aid (Crépeau & Nakache, 2006). Second, good information about how to navigate the refugee system is of utmost importance in building a good case. As I have seen in my work, most refugee claimants experience a deficit of information. Women are less likely to have access to information and counsel (Bombardier, 2007; Canadian Council for Refugees [CCR], 1999). This means women are less likely to understand the legal process and take advantage of available resources. Places that provide information services about the legal process are in high demand and often cannot meet expectations. Most of the study participants knew very little about the refugee determination process and how to navigate it. Third, little knowledge and sensitivity about the effects of trauma can lead Immigration and Refugee Board (IRB) members to make faulty judgments about people's narratives. Claimants do not always tell all the details of their assault to immigration officers and their legal representatives (CCR, 1999, 2010). Among those in my journal, I found this situation happened because they felt intimidated by immigration officers, lawyers, and consultants. They felt ashamed and afraid and did not always know that what they were omitting was relevant to their case. For women who suffered violence from male perpetrators, talking to male lawyers or male interpreters could be difficult, preventing them from telling their stories in full.

Counselling and therapy are important services for survivors of violence. It is often in this setting that people can speak about their stories without the pressure and intimidation of the legal system. Time is also critical. People need time to build trust with their legal representatives and their therapist, and they need time to process traumatic experiences in order to make sense of those events. Traumatic experiences can affect one's ability to testify and, when not processed, can lead to narratives that seem inconsistent. In my practice, clients who have engaged in therapy stand a greater chance of getting a positive outcome from their refugee hearings. Claimants do not always know about the importance of therapy services in relation to their refugee case. When they are encouraged to seek them, usually by lawyers, consultants, community workers, or friends, they find these services are not available because of long waiting lists. Very few of the research participants who suffered violence had a therapist help them process traumatic experiences.

Fourth, problems with and abuse by those representing the system go unchallenged. People often do not report abuses of authority by unscrupulous lawyers and consultants because of their perceived authority and social standing. Furthermore, many claimants arrive in Canada with a fear of authorities. They do not report their legal representatives despite their failure to do their job (e.g., failure to show up for refugee hearings and other appointments, poorly written narratives in the PIF, meeting with clients only once or twice before their hearing, or forgetting to present crucial evidence given to them well in advance) for fear of reprisals. Having attended many refugee hearings, I have seen board members notice how badly clients are represented, yet they turn a blind eye.

Most of the interview participants in this research felt they were badly represented by their lawyer or consultant. In two cases the consultants did not appear for their hearings, leaving claimants stranded. Bill C-35 promises to deal with fraud from "ghost" consultants and anyone giving misleading legal advice for a fee (Saint-Cyr, 2010). However, it does not address other factors that prevent people from reporting their concerns, such as fear of retaliation.

The pathway that leads people to fall out of status is further facilitated by key structural changes in the refugee determination system. The government's decision to move from two IRB members to one has been of great disadvantage to refugee claimants (CCR, 2006). Before, disagreement between two IRB members concerning a claim led automatically to a positive decision. This helped to minimize possible biases and subjective negative judgments, such as those based on gender and race. Not long ago I witnessed this in the hearing of a Mexican woman who had escaped a very traumatic situation. Her ex-partner severely assaulted her physically and sexually. She had three children resulting from rape. The board member asked her why she had three children if her husband was raping her. She became confused and could not answer. This board member questioned the truthfulness of her story based on his own bias. He did not take into account the fact that she came from a rural and religious area where birth control is simply not practised, and marital rape is not considered rape. Faced with this question, she felt confused, guilty, and embarrassed. If there had been two board members at this hearing, this situation might have been prevented.

The Second Stage

The negative outcome for refugee claims is high: the overall rejection rate in 2009 was 45 per cent. The rejection rate for some Latin American countries is higher still: 89 per cent for Mexico and 67 per cent for El Salvador (CCR, 2009c). Once people receive a negative outcome from their refugee hearing, it is very difficult to overturn the decision. There is no appeal system on the merits of the case.[4] People can apply for a Judicial Review: if they are granted leave by the Federal Court, their case can be reviewed to evaluate whether the board member followed all the rules in making the decision (CCR, 2009b; Federal Court, Canada, 2006). About 75 per cent of those initially denied apply for leave; of those, about 10 per cent are granted leave, and less than half (40 per cent) have their original decision changed. This works out to a success rate of 4 per cent (Macklin, 2009). People have only fifteen days after the initial negative decision is given to apply for a judicial review. For those without access to legal aid, the cost is astronomical, about three thousand dollars. Half of those interviewed applied for a judicial review, but all were denied leave. The rest did not apply for economic reasons, except in one case where the lawyer missed the fifteen-day deadline.

Denied refugees have access to the Pre-Removal Risk Assessment (PRRA). For a PRRA application to succeed, the applicant must demonstrate that being returned to the country of origin would mean facing a serious risk not faced by others residing there. Only new evidence can be presented for this application. The cost for a PRRA application can range from one to three thousand dollars, since most applicants do not have access to legal aid. In 2006 there was only a 2.1 per cent acceptance rate (CIC, 2009c). Nine of the study participants applied for a PRRA but all were denied.

Humanitarian and compassionate applications (H&C) can provide a final but slim opportunity for people to regularize their status. People can apply at any time while they have some form of authorized precarious status or after they fall out of status. The submission of an H&C application does not stop a deportation order. In completing an H&C the individual must prove he or she has successfully established him or herself in Canada, which means demonstrating financial independence. Applications usually take less time to process when people apply while still in the refugee process; if made after people fall out of status or after the outcome of the PRRA, it can take three to five years. An H&C is not normally viewed as a priority application by Citizenship and Immigration Canada (Scott, 2010; Stothers, 2010), and the acceptance rate is low – between 2.5 and 5 per cent (Goldring, Berinstein, & Bernhard, 2009). If people are denied, there is no recourse but to apply again and wait another three to five years. For a family it typically costs three to seven thousand dollars to apply. This includes government and legal fees. Women without partners find it very difficult to qualify for an H&C because they usually earn less money than men. After falling out of status they earn even less. For some women, this means staying in abusive relationships in order to have a higher chance at qualifying.

In this study, five interview participants applied for an H&C. Three had their application denied, and two reapplied. Five of the research participants had experienced fraud. They paid thousands of dollars to consultants who literally took off with their money without doing anything. Those who had not applied for H&C were currently saving money to apply. One woman who was experiencing abuse by her partner decided to stay in the relationship until a decision was reached on her H&C application.

Legislation introduced in February 2012 (Bill C-31) will further contribute to people falling out of status: instead of having twenty-eight days to complete the PIF, they will be given only fifteen days to fill out what will be called the Basis of Claim form after their port-of-entry interview. There will no longer be a PIF. If people come from a Designated Country of Origin (DCO), meaning a country considered by the minister to have the democratic institutions necessary for people to live in safety, they will have thirty days for a hearing. If, on the other hand, people come from a country not considered to have these democratic institutions, they will have sixty days, and no longer than ninety days, to have a hearing. Only those from non-DCOs will have access to an appeal system (Canadian Association of Refugee Lawyers, 2012). This proposed legislation will not allow claimants to process their case adequately. They will not be given sufficient time to process their claim, nor the resources needed to do so. Dividing claimants into two streams based on their country of origin will further discriminate against applicants such as women and minorities who face danger based on their minority status rather than whether or not they come from a safe country (CCR, 2010).

Legal Non-existence and Exclusionary Practices

Many people decide to stay after exhausting all avenues for regularization. They stay because they seek safety, a better future for their children, and better economic opportunities. Two seemingly contradictory realities affect them after overstaying a deportation order. First, they enter the space of legal non-existence in which personhood is erased and a disjuncture between physical and legal presence emerges (Coutin, 2000). As they become legally absent, the state no longer grants them rights and entitlements. Second, their visibility becomes heightened as the state apparatus attempts to deport them. Consequently, they experience danger and need to make themselves invisible to avoid deportation (Villegas, 2010). Legal non-existence and hyper-visibility were apparent in all research participants. Dorian speaks of non-existence:

> Yes, it is as if you existed before, and then you did not anymore. From the moment that you have to hide under the shadows you understand that

you cease to exist, you cease to belong in the system, you cease to belong to society, you cease to belong. Then, somehow, you lose your dignity.

At the same time, they begin a life full of risks, where the police now represent danger. Dorian explains:

From the moment you become illegal you have to tell your children to beware of the police because the ones that once protected you [when you had status], no longer do it because they now represent danger. It all is very confusing; it changes your life.

The exclusionary policies implicated in producing legal non-existence (Coutin, 2000) deny people access to many of the elements identified as social determinants of health. This significantly reduces people's ability to gather the resources needed to live in this society. In my research, I identified two key exclusionary policies: denial of state-sanctioned identification and reduced access to public goods and services. People simply did not have a way to obtain state-sanctioned identification, and access to services was extremely limited (Berinstein et al., 2006; Chakkalakal & Neve, 1998; Oxman-Martinez et al., 2005; Paradis, Hulchanski, et al., 2008; Young, 2007).

Study participants were hampered in accessing health care services, a very important determinant of health. They only had access to community health clinics, not on the basis of entitlement but based on the clinic's criteria for eligibility, provided the clinic had space (Pashang, 2008; P. Villegas, in this volume). If they ended up in the hospital, they had to pay thousands of dollars in fees. They did not have access to public housing, social assistance, legal aid, work permits, and employment protections. Day-care subsidies were not available to them, even if their children were Canadian born (Bernhard et al., 2007). They did not have access to English language classes, skills-training programs, college and university programs (unless they paid international student fees), and community programs where identification and status were required. Only the children were able to go to school regardless of their status. Nevertheless, research shows that some children are still not allowed in schools, and parents face difficulties before their children can attend school (Bejan & Sidhu, 2010; Sidhu, 2008; F. Villegas, in this volume).

In 2006 the Toronto police board adopted The Victims and Witnesses Without Legal Status Policy or, as it is known, the "Don't Ask" policy (Toronto Police Services, 2007). It was meant to offer protection to victims of crime. In theory, people who have fallen out of status can have police protection as long as their status does not become known to the police. What usually happens, however, is that police ask for immigration status. Even if they did not ask, and the guilty party decided to make known the other party's lack of status, the police would be required to let immigration know (Doolittle, 2008). This has happened to women who called the police for protection from domestic violence (Berinstein et al., 2006). An attempt by the police board to study the possibility of adopting a "Don't Tell" policy, which would have protected women against violence, was rejected in November 2008 (Doolittle, 2008; Hanes, 2008). In my practice, it is very difficult to advise women experiencing violence and lack of immigration status to seek police protection because of the risk of deportation.

Public workers such as doctors, nurses, social workers, children's aid case workers, and therapists are not required to call immigration authorities. Yet some do. The lack of an official policy and protocol to work with people with precarious status results in inconsistent and unreliable services. More importantly, workers can make a personal decision to call immigration on people without any consequence to themselves (Berinstein et al., 2006). This illustrates the role of service providers as players implicated in the conditionality of presence for people without status.

For those who have fallen out of status there are other deterrents to seeking public services. Fear of being reported to the police, child protective services, and immigration can act as barriers to seeking services (Berinstein et al., 2006; Chakkalakal and Neve, 1998; Pashang, 2008). Many study participants did not go to community agencies fearing that if they gave their names and contact information, agency staff would send the information to immigration. Some believed they were not even eligible to receive services from community agencies. Organizations committed to working with this population (Social Planning Toronto, 2010a), including agencies and churches that have little to no funding from the government, were places where research participants found more services and support to be available. These places did not require identification and status to participate in most programs.

Legal Non-existence Creates Vulnerability

These exclusionary policies compromise access to the conditions necessary for health and well-being and create vulnerability to exploitation. My research shows that people found themselves vulnerable to various forms of exploitation in the workplace and with consultants and lawyers. At work, they complained about overwork, employers changing the terms of employment at will, being paid much less than other employees with status, and, in some cases, not being paid at all (Landolt & Goldring, in this volume). Regarding legal consultants and lawyers, participants complained about the large sums of money paid for legal forms, and negligence in submitting forms on time and with the right information. Some consultants ran away with thousands of dollars without performing any service. These injustices were not reported for fear of deportation.

Gender-Based Vulnerability

Women are vulnerable to gender-based exploitation and violence that can occur at home, work, or anywhere else. In general women earn less money than men, and jobs tend to be gendered (Picchio, 1992). For women with no status the situation is graver still. The underground economy is gendered, and women end up taking jobs cleaning homes and offices, cooking in restaurants, or taking care of children; these jobs pay less than those held by their male counterparts. Men often find work in the construction industry, as floor polishers, or in other such jobs. Although those jobs pay less than jobs held by men with status, they still pay more than jobs typically held by non-status women (Magalhaes et al., 2010). Women with children are particularly vulnerable: when they take on reproductive work they depend on their male partners for survival needs. And women in abusive relationships, especially those with children, are the most vulnerable. They experience multilevel disadvantages: they have little or no access to public services such as daycare and social assistance, there is a real risk of deportation if they call the police for protection, and they do not earn enough money to manage on their own. Most of these women do not see going back to their country of origin as an option because of insecurity and lack of opportunity for them and their children. They would rather live in fear with an abusive partner while experiencing fear of deportation, and hope to have status one day. Only then, with status, will they have the option to call the police.

Mental Health Impact

Falling out of status negatively affects the mental health of individuals and families. The loss of social entitlements, the experience of vulnerability to abuse and exploitation, and the overall sense of being persecuted and in danger create the conditions for people to experience trauma. According to Briere and Scott (2006), traumatic conditions are characterized by danger and vulnerability. These characteristics were present in the lives and narratives of the participants in this research.

Trauma is often understood as a one-time event such as a horrible violent attack. However, trauma can also be caused by ongoing stress, such as living in a crime-ridden neighbourhood (Smith & Segal, 2008) or, as my research demonstrates, living in fear of deportation. Trauma produces debilitating emotional symptoms (Le Page, 2010; Smith & Segal, 2008), and these symptoms are likely to be more severe if a person has experienced trauma previously (Smith & Segal, 2008). Research demonstrates that trauma compounds with insecurity to increase the psychological toll in the lives of migrants with precarious immigration status (Khanlou et al., 2010; Simich et al., 2007). The majority of the research participants said they experienced violence prior to migrating to Canada. This is more likely to affect them in their present condition of "no status," increasing the mental health impact. As seen in this research, the mental health impact is characterized by fear, powerlessness, helplessness, and other mental health reactions. I will now discuss how research participants, families, and children were affected.

Fear

Fear is something research participants experienced before migrating and throughout the refugee process. With the loss of status, the magnitude of fear increased exponentially. Research participants feared they could be deported at any moment, which would dramatically change the course of their lives. They also feared they would be treated like criminals, their families would be separated, and their children would be taken away. Since the interviews took place, four of the ten interviewees were deported without any warning. In each case, the families were separated (in one case a parent stayed with the children and was deported later on). Although children are not taken away from their parents, the fear that this might happen increases anxiety levels. This fear is real, it affects the way they live, and it causes them to view events around them with suspicion and apprehension. Mario describes this fear:

I mean, you stop behaving like a normal person. You are paranoid the entire day, paranoid. Sometimes you relax and forget, but you remember that [fear of deportation] at least once a day.

People feel hunted by the authorities, yet they know they did not commit a crime. This ambivalence is heightened when they hear of immigration raids. Martha explains:

I felt like a delinquent but at the same time not; why delinquent if I had not killed anyone. I have not done anything bad … yet, you feel persecuted.

Helplessness and Powerlessness

The level of uncertainly among the participants is so great that for some of them it is better not to think of or plan for the future. They find themselves in a state of limbo. Menjívar (2006) calls this a state of "suspended lives." This indefinite suspension minimizes the control people can assert over their lives. Yet according to Health Canada, "the degree of control people have over life circumstances, especially stressful situations, and their discretion to act are the key influences" to health and wellness (2003, p. 3). Discussing issues related to social inequality and exclusion, Galabuzi (2004) affirms that these translate into powerlessness, hopelessness, and despair, contributing to the emotional and physical impact on health.

The research participants repeatedly expressed their sense of powerlessness in specific situations where they could not assert their rights and did not have a high degree of control over their circumstances. For example, Ramón could not do anything to protect his young son when he was attacked by the owner of a go-karting business, except run away. For Mario, this level of powerlessness was like being a prisoner. When Dorian's boss changed his mind and paid her less than agreed, she could not do or say anything other than accept his new terms. She added:

When you feel you have no rights you annul certain parts of your temper. If you [are] like me that cannot see injustices and quickly jump in and get involved, and say that is not fair, that is not good. But when you know you cannot raise your voice because it is dangerous, then you annul aspects of your own personality. Then you become more submissive. It is like … it is exactly that, you stop being yourself, you stop being yourself.

The research participants felt they could not make future plans, however big or small. They experienced a great deal of frustration because they could not better themselves. They did not have access to education to improve their English language skills, formal education, or other training. They could not improve their economic situation or their jobs. Mario felt that he was only good to work and benefit someone else, and that he could not improve himself:

Right now I am like a useful idiot: I do not use the hospital. I am cheap [my labour]. I cannot do anything: I cannot study. I cannot work. I cannot realize myself as a person.

Other Mental Health Impacts

Fear and helplessness were often accompanied by a wide range of symptoms such as depression, anxiety, low self-esteem, guilt, frustration, anger, self-blame, and constant worrying. All research participants experienced a number of these symptoms: "I feel very depressed, very depressed and very powerless," stated Arnold. Elsa also experienced depression: "Well, yes, sometimes I do, I get depressed and begin to think … what can I do." For Martha losing status created anxiety, insecurity, fear, depression, and powerlessness: "I mean, I became a very insecure person, fearful of many things especially at the beginning. I became ill, I got depressed. I saw myself very ill, very desperate for not knowing what to do." Daniela's self-esteem was also affected: "Here, one feels worthless, inferior, belonging nowhere. I feel like I am worthless, I cannot do anything here."

Parents feel guilty because they cannot provide for their children's needs (Pashang, 2008). Parents in this research dealt with a sense of guilt and concern for their children. They felt they could not provide them with security, safety, stability, and material goods they needed. As Hilda succinctly put it:

Those are things that, although one might have trust in God, they destroy you inside because, at least to me, it pains me to have to be saying to them [my kids], "look, you cannot because you do not have papers." It is very difficult and very painful for a parent. It is very painful because to our children we want to,… as long as it is at our financial reach we want to give them the best.

Impact on Children

Like the adults, children are subjected to experiences of fear and danger. They worry about the uncertainty of their status and the thought of being deported (Young, 2007). Although parents try to protect their children from suffering, it is hard for children not to carry the burden of seeing their family deported and thinking it happened because of something they did. This happened to Dorian's twelve-year-old son, who suffered the trauma of seeing his father deported. Someone called the police at his school for something minor he and other boys did, but because he had no status he was taken to the police station. When his father went to pick him up, he was apprehended and deported in a matter of hours. A few months later, they were all deported, but not without this boy carrying the burden that he caused his family's deportation. As was the case with this boy and his family, the threat of deportation may force children and their families to move suddenly to a different home and school, leaving their friends behind without an explanation. Living with such insecurity and fear is particularly hard on children who are in their developmental years, increasing their risk of mental health issues well into adulthood (Smith & Segal, 2008; Wheeler, 2009).

Impact on the Family

Living without status and legal exclusion also have negative effects on relationships in the family, creating acute stressors (McDonald, n.d.). I found that the stress of losing status, insecurity, and living in fear disrupts family life and erodes family well-being. As refugee claimants, the participants said they experienced a lot of stress, uncertainty, and fear from not knowing what would happen. Yet they built their families in the hope of having a positive refugee outcome. They felt free to engage in recreational activities as a family. They went out freely to the mall, to parks, on walks, and other outings. They also had more resources, including money, better jobs, and access to public services. Having refugee status decreased their need to struggle for survival and optimized their options for family activities and resources.

After they lost their refugee claim, uncertainty and fear increased significantly. They experienced what I call *non-status stress*, which is produced by the risk and fear of deportation and the constant struggle to survive. Because of fear of deportation, people in this research went out much less and only to specific places with people they trusted. Whenever they perceived a high degree of threat of deportation, they moved, left their jobs, abandoned friends, and moved their children to a different school. All of the study participants had already moved at least twice by the time I interviewed them. Isolation is inevitable in conditions of fear and danger. In addition, living in constant survival mode (where they have less money and no access to a safety net to fall back on in the event of financial crises) demanded that they work longer hours to make ends meet, introducing further stress. They experienced fear and anxiety when confronted with the risk of losing their job. This, and the fear of deportation, constrained the time and energy of the participants. They said they engaged less in family recreational activities than before because these restrictions did not allow them to be free to enjoy themselves with their families.

The conditions described above constitute the perfect setting for violence and aggression to manifest. Research in the United States has found that the stress and helplessness of those who are "undocumented" lead to feelings of frustration and anger (Cavazos-Rehg, Zayas, & Spitznagel, 2007). My research corroborates this: aggressive physical and non-physical behaviours intensified after people fell out of status. While this study suggests that women are the primary targets of physical aggression, most research participants (men and women) reported an increase in conflict and arguments. My findings suggest that repressed anger and frustration are the main causes for aggressive behaviours. Arnold's comments illustrate how stress and powerlessness due to lack of status increased his irritability:

> Perhaps [not having status] might cause me to be a bit irritated, and anxious. Yes, yes, because things do not work out as one would like, and one cannot plan. Then, one feels bad, one gets negative or maybe a fly goes by, in a matter of speaking, and one gets irritated because you are already sensitive; because it is something that escapes you and you cannot control it.

Repressed anger and frustration can lead to outbursts of anger, which often manifest among those with whom one does not feel at risk of deportation: the family. This was illustrated by Dorian:

> It is dangerous because of those around you. Because you know to repress anguish, to repress raising your voice, to repress continuously many human attitudes ... We are like in a pressure cooker. Then comes a time

when that pressure cooker can explode with the only people with whom it can explode, with whom you feel safe, with the members of your family. Then, everything that you have repressed, because you cannot release it outside, you release it inside your family nucleus. So, for example, while I never raised my voice to my children [before] I raise it [now]. [Before] we did not argue with my husband, but now we do. Because all that [not having status] affects you.

For Martha, it was the desperation of not finding a way out that made her feel irritated and tense, and caused fights with her partner: "I fought more with my partner because of my desperation of not knowing where to run to. I was very tense and irritable with him. He is a very peaceful and relaxed person, but later he also became desperate."

All these negative effects make one wonder how it is that people can live under such conditions. I have shown that the psychosocial impact of living without status is severe for both individuals and families. Nevertheless, I found that people's needs and desires to stay and make a better life for themselves and their children gave them the courage and strength to continue the struggle for status. Although they lacked access to most conditions that positively affect health and well-being, they still managed to gain access to some resources. Paradoxically, the flexible nature of the labour market allowed them to find work, although it was precarious. Many of the research participants said that community agencies, community clinics, churches, and good people provided them with some support, especially at critical times. In my research, faith played a major role in helping the majority of families cope. Support and faith, then, act as protective factors (Grunert & Adomatis, 2008), allowing families and individuals to continue to survive and hope for regularization.

Conclusion

I have shown how the production of illegality through the refugee determination system negatively affects the health and well-being of individuals and families. Their need for safety and desire to give their children better opportunities embeds them in a system that makes them legally non-existent, without rights and access to the conditions that determine health. At the same time, they become targets for deportation, thus creating risk and danger. As a result, they become vulnerable to abuse and exploitation as they enter the realm of the underground where gathering important life resources is precarious. In this system exploitation and vulnerability are gendered; women, particularly those with children, experience greater precariousness.

The experiences of insecurity, legal non-existence, and exclusion create traumatic conditions that severely affect the mental health of adults, children, and the family. Under these conditions people live in a state of fear and insecurity where powerlessness and helplessness, depression, isolation, anxiety, despair, low self-esteem, guilt, frustration, anger, and self-blame permeate their everyday lives.

The very presence of these people in situations of such adversity issues a threefold challenge. First, global inequality will continue to produce vulnerable migrants. Second, the production of illegality through the refugee determination system contributes to vulnerability and ill health. We need to build a refugee protection system that is fair and relevant for people. This system needs to consider people's social location, and the impact of violence and global economic disadvantage. We need a system that creates a pathway to permanent immigration status, in other words, a system that empowers people instead of bogging them down. Third, policies such as "Don't Ask Don't Tell" need to be set in place, enabling non-status people to have access to public services. Without addressing these three challenges, people will continue to fall out of status and find themselves in positions of vulnerability. They will become vulnerable to poverty, exploitation, and abuse, and their experiences will continue to be detrimental to their mental health and family well-being. For this reason, I maintain that immigration legal status is a determinant of health, one of particularly significant importance because it shapes access to other determinants of health.

NOTES

1 This chapter is based on research conducted for my MA thesis (Saad, 2011).
2 I have been working as a counsellor and program coordinator at a community organization in Toronto since 1989. As part of my practice, I work with individuals and families with precarious status.
3 Under Bill C-31, the PIF will be replaced by an interview.
4 Under Bill C-31 an appeal will be implemented. We still do not know how this will be carried out.

8 The Social Production of Non-citizenship: The Consequences of Intersecting Trajectories of Precarious Legal Status and Precarious Work

PATRICIA LANDOLT AND LUIN GOLDRING

The global age of migration has transformed the boundaries between citizenship and non-citizenship and how legal status, migratory movements, and employment relations intersect. Four interrelated trends are involved in this transformation: the absolute growth in the global population of irregular and undocumented migrant workers (Bacon, 2008; Dauvergne, 2008); the increasingly complex national and international regulatory framework that sometimes regularizes and at other times irregularizes migrant workers (Calavita, 1998; Goldring & Landolt, 2011); the proliferation of temporary migrant worker programs worldwide and their notable expansion into countries such as Canada and Australia with a decades-long focus on meeting labour market needs through permanent immigration (Castles & Miller, 2009; Ruhs, 2006; Sharma, 2006); and an increase in precarious work across a range of sectors and occupations, and throughout the Global North (Kalleberg, 2008; Munck, 2008; Vosko, 2010).

These broad trends are in turn associated with a revamping of the legal and normative framework that organizes migrant legal status as a source of state control and employer strategies of exploitation and labour market segmentation. Migrant worker legal insecurity and economic vulnerability is rooted in the combination of (1) unpredictable, nonlinear, and not always voluntary movement between various points in a continuum of precarious legal status (Goldring, Berinstein, & Bernhard, 2009); (2) precarious work situations generated by employer strategies of flexibilization (Bernhardt, Boushey, Dresser, & Tilly, 2008); and (3) the potential for this intersecting location to produce experiences that have cumulative, nonlinear, and long-term path-dependent effects

(Goldring & Landolt, 2011). In other words, migrant workers across the Global North and in pockets of the Global South are spending more time navigating through various forms of insecure migratory legal status – the chutes and ladders of legal status, making them particularly vulnerable to employer exploitation and abuse. At times, some migrant workers who are in transit or in a destination country move into more secure legal situations, but these shifts are often not permanent and may not ensure gains on the work front.

In this chapter we draw on our research about the work experiences of Latin American and Caribbean migrant workers in the Greater Toronto Area (GTA) to explore how the intersecting vulnerabilities of precarious legal status and precarious work exert long-term, negative effects on work. We will focus on the social production of non-citizenship to explain why migrant workers who regularize, moving from insecure to secure legal status, often fail to make significant gains in their work situation.[1] Our analytical focus on legal status differs from most research on the impact of regularization on work, which focuses on the character of the labour market and the organization of work to explain post-regularization work outcomes. However, a singular focus on work is insufficient: the current age of global migration is distiguished by compounding insecurities generated at the *intersections* of precarious legal status and precarious work (Castles & Miller, 2009; Goldring & Landolt, 2011; Munck, 2008). As such, a focus on one dimension of migrant vulnerabilty at the expense of the other will produce a partial understanding of the current problem. Thus, we consider how the experience of precarious legal status or non-citizenship imposes severe limits on migrants' post-regularization work experiences. We will demonstrate that non-citizenship is socially produced – and not simply as a residual category opposed to citizenship, but in the sense that social relations and practices mediate non-citizenship, turning an insecure legal category into a social location and lived experience that has long-term negative outcomes that shape post-regularization life.

The next two sections of this chapter review previous research about how legal status regularization affects work, and scholarship that conceptualizes citizenship as a relational and contested practice. In the third section we draw on qualitative interview data from our research project to capture three aspects of the social production of non-citizenship: the regulatory context that frames the life chances of precarious legal status migrants in Canada; the character of social relations between precarious legal status migrants and a range of actors including employers, government agents, family, and friends; and the consequences of the regulatory context and social interactions for the well-being of migrants navigating non-citizenship. The chapter ends with a brief discussion of what our findings reveal about the social production of non-citizenship and its relationship to citizenship, both in practice and in theory.

The Impact of Legal Status Change on Work

A long history of scholarship has focused on the relationship between citizenship and work, examining legal status, race, class, and gender as they relate to labour market segmentation in several regional contexts (Burawoy, 1976; Castles & Kosak, 1973; Piore, 1979; Thomas, 1981). Most systematic research about the wage effects of being undocumented has been conducted in the United States; researchers have demonstrated that undocumented migrant workers in that country earn significantly less than documented workers, controlling for factors such as education and time in the country (Capps, Fix, Passel, Ost, & Perez-Lopez, 2003; Phillips & Massey, 1999; Rivera-Batiz, 1999). Similar findings have been reported in other parts of the world (Bloch, 2010; Burgers, 1998; Vicente, 2000). These findings about the wage penalties for being undocumented have laid the foundation for research about regularization, where the focus is on work outcomes among migrants who move from an unauthorized and insecure (irregular) legal status to a more secure, authorized status (Cobb-Clark & Kossoudji, 1999).

Research about the employment effects of regularization yields a fairly consistent picture: regularization has a limited effect on work conditions or wages. In the United States, the Legalized Population Survey (LPS-1 and LPS-2) tracked people regularized through the 1986 Immigration Reform and Control Act (IRCA). It collected information about work at four points in time: prior to migration, upon arrival in the United States, at the time of the application (about 1998/88), and in 1992 when a follow-up survey was conducted. The LPS surveys revealed that legalization was associated with limited upward mobility, "job churning," and minimal, highly gendered positive wage effects (Cobb-Clark & Kossoudji, 1999; Kossoudji & Cobb-Clark, 2000; Kossoudji & Cobb-Clark, 2002).

More recent European studies about the effects of regularization programs also reveal limited improvements. In Spain, for example, agricultural workers must pay expensive fees to employers and intermediaries to obtain the employment contracts required for regularization, and employment conditions and wages do not improve in the short term after regularization (Martínez Veiga, 2007). The Undocumented Worker Transitions Project conducted a comprehensive analysis of immigrant work experiences and the transition to regularization across seven countries in the European Union. It found that workers may experience immediate improvements in terms of psychological well-being together with the right to access state welfare and service provisions. However, improvements in employment and conditions of work are minimal and subject to a time lag. More significant improvements in work or wages require workers to work outside the sector in which they were employed when they had irregular legal status – a shift that is extremely difficult to achieve (McKay, Markova, Paraskevopoulou, & Wright, 2009).

Our survey of 300 Latin American and Caribbean migrant workers in the GTA found similar results in the Canadian context.[2] We focused on the relationship between precarious legal status and precarious work, defined as a job that is unstable and insecure, offers limited rights, protections, and benefits to workers, allows workers little control over their schedules, and gives workers little say in decisions of how work will be done (Goldring & Landolt, 2009b). Logistic regression on the likelihood of having a more or less precarious job revealed that precarious legal status has lasting negative effects on work outcomes, controlling for other variables including education, gender, family composition, English competence, or time in Canada (Goldring & Landolt, 2009c). People who entered and stayed in Canada with precarious legal status (e.g., students, tourists, refugee claimants, and temporary foreign workers) were more likely to have highly precarious jobs at the time of the survey compared to those who entered and stayed in a secure legal category (e.g., landed immigrants). Respondents who entered with precarious status (temporary permits or no work permits) but eventually obtained secure status (those who were regularized) were also more likely to have more precarious jobs than immigrant workers who entered and stayed secure.

The vast majority of research about how regularization affects work has focused on the character of labour markets and the organization of work to explain the absence of significant work improvements post-regularization. The industrial relations environment has been identified as an important determinant of post-regularization work outcomes (Goldring & Landolt, 2009d; McKay et al., 2009). Particularly significant factors include the strength of unions, the existence of collective bargaining and general applicability of collective agreements, effective enforcement of labour standards, the extent to which a casual or temporary labour force is normalized in the sector, the presence of ethnic entrepreneurship and co-ethnic employers, a large informal sector, and employer strategies. Labour market segmentation is associated with sectoral troughs that make moving into a better job difficult, regardless of legal status or changes in status (Hiebert, 1999). A third important factor is resource-poor social networks among workers, which limit their ability to move beyond the sector in which they were employed while in a precarious legal status (Menjívar, 2000).

Few studies have assessed how non-citizenship legal status affects post-regularization work outcomes. Scholarship about regularization tends to conceptualize a change in legal status as a fairly straightforward change from a precarious to a more secure legal status. As a result, it tends not to examine how non-citizenship as a social experience might help explain why regularization has such a limited effect on work. We focused on non-citizenship and its relationship to citizenship to capture how work and (non-)citizenship intersect to generate compounding insecurities, and why these intersecting vulnerabilities make it difficult to shed non-citizenship as a social experience, even as a migrant crosses into the realm of citizenship.

Problematizing Non-citizenship and Legal Status Boundary Crossing

Citizenship has typically been understood as an achieved and discrete category, with clear and relatively firm boundaries (Bosniak, 2000b). Citizenship laws and nation-building traditions regulate who is granted birthright citizenship and who can be permitted entry into the status of citizenship. The idea of citizenship as an achieved status results in the typical framing of questions about the effects of regularization; that is, does legal status boundary crossing lead to a change in work? In contrast, scholarship about substantive citizenship challenges this fairly static approach to citizenship as an attained status, and has made two important contributions to the field.

First, citizenship is conceptualized as a negotiated and relational practice (Stasiulis & Bakan, 1997, 2005). This framing opens up two analytical possibilities: first, that social dimensions such as gender, race, racialization, class, sexuality, and disability intersect with formal legal status to produce varying experiences and practices of citizenship for particular individuals and social groups of citizens; and, second, that citizenship is never fully fixed, permanent, or stable and can be eroded in practice, meaning in specific encounters. Citizenship conceived as relational practice helps reveal the social production of citizenship boundaries that can be enforced and contested in the points of contact between the state and those who make claims on the state. It also clarifies the politics of citizenship boundary-making over time, revealing how boundaries include and exclude changing configurations of gendered and racialized citizen-subjects (Bakan & Stasiulis, 1997; Lister, 1997; Ngai, 2002).

Second, citizenship is conceptualized as a relational practice with spatial and scalar dimensions (Painter & Philo, 1995). Citizenship is posed as an uneven, multilayered construct in which the layers or scales – local, regional, national, supranational, transnational, etc. – are interconnected (Basok, 2004; Nakano Glenn, 2002). The spatially uneven and multi-scalar form of citizenship suggests that the exercise of rights associated with citizenship at one scale may be eroded or restricted at another scale and that a given individual or group's citizenship practices may vary across locations. This introduces spatiality and scale as sources of uncertainty and unevenness in the uniform exercise of citizenship, as potential sources of distance between formal citizenship status and the actual practice of citizenship. The relational practice and lived experience of citizenship varies across local and social settings and at different scales. Individuals may exercise citizenship more easily in some contexts than in others, and not all individuals in a specific space experience citizenship equally or uniformly.

However, this kind of scholarship is rarely applied to non-citizenship or to the citizenship/non-citizenship boundary: the discreteness of citizenship as a conceptual category and the sharp boundary between citizenship and non-citizenship persists in the analysis of non-citizenship. Changes that determine who falls into one or the other categories of citizenship or non-citizenship are associated with movement, rather than a blurring of boundaries (cf. Alba, 2005; Zolberg & Woon, 1999). Thus, some national citizenship boundaries are considered more inclusive and permeable than others, but boundaries remain discrete and container-like. From this perspective, moving from one category of legal status to another still implies a break, a movement from one state to a new, clearly differentiated state. Individuals presumably shed the category of non-citizenship as they cross the boundary to citizenship.

This binary framing of the boundary between citizenship and non-citizenship underlies the bulk of scholarship on the relationship between regularization and work, and explains why scholars have not problematized non-citizenship as part of the explanation for the failure of migrant workers to make considerable gains in work outcomes post-regularization. Our analysis applies the idea of citizenship as an uneven and relational practice, drawing on qualitative data from our research about immigrants and precarious employment, to examine the social production of non-citizenship. We asked whether, and why, formal boundary movement across legal status categories is fuzzy and non-discrete, focusing on the social experience of non-citizenship and its production as more than a bounded category, and framing it instead as a sticky social category that is not easily shed with regularization.

The Social Production of Non-citizenship

From 2005 to 2006 we interviewed 300 Latin American and Caribbean immigrant workers using a mixed-method questionnaire. Respondents were asked about the contexts of exit and reception of their migration process, the strategies they used to deal with employment challenges and opportunities in Canada, and the patterns of contact (or lack of contact) with social institutions and community organizations during early settlement. In this chapter, we draw on responses to open-ended questions about whether and how their immigration status has affected their work opportunities, the strategies they used to regularize their situation, and any impact that a change in legal status (to more or less secure status) has had on their life and work experience in Canada. Specifically, we focus here on the responses provided by the 112 respondents who regularized their status; this represented 37 per cent of our total study population ($N = 300$). We used open and focused coding to analyse the data; we include direct quotes here as representative data trends because we found considerable agreement across this subgroup of participants with regard to the economic and social impacts of living and working with precarious legal status.

Here, we examine three dimensions of the social production of non-citizenship: the regulatory framework that organizes the lives of migrants with precarious legal status in Canada; the often negative social relations between these migrants and employers, government workers, family, friends, and those involved in the immigration-related legal apparatus; and how regulatory restrictions and predatory social relations can work to generate fear, stress, and social isolation among these migrants.

A Restrictive Regulatory Context

Precarious legal status migrants live in a restrictive regulatory context that has cumulative and highly corrosive consequences. Unauthorized precarious legal status migrants, such as tourists who overstay their visa or rejected refugee claimants, face blanket restrictions in social and economic spheres. Authorized precarious legal status migrants such as refugee claimants, international students, and temporary migrant workers are legally entitled to certain public goods. However, temporary authorized residents are assigned a social insurance number (SIN) beginning with the number 9, a highly visible marker of their temporariness (cf. Montgomery, 2002). For some temporary workers, such as those in the seasonal agricultural workers and live-in-caregiver programs, the right to live and work in Canada is conditional on continuing to work with a given employer (Basok, 2002; Nakache & Kinoshita, 2010). Unauthorized migrants have more labour market mobility, but less regulatory protection (Basok, 2002).

Precarious legal status migrants, both authorized and unauthorized, face restrictions that condition their engagement with public and private institutions in Canada. They are denied entry into federal and provincial government-financed immigrant settlement programs and services, such as free English language classes and employment counselling. They are also charged international student fees at all post-secondary educational institutions, making recertification or educational advancement financially prohibitive. Authorized migrants with a SIN that ends with a 9 also have difficulties opening a bank account, getting a landline telephone, accessing bank credit, or applying for a credit card.

The regulatory restrictions, and the inconsistencies they generate, did not go unnoticed by our survey respondents. One Caribbean respondent commented about how having a SIN starting with 9 affected the search for work:

> First of all when you have a work permit it specifies you either have to get an open [work] permit or a specific permit that says you're only allowed to work in this field. With an open permit you're allowed to explore all the jobs that are there but more than likely very few people are going to hire you with a 9, which means [that] your temporary status ... it kind of limits

you, even though it gives you an open permit that says apply for how many jobs you want when you come with your qualification then you put a nine in front of that it changes the dynamics of what you are entitled to get you know what I mean. (#265).

Having a SIN ending with 9 restricts job searches for workers with temporary permits, reflecting a clear gap between the formal rights associated with authorized but temporary status and employer practices associated with non-citizenship.

Another respondent noted that the immigration system effectively pushes migrants to work outside of state regulations.

I found that the system here was so disjointed … While they're rejecting me [for a work permit] and not giving me a work permit they were kind enough to give me visitor status so that I could pursue my legal papers. Now how ridiculous is that? You don't want me to work but I can sit around in your country, I consider that a load of bull. (#242)

This comment reveals how the regulatory framework creates the conditions for migrant's irregularization (cf. Goldring, Berinstein, & Bernhard, 2009).

Finally, an asylum seeker whose refugee claim was eventually accepted reflected on how the social assistance caseworker had helped generate work-related insecurities for newcomers:

At the welfare office we find two kinds of people. People who are very professional, who understand perfectly the purpose of welfare … who assume it is a way to help insert us into society … and other people that I feel are not prepared for this kind of work. There were a couple days when I left very, very sad because one person [case worker] told me I had to go out and work. They said I had to go out and work and I said no but I didn't know what to do yet. And in the kinds of jobs the person offered me well I really couldn't do them … I had just arrived. I still wasn't ready to go out to do cleaning, yes? Because we really needed more time to learn a bit more English, to get to know the city … to become familiar with things. (#21)

On-the-ground encounters between social assistance caseworkers and authorized precarious legal status migrant workers illustrate the uneven and contingent experience of non-citizenship. Caseworker discretion rushes precarious status migrants into the labour market before they are "job ready," which can lead to de-skilling and pigeonholing into precarious work.

Regulatory barriers have cumulative impacts: restrictions in one sphere compound vulnerabilities in other spheres. As noted above, respondents with precarious legal status are excluded from government-funded English language programs, even though like most immigrants they identified language and accent as central barriers to securing a decent job:

> What I felt affected me [looking for work] was my English. It was not fluid. Even now, the accent, there are some people that make "remarks" to point out your accent; they mention it to you, they have mentioned it to me ..., at my last job I had to quit because he placed too much emphasis on my accent and my race. (#111)

Without "standard" Canadian English, precarious legal status migrants felt they were unable to advocate for themselves at work and beyond.

The restrictive regulatory context imposes further conditions that shape intersecting employment and legal status strategies and trajectories. Regardless of education and work experience prior to coming to Canada, lack of a work permit or having only a temporary work and residence permit meant that respondents with precarious legal status settled for any job they could get, often cash jobs in cleaning or construction or as caregivers:

> People are willing to hire illegal people, but like the type of work, of course you have to take what you get, the type of employer, you take what you get ... you don't have a wide variety right, because you don't have a social number you're illegal right, so when um, a job situation arise, it might not be much but you're willing to take it because, what else is there? You're not going to be able to go through unemployment insurance or anything so, social services, no, so you take what you get, because who's going to take care of you? (#226)

Lack of work authorization meant a self-imposed limiting of the job search, focusing on jobs one would be likely to get and where few questions would be asked:

Prior to becoming a landed immigrant the only jobs, even though I knew better and I had skills and I knew that I could do all these things, but the only jobs I thought were within my range were cleaning people's houses, working in a factory, or taking care of people's kids in their house right, um those were also the jobs that you were less um ... intrusive, people weren't going to ask you about your personal business, they weren't going to ask you how you got there, can I see your proper insurance number. (#265)

Initial and subsequent job searches were further constrained by the need to find or keep a job for financial reasons:

For me it was keeping [an] employer, if you working in a job and you're being exploited you want to leave right, you want to leave but you don't want to leave because you have bills so you always look for something before you move on, and they may take a while, and then you're stuck there for a while, while looking for a next employer and hoping that when you find this new employer you're not going to [be able to] make the bills. (#237)

In settling for what they could get, many respondents found themselves in jobs that meant de-skilling; they, and often their spouses, were doing work they would not have done before coming to Canada:

My husband ... had always had his own business, worked in an office. He didn't know anything about carpentry; in his life he'd never held a hammer except to hang something at home ... He had never done that, and it pains me that he is doing this, because he never had to do it in his life, so he never had a chance to study. [He] always had to work to sustain us, so that we could live here. (#22).

In the search for livelihood precarious status migrants sacrifice respect, taking demeaning jobs, in order to meet financial needs.

So it's that constant looking for something that you're going to be really comfortable with and stable, and people respect you not just because you're in the house as a nanny or clean the house. (#237)

Look, at first I looked for cleaning jobs. I said to myself, if I don't know how to speak English, so I have to ... but it felt demeaning, it didn't fit, you know? (#22)

Our study participants were clearly aware of the poor quality of their jobs but saw it as a necessary strategy for making ends meet.

Predatory Encounters between Citizens and Non-citizens

Relations between precarious legal status migrant workers, whether authorized or unauthorized, and citizens or those with secure legal status are characterized by predatory patterns of abuse in various settings, including the workplace, the legal system, and with family and friends (Saad, in this volume).

Precarious status meant that our respondents were placed in precarious jobs and work situations characterized by limited workplace regulation, little worker control, and virtually no recourse in the face of abuse or exploitation. Employers who hire people without work permits can get away with illegal and/or unfair practices. Respondents provided examples of harassment, intimidation, cash payment, and wage theft.

Employers also use the temporariness of refugees' status, and specifically the nine-SIN, to generate uncertainty and secure worker compliance. A Mexican man remembered an early employer's strategy to keep refugee claimants working for him:

> Another thing he said to me was that because of my status – when I was a refugee claimant – that companies in general discriminate against people with a nine on their SIN because they don't have the certainty that the person will be staying in Canada. He would say these kinds of little things, and of course it made one scared. And we would limit our looking for other work opportunities. (#51)

Employer harassment reflects the social practice of a restrictive regulatory environment. Having a SIN beginning with 9 is intended to clearly demarcate the boundaries of migrant participation in Canadian labour markets and society. It puts migrant workers in abusive and vulnerable work situations.

The vast majority of respondents experienced non-payment or underpayment of wages, particularly when they first entered the Canadian labour market: "That happened to me a couple of times. I lost about 3,000 dollars" (#4). Wage theft was often compounded by lack of information about their rights and their vulnerability as precarious employees:

I think in my first year they stole from me maybe more than 60% of the times I worked; that it was a very precarious situation; that even though I spoke English – I spoke English when I arrived here – my lack of knowledge of the context, the surroundings. (#136)

Employers they over work you and then they underpay you, "oh your salary is xyz" but when the end of the week comes it ends up being abc, so they give you less than what they planned on giving you, if you talk they get angry and fire you. (#237)

For some Latin American respondents, limited English intersected with and compounded legal status vulnerability; their lack of voice translated into limited information and recourse:

In the beginning because I didn't know the language I had to accept everything; one time they didn't pay me … in this company where I did occasional work. I did a job but I did not know my rights so when I went to ask for my pay they had discounted, and it wasn't for the government it was a fine or something like that. Really they never explained it to me, they didn't explain and they never paid me the money that they should have paid me. It was a dirty trick … I worked all day and they did not pay me. (#146)

Employers sometimes rationalized underpaying workers by arguing that they were helping the worker in some other way. One respondent was sponsored by her employers for the Live-in Caregiver Program (LCP); the employers then used that relationship to underpay her:

I told them all the time, and she was like "oh we have 3 kids and we have the mortgage and that's all we can afford," and then this is the part that humiliated me, they would always make you feel because they sponsored you they can just pay you $250 because she would say stuff like "remember we sponsored you and we're helping you in some way," so that probably, they thought that they did that so they could pay me $250 and I shouldn't complain but I told them all the time this isn't adequate, it's not enough … but because they sponsored me they thought ok we can take advantage of her .(#261)

Respondents clearly identified the relationship between precarious status and aspects of precarious work such as cash payment and wage theft:

What happens is that as long as you don't have your work permit and you work for cash, people abuse you. And well the truth is yes I was exploited a lot as well. I worked for very little money and I worked a lot of hours and a lot of those hours I was never paid ... you would do the job just like any other person ... but because of the papers ... a person needs to eat, needs to buy stuff ... you have to earn something ... you accept and you accept ... and it's that way and the government should know about this. (#7)

Some workers and employers may prefer cash to avoid paying taxes, but cash payment generally means that employers have control over when, how, and how much the workers get paid. One Caribbean woman recalled her first job as a nanny:

I consider them the family from hell because like they pay me like $100 every 2 weeks. I work from like 7 o'clock Sunday night and Saturday morning I have to wake up and sit on the steps and wait for these people to wake and give me a pay cheque and when they woke up they would say I'm sorry Elizabeth I don't have any cash to give you. And then I have to wonder how I'm going to get home because I don't have any money to take the bus so a lot of the times my sister would send her husband to come pick me up, [this] was like an every week thing. (#280)

Unsurprisingly, the search for work with precarious status leads to precarious work, but it is interesting that low-wage temporary authorized migrant workers are also subject to this sort of precarious work. Those who spend prolonged periods of time in such conditions of vulnerability are likely to remain poor and have limited opportunities to improve the terms and conditions of their employment or invest in education as a stepping stone to less precarious, more decent work (Goldring & Landolt, 2009c).

Predatory relations are not confined to work. Our respondents confirmed that migrants are vulnerable to abusive, incompetent, and at times inexperienced immigration consultants and lawyers. One Mexican refugee claimant recounted his experience with legal aid:

My experience with the first lawyer ... with a not-for-profit lawyer, they don't charge. The only thing I needed was for someone to translate my story into English using proper legal terminology, nothing else. And they said: yes we can help you, I did not know how legal aid worked right? Legal aid handed me a letter that they wanted me to sign where, as I understood it, I authorized this person to be my lawyer and they needed a credit, which would be given by legal aid to the lawyer. And it seemed a bit dishonest to me. I laughed, my story was translated incorrectly and in fact I did not sign. Even without my signature they sent my papers to the refugee board, which scheduled me for a hearing ... without my signature. And I said simply that this was not the letter I had submitted, and the translation was incorrect and I made them see that the lawyer was at fault. In fact because it did not have my signature, it was not valid. I decided to change my lawyer ... I tried to do it myself but I didn't have the tools, the English especially to translate things properly ... Then I looked for another lawyer and I told someone who worked with Amnesty International and the Red Cross and I requested legal aid again ... fortunately everything worked out. (#51)

Similarly, an Argentine respondent who worked in Canada for ten years without a work permit noted the difficulties he encountered when he tried to become regularized:

Oh yes there were many errors in my case. At first I listened to my cousin and other friends from work who told me to make a refugee claim. So when the lady from legal aid did my paper work, she started to keep my welfare cheques and cashed them because I did not know what they were. Then they made us lie in immigration; make up a story so that I could attain refugee status. Afterwards the lawyers – a mafia – would make me go to the interviews and then they would look at me and say "okay you can go now." I did not understand a thing of what they were saying to me and they had me by the tail, they charged me $600 for an interpreter. And they would pass my case from lawyer to lawyer and when they had to go to court they would not show up. (#131)

Respondents also commented on the negative impact of informal sources of information. One Argentinean woman recounted how her brother-in-law made her feel that being a refugee claimant was a form of stigma, a dirty secret that tainted and restricted her dealings with state agents:

Like being a refugee was a dirty word ... we didn't want to tell anyone that we were refugees because we were ashamed, embarrassed. Do you understand? Besides my brother-in-law said that we should not tell anyone we were refugees because people don't like refugees. So we didn't say anything; we thought people would discriminate against us ... [He also told us] to not go on welfare [although we were entitled] because if we went on welfare our refugee claim would be denied. So we did not apply for fear that they would say no [to her claim]. (#22)

Working to achieve regularization is very slow and requires a huge investment of cash and time – both of which are scarce among precariously employed workers. Our subgroup of respondents that regularized said they spent between one-and-a-half to ten years in various forms of precarious legal status, during which time they were putting money and time into their efforts to be regularized. Refugee claimants who were eventually granted asylum typically spent an average of two years in some form of precarious status, and some waited as long as five years from presenting their claim to receiving their permanent residence card.

The Impacts of Non-citizenship on Well-Being

Regulatory barriers and predatory relations prolonged work and legal status precarity, and also drained the confidence of respondents. Together, these processes generated stress and insecurity, and had a long-term and profound impact on respondents' ability to integrate and settle successfully in Toronto. Plans were delayed and derailed by legal status–associated forms, barriers, and costs. Precarious legal status produced a deep sense of uncertainty, fear, and anxiety (see Saad and Brasch, in this volume).

Respondents characterized their first year(s) in Canada and the period that they lived with precarious legal status as extremely depressing. Gruelling work schedules and a lack of social networks generated social isolation. One Colombian man who made a refugee claim recounts:

What can I tell you? [My first year] was extremely hard, extremely sad; it was a year with lots of loneliness because I was living alone in a basement. I didn't have time for anything different, just time for work. (#136)

Another refugee claimant talked about the stress and insecurity he felt waiting for the outcome of his case; the uncertainty of not knowing produced a constant sense of being in limbo:

> On top of the insecurity, you don't know whether they are going to say yes
> or no to you ... are they going to tell you tomorrow? And they might tell
> you: "no" and you have to leave and you don't even have the money for
> the plane ticket to leave ... It was mainly the first year, year and a half that
> I didn't have my status ... my status was like a refugee claimant ... I didn't
> have the security/certainty that I was going to stay. (#51)

Respondents noted feeling a sense of "hurry up and wait" while in
legal limbo: everything was on hold and yet life was passing them by.
One Caribbean woman who married to regularize commented on her
feeling of being suspended in time:

> Yes, you feel like you just have to wait ... you just have to look and wait
> and try not to get sick, and try to, you are almost in a suspense you don't
> know if you're going to get through or not, that paralyze you for a while,
> and you lost out on some good years of your youth there. (#212)

The period of legal uncertainty and the fear, isolation, and stress it
produced had long-term effects on social and emotional well-being. Respondents felt they had lost time and that when it was finally over, they
were financially drained and did not have the social, financial, or emotional resources to make significant changes in their social and work
lives.

Conclusion

Legal status plays a fundamental role in immigrant incorporation
and well-being because it intersects with language, accent, racialization, gender, and other dimensions of stratification to channel precarious status workers into particular jobs and conditions at the bottom of
the labour market. Our qualitative data revealed how precarious legal
status intersects with precarious work and the mechanisms that make
non-citizenship a sticky social category, with long-lasting negative effects on workers' legal status trajectories and work outcomes.

One important mechanism is the (increasing) segmentation of the
labour market by legal status. This occurs through the selective application and practice of regulations regarding work authorization:
individuals are hired for particular jobs and under specific conditions
because of their precarious legal status. More specifically, newcomers with precarious status settle or search for particular kinds of job

situations, and employers hire these workers fully aware of their legal status. The process of finding work is gendered, with men often settling for jobs as labourers in construction or manufacturing, and women working as nannies or other forms of caregivers and in services. They are vulnerable workers with precarious terms of employment, working at the bottom of the labour market with limited opportunity for mobility.

Precarious employment is certainly not limited to individuals with precarious migratory status (Vosko, 2006). However, precarious status has certain specific features rooted in the vulnerability of temporary authorized status and unauthorized status: precarious status workers usually cannot afford to complain about work and related violations, nor can they easily train or retrain for better work, or in some cases, even search for new jobs. Their legal status constrains opportunities for getting better work, as they need to continue to earn money to negotiate a ladder to more secure status.

Additional mechanisms operate to keep precarious status workers poor and in precarious work, even as they try to regularize their status. Employer strategies include wage theft and underpayment, manipulation, and misinformation. Institutionally, SIN numbers limit occupational mobility. Not having a number means settling for a narrow range of jobs, and having a number that starts with a 9 does not help, as employers use its presence either not to hire or to hire for specific kinds of low-end work. As a result, precarious status migrants remain in low-wage precarious work over time, as part of the vulnerable working poor, and cannot invest or build up assets.

Once precarious status workers are caught in precarious work, the specific intersectionality of their situation helps establish pathways that are difficult to leave, even as time passes and although they may make efforts to regularize. Several barriers are particularly noteworthy: the fear and stress caused by needing to keep a job; not wanting to reveal one's status; not qualifying for income support (employment insurance, daycare subsidies) or state-run programs (English language courses, student loans); and the challenges posed by efforts to regularize, including costly fees, losing money to predatory intermediaries, and revealing one's status. If and when a transition to more secure status is achieved, it takes a long time and considerable effort to overcome these multiple challenges. Questions about the effects of regularization do not adequately take these conditions – a product of non-citizen legal status – into account.

Crossing the boundary into secure status does not guarantee less precarious work, although it offers some relief by lessening fear and stress, particularly for those who were in unauthorized forms of precarious status. Our data reveal that living in the intersections of precarious status and precarious work involves negative effects that continue long after a legal status boundary is crossed. Legal status operates as a dimension of social location on life-chances in a way more akin to gender and racialization, and less like an achieved – and changeable – status such as that conferred by a recognized professional degree or a high rank earned by progressing through an institutional hierarchy.

Time is also an important dimension as newcomers navigate the intersecting challenges of status and work. Time may eventually be associated with an improved employment situation, but it does not generate consistent, predictable, and matched shifts in status and work. Legal status can and does change without an accompanying improvement in work. Our data reveal some reasons for this: prolonged experiences of poverty or low-income create a "stickiness" that is difficult to escape; low income affects social and economic realms; and social networks, institutional contacts, financial situations, and work experiences become so enmeshed with legal status that significant investment and/ or income support is required (and perhaps additional social and institutional contacts) to move into better work – assuming less precarious jobs are even available.

Our research yields several main findings relevant to current debates on stratification, legal status, and citizenship/non-citizenship. First, we confirmed that legal status is becoming institutionalized as a dimension of stratification in Toronto labour markets, and perhaps beyond. Second, our results provide a basis for questioning the sociological category of legal status and the boundaries of citizenship. In addition to understanding citizenship boundaries as dynamic and negotiated, it is also important to consider how these boundaries are crossed and what happens as people navigate across them. Negotiated citizenship boundaries tend to continue to be understood as discrete; if they are instead conceptualized as fuzzy and permeable, and if the social relations that accrete in them are seen as somewhat sticky, then crossing them can be understood as a shift that may be accompanied by baggage from the "previous" side of the divide. A racialized immigrant may experience occupational mobility, but will always be racialized. Similarly, precarious status migrants can change their status, but they will continue to carry many of the trappings they developed while living and working with precarious status. These will limit their opportunities and shape their chances of moving into decent work – within the context of broader labour market constraints.

We conclude by underscoring the importance of recognizing legal status as a dimension of stratification, with the caution that it matters how legal status is conceptualized. Boundaries of citizenship categories are negotiated and reproduced, and can be crossed – but not without social baggage. A range of actors and institutions participate in shaping migrant legal status trajectories and work experiences as precarious status migrants navigate the chutes and ladders of legal status. Transitions over time reveal how trajectories and efforts to gain more secure status occur: individuals may move between forms of precarious status and transition to a secure status only to enter heterogeneous spaces of citizenship, where recency, racialization, gender, social capital, and education produce differentiated experiences of citizenship. The unevenness of secure status and citizenship accounts for the uneven citizenship of former non-citizens, including precarious legal status migrant workers. However, the social experience of entering secure status from the other side of the citizenship/non-citizenship divide also needs consideration. We demonstrated that shifts in legal status involve crossing boundaries that are blurry and sticky, in the sense that moving across a boundary does not preclude bringing attributes associated with the previous "status" or configuration of citizenship/non-citizenship rights to the "new state." As individuals and groups navigate work and citizenship intersections over time, their movement may be multidirectional, involving irregularization and regularization – and movement from one legal status to another may not bring concomitant shifts in the quality of work. Their interaction with gatekeepers, employers, legal advisors, service providers, and others also shapes their trajectories.

NOTES

1 "Regularization" is not an ideal term for capturing boundary crossing from unauthorized status to permanent residence because it frames unauthorized status as deviant, irregular, and not normal, and because the focus on moving from undocumented to documented sidelines transitions among forms of precarious status, which may offer temporary improvements. We use it in spite of these limitations, for lack of a better term.

2   For details on the research project, including key research questions, project methods, sample description, a copy of the survey instrument, and
plain language research briefs based on the statistical analysis, see the
project website: www.arts.yorku.ca/ine/index.php.

9 Pathways to Precarity: Structural Vulnerabilities and Lived Consequences for Migrant Farmworkers in Canada

JANET MCLAUGHLIN AND JENNA HENNEBRY

The expanding reliance on migrant labour in Canadian agriculture is part of a larger international trend in labour relations, which increasingly enables employers to evade or violate labour standards to maximize profit amid globalized competition. At the same time, state structures that are in place to monitor and enforce workers' protections are further eroded in response to pressures towards deregulation (Bernhardt, Boushey, Dresser, & Tilly, 2008). Agriculture is among the most dangerous industries in Canada, yet farmworkers in general, and migrant farmworkers (hereafter MFWs) in particular, have historically been less protected than workers in other industries (Tucker, 2006). This is in part because there is no meaningful incentive for employers or the Canadian state to protect MFWs' rights, health, and safety. To the contrary, the current system is structured to provide the ideal workforce in the form of a limitless and constant source of fit, healthy migrant labour, which can be easily removed, returned, and replaced the moment any problem or concern arises.

This chapter explores the insecure circumstances that surround MFWs' lives and work in Canada, with a focus on workers with health concerns who shift from Temporary Migrant Worker (TMW) status to other, more precarious forms of status, including unauthorized status. Through a comparison of two of the program streams that comprise Canada's Temporary Foreign Worker Program (TFWP) – the long-standing Seasonal Agricultural Workers Program (SAWP) and the more recent Pilot Project for Occupations Requiring Lower Levels of Formal Training (hereafter referred to as NOCCD)[1] – we argue that

MFWs, even with *authorized temporary legal status* in Canada, live and work under precarious circumstances.

The term "precarious" has been used to analyse immigration status (Goldring, Berinstein, & Bernhard, 2009) and employment relations (Vosko, 2006; Vosko, Zukewich, & Cranford, 2003). For MFWs the term is particularly relevant since both their migration and their employment status are contingent and temporary. In this chapter we explore the nexus of precarious immigration and employment status for MFWs, and focus on the effects of precarity on their everyday lives, and particularly on their health. Through detailed case studies of workers who have experienced serious health concerns, we further demonstrate how and why authorized migrant workers may shift into even more precarious status with compounded vulnerabilities. By focusing on the intersections of health concerns, access to health care, and broader circumstances of precarity, we hone in on a central contradiction of temporary foreign worker programs. We suggest that the restricted nature of such programs, and employer tactics commonly employed within them, may in fact facilitate the push towards the illegalization of workers – the very outcomes that these authorized migration programs are intended to avoid – all the while leaving workers with serious health concerns abandoned as they negotiate survival on the margins of this system.

Research on MFWs, mostly focused on Mexican workers in the SAWP, demonstrates their high level of vulnerability. It has documented the structural constraints of MFWs' employment circumstances, the high level of risks associated with their living and working conditions, the gendered and racialized dimensions of their employment, and the conditions and effects of their social and political exclusion from Canadian communities (Basok, 2002; Becerril Quintana, 2007; Binford, Carrasco Rivas, Arana Hernandez, & Santillana de Rojas, 2004; Hennebry, 2006; McLaughlin, 2009b; McLaughlin, 2010; Preibisch, 2004; Preibisch & Binford, 2007; Preibisch & Encalada Grez, 2010). This research has also made clear that temporary migration programs assume migrants will follow the expected trajectory of their program, returning home and then back to Canada the following year. What has been missing thus far is a detailed analysis of the contexts wherein migrants deviate from this expected pattern.

MFWs' legal status, which is contingent on their employers, can quickly become further eroded by employer practices, which push workers into deeper circumstances of precarity, including illegality, with significant consequences. For example, employers push workers into further precarity by threatening to fire them for engaging in labour conflicts, dismissing workers who complain of sickness or injury, or without proper authorization "loaning out" workers to colleagues in the industry. Such instances, while not universally experienced, are very common. Regardless of frequency, we argue that the structures of Canada's TFWP facilitate the further precarization of workers. Many migrant workers come to Canada with the hope of earning enough money to support their families. When something goes wrong – if they have a conflict with the employer, if they become sick or injured, or if their contract ends prematurely for any reason – many fear returning to their countries of origin as this will mean a loss of expected income or the ability to access needed medical care. Some workers therefore opt to stay in Canada, but, under the legal restrictions that govern their program, there is no direct transition for them to become permanent residents or to stay on indefinitely (Nakache, 2010); hence they may fall into deeper forms of precarity, without legal status in Canada or access to work or safe housing (Nakache, in this volume).

By documenting the principal pathways between forms of precarious legal status that have emerged in our research, we demonstrate the fragility of migrants' temporary legal status and the conditionality surrounding their presence. While we focus on the varied experiences, adaptability, and agency of individual migrants, we also contend that the construction of precarious status – and the vulnerabilities such forms of status engender – are primarily defined and facilitated by state policies and regulations and employer practices, rather than by migrants themselves (cf. Goldring, Berinstein, & Bernhard, 2009). With very limited options and from highly constrained positions of power, migrants use whatever strategies are available to secure their interests, but often with difficult consequences for themselves and their families (Goldring & Landolt, in this volume).

Our analysis draws on more than ten years of combined ethnographic research involving standardized questionnaires ($N = 576$), qualitative interviews (over three hundred) and participant observation with MFWs (working on Canadian farms as well as living with workers and their families in Jamaica and Mexico). These data were complemented by archival research and, focus groups and interviews with employers, government agents, health care providers, labour and community groups, and others (Hennebry, 2006, 2010a; McLaughlin, 2009b). Our earlier work focused on MFWs in the SAWP, but our more recent and ongoing research involves participants in both program streams.

Workers' motivations for changing status or staying in Canada beyond work contracts have not been the focus of our previous investigations, yet our research has revealed numerous reasons why MFWs may wish to do so. The most prevalent include health complications (including those who wish to stay in Canada to receive medical treatment that they do not think will be afforded to them in their countries of origin); the development of personal relationships in Canada (including wanting to stay with families, friends, children, or romantic partners); fear of returning home (due to persecution, domestic conflicts, lack of resources, debts to unscrupulous third parties, etc.); employment factors (including early contract dismissals, poor living or working conditions, or conflicts with employers or co-workers); and economic factors (such as poor economic resources and wanting to remain in Canada to earn more money before returning home). Such motivations are not mutually exclusive, and indeed they often intersect or overlap.

The case studies we selected for this chapter were not based on their representativeness for all migrant workers, or an attempt to illustrate each of the factors identified above; instead, we chose them as particularly illustrative and compelling cases that demonstrate some of the most common (and what we argue are the most consequential) pathways to legal status precarity for migrant workers. In particular, we selected cases that demonstrate the *recursive* role that health complications play in precarization for two reasons. First, there are the very tangible and often permanent ramifications of health complications for migrants and their families, whose precarization can have very serious consequences resulting not only in a lack of rights, income, and so on, but also in severe pain, lifelong illness, and even loss of life. Second, evidence from our previous research indicates that MFWs are particularly vulnerable to health risks and that those who encounter health complications have a greater likelihood of moving into more precarious migration and employment situations (Hennebry, Preibisch, & McLaughlin, 2010; McLaughlin, 2009b; Preibisch & Hennebry, 2011). Thus health represents intersecting and reinforcing forms of precarity and vulnerability: precarious circumstances produce poor health, and health concerns produce further precarity.

The next section provides background information on temporary agricultural migration in Canada; this is followed by a theorization of why and how we understand MFWs through the lens of precariousness. We then enter into a more focused discussion of the structural factors that create conditions of precarity, followed by an analysis of pathways to further precarity for MFWs in general, and three case studies in particular.

Background on Temporary Agricultural Migration in Canada

Policy makers and analysts often label guest worker programs as a "win-win" solution to the dilemmas of perceived regional labour shortages and surpluses. The use of TMWs in Canada, both within and outside of agriculture, has grown dramatically over the past decade. One of the principal advantages of the TFWP is that it offers a seemingly safer and legal migratory alternative to the increasingly perilous and securitized routes to the United States and elsewhere, especially for Mexican and Central American migrants who have long relied on unauthorized migration to the United States (Binford et al., 2004). Over thirty-five thousand TMWs are now employed in agriculture between the SAWP and the NOCCD. These two program streams are part of the broader Temporary Foreign Worker Program. The two programs employ workers designated as "low-skilled" who are generally ineligible for immigration streams leading to permanent residency, yet they also differ in significant ways (Hennebry & Preibisch, 2010b; Nakache, in this volume).

As a managed migration program, the SAWP employs workers from Mexico and several Commonwealth Caribbean countries for up to eight months each year through annually negotiated contracts with these countries. Sending countries are responsible for the recruitment and selection of participants, and act as legal representative of workers in the country through consular officials in Canada. The NOCCD is less regulated, employs workers on twelve-to-twenty-four-month work permits (with a maximum of four consecutive years in Canada, after which migrant workers must return home for a minimum of four years), draws them from any country in the world, and relies on employers, often through private contractors, to recruit and hire their own work forces. Migrants coming through the NOCCD are subject to a three-month waiting period for access to provincial health care; SAWP participants are eligible for provincial health care upon arrival (though their access to this care is mediated by employers) (McLaughlin, 2009a; Pysklywec et al., 2011). The mobility rights of workers in both programs are highly restricted. In the SAWP, workers are bound to work for one employer unless they receive permission from their employers and appropriate government agencies for a transfer. In the NOCCD, switching employers is contingent upon workers finding another employer with a valid labour market opinion. In both programs, workers who want to switch employers are often unable to do so in practice.

Neither program provides a pathway to permanent residence for participants, though some participants in the NOCCD may be able to apply through the Provincial Nominee Program (PNP) (though typically, farmworkers are *not* nominated through this program). However, use of the PNP in this context can heighten MFWs' precarity, as workers vie for the requisite employment offer and may be willing to accept unsafe work or mistreatment to get it (Hennebry, 2010b). In general, however, MFWs are treated as temporary guest workers who are not meant to stay beyond their contracts or to immigrate to Canada. Although the labour shortages they fill are said to be temporary, it is clear that MFWs' integration into Canadian agriculture over the last half-century has become permanently entrenched.

The Cycle of Precarity: Why MFWs Are Precarious

Following Goldring, Berinstein, and Bernhard (2009), we use the term "precarious status" to reflect the dynamic and variable forms of irregular status of migrants in Canada. Goldring, Berinstein, and Bernhard (2009) propose that precarious status is marked by the absence of any of the following components typically ascribed to permanent residents (and citizens) of Canada: (1) work authorization; (2) residence permit (the right to remain permanently in Canada); (3) not depending on another person (e.g., an employer) to remain in the country; (4) access to social rights and services such as education and health care; and (5) not being able to sponsor family. MFWs only have access to the first criterion (work authorization), but even this work contract, and their residency, are tenuous and depend on relationships with employers (component 3). They are typically unable to access a residence permit (category 2) and have only limited and temporary access to social rights and services (category 4). They are unable to sponsor family to join them (component 5) and normally cannot even visit with family members during the duration of their stay in Canada due to logistical and visa restrictions. Reviewing which criteria apply to MFWs highlights the conditionality surrounding the terms under which they are able to remain in Canada (Goldring & Landolt, in this volume).

MFWs' experiences of precarious immigration status are compounded by and intersect with their precarious employment relationship. Vosko and colleagues (Vosko, 2006; Vosko, Zukewich, & Cranford, 2003) have analysed the situation of precarious work/employment in Canada. They draw on the work of Rodgers (1989), who identifies four elements to determine if a job is precarious. These include: (1) the certainty of sustained employment, including length of job and potential for job loss; (2) the amount of control over labour and employment conditions, including whether or not a trade union is present and corresponding influence over working conditions, wages, and the like; (3) the amount of regulatory protection through laws or union representation; and (4) income – whether wages are sufficient to support the worker as well as any dependents (Vosko, Zukewich, & Cranford, 2003).

Using these criteria, it is clear that MFWs' positions are deeply precarious in all four categories. First, migrants' jobs are not permanent and there is no provision of job security protecting current or future employment; they can be fired at any time and the firing often results not only in job loss but also in loss of the right to remain in Canada, access services, and so on. Second, workers have almost no control over labour and employment conditions, and in Ontario, the principal province of MFW employment, agricultural workers are legally forbidden from bargaining as part of a union. Even in provinces where unionization is legal for agricultural workers, they have faced intimidation and threats, not only from employers but also from their own government agents, who are meant to represent their interests. Employer tactics such as firing and repatriating workers just before a union certification vote, or replacing workers who had shown interest in joining a union with another work force the following year, serve to threaten workers and render this right largely meaningless (see Sandborn, 2009; Stueck, 2008). Finally, as recipients of minimum, seasonal wages with multiple deductions, workers also experience income insecurity and poverty. Typically, employment options in their countries of origin are even less secure, which explains why they are driven to work abroad. Furthermore, short-term jobs are difficult to attain upon return to their countries of origin in between seasonal work in Canada. This lack of stable, continual income increases their vulnerability, as they fear the consequences of losing much-needed Canadian employment, and thus are willing to endure demanding, distasteful, difficult, and even dangerous conditions in order to keep their jobs (Basok, 2002; Hennebry, 2010b; McLaughlin, 2009b). At the same time, as we have described in detail elsewhere (Hennebry, 2006; McLaughlin, 2009b), the vast majority of MFWs come from poor economic backgrounds, from countries in the Global South that have faced enduring economic crises and rising levels of inequality. Within this larger world system, many migrants describe a deteriorating economic reality and a rising dependence on migration for family survival (Hennebry, 2006; McLaughlin, 2009b).

Recent research in Canada has documented the relationship between precarious migration status and compromised health care access (Khan, Lalani, Plamadeala, Sun, & Gardner, 2010) and precarious work and poor health outcomes (Lewchuk, Clarke, & de Wolff, 2008). Certain aspects of precarious employment that are particularly relevant to migrants' experience (e.g., workers' efforts to stay employed and their experience of constant evaluation) are strongly associated with negative self-reported health outcomes in the Canadian context (Lewchuk et al., 2008). The World Health Organization (2010) has also acknowledged the particularly vulnerable circumstances of migrant populations (particularly those working in lower-skilled jobs) that often lead to poor health outcomes. A recent literature review of the Canadian context found that MFWs' vulnerability to health concerns is amplified by multiple social determinants associated with poorer health outcomes, including low income, poor living and working conditions, barriers to accessing health care, and poor social support and integration (McLaughlin, 2011).

Indeed there are many factors that heighten MFWs' vulnerability to health risks in Canada. Ironically, some of the perceived advantages of the TFWP in relation to more perilous forms of migration, as noted earlier, render workers more willing to accept poor conditions in order to maintain their coveted positions. MFWs thereby find themselves integrated into a system in which they are deeply and *structurally vulnerable*: the mechanisms behind these programs, and migrants' position within them, institutionalize their vulnerability and limit their power to change poor circumstances. MFWs are essentially bound to their employers and must reside on their property and live under their rules, which may be arbitrary or unjust. Workers can be dismissed from their employment without recourse to appeal and repatriated at any time; their readmittance to the program greatly depends on the recommendation of their employers. The existence of these measures is justified by the exceptional needs of the agricultural industry to stay competitive amid globalized pressures (e.g., to have workers readily available to work flexible hours who are unable to organize and to demand better conditions and pay) (Basok, 2002; McLaughlin, 2009b). With respect to health risks faced by MFWs in Canada, our research has demonstrated that it is not the case of a few "bad apples" or unscrupulous employers who exploit workers or put them at risk while working or living in Canada; rather, it is the structural realities of the TFWP and agricultural employment that lead to pervasive and persistent health risks and barriers to care among MFWs (Hennebry, 2010b; McLaughlin, 2009b).

In general, farm work is recognized as difficult, tedious, and precarious (Tucker, 2006) and ranked as the most dangerous sector after mining and construction (Basok, 2002). As foreigners, MFWs often feel that they are given the most difficult tasks and are expected to work harder to impress employers. The work is also highly variable across industries and seasons – involving intense peaks of continual work and slower periods of relative inactivity. Furthermore, MFWs' construction as disposable, interchangeable workers facilitates dynamics of competition and vulnerability. MFWs are positioned at the bottom rung of Canada's agricultural labour force, providing a contemporary illustration of Bonacich's (1979) early split labour market theory in which non-white workers from peripheral regions take on the least desired and lower-paid positions while white workers from core regions monopolize jobs with higher pay and benefits, greater labour market mobility, and job security. Though the quest for the "ideal" labour force in agriculture has long been structured and differentiated along lines of race and ethnicity, gender, immigration, and citizenship (Thomas, 1992), the growing segmentation of Canada's labour market, with TMWs concentrated at the bottom of the scale, takes labour market segmentation to a new low. Workers constantly feel threatened that if they do not perform adequately, they can be replaced – either by those waiting at the queue in their countries of origin or by other groups of workers from different racialized or gendered groups (Hennebry, 2006; McLaughlin, 2010; Preibisch & Binford, 2007; Preibisch & Encalada Grez, 2010). They therefore feel pressured to accept work under difficult conditions, which may pose health risks, and when problems do emerge, workers are invariably reluctant to report them or to have medical conditions treated (cf. Landolt & Goldring, in this volume).

Migrants' living conditions further entrench their precarity. Their accommodations, which are typically provided by employers, are considered temporary residences, and thus often lack the infrastructure of permanent dwellings. Workers often cite a lack of adequate resources (e.g., fridges, stoves, private space, washing machines, fans) in order to lead healthy lives (Hennebry et al., 2010; McLaughlin, 2009b), yet they have very little recourse to improve shortcomings, because their landlord is also their employer. This problematic integration of the roles of employer and landlord gives employers an exceptional amount of control over the lives of MFWs outside of the workplace.

This situation is exacerbated by workers' fundamental exclusion from Canadian society, which renders them largely isolated within rural communities and further deepens their vulnerability and dependency on employers. While community, labour, and religious groups have over the past decade expanded their efforts to include and support migrant workers (McLaughlin, 2009b; Preibisch, 2004), in general the various levels of government have made no concerted effort to include or integrate migrant workers in Canadian society (Nakache, 2010). This social exclusion and lack of community integration is largely because these temporary workers are not seen as future immigrants, and as such are not typically eligible for support services that are designed to integrate and support new Canadians. Therefore if MFWs decide or are forced to change their temporary legal status, they have few resources to help them navigate this transition, further heightening their precarity.

In sum, MFWs in the TFWP have very little control over when and to where they migrate, the duration of stay, or the conditions of their employment and residence. Their precariousness is heightened by conditions that fundamentally limit their ability to be mobile, to organize or to settle and form communities of their own choosing, or to actively resist or change negative circumstances. Those participating in such a system of managed migration may have more *rights* than their non-status counterparts (e.g., access to health care, a secured place to live), yet they arguably experience considerably fewer *freedoms* (Basok, 2002; McLaughlin, 2009b).

These structural factors add to the conditions in which MFWs in Canada are caught in a "vicious cycle of precariousness" (Tucker, 2006, p. 157). The cyclical nature of this precarity is important to note, since migrant workers start from vulnerable positions in the global political economy and enter Canada with precarious immigration status to perform precarious work; these intersecting processes in turn heighten their vulnerability to health risks, exploitation, and abuse – all situations that push them into heightened precarity with threatened loss of employment or immigration status. When health problems emerge, such as those profiled in the following sections, regardless of whether workers stay in Canada or return to their countries of origin, vulnerable circumstances continue.

Pathways to Further Precarity

Workers in the SAWP are extensively screened by their countries of origin in part to ensure their likelihood of return (McLaughlin, 2010). This helps to ensure that the vast majority of SAWP participants return home following contracts, although as we demonstrate below, this is a far from universal experience. Furthermore, as increasing numbers of workers enter Canada under the NOCCD – which does not involve the sending countries in recruitment, selection, screening, tracking, and representation of migrant workers as does the SAWP – analysts antici-pate that growing numbers of workers will overstay their work permits and thus experience heightened precarity (Goldring, Hennebry, & Pre-ibisch, 2009; Hennebry & Preibisch, 2010a).

The significant differences between these two program streams have distinct consequences in the various pathways to precarity. In particu-lar, the often celebrated strengths of the SAWP (such as involvement of the sending country), have not been adopted in the NOCCD, leaving migrants more vulnerable to exploitation from not only unscrupulous employers but also a growing migration industry aiming to capitalize on brokering migrants in Canada (Hennebry, 2008; Hennebry & Pre-ibisch, 2010a). The introduction to this volume describes dependency on such third parties as a form of conditionality that also heightens MFWs' vulnerability and precarity.

Migrant farmworkers may come to Canada with the hope of settling here. Our recent survey of Mexican and Jamaican MFWs in Ontario found that 60 per cent indicated they were interested in gaining per-manent residency in Canada (Hennebry et al., 2010). However, unlike migrants in the Live-in Caregiver Program and other TMWs classified by higher skill levels, it is almost impossible for MFWs, in either the SAWP or the NOCCD, to ever be able to immigrate to Canada (Na-kache, in this volume). Workers who wish to stay in Canada have few legal pathways, and those that do exist are not easily accessed. In very select cases, workers may be sponsored to immigrate through a Cana-dian employer or spouse. In other cases, some MFWs may apply for refugee or humanitarian and compassionate (H & C) claims to remain in the country, but these are very rare and the countries from which mi-grants originate (Mexico, Jamaica, etc.) are not recognized by the Cana-dian government as countries with high levels of political persecution; accordingly, the acceptance rate in Canada is very low. At any point along these processes, would-be immigrants may lose sponsorship or

Figure 9.1. Primary Routes between Forms of Status for Temporary Migrant Workers

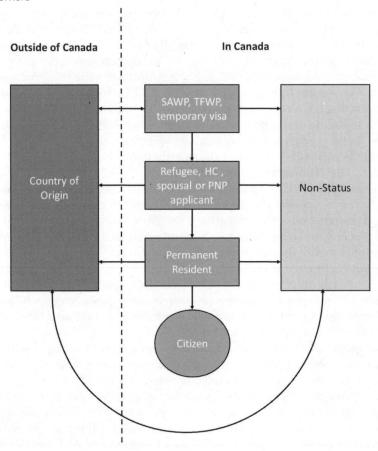

Source: Figure prepared by authors.

be denied refugee claims and again slip out of legal status (see Goldring, Berinstein, & Bernhard, 2009). Otherwise, TMWs who wish to stay in Canada have little choice but to become non-status (see Figure 9.1).

While it is difficult to obtain exact statistics, analysts speculate that a significant number of workers in agriculture may be working without legal authorization, either without any authorization to live or work in

Canada or with some form of status that does not permit their employment (for example, people on tourist visas, or current or former TMWs who do not have a valid work permit for the job). Such workers are easily absorbed within agriculture, an industry that, due in part to the changing nature of the seasons and demands of the crops, has long relied on flexible, temporary, and informal labour arrangements. It is thus also common for agricultural employers to informally "share" workers as their demands change. Such informal arrangements, however, can have serious consequences for workers, who can face deportation for violating their visa conditions when working without authorization. The more frequent occurrence of immigration raids in agricultural workplaces over the past several years indicates this trend and demonstrates the reality behind this threat (e.g., C. Cook, 2009; Hill, 2009).

The issues of legally employed TMWs and unauthorized workers in agriculture are deeply interrelated. The existence of both groups stems from an immigration regime that does not value the contributions of manual labourers in its point system, effectively prohibiting this "class" of people from ever becoming citizens. It also has to do with the problematic features of the SAWP and NOCCD, which do not allow workers to easily change employers (or work for more than one employer simultaneously) or to receive health care for long-term problems, let alone have an appeals process before being fired and repatriated. The line between being a "legal" migrant and one labelled as "illegal" can be quite easily blurred, consistent with the processes of "alienage" theorized in Bosniak's (2006) examination of non-citizenship in the United States. This is true even for workers who never intended to stay on in Canada past their visas, as the following case studies demonstrate. The three examples, all of which share the added complication or trigger of health concerns, provide a glimpse into the broader contexts and everyday lived experiences for those who follow pathways to further precarity from the already tenuous position of migrant workers.

Case Studies of Status Changes

Case 1: Steve – SAWP to Non-status to Return

Steve[2] worked as a farm labourer on rented land in his native Jamaica. With almost no education, few job prospects, and a wife and two children to support, he journeyed to Canada with the hope of saving money to buy a home and his own piece of land in Jamaica. During his first year of working in the SAWP, he suffered a serious workplace injury. One day when he was riding on the back of a farm vehicle that had no seat and no barriers, the driver took a sharp right turn and Steve fell backwards off the vehicle onto his head and was rendered unconscious. He was taken to the hospital, where he was diagnosed with a serious concussion and received stitches for his injury. He received some workers' compensation for the work days lost, but when his doctor said he could try doing light work, he was told to go back to work and his compensation stopped. Even the proposed "light duties" assigned by his employer aggravated his pain. "I couldn't even sit without being in agony," he recalls, and soon after starting the work he told his boss that he was in too much pain to continue. Unfortunately, his medical situation was not re-evaluated. Instead, his employer told him he had breached his contract and would be going home that week.

Steve's doctor had recommended physiotherapy and had booked an MRI to determine the extent of his injury. The MRI was scheduled just days after the date of the return ticket that had been thrust upon Steve. Steve knew that these treatments and tests would not be affordable to him in Jamaica and he feared suffering from a permanent injury without any support at home, so on the day he was to be sent home, he instead ran away to a friend's house. Because he did not go home on his designated flight, he was labelled "Absent without Leave" – AWOL – a classification that essentially deemed him to be without legal status in Canada and forbidden to ever re-enter the SAWP. The next week he showed up to his MRI appointment and was told it had been cancelled, and that he was ineligible to receive more treatments.

Steve spent many months in Canada trying to seek compensation and medical care, or even enough money to fly back to Jamaica, while becoming increasingly homesick. Finally, with the help of a friend, he purchased a ticket to Jamaica, where he arrived in a great deal of pain and unable to work. With the assistance of a community legal advocate in Canada, Steve appealed the decision to terminate his compensation. The adjudicator refused his claim, saying that he should have had an MRI in Canada, and now too much time had passed. It is now over five years since his accident; he is still injured, unable to work, and ineligible for compensation. Steve's wife has become the sole support for the family, working daily growing yams, bananas, and vegetables on their rented land, while his daughter had to leave school because the family could no longer afford the expenses.

Case 2: Enrique – SAWP to Refugee Claimant

Enrique had annually migrated from Mexico to Canada for nearly a decade through the SAWP, saving enough money to build a large home in his rural village and to support a growing family. He had attained a good grasp of English and was often assigned to leadership roles by his employer, with whom he had a good relationship. One day while working he came down with sudden, severe, and unusual symptoms. Rushed to the hospital, he was soon diagnosed with kidney failure. Enrique was then told that he would not be able to survive without regular dialysis treatments and/or a kidney transplant and a lifetime of costly follow-up medications and treatment. Learning of his illness, the Mexican authorities began to exert pressure for Enrique to return home. Unfortunately, the very costly medical services he would require are not readily available to the poor and uninsured in Mexico, and Enrique feared that if he did return, he would die.

Upon learning of the gravity of the situation, Enrique's employer intervened. Citing Enrique as an excellent worker, he did not want to "send him home to die." He hired a lawyer for Enrique, who filed for refugee status, enabling him to prolong his stay in Canada, even if it came at the expense of a long and painful separation from his wife and children. As a refugee applicant, Enrique has been able to have all of his life-sustaining dialysis and medical expenses covered under the Interim Federal Health Program. However, Canada does not normally accept refugees on medical grounds, and despite innovative legal arguments, he lost his case. Five years since the incident, Enrique has exhausted all of his appeals and is now awaiting a deportation order. His final hope is a humanitarian and compassionate claim, which as of 2011 remains outstanding. If he loses this, his choice will be either to return to Mexico, where he does not have access to health care, or stay on in Canada without status or legal access to health care (McLaughlin, 2009b).

Case 3: Eliana – NOCCD to Unemployment to Non-status

Eliana arrived with approximately twenty other women from Guatemala to pick mushrooms at an Ontario farm, for what they thought was to be a two-year contract under the NOCCD program.[3] After only one month of being in Canada, Eliana experienced severe abdominal cramping and bleeding. Fearful to tell her employer, she kept working and did not request medical attention, nor did she request information on her private health care insurance provided by the employer. Without independent access to insurance, Eliana would have had to pay for services upfront and then submit a claim to the employer. Fearful of employer reprimand, Eliana sought assistance through community volunteers, who found a doctor willing to see her without charge. The doctor determined that she was three months pregnant and recommended that she refrain from heavy lifting or strenuous work and that she have further tests to determine that her and her baby's health were satisfactory. Fearful of losing employment, she did not tell her employer about her pregnancy, and she did not get the requisite medical tests. Eliana's fear of loss of employment was further compounded by other factors that contributed to her economic insecurity and dependency on this job. Eliana described her particularly tenuous position:

> I did not know I was pregnant when I came to Canada. I can't tell my employer or he will fire me. I can't get the insurance to go to the doctor, because he will know. I also can't go home to Guatemala. I am not married and I have no one to help me. I borrowed money to pay for the IOM deposit, and he [the lender] will take my grandmother's house if I cannot pay it back, plus interest. I have not made enough money to pay it back yet. I have to stay and find other work until I can pay. I planned on coming for two years, I can't return home with less money and pregnant after only two months. I have no choice but to try to stay in Canada. I don't know who can help me.

Eliana and the other Guatemalan women explained that they had to work for at least three months just to pay back money they had borrowed to cover the upfront deposit (four hundred Canadian dollars) paid to the International Organization for Migration (IOM), which had an agreement with Guatemala to recruit and place workers in Canada. In addition, migrants also paid into a medical service plan - a mandatory plan that provided access to health care for families of migrants in Guatemala (IOM, 2008). Because this insurance was paid for by migrants, this made coverage for migrant households wholly reliant on obtaining and fulfilling a work contract in Canada. Access to health services for migrant families in Guatemala thus became contingent on maintaining employment in Canada, which added additional pressure on workers to remain in exploitative or dangerous working situations, since coverage was terminated if a worker was laid off or was not selected for another contract.

Termination of the health coverage is exactly what happened to Eliana and her co-workers only a few months after their arrival when they were let go in two mass firings. Just two days before Christmas, Eliana and her co-workers were out of a job and told they would be evicted from the apartment they rented from the employer (see Tambar, 2008). They were issued plane tickets the next day and told they had to leave in less than one week. Overnight, these workers found themselves without employment, homeless, and being sent back to their countries of origin. Their families in Guatemala also found themselves without access to health insurance, and with no remittance money to pay off debts incurred by coming to Canada.

Eliana and many of the other MFWs employed at this farm chose to stay in Canada and look for a legal change of employment. However, since there is no mechanism in place to assist TMWs in locating another employer with a valid labour market opinion (LMO), many spent the following months simply using up whatever savings they had and surviving on the support of community groups, such as Justicia for Migrant Workers,[4] volunteers, and friends. Without alternatives, some chose to pay for another plane ticket home, and many opted to find work "under the table" across the country. Though NOCCD workers have the legal right to remain in Canada until the duration of their work permit expires (unless specifically terminated by Citizenship and Immigration Canada), they cannot work for an employer without a valid LMO and have no access to permanent residency – leaving these migrant workers with very few options. Clearly, four of the five factors that we identified previously converged to lead Eliana into greater precarity: health complications, economic factors, employment factors, and fear of returning home. Eliana and her *compañeras* came to Canada in search of an avenue for greater economic security, but Canada's TFWP proved to be nothing more than a pathway to precarity for these migrants and their families.

Conclusion: The Consequences of Precarity

This chapter has shown how precarious forms of immigration and employment intersect and render MFWs structurally vulnerable. The situation of MFWs supports the argument put forward in this volume that *authorized* temporary status can also be extremely precarious, resulting in blurred distinctions between authorized and unauthorized status captured in the term "precarious." We have also unpacked some aspects of the myth of circular, predictable migration, supposedly ensured by temporary migration programs, and we have demonstrated some of the limited ways in which, and reasons why, migrants may seek to change their immigration status or become non-status. Without a clear, established pathway towards immigration, and/or institutionalized support to navigate a complex and confusing employment and immigration landscape, TMWs who wish to stay in Canada beyond their contracts rely on a number of strategies, which have additional risks, compounding precarity.

Using health as a common theme, these cases demonstrate the intertwining factors that lead to precarization for MFWs. Steve's story provides one example of how the workers' compensation system breaks down for injured workers and how workers' tenuous immigration status can compromise their long-term health and access to health care. With various types of machinery and vehicles used throughout agriculture and a lack of worker training, workplace injuries are common among MFWs (Hennebry et al., 2010; McLaughlin, 2009b). Injured workers are often told they can do "light duties," only to be fired the minute they indicate they are in too much pain to continue. Having no legal recourse to remain in the country, workers are often repatriated immediately, before their injuries can be further investigated or treated (McLaughlin, 2007). Those who stay in Canada are left with nowhere to live, no income, and a lack of access to services.

Enrique's case, while rare, is not unique. Several other workers identified in our research have experienced kidney failure ($n = 5$) and dozens of others have developed other serious conditions, such as advanced cancer, heart disease, and AIDS, while in Canada. Some have been repatriated to their countries of origin, where, without access to medical care, they have since died. Others have stayed in Canada by changing status, either as refugee claimants, or with visitor's visas. In some of these cases, permanent residency applications or refugee determinations are still pending. As a result, their life-sustaining treatment continues at least until their cases are decided. In most other cases, however, workers are deported or pressured to leave before they can receive support or care. The fact that Enrique's struggle continued despite the assistance of his sympathetic employer demonstrates the limits of the *system* in supporting workers in vulnerable situations (McLaughlin, 2009b).

Eliana's case touches on some of the specific issues within the NOCCD involving health insurance, debt, and difficulty switching employers. It also highlights the particular concerns facing women workers, many of whom are migrants during their reproductive years. If pregnant, most are fearful to tell employers and risk losing employment. They are thus unable to modify tasks appropriately at work or to seek prenatal care (McLaughlin, 2008). This is a major problem for women MFWs that, in part due to its very invisibility, has been largely neglected by policy makers, researchers, and community resources.

Collectively these cases demonstrate how precarization is particularly pronounced for workers who develop long-term or serious health issues. In the absence of sustained, transnational, or portable health insurance plans, such workers are in a highly tenuous position. They are afraid to return home without the guarantee of care, but at the same time find themselves in Canada without secure legalized status, a job, assistance with interpretation and communication, their families or any support system, or often even a place to live. These workers are pushed to the margins, attempting to secure medical care and survival in whatever ways they can, living with profound uncertainty and stress. With no viable options, they may be forced into situations that only further deepen their precarity (Saad, in this volume).

Many MFWs experience precarization from the moment they enter Canada, despite legal (though temporary) migration status. Several policy changes could be considered to address the vulnerabilities that lead to precarity for MFWs. Providing all temporary migrant workers with a path to regularized status, open work permits, portable comprehensive health insurance, support to access rights and benefits (both during and after their employment), and an appeals process prior to repatriation are all potential strategies. To be effective and meaningful, any changes must address the root causes of workers' underlying vulnerabilities. Without these changes, the expanding employment of TMWs across Canada will likely result in increasing numbers of workers who will stay in Canada at their own risk, as they traverse through tangled and narrow pathways to precarity.

NOTES

1 NOCCD refers to the National Occupational Classification (NOC) C and D – categories of employment in Canada that require lower levels of formal training. The program is now called "Stream for

Lower-Skilled Occupations" (August 2012). See http://www.hrsdc.
gc.ca/eng/workplaceskills/foreign_workers/lowskill.shtml for more
information.

2 Workers' names are pseudonyms. This case study was adapted from
McLaughlin (2007).

3 This worker (along with nearly three thousand others) was recruited
through an agreement with the International Organization for Migration
and the government of Guatemala. As of 2012 this agreement is no longer
is place; however, the Fondation des entreprises en recrutement de main-
d'œuvre agricole étrangère (a conglomerate of employers associations in
Quebec) is now directly recruiting workers in Guatemala.

4 More information on this group can be found at www.justicia4migrant-
workers.org.

10 Precarious Immigration Status and Precarious Housing Pathways: Refugee Claimant Homelessness in Toronto and Vancouver

PRIYA KISSOON

Approximately 2.5 million homeless people currently live in Canada (Wellesley Institute, 2010). The vast majority (2.2 million) are "hidden," meaning they are invisible for enumeration because they are "relatively homeless": living in illegal, temporary, or inappropriate accommodation that is not meant for habitation or is not conducive to good health – doubled up in overcrowded dwellings, couch surfing, and at high risk of "absolute homelessness." Research has shown that new immigrants are over-represented among the hidden homeless (Enns, 2005; Fiedler et al., 2006) and are at high risk of using shelters or sleeping rough (City of Toronto, 1999). Poverty and a shortage of adequate and affordable housing affect all groups, but for newcomers, finding housing is even more difficult due to language barriers, lack of knowledge about Canadian housing, and limited social networks, financial resources, and

This project was funded by a SSHRC Postdoctoral Fellowship and Metropolis British Columbia – Homelessness Partnering Secretariat research grant. The research would not have been possible without the support of FCJ Refugee Centre in Toronto and Inland Refugee Society of British Columbia, amongst other organizations serving beyond their capacity to help fleeing and displaced persons and facilitate awareness on issues facing refugee claimants in Canada. Thank you to the editors of this important volume for inviting my submission and to Patricia Landolt in particular, whose patience in helping me to prepare this chapter has been seemingly infinite. Most importantly, I would like to acknowledge and give thanks to migrant participants for sharing some part of their life stories so that readers might have an alternative perspective of Canada as a country of immigrants and of homelessness in its cities.

information. Refugee claimants are particularly disadvantaged by their temporary status (Hiebert et al., 2005; Miraftab, 2000; Murdie, 2008; Sherrell & Immigrant Services Society of BC, 2009), and recent studies have documented the challenges faced by individuals without authorized immigration in negotiating the housing market and coping with homelessness (see Paradis, Hulchanski, et al., 2008).

Refugee claimants also face obstacles to work, including delays in receiving work permits and being assigned social insurance numbers that begin with a 9, which tag them as temporary workers (see Landolt & Goldring, in this volume). They are also ineligible for social assistance until their claims are referred for protection determination, which legislatively should take no more than three days, but in reality can take several weeks. They must also cope with varying degrees of post-traumatic stress and poor health from experiences of persecution, the pain of lost or left loved ones, and the expense and stress of the journey to Canada (Hiebert et al., 2005; Junaid, 2002; Mattu, 2002; Miraftab, 2000; Kilbride and Webber, 2006; Klodawsky et al., 2005; Murdie, 2008; Murdie et al., 1996; Paradis, Hulchanski, et al., 2008; Zine, 2002). The Canadian Centre for the Victims of Torture reported that "30 percent of refugees who come to Canada are survivors of torture, war, genocide and crimes against humanity" (CCVT, 2010).

When newcomers arrive in Canada, one of their first priorities is finding shelter; housing is widely recognized as the cornerstone of settlement because safe, accessible, appropriate, and affordable accommodation offers a stable home base to re-establish careers, networks, and a sense of security. However, Canada's major cities are critically short of affordable rental accommodation in the private and public housing sectors (Carter, 2008; Hulchanski, 2004; Murdie, 2008). Social housing accounts for only 11 per cent of Vancouver's housing stock and the wait time for social housing is close to ten years. In Toronto, vacancies in market rents were under one per cent from the mid-1990s to 2002 (Canada Mortgage and Housing Corporation, 2006), and the larger units (three or more bedrooms) that are vacant are usually either derelict or out of the price range of most newcomers (Carter, 2008; Miraftab, 2000).

Refugees reportedly experience exclusion and vulnerability within the public housing sector as a result of their not understanding allocation procedures, discrimination from gatekeepers, and culturally unresponsive placement policies (Carter, 2008; Sherrell & Immigrant Services Society of BC, 2009); together, these factors can result in some families being refused a unit. Systemic discrimination and exploitation, particularly against large families, immigrants from non-European backgrounds, and immigrant women, especially single mothers (Carter, 2008; Hiebert and Mendez, 2008; Murdie, 2008; Novac, 1996; Rose & Ray, 2001; Sherrell & Immigrant Services Society of BC, 2009), combined with the stigma of welfare or low income (Dion, 2001; Murdie, 2003; Zine, 2002), create tremendous disadvantages for refugee newcomers competing for housing at the lower ends of the rental market. This increases distress and risk of homelessness (Carter, 2008; Hiebert et al., 2005; San Pedro, 2001), and ultimately focuses refugees' energy and resources on survival, subsistence, and supporting basic needs, rather than on socio-economic development and integration. A lack of knowledge about rights, and sometimes a lack of confidence or ability to exercise those rights, can force refugees to accept housing that is unsafe, inappropriate, difficult to access, and even unaffordable (Francis, 2009; Hiebert et al., 2005; Sherrell & Immigrant Services Society of BC, 2009). Consequently, refugees are more likely than other immigrant groups to be at risk of hidden homelessness. Visible minority refugees are also more likely to live in substandard housing that is segregated (Carter, 2008, p. 17; Sherrell & Immigrant Services Society of BC, 2009). Using a pathways approach, this chapter explores the relationship between homelessness and precarious status among refugee claimants. It will help clarify the complexities of homelessness among refugee claimants by demonstrating that unauthorized or undocumented residence may be one characteristic of precarious immigration trajectories. It will also explore whether immigration status may in turn affect, or be affected by, housing stability or homelessness.

By applying a pathways framework, we assess homelessness and precarious status as episodes in a housing and immigration career, respectively. This approach involves a longitudinal perspective of homelessness and lack of status, revealing the complex and dynamic processes involved, particularly the precipitates to instability and precariousness and the stabilizing factors that affect migrants' housing and refugee claim experiences and decision making over time. It is able to capture accommodation and legal status as geographical panoramas – snapshots of trajectories over time and space as opposed to static categories. This is extremely helpful when applied to the experiences of individuals with precarious immigration status (see McLaughlin and Hennebry, in this volume). Its analytical value has been confirmed: exploratory research on shelter use by homeless immigrant women, for example, revealed that women with unauthorized precarious legal status (e.g.,

visa overstay, expired work permit, rejected refugee claimant) initiated a process of regularization (e.g., refugee claim, humanitarian and
compassionate review) when they entered the shelter system (Paradis,
Novac, et al., 2008). This suggests that the relationship between homelessness and precarious immigration status is complex and potentially
multidirectional.

I based this chapter on the results of in-depth semi-structured interviews and detailed housing histories conducted in 2008 with thirty-
four migrants in Vancouver and Toronto and approximately fifteen key
informants from non-profit agencies and non-governmental organizations. Although I draw from all of these interviews in this chapter, I
profile the cases of five migrants who experienced multiple changes in
their legal status and housing situation, to clarify the shifting and often
unexpected relationships between these overlapping arenas of social
experience. The case studies will illustrate the importance of migrants'
agency and decision making in coping with precarious housing and
immigration status.

I will begin with a brief discussion of the concepts of housing and
legal status careers, particularly homelessness and Canada's refugee
determination process. This will be followed by a discussion of the research methods and some of the challenges of tracking and interviewing a doubly vulnerable migrant population across two urban centres,
Toronto and Vancouver. Next, I will present a profile of the housing
and legal status trajectories for the entire sample, followed by the five
in-depth cases. I will conclude with a few observations about the refugee claim process, unauthorized residence, and vulnerability to homelessness, especially among refugee newcomers.

Housing Careers and Changes in Legal Status

A pathways approach frames information about events – becoming
homeless or losing status – as processes in the context of a person's
whole residential history and his or her passage through various immigration categories. In this section I will draw on the concepts of a
housing career and precarious legal status to build a longitudinal
framework to analyse the intersections of housing, homelessness, and
legal status changes.

Scholarship about housing and homelessness has developed the concept of a "housing career" to highlight the changes in quality, mobility, social practices, and meaning that constitute housing consumption

over time and space (Clapham, 2002). The housing career is an analytical category that encapsulates different aspects of housing and foregrounds the meanings and practices of housing, the dynamic nature of the housing experience, and interrelatedness with other careers, such as family, employment, and education (Clapham, 2002). According to Clapham (2002), "One of the major strengths of the pathways approach is the recognition that changes in housing can involve a different set of social practices as well as the more widely recognised physical changes. In addition, the consumption of housing can be modified substantially even without mobility because of a change in social practices" (pp. 63–4). Recognizing the importance of subjective evaluation in assessments of the housing career, Murdie (2008) suggested that while housing outcomes include physical and social qualities of home and neighbourhood, increasing levels of satisfaction are the best indicator of a "progressive" housing career (Murdie, 2008, p. 84). The concept of a housing career also captures how a person's residential history shapes their current experience of homelessness (Daly, 1996; May, 2000; Piliavin, Entner Wright, et al., 1996). For example, patterns of constrained moves and protracted stays in unsatisfactory accommodation are characteristic of hidden homelessness and often precede absolute homelessness (May, 2000; Piliavin, Entner Wright, et al., 1996; Piliavin, Sosin, et al., 1993).

Precarious immigration status is an emotional and tangible obstacle to maximizing residential choice and agency (see Saad, in this volume). It is not only an administrative barrier to access programs, housing, work, education, and health care; it is also imbued with stigma and discriminated against socially and institutionally. Unauthorized residence is linked to service avoidance because some people will refuse to seek help for fear that loss of anonymity will result in detention and deportation; it can also intensify post-traumatic stress and medical conditions in cases of asylum seekers (Saad, in this volume).

Research has documented the vulnerability of refugee newcomers and the housing circumstances of persons affected by both precarious housing and precarious status, revealing that these individuals often spend more than 50 per cent of their income on rent; are forced to compromise on health and comfort (quantity and quality of food, use of public transportation, buying seasonal clothes or medicine); and are unable to reunite their family or obtain permanent residency due to the financial cost and fear of authorities (Francis, 2010; Hiebert et al., 2005; Kissoon, 2010a, 2010b; Miraftab, 2000; Murdie 2005, 2008; Ryan and Woodill, 2000; Sherrell & Immigrant Services Society of BC, 2009; Zine, 2002).

Like the housing career, precarious legal status can also be conceptualized as a pathway or "career." The pathways approach highlights how policy shifts and institutional negotiations produce variable categories of precarious legal status, as well as movement across categories. Variable authorized and unauthorized forms of precarious legal status can be framed as interlinked moments in a person's legal status career. By revealing the trajectories of migrants' legal status, the pathways concept highlights both the institutional production of legal status and migrants' agency and decision making. This kind of analysis requires investigating how migrants' decision making builds on previous decisions, efforts to regularize or obtain a status that appears to offer greater security, or the decision to move out of status and remain in Canada as an unauthorized resident. A pathways approach recognizes that today's citizen may have been an "illegal immigrant" or unauthorized resident, or that he/she could have been a refugee claimant or authorized non-resident.

A Snapshot of the Refugee Claimant Process

In Canada, the federal Ministry of Citizenship and Immigration Canada is responsible for the refugee determination process. The Immigration and Refugee Board, an independent quasi-judicial body created in 1989, manages asylum claims to guarantee due process for all refugee claimants on Canadian soil, including full right of appeal. People who arrive in Canada at the border and seek asylum, or who are already in Canada and decide to make a refugee claim after a change in country-conditions or learning about the determination process, are referred to as "in-land refugee claimants." If these claimants are deemed eligible to apply for asylum, their cases are referred to the Refugee Protection Division of the Immigration and Refugee Board, and if they are found to be in need of protection, they are given "convention refugee status." The determination process can take months or years; it can be legally complex and very expensive. With a positive decision and the granting of convention refugee status, an individual is eligible to apply for permanent residence. While the procedural timelines for claimants to submit documentation in support of their applications are tight, the backlog of decisions from the Refugee Protection Division means that refugee claimants are in legal limbo for the duration of their claim.

Research has shown that this has a negative impact on integration, as well as the claimant's mental health and well-being (Alfred, 2002; Hiebert et al., 2005; Klodawsky et al., 2005; Murdie, 2005; Ryan and Woodill, 2000; Zine, 2002).

During the refugee determination process, claimants are issued a conditional departure order along with a stay of removal until their claim is decided. If the decision is negative, the removal order becomes enforceable. While the decision is pending, refugee claimants are eligible for the same provincial welfare assistance as Canadian nationals. They are also eligible for emergency shelter and social housing. However, they are excluded from a range of federally funded social services associated with settlement and integration, including language classes, employment counselling, and job readiness programs. Once refugee claimants have completed their medical examination, they are eligible to attend school while awaiting a decision on their claim, although they are typically charged international student fees if they attend college or university. Refugee claimants are eligible to work, are provided with a temporary social insurance number, and receive basic and emergency health care under the Interim Federal Health system.

Researchers and advocacy groups have identified systemic issues within the refugee determination system that generate uncertainty and instability for migrants and contribute to illegality (Dauvergne, 2008): variation in acceptance rates by region; protracted legal limbo due to an increasing backlog of cases; the reduction of Immigration and Refugee Board hearing panels from two members to one; politically motivated selection of members; expedited hearings for targeted nationalities with large numbers of applications but low probabilities of acceptance; pronounced delay in implementing a refugee appeals division; possibility of extradition; chronic lack of funding to the Immigration and Refugee Board and Refugee Protection Division; and provincial cuts to legal aid (Canadian Council of Refugees [CCR], 2006, 2007; Goldring et al., 2007; Stoffman, 2002).

Under the 2002 Immigration and Refugee Protection Act, prior to the introduction of Bill C-11 (which introduced the Refugee Appeals Division of the Immigration and Refugee Board), if a person's refugee claim was denied, two ad hoc post-hearing mechanisms of quasi-appeal were available. First, a rejected claimant could request a Pre-Removal Risk Assessment (PRRA) to evaluate any new evidence that might indicate that removal to their country of origin might result in violence or put them in harm's way. A person undergoing a PRRA has a stay of removal until their application is assessed, but the success rate on the PRRA is less than 2 per cent. Second, a person can apply for humanitarian and compassionate (H&C) consideration, which requires that they prove they have already successfully integrated in Canada and that removal to their country of origin would result in undue hardship. However, neither integration nor undue hardship alone are sufficient to stay removal during the H&C application assessment. This makes people who fear harm if returned to their country of origin, and who may have made life-changing sacrifices for their escape to Canada, particularly vulnerable. The H&C application is also expensive,[1] which places lower-income applicants at an extreme disadvantage. Accessing social welfare supports can be detrimental to demonstrating integration, and rates of H&C acceptance are low – about 20 per cent according to lawyers, but 50 to 70 per cent according to a Citizenship and Immigration Canada spokesperson who may have been including family sponsorship and spousal sponsorship applications in the calculation (Keung, 2008a, 2008b).

A longitudinal or pathways perspective on migrants' legal status career situates the formal refugee determination process and ad hoc appeals mechanisms in relation to people's lives before launching an application and/or after receiving negative decisions on the PRRA or H&C application. Frontline workers and immigration practitioners widely acknowledge that unauthorized residence with precarious legal status (e.g., an expired tourist visa) is common among migrants who subsequently decide to make a refugee application, which is an uncertain and legally complicated process. Migrants may also flee underground if they feel their traumas and circumstances have been delegitimized by a negative refugee decision and appeal or review options have been denied or exhausted (see Saad, in this volume).

In the next section I explore migrants' decision making as it pertains to shifts between the refugee claimant process and unauthorized forms of precarious legal status, and how these shifts are related to the risk of homelessness, based on case studies collected during my research. The next section contextualizes these case studies, beginning with a brief description of the study's design and participant recruitment and an overview of the key characteristics of all interviewees.

Profile of a Doubly Invisible Migrant Population

In 2008 I conducted thirty-four in-depth semi-structured interviews with migrants who had made a refugee claim and had lived in Canada without authorization before or after making their refugee claim. The interview guide covered a number of issues: the circumstances of their journey and entry into Canada; the reasons and circumstances under which the refugee claim was made; their social networks, including their awareness of and access to support and resources in Canada; and their housing experiences. Housing experiences were collated to capture the details and characteristics of each dwelling in chronological order, including location, dwelling and neighbourhood satisfaction, affordability, reasons for leaving, and resources used to find the next home.

Interpreters were made available to participants, and interviews were taped, transcribed, and coded for analysis. Participants were offered a stipend for participation, and were mainly referred to the study by a few key agencies in Vancouver and Toronto, although I also advertised through posters in laundromats, on community bulletin boards, and in support agencies, and by participants' word-of-mouth referrals to family or friends. Recruitment was a slow process; one major barrier was the vulnerable position of migrants and issues of ethics and trust (see Young, and Bernhard and Young, in this volume).

The thirty-four participants originated from twenty-three countries across six regions: North America, Central and South America, the Caribbean, Africa, Asia, and Europe. Routes between unauthorized residence and refugee claimant status differed, although most participants had lived without status before making an in-land asylum application case (79 per cent). Of the thirty-four participants, five had entered Canada clandestinely and resided for months without papers, two lived with false documents, two were inadmissible or excluded from the refugee determination process, and eighteen had overstayed a visitor's visa or work permit. Overall, 20 per cent were residing in Canada without authorization after a negative decision on their PRRA.

At the time of the interview, 26 per cent of the thirty-four participants were refugee claimants ($N = 9$), 24 per cent had more permanent status (convention refugee, permanent residence, or citizenship) ($N = 8$), and 32 per cent were without status but undergoing a legal process such as the PRRA or H&C ($N = 11$). Of all participants, 18 per cent ($N = 6$) were without status and not going through a legal process such as PRRA or the H&C. These varying forms of status and precarious status were associated with variable lengths of residence in Canada. Of all participants, 18 per cent had arrived in Canada before 2000, 35 per cent had arrived within three years prior to the interview, and 9 per cent had lived in Canada for more than 12 years.

While all participants struggled to pay their rent, for many participants this was a preoccupation that had taken a pronounced emotional and physical toll on their health and well-being. Absolute homelessness was experienced by 44 per cent of participants at some point since arriving in Canada, meaning they were sleeping outside ($N = 6$) or in shelters ($N = 15$). Calculated across multiple episodes of homelessness, these participants spent an average of forty-one weeks in shelters and an average of two weeks sleeping outside. In terms of hidden homelessness, 59 per cent spent an average of sixteen weeks doubled-up and not paying rent. Overall, 62 per cent had spent an average of thirty-three weeks in residences in which they were unhappy, rating the experience as less than five on a ten-point scale. Only three participants stated they were always well housed and satisfied with their accommodation.

Of the 44 per cent of participants who had stayed in homeless shelters, all had been living without authorization to reside in Canada. Every participant who used the shelter system did so because their economic and social welfare had deteriorated to the point that they could no longer subsist without support. For these participants, initial exits from homelessness were the result of launching a process of regularization through either a refugee claim or an H&C application, which made them eligible for assistance programs. In certain cases, these programs provided short-term solutions to survival and stability issues, but a few participants later experienced absolute homelessness when their applications were denied and their vulnerabilities remained unchanged.

The vast majority of participants experienced some sense of a positive housing career in Canada, with an increase in satisfaction from arrival to their current accommodation. A positive direction in housing career may be linked to a positive legal status trajectory, because 82 per cent of participants shifted from a period of unauthorized residence to a process of regularization, or temporary or permanent residence in Canada. This shift towards less-precarious legal status also afforded them greater access to state-funded health and social services, and helped to increase confidence. This suggests a positive correlation between legal status stability and housing stability.

The following section provides five case studies that illustrate migrant decision making and constrained agency situated at the intersection of the housing market and precarious immigration status.

Snapshots of Legal Status and Housing Careers

The heterogeneity of circumstances and decision making at the intersections of housing and precarious immigration status is well illustrated through the five case studies I present in this section. All five participants arrived in Canada in 2002, and all entered as visitors to either Vancouver or Toronto. Although participants shared some broad characteristics (year of arrival, city, periods of unauthorized residence, and the refugee claims process), the individual circumstances related to their legal and housing decisions varied considerably. They did, however, all face systemic and structural barriers to stability in their housing and immigration status careers. They also shared the common experience that short-term improvements to their situations often resulted in unexpected complications in the longer term.

Table 10.1 presents an overview of the case studies; it lists individual traits and highlights their housing and legal trajectories, including their current living situations. As shown in Table 10.1, three of the five profiled participants arriving in 2002 resided in Vancouver (Frank, Luke, and Mary) and two resided in Toronto (Tania and Luisa). Each arrived from a different country and resided with a different current status, ranging from unauthorized resident to citizen. Each of the five had allowed their entry visas to expire and lived without status before making refugee claims, with the exception of Luke, who shifted from a refugee claim to living in Canada without status. The period that preceded the claim was longer than the period without status for everyone except for Luke, which was related to his unauthorized status after a negative refugee decision. Frank had a temporary residence permit, Mary and Tania were awaiting decisions on applications, and Luisa was a citizen.

Table 10.1 shows that for each of the profiled participants, social networks were integral to having shelter on arrival. The length of time spent being hosted ranged from about two weeks (Luke) to a few years (Mary). The final column lists the total number of moves since arriving in 2002 and the interview in 2008 (approximately a six-year span), together with the level of satisfaction in the first place compared to the current accommodation. Satisfaction was rated on a ten-point scale, with one being the worst place imaginable and ten being the best. Frank, Luke, and Luisa each moved a total of five times. Mary and Tania moved considerably more: ten and twelve times, respectively. Everyone except Frank enjoyed their current accommodation. Frank's

Table 10.1. Participant Legal Status and Housing Profile

	Snapshot of Participants and Current Status	Route to Unauthorized Residence	Amount of Time before Claim	Amount of Time Non-status	First Place	Current Place	Total Moves and Satisfaction in First and Current Residence
Vancouver	Frank: *Temporary status, Malawi, 50+ yrs old, wife and children in Malawi	Visa expired	1.5 years	6 months	Hosted by acquaintance 18 months	Transitional housing / AIDS hospice 1 year	5 moves; 5→5
	Luke: No status, Spain, 24 yrs old, common law w/ one child in Canada	Failed claim	Few weeks	3 years	Doubled up with friends 4 years	Co-op, ownership 3 years	5 moves; 3→8
	Mary: Refugee claimant, Trinidad, 33 yrs old, lone parent, two children in Canada	Visa expired	4 years	2.5 years	With partner 4 years	Transitional housing / domestic violence 1 year	10 moves; 1→8
Toronto	Tania: PRRA, Costa Rica, 20 yrs old, common-law, 2 children in Canada	Visa expired	6 months	3 months	Parents + 9 people in 3 bdrm 1 year	One bdrm. apt rental with partner 1.5 years	12 moves; 3→9
	Luisa: Citizen, Brazil, 33 yrs old, single, no children	Visa expired	9 months	3 months	Couch 1 month	Shared flat 4 years	5 moves; 9→9

* All names have been changed to protect identity
Source: Author's data

satisfaction in his first and current place remained low, both rated at five. Luisa's satisfaction in her first and current place remained high, both rated at nine. The next sections explore the individual experiences of each of the five migrants. Together, these cases illustrate the importance of migrants' agency and decision making in coping with precarious housing and immigration status.

Frank

Frank was fifty-four at the time of the interview and had lived in Victoria, British Columbia, for a year before moving to Vancouver to be nearer the resources he needed to regularize his status. He was from Malawi, where he had been a teacher and political hopeful. He came to Canada to upgrade his education, invited by a Canadian friend, but he misunderstood his prospects for study, and on arrival was confronted with ineligibility for tuition support and high international student fees. Neither he nor his friend realized that visitor status could not be converted to a more permanent status, and after receiving one extension, he was denied a second. During this period, school fees were beyond his reach and he was ineligible for a work permit, leaving him destitute and dependent on his host-friend. Frank said, "I was anxious because I had no money, not even to buy a ticket back home, nowhere to go, nobody to talk to. The first thing being that I wanted to achieve certain things in life and the things didn't work out that way." To arrive in Canada, Frank had sold household items, borrowed from his savings, and borrowed money from lenders, spending thousands of dollars beyond the cost of the airfare for the promise of an education in Canada. For Frank this was an investment in the future. He thought of Canada as a door to further opportunities in his country, explaining that he was "quite energetic to go and do some study. It's to have the opportunities. But, there were no opportunities for me. I just ended up somebody with nowhere, with no money, and almost like destitute."

When Frank moved to Vancouver to find a solution to his immigration problem, he quickly ran out of funds and found himself in a state of absolute homelessness, where his only option was to enter the shelter system. Up to this point, Frank had never considered himself a refugee or believed that the refugee determination process would be the only pathway to remain in Canada. His perception of a "refugee" was as a vulnerable "other," what he called "refugees of a different kind," which he could not imagine himself as, since "back home, in my country ... just like bordering Mozambique, we have so many refugees who would stay within our country. But here, to make a refugee claim, I had no idea." The shelter staff introduced Frank to someone from legal aid, who told him that the refugee process was the "only alternative" for him to stay in Canada. In Frank's mind all he could think of was his humiliation if he returned to Malawi without achieving anything; he said, "I didn't want to go back as a failure just to say everything failed and then I'm here, I'm home. There's nothing. So, the only alternative was making a refugee claim."

Through the mandatory medical examination required for the refugee process, Frank discovered he had HIV-AIDS. This made Frank eligible for a subsistence income through welfare, from which he had previously been excluded. Frank was also assisted by local specialized health agencies, one of which managed a housing association that gave priority to people with HIV-AIDS. The process of stabilizing his legal status through a refugee claim also helped stabilize his housing; it allowed him to move out of the shelter system into transitional housing, where he lived for the duration of his refugee claim, and where he was living at the time of the interview.

Frank received a negative refugee decision, and subsequently applied for temporary status. Although his current status was renewable and precarious, the refugee claims process gave him some relative stability, including a move from homelessness to housing. Still, when asked whether he felt more or less stable when he made the refugee claim, Frank responded, "Less stable because I wasn't just too sure about myself. I couldn't even focus. It was, 'Whoa, I'm just a failure.'" Frank's emotional life was also strained by his family in Malawi's disbelief of the difficulties he had encountered in Canada, which he found "really, really, really very distressing," and "like living in a life like in a limbo. You don't know what's going to happen next."

Luke

Luke made a refugee claim almost immediately upon arriving in Vancouver. At the time of the interview, Luke was twenty-four years old and had been living clandestinely in Canada for almost three years in exceptionally good housing, and had relatively stable and well-paying employment.

Luke was a Spanish citizen with a Mexican partner. Along with a child from his partner's previous marriage, they had travelled to

Canada with the intention of applying for refugee status. While Luke's refugee claim was denied, his partner's was approved. He was ordered to leave Canada, so he left and worked in the United States for some time before the financial pressure in Vancouver began to overwhelm his partner, who pleaded for him to return. Travelling with a group of friends, he avoided scrutiny at the border, and has since been living in Vancouver without status.

Before he left Canada, Luke and his partner had bought a two-bedroom co-op apartment; after he left, she was left with the payments and repaying loans. With his return they were able to stabilize their housing, with difficulty. Because Luke and his partner have been economically viable despite his lack of status, he has no urgent plans to try to resolve his status.

Like most participants, on arrival in Canada Luke lived with friends for a short period until he could find a place of his own. For two weeks he slept on their couch or in the den; the two-bedroom apartment was shared with five other people. He was extremely dissatisfied with this housing, rating it a three out of ten in satisfaction. Immediately upon filing his refugee claim, he applied for welfare, with which he rented a bachelor apartment in the neighbourhood. He and his partner and her child lived there for six months and then moved to a larger apartment in the same building. His level of satisfaction did not increase with the larger apartment because it was rat infested, so he rated both units in the building a four out of ten. They remained in the larger apartment for one year and then moved because of the infestation. Cost and unit size were their main considerations for their next move.

The couple found an apartment in the same area with one bedroom and a den. When they moved in, Luke was still awaiting a decision on his refugee claim, and during this year he supplemented his welfare by working as a telemarketer, construction worker, and in a restaurant. He rated this residence a seven out of ten, which was a significant improvement in his housing experience; the family stayed there for one year. Luke described the unit as "clean, close to everything, a decent building, and in a great area." However, during their stay in this residence, Luke learned he had failed in his refugee claim, and shortly thereafter he also failed in his Pre-Removal Risk Assessment.

Luke's negative decision did not deter the couple from pursuing their dreams in Canada, because his partner's decision was positive. Based on her ability to stay in Canada, and his ability to find employment despite his lack of status, they purchased a recently vacant remodelled co-op. In the few months preceding their move from renting to owner-ship, Luke received a notice to remove himself from Canada, and left. Since returning to Canada, Luke has worked in landscaping to help support the family. They rate their current residence as an eight out of ten, enjoying both the dwelling and neighbourhood, but they also acknowledged that their accommodation is not as fancy as what they were accustomed to in Mexico, nor is it their dream apartment in down-town Vancouver.

Although Luke's legal and housing trajectories are not positively correlated, his apparent stable ascendant career masks the instability, stress, and vulnerability his own legal instability placed on his partner. His precarious legal status did not affect his positive housing career because his spouse carried the burden of the housing cost and manage-ment. Thus, although Luke was able to manage his unauthorized resi-dence and intersecting careers, the uncertainty of his status placed an undue burden on his family.

Mary

Mary was thirty-three at the time of the interview and was living in transitional housing for abused women with her two young Canadian-born children. She was from Trinidad and had a US green card. She had lived in the United States for fourteen years before falling in love and moving to Canada to live with her boyfriend. They lived together for about four years, of which two and a half were without status:

> Yeah, when my status expired, I just kind of given up a bit so there's no-where for me to go and my partner kind of regurgitated that … He actu-ally knew my status and kind of kept it that way because he could control [me] – "You can't do anything because I'll [report] you."

Mary was in Canada for some time before making a refugee claim. Her boyfriend had been abusive, but this seemed to escalate when she lost her status. When she discovered she was pregnant, and was still abused, she fled to a women's shelter, where she spent three months. During this time, she made inquiries about ways to regularize her sta-tus, and learned that she could make a refugee claim, which surprised her since she had been living in the United States for some time. She delivered her baby without status, and then made a refugee claim to receive income support. About this same time, she also applied for and was accepted into transitional housing due to the abuse she suffered, and because she was caring for her newborn baby.

Mary described the intersection of status and housing stability in relation to the kind of assistance she had received: "[without status], it was very big struggle because I was getting help from family and friends and what not. And here, I am getting help without having to struggle." Making the refugee claim improved her situation by expanding her choices and giving her options she did not have while living without status. She directly attributed her homelessness experience to having no status because she assumed that status would have afforded her a job and opportunities that were otherwise unavailable to her. Mary was university educated, had worked as an editor for a public relations firm in the United States, and was highly articulate. Consequently, even though she was more vulnerable as a result of her precarious status, she described a proactive approach to ensuring her needs were met, beginning with the recognition that a lack of immigration status did not diminish her worth as a human being:

I'll call around with phone numbers and ask questions ... about housing and co-op – different – some co-op applications and immigration service numbers – because I was questioning about work permits and – programs for the kids and for myself. I've asked them on the phone, "Is it a dormitory? It is this way, is it that way?" They would recommend, "You shouldn't come here. We recommend this place." So if you ask the right questions – being strong enough and not accepting pitfalls, you know – just saying, "Yes, I need proper housing." I know I'm in this position but I deserve it because I'm human. So a lot of women don't do that. They think, "Oh, okay. Bye. What am I going to do now?" [I would say to them], "You can't be that way."

When asked to describe how her circumstances changed on making the refugee claim, she listed access to housing co-ops, immigration services, a work permit, children's programs, and daycare. Mary's refugee claim was the main reason that her housing trajectory stabilized; it was how she obtained the three-bedroom transitional housing unit she was in at the time of the interview, and how she was eligible to be waitlisted in priority status for BC Housing. She was very satisfied with her apartment, rating it eight out of ten for size, location, and affordability. Regarding her claim, she explained that she was ready to accept whatever decisions were handed down in her refugee case, while also being prepared to exhaust all avenues available to her to remain in Canada.

Tania

Tania is a twenty-year-old woman from Costa Rica who lives with her partner and their two Canadian-born children in a one-bedroom apartment in Toronto. She looks after her children at home while her partner works outside of the home. At the time of the interview, she had received a negative decision on her refugee claim and was awaiting the outcome of her Pre-Removal Risk Assessment.

Upon arrival in Canada in 2002, Tania was fourteen years old. She stayed with her parents and siblings in a three-bedroom apartment, which was home to nine people in total. When Tania arrived, she was issued a visitor's visa of only two months, and when this expired she remained without status for four months before making a refugee claim. Tania had relatively high residential mobility for her age and in comparison to other participants. This is explained in part by volatile relationships that ensued between her parents and her boyfriend as a result of her unexpected pregnancy shortly after arriving in Canada. She was kicked out of her parents' home and moved in with her boyfriend, where occasional conflict would cause her to return to her parents' home, such that each place was an inadequate but functional respite from the other. Tania had moved twelve times in the six years she had been in Canada, and half of these moves were forced returns to shared accommodation with her parents or siblings after experiencing conflict with her boyfriend.

Tania's family members were in different stages of separate claims. On various occasions the Canada Border Services Agency would appear, forcing certain family members to flee to the homes of friends and extended family. As a result, Tania explained that there was constant tension in her parents' residence, where no one was truly "at home." I asked Tania how things changed for her once she made the refugee claim. She said that her change in status opened up her access to services, "Well, it was a lot easier because we got into school and we got help from government, welfare, social services. So it was easier." Tania noted that she did not attend school for the six-month period she was in Canada before making the refugee claim. This changed once she made her refugee claim. She also observed, and was critical of, their landlord's exploitation of the family's lack of status for his own gain: "The place that we were living, because we were – how do you say – without status, they were threatening us that if we leave, they're going to call – just not to lose the tenants, they will also always threaten. So it was hard." This affected not only their freedom to leave their accommodation, but also their security of tenure, and their sense of immigration security. Tania further commented on the condition of her parents' house, saying, "The conditions of the house [weren't] very good so [the landlord] knew that he wasn't going to find nobody to live there because it was very disgusting." Tania's older brother had come to Canada ahead of the rest of the family and secured the unfurnished apartment in a house for everyone to live. This was also directly related to status, because her brother had said, "It was the only house that he could get for all of us where they didn't ask for Social Insurance or anything like that."

Tania recalled the stark beginnings of her housing history in Canada, and their sparse comforts:

We didn't have [any]where to sleep. We had to go look for mattresses from the streets. And I remember me and my brothers, the first night we slept on the floor just with a blanket. And the next morning, we went through the neighbourhood hoping to see a mattress because the floor was very hard [but] we didn't – Yeah, so that was – we didn't have a phone because there was no money, [and there was] nowhere to sit.

While the family's lack of immigration status restricted their choices to the least formal and least desirable residences, their status as renters improved as their immigration status did. Tania explains:

To rent an apartment or to rent a house, they're always asking for Social Insurance and reference letters, financial statements. So it was difficult … But making the refugee claim changed things [because] they asked us for the Social Insurance; we provided that. They asked for financial statement; we provided that because my dad already had opened a bank account and our status, they asked for status.

Positively correlated with the refugee claim; the family moved to better but more expensive accommodation, reflecting mutually reinforcing ascendant careers. Although Tania's housing career is closely interlaced with that of her parents, as a newcomer and a teenage parent she faced massive challenges with precarious immigration status, struggling with language, work, school, and relationships. Her vulnerability as a refugee claimant newcomer was exacerbated by her pregnancy, her parents' rejection, and conflict with her partner, "When I got pregnant, my dad kicked me out ... – he kicked me out so I didn't have [any]where to go – nowhere to go. And I didn't know about that I could get social services or welfare." Seeing no options at the time, she explained, "I went to my boyfriend's house. After one year living with him, my friend told me, 'You know what, you can apply to social service. You are sixteen. You're not living with your parents.'" Although Tania was a refugee claimant at this time, she did not know what services were available to her, so she bounced back and forth between her parents and boyfriend as primary financial supports instead of availing herself of state support and becoming her own head of household with her child. She described this period, which includes her and her newborn baby sleeping on a friend's couch:

> Well, after me and my baby's daddy separated – I left him. My dad didn't want to know nothing and "don't bring any problems to me" so I had to stay with my friend for a week or so with my kid. So my mom was the one who told me to [come home] because I didn't have welfare. I wasn't in welfare, [and] I didn't have no one, no place to go [to], and didn't have money for rent.

She evaluated this early accommodation with her parents as a three out of ten compared with her current accommodation with her partner and children, which she rated as a nine out of ten, with no immediate plans to move. Tania's short history of unauthorized residence preceded the refugee claim, but it was her relationship with her boyfriend that eventually stabilized her housing trajectory.

Luisa

Luisa was thirty-three at the time of the interview; she came from Brazil and was a Canadian citizen. At the time of the interview, she was living in an apartment she loved and working for a Canadian bank in securities. She had spent a few months in Canada without status before making a refugee claim. Despite poor housing quality during times of precarious status, she had a relatively stable housing career in Canada, with few moves and a high level of satisfaction. Luisa had not considered making a refugee claim in Canada. She said, "when I came,

I didn't have idea about refugee claim. I had [at] that time idea that I stay here and try to stay legal but here, I have to start first, right? I had plans to stay here just to study and wait for the papers." Luisa had the financial resources and ability to leave and re-enter the country if she wished, but she learned about the refugee claim process and realized that problems she faced in Brazil might make her eligible for this route to residence. She used her own human capital and education to leverage further resources: "When I decided to come to Canada I went to Yahoo! Group of people who lives here. And I send email. I said, 'I'm going to Toronto. I need some help.' And one lady reply my email and said, 'Oh, I can help you. Send me your information, the date, and the plane.' And I send it her and when I arrived, she was in the airport. She took me and we went to her house. I stayed there for one month." Luisa considered that she was more stable living in Canada without status than as a refugee claimant. She described her experience in the following way:

> When you don't have status, you can work anywhere. You can make money and pay the house. But when you are not sure if you can stay or not, it's strange, you know. I cannot explain exact what you feel but it's something that limit you to do the things to have find, for example, not a house but a comfortable house or cleaner house. You want to be in – you don't want anybody to pay attention you because today you can stay here but tomorrow you have to leave. You never know. I didn't exist if you don't have status. It's very strange, you know, some situation. For example, if they send a letter to you [as a refugee claimant] and your landlord see – usually, they have these in the envelope. [The landlord] will start to talk. They make complain. They make a comment just because the people has wrong idea about refugee. They think if you are a refugee, you are a bad person in your country. That's why you are here. It's strange because every day you have to think about this and now I have to check my mail.

Luisa had a number of bad experiences with Brazilian and Portuguese landlords who assumed she had no legal status because of her nationality and newcomer status. Luisa was refused adequate heating, the freedom to shower at night, and the right to have visitors. On one occasion her landlord entered her apartment to see its condition without realizing she was inside, asleep. Luisa also described two situations in which she called the police to intervene in what she considered her landlord's harassment of her. Both times she had no status, and both times the police improved the situation. She stated that newcomers needed to voice their complaints so that landlords would stop mistreating them. Similar to the others, Luisa's case captures the intersection of precarious status with precarious housing. Although Frank and Mary's experiences of unauthorized residence led to absolute homelessness, each of the cases profiled and all of the migrants interviewed experienced hidden and poor-quality housing in Canada.

Conclusion

Managing to survive in Canada with precarious status requires the ability to navigate informal housing and labour markets, but under what conditions, and to what end? The case studies presented here show that individual decision making, vulnerabilities, traumas, and coping mechanisms affect the meaning of precarious housing and immigration status, and that migrants' vulnerabilities are exaggerated by their unauthorized residence.

A longitudinal and detailed approach to the entire housing history, the realities of pre-refugee claims and post-PRRA situations for unauthorized residence reveals how fear, stigma, and exclusion affect housing stability. The careers approach contextualizes non-status migrants' housing and migration trajectories and generates a more nuanced understanding of lack of status. Exploring pathways moves analysis away from a narrow understanding of migrant illegality or periods of unauthorized residence, and shows how people move through different statuses and how these affect, and are affected by, housing insecurity, destitution, and the risk of homelessness. As these case studies illustrate, routes to citizenship, especially through the limited window of the in-land refugee determination process, may include lack of status. This chapter demonstrates that by virtue of their precarious status and invisibility, non-status migrants are not only vulnerable, but also likely to experience intense and protracted forms of both hidden and visible homelessness. Moreover, periods without status make people highly vulnerable in the refugee determination process.

Future research will need to clarify the potential effects of in-land programs for regularization, for supported return, and for fee waivers on immigration processes for destitute persons. In addition, all levels of government and service providers need to focus on gender sensitivity, the racialization of lack of status, and the deleterious effects on mothers and children cared for in Canada and left abroad. This issue is highly problematic given the protracted visible homelessness, the detrimental effects of homelessness on children in shelters (Decter, 2007), and the pervasive hidden homelessness, all of which disproportionately affect the poorest communities and neighbourhoods in Canadian cities. Research should also be conducted on the ramifications of a partial or non-existent "Don't Ask Don't Tell" policy for emergency and police services on non-status women's vulnerability to hidden homelessness and domestic violence (Bhuyan, in this volume).

This chapter has shown that decisions about legal status intersect with other social and political conditions of well-being, where lack of status is only one period in a whole immigration trajectory. Living "underground" can be a precondition for exploitation, especially for migrants who feel compelled to accept poor living and working conditions to avoid contact with authority figures, for fear of detention and deportation. Being an "unrecognized refugee," one whose claim has not been legitimated by the state or some other appointed third party, while also managing some degree of post-traumatic stress, is tantamount to being a "non-person," because a "normal" life is all but impossible with the pervasive threat of removal or deportation. Yet, migrants manage not only to survive, but to succeed through resilience and perseverance.

NOTE

1 The payment of the processing fees must be included in the application ($550 per adult, $150 per child, and the Right of Permanent Residence fee is $490 per adult).

PART THREE

Institutional Negotiations of Status and Rights

11 Negotiating the Boundaries of Membership: Health Care Providers, Access to Social Goods, and Immigration Status

PALOMA E. VILLEGAS

On 2 October 2009 a seven-year-old refugee claimant suffering from a head injury was turned away from a Toronto area emergency room. While refugee claimants are provided health coverage under the Interim Federal Health system, at the time of the incident the boy's health benefit card had expired and he was awaiting its renewal. Unsure of her son's eligibility for care, the boy's mother called the health information line, Telehealth Ontario, where she was assured that her son would receive care. At the hospital registration desk, she was asked to pay a fee before her son was admitted. She explained the incident in a *Toronto Star* news article:

> The woman at the registration desk said to me, "No, if you want somebody to look at your son, you have to pay the service fee." She said it would cost us $650 ... The woman then said to me, "I have to pay taxes. [My colleague] has to pay taxes. If you want service, you have to pay." (Keung, 2009a)

Because they could not afford the $650 fee, the family was denied access to emergency services and referred to a walk-in clinic.

The example presented above captures the insecure and negotiated quality of access to health care that characterizes the lives of precarious status migrants in Canada. The admissions clerk at the hospital emergency unit drew on a framework of fiscal (and moral) responsibility to determine a child's right to health care. She linked tax contributions to membership and rights, and assumed that precarious status migrants do not contribute and therefore do not have these rights. The hotline operator at Telehealth assured the family that the child could not be denied care at a hospital emergency unit; she assumed that health care was a right for all. Along the way, nurses and doctors would also participate in decisions that would condition access. Their decisions would likewise be shaped by the policy directives that govern the sector and by the procedures and budget allocations that organize their places of work.

Precarious status migrants, whether authorized or unauthorized, have insecure access to a range of goods and services that in Canada are considered essential and linked to the basic rights and entitlements of citizenship. Universal health care is a defining feature of Canadian citizenship and considered a basic human right. Canadian law states that emergency services cannot be denied to anyone regardless of their ability to pay for the service (Elgersma, 2008). Precarious legal status migrants, whether authorized or unauthorized, have insecure access to health care in Canada and often only access care through informal and uncertain negotiations with providers. As such, health care is an important institutional site in which to examine how the boundaries between citizens and non-citizens are regulated and negotiated.

In this chapter I analyse the role of health care institutions and their workers, as advocates and gatekeepers in producing varying degrees of access to health care for precarious status migrants in Toronto. The analysis reveals two features of the relationship between precarious legal status and health care: (1) immigration status is flexible and shifts over time, making it difficult to map precarious status migrants' eligibility for health care in Canada; and (2) precarious legal status migrants' access to health care is contingent on health care workers' resources and, more importantly, on their understandings of immigration and health care policies. I also examine what health care workers' varied and at times competing frameworks for understanding health tell us about the ways in which the boundaries of access and citizenship are drawn. Ideas of universal health care access inform ideas of citizenship and its entitlements. It is citizens who are the imagined recipients of such policies. Yet precarious status migrants are able to garner some access, which leads to important questions about how the boundaries of citizenship are produced and maintained.

The chapter begins by briefly outlining the scholarship on citizenship that informs my analysis. I then discuss the regulatory framework that organizes health care delivery in Ontario, and specifically in Toronto, to identify sites where negotiated access to health care might occur.

This is followed with a discussion of the ways in which two types of workers in health care seek to expand access to care for precarious status migrants. Frontline workers develop strategies to secure some access in the course of their daily work routines. Middle-level managers in the sector, specifically community liaisons, develop advocacy strategies to insert the right to health care for migrants into the broader equity agenda. I consider the limitations they all face in doing this kind of political work. Finally, I consider what health care workers' ideas about rights to health care and negotiated practices of access tell us about membership and citizenship more broadly.

Citizenship's Gatekeepers

As Linda Bosniak (2009) argues, citizenship has been normatively understood in terms of binaries. One example is the notion of citizenship as either thin or thick. Thin citizenship refers to citizenship as a status only, without rights or obligations. One can contrast this version to a thick notion of citizenship that incorporates "more robust, substantive conceptions – whether based on rights, democratic participation, or identity/recognition" (Bosniak, 2009, p. 142). It is this thick or substantive citizenship that I am interested in, for it is what is invoked when referring to benefits and entitlements such as universal health care for non-citizens.

Discussions of citizenship do not always take into account the experiences of "non-citizens" (Bosniak, 2006). People with this status of "alienage," or precarious immigration status (Goldring, Berinstein," & Bernhard, 2009; Goldring and Landolt, in this volume), may enjoy some rights as a result of their presence and participation in a territory, but these rights are often not guaranteed. It is this division, between substantive rights and entitlements for citizens and their uneven application to "non-citizens," that needs to be examined. One way to think about this is to examine how the borders of citizenship extend into the internal activities of the nation-state (Bosniak, 2006). It is in those moments that non-citizens can take part in some citizenship practices. This does not mean that full citizenship, in terms of either status or substance, is suddenly extended to non-citizens, but only that the rights and entitlements afforded through citizenship are sometimes applied to non-citizens. In that sense, citizenship becomes flexible. Bosniak (2006) develops this idea when she suggests that "citizenship is not a unitary or monolithic whole: the concept is comprised of distinct

discourses designating a range of institutions and experiences and social practices that are overlapping but not always coextensive" (p. 3).
Similarly, Daiva Stasiulis and Abigail Bakan (2003) argue that citizenship is a negotiated process:

> Citizenship exists on a spectrum, involving a pool of rights that are vari-
> ously offered, denied, or challenged, as well as a set of obligations that are
> unequally demanded. The terms and conditions of citizenship rights and
> responsibilities are the product of active and ongoing negotiation. This
> process of negotiation involves numerous actors, where human agency
> on the part of non-citizens operates through a combination of individual
> and collective strategies within a matrix of relationships and institutional
> practices over space and time. (p. 2)

Because citizenship and access are negotiated, we need to look
to their points of operation – in this case the interaction between
health care institutions and their workers and patients – to understand how they are negotiated. This is why the role of gatekeeper
is important.

Gatekeepers, as the name implies, are responsible, implicitly or explicitly, for maintaining the boundaries of access and citizenship. For
instance, Stasiulis and Bakan (2003) refer to immigration gatekeepers
as those who "select, reject and restrict the conditions of entry" (p. 63).
As actors (and citizens) within the nation, gatekeepers also "help structure … subsequent options for access to, and fulfillment of, citizenship rights" (Stasiulis & Bakan, 2005, p. 63). Similarly, Franca Iacovetta
(2006), in her analysis of gatekeepers in Cold War Canada, conceptualizes gatekeepers broadly, arguing that their roles extend beyond "those
authorities who determine admission requirements and regulations for
a country or institution" (p. xii). This more fluid definition allows for
the inclusion of those who do not determine the boundaries of access
for health care institutions officially but who, explicitly and implicitly,
negotiate boundaries in their day-to-day work. Therefore, while gatekeepers may not necessarily change citizenship law through their determination of access, they do affect citizenship practices. There is a
degree of conditionality between precarious status migrants and health
care gatekeepers (Goldring and Landolt, in this volume). The result is a
complex "matrix of relationships and institutional practices that is flexible and contingent" (Stasiulis & Bakan, 2005, p. 2).

Methods

The data for this chapter were primarily collected for a research project that examined the opening and closing of access for precarious status migrants in Toronto's health and education sectors.[1] In the first stage of the project, we collected newspaper articles, reports, and documents by and about health care institutions in Canada, paying particular attention to those that referenced precarious status migrants. The second stage involved preliminary key informant interviews and two focus groups with health care workers. Interviews were conducted with a hospital worker who was later a participant in a focus group; a researcher who had conducted a study on precarious status migrants' health experiences; an executive director at a community health centre; and a frontline worker at a community centre. These interviews helped to contextualize the sector as well as identify potential focus group respondents.

Focus groups were organized according to two job descriptions in the health care field: frontline workers, who engage with patients on a regular basis, and community liaison workers, who work in middle-management positions and have less interaction with patients. The first focus group brought together four frontline workers. Two of the participants worked in community clinics (one was a community health centre), one as a nurse and the other as a community worker. Another respondent worked as a midwife, and the fourth participant worked for the municipally funded public health department. The second focus group was composed of five community liaisons. Three community liaisons worked in middle management for different hospitals and the other two worked for community clinics. In addition, one respondent had also worked for provincial health policy makers. All respondents, except one community liaison, were women and all elected to remain anonymous.

In practice, the two groups – frontline workers and community liaisons – are not always mutually exclusive, but the division is useful to capture the relationship between individuals' strategies and policy positions and their different institutional locations. In other words, the division allows me to ask whether institutional location produces different frameworks for access. Respondents were asked to discuss a range of topics, including the history of access to health care for precarious status migrants; the routes differently situated precarious status migrants undergo to receive care (and how the sector responds to the process); the challenges and impact focus group respondents experienced in negotiating access; and their recommendations to improve the process. Interviews and focus groups were transcribed and coded according to themes, focusing on how respondents conceptualized access, how they defined and imagined differently situated precarious status migrants (refugee claimants, visitors, etc.), and what strategies and limitations they encountered in their day-to-day work.

The Regulatory Landscape of Access to Health Care

Although access to health care for precarious status migrants in Canada is largely under the public radar, there is important research on the topic. They include guidelines as to who can legally receive health care benefits (Elgersma, 2008); general discussions of the situation (Berinstein et al., 2006; Bernhard et al., 2007; Caulford & Vali, 2006); case studies of the effect of limited access on precarious status migrants and health care workers (Rousseau et al., 2008; Simich et al., 2007); the costs incurred when seeking healthcare (Morris, 2009); the effects on treating particular illnesses (Committee for Accessible AIDS Treatment, 2006; Li, in this volume) or particular populations (Oxman-Martinez et al., 2005); and plans to improve access (Community Health Centres of Greater Toronto, 2008). There has been less research conducted around the role of health care workers in negotiating various degrees of access, particularly in relation to questions of membership.

The issue of health care access for precarious status migrants brings the health care system into dialogue with the immigration system. Although Canada ostensibly has a universal health care system, the conditions and degree of access to health care for precarious status migrants are complex and confusing and certainly not universal. Coverage is piecemeal and does not account for people tracking through more precarious or more secure forms of legal status, often in unpredictable and unexpected ways and directions (Goldring & Landolt, this volume). Citizens and permanent residents in Canada receive health care through provincially organized systems (in Ontario this is the Ontario Health Insurance Plan, OHIP). However, newly arrived permanent residents in Ontario have to wait three months before they become eligible for OHIP. With a few exceptions, during the three-month wait permanent residents, people en route to citizenship, remain uninsured. Alternatively, the federal government, not the provinces, manages health coverage for convention refugees and refugee claimants who receive coverage through the Interim Federal Health Program (IFHP). While this plan provides a number of services, it is not as extensive as provincial health plans. The IFHP also requires health care organizations to complete separate and additional paperwork for reimbursements for costs incurred in providing care to this precarious status population. Finally, unauthorized precarious status migrants (e.g., visa overstayers, failed refugee claimants) and some authorized ones (e.g., international students) are not eligible for federal or provincial health plans. They fall into the category of uninsured, and are expected – particularly in the case of students – to purchase private health insurance.

"Uninsured" in this case refers to anyone temporarily or permanently ineligible for provincial or federal health plans. While initially designated for homeless persons and those who may have lost a health card, the designation and its associated services have extended to include precarious status migrants. Therefore, in a context in which the population of uninsured precarious status migrants is growing, "uninsured" is often used interchangeably with "precarious status" in this sector. The term is also less contentious than "non-status" or "precarious status," making it a more palatable option for some advocates, particularly in anti-immigrant contexts.

Under the rubric of the "uninsured" emerges the institutional point of access to health care for unauthorized and authorized precarious status migrants. Access and care are piecemeal and resource poor. One option for coverage is Toronto Public Health, which is funded by the municipal government and does not require proof of OHIP or legal status. A second option is the Scarborough Clinic, which runs on donations and volunteer medical professionals to offer services for the uninsured; the bulk of their patients are precarious status migrants, including permanent residents in the three-month wait period (Caulford & Vali, 2006). Third, some of Ontario's community health centres (CHCs) receive funding to treat uninsured patients. That funding is the most often used example of an opening for access for precarious status migrants in Toronto. Because the use of those funds is discretionary, CHCs have the power to use the funds to treat any uninsured patients. However, although "uninsured" funds are largely regarded as an opening, not all CHCs use that money to treat precarious status migrants. Other restrictions also apply. For instance, the funding itself is often not enough to treat all those in need or to provide comprehensive care. Another restriction is catchment area. If a person does not live in a CHC's catchment area and catchment is a requirement to receive care, they may not be served. Furthermore, as I discuss below, differently situated precarious status migrants maybe be given preference over others. There is, of course, always room for negotiation within these "official" and informal policies.

CHCs, like emergency rooms, can be the first place that precarious status migrants seek care. However, they are not equipped with the health care technology and long-term facilities to treat patients with more complicated needs. As a result, some CHCs have created specific arrangements with nearby hospitals that allow them to refer CHC members for more specialized care, often paid for by the CHC. The arrangements also allow CHCs the use of a number of free hospital beds each year (Community Health Centres of Greater Toronto, 2008).

A few hospitals have also created internal policies to provide better care for precarious status migrants. These include making immigration status a part of the equity agenda, as well as strategizing on concrete ways to increase access. For instance, in 2008–2009, hospitals in the Toronto Local Health Integration Network (LHIN) documented and evaluated their equity policies (Edwards, 2009; Gardner, 2008; Women's College Hospital, 2009). In addition, in 2007, the Hospital Collaborative on Marginalized and Vulnerable Populations was created in Toronto. This group brought together members of nine hospitals with the overarching theme of health equity. Members of the collaborative have also discussed and presented on the conditions and differential access that precarious status migrants face (Atungo et al., 2010).

There are always limitations across these informal and formal arrangements and policies. The level of need often surpasses the ability to provide care. Waiting lists are very long at the few CHCs that admit precarious status migrants. Entry into a CHC does not ensure comprehensive coverage or care, and only some CHCs have partnerships with hospitals that might extend care. The bulk of arrangements within and across institutions are informal and contingent, making it difficult to maintain them on a permanent basis. In this context, the responsibility for negotiating access falls on health care workers and precarious status migrants and is achieved in daily encounters and through case-by-case strategies.

Frontline Worker Strategies for Securing Access

The regulatory framework generates gaps and contradictions in care, but also openings and possibilities for negotiating access. At this

political juncture, it is these windows of access that frontline professionals "work" to secure access for their clients. Each institution and
workplace presents a different set of procedures and local openings for
securing some degree of access. Some health care centres (clinics and
hospitals, for instance) have clear policies and mission statements to
provide care to uninsured or not fully insured patients. Others may
not have anything written down but there may be an unspoken understanding about who receives care. And while there may be written
or unspoken directives to serve precarious status migrants, all health
care centers also have to negotiate a climate of limited resources and
increased hostility towards precarious status migrants.

In this troubled context, frontline workers develop their own strategies for providing or increasing access to health care for precarious
status migrants. Networking with other health care workers is one of
the most important. These relationships allow them to stretch their resources beyond their workplace, finding, for instance, an extra hospital
bed or a physician willing to work pro bono. One frontline worker explained it this way: "there's a core group of us ... each person knows
a huge network ... it's very informal ... we don't go looking for them,
it's also mercenary." In order to be part of the network members have
to be reliable and have similar modes of care delivery, including opinions about who is eligible for care, because participating also implies
a degree of trust and reciprocity. Contacts must be ready to return the
favour in order to keep the relationship going. Building these relationships takes time, which is difficult because the sector experiences a large
amount of worker turnover. This means that some people do not stay
in their position long enough to join a network, and those who are part
of a network and leave are sorely missed. Also, as the frontline worker
identified, networking can be a mercenary practice, particularly when
the strategies and actions mobilized by frontline workers are not universally approved in the sector. Being part of a network does not guarantee success. For instance, one respondent said, "I got a long history of
knowing who to phone and can *usually* get the phone call taken." She
understands that there is a limited number of favours she can expect
from each of her contacts and that this necessarily translates into access
denial for some of her clients.

Second, frontline workers make informal referrals when demand
exceeds their capacity. Frontline workers are overworked and overburdened, and have to prioritize who receives care. Those who fall off
their plate and cannot be treated are advised of other clinics or places

where they may be taken. Informal referrals can occur in conjunction with formal ones, increasing the possibility that a patient may be able to access health care. However, because referrals (and networking as a whole) are informal, they never come with a guarantee of access. Access to health care is thus in large part predicated on health care workers' and precarious status migrants' ability to strategize and build their own networks.

Finally, health care providers negotiate with partner health care organizations on behalf of individual clients to waive fees and reduce the price of services. In some instances, the strategy is stable, as in relationships between CHCs and hospitals that provide a number of free beds per year. In that scenario, a route for action is in place. However, as with the networking strategy, access and the pathway to achieve it are not guaranteed; they are also unstable and time consuming.

Community Liaison Worker Advocacy for Procedural and Policy Change

Community liaisons include middle management staff and those involved in diversity and equity work within health care organizations. For this reason, liaison workers do not necessarily see patients day to day. Instead, they act as bridges between management, frontline workers, and other organizations, committees, and networks. Community liaisons perform two key roles to negotiate access: they work as advocates within their institution and mobilize to change the agenda on precarious status migrants in the health sector more broadly.

As advocates within their own institutions, community liaisons draw on institutional histories and vision statements to try to advocate for an agenda of access. Liaisons working in hospitals with roots in traditions of Catholic charity draw on this history to push for greater generosity towards precarious status migrants. This is a challenge, as hospitals across the province, regardless of particular traditions, now emphasize efficiency, risk management, and fiscal responsibility. Liaisons are constantly participating in meetings where they place the issue of uninsured clients and/or precarious status migrants on the table.

Sectoral networking allows liaisons to go beyond the immediate restrictions of their own institutions to forge relationships with other players in the sector and to coordinate conversations. In this way they disseminate existing best practices and effective strategies and push for concrete procedural improvements on the frontlines of care. One example is the organization of formalized networks that come together to discuss strategies and policy directives regarding uninsured and precarious status patients. One such network brings together people working or engaged with community health centres in Ontario (Community Health Centres of Greater Toronto, 2008). Another brings together a variety of different advocates and health care workers interested in the topic (Women's College Hospital, 2010).

The strategy for these networks is to advocate for better access. Such advocacy is mostly put forth on the grounds of increasing equity, although access is also conceptualized as an "urgent community health concern for the Greater Toronto Area," perhaps also alluding to a public health issue (Women's College Hospital, 2010). The strategies of these more formalized networks include the creation of informational and policy documents (Community Health Centres of Greater Toronto, 2008; Gardner, 2008) and organizing conferences (Women's College Hospital, 2010).

They also work on targeted approaches, such as advocating equal rates for services rendered regardless of immigration status. The issue of fees is a good example of their work because it demonstrates a multilevel process in which access becomes restricted. Physicians treating patients under a provincial health plan charge the government specific rates for services. However, they are not regulated to charge those same rates when working with uninsured precarious status migrants, since the government does not pay for those services. Respondents reported hearing of physicians who charged as much as three times the going OHIP rate. Therefore, within their networks community liaisons are working to push for standardized rates, so that uninsured clients are not overcharged.

A related issue is that of double billing. In this example, it is not only physicians who become involved, but also hospitals and collection agencies. Patients may be billed separately by the physician and hospital, creating confusion and added stress. One respondent working at a hospital explains the process:

> As I understand it ... the physician has to follow up for their payment and then the hospital follows up for their payment. One of the key complaints that we heard from folks ... [is that they] will end up getting two different bills which completely confuses them too. So for some folks it's not an issue about paying but it's the process and administration.

Finally, when patients are not able to pay the exorbitant fees in the allotted time, some hospitals employ collection agencies, adding to the stress and confusion.

Limitations

It is worth discussing some of the limitations to frontline workers' and community liaisons' current strategies because they may help to identify avenues for immediate procedural improvements. Furthermore, in the same way strategies to provide access make the boundaries of access less strict, the limitations frontline workers and community liaisons experience foreclose some of those opportunities, reminding us that negotiated citizenship is contingent, often temporary, and may expand and restrict access.

One limitation is the lack of resources. Resources in this sense are more than just funds; they include time and contacts, though these are linked to limited funding. Resource limitations range from those experienced within a specific health care organization (the cost of procedures, increasing number of clients) to those that involve networking (creating and maintaining networks and lack of resources to do large-scale advocacy). Time is also an important resource. The time it takes to generate contacts and networks and the stress of knowing the limits of what they achieve means frontline workers and community liaisons are often overworked and overburdened. Furthermore, the lack of resources forces health care workers, clinics, and hospitals to make discretionary decisions about who should have access and the types of services that access entails. Such decisions can be based on a range of criteria – the nature of the immediate health care demand (e.g., a work injury, late-term pregnancy, or cancer diagnosis) and/or the type of legal status the person has (refugee claimant covered by IFHP versus visa overstayer who is uninsured).

Another limitation involves the transient nature of government, including turnover among government staff and political shifts across time. While some liaison workers felt that the best way to improve access was to advocate at regional and provincial levels, the constant shifting of ministerial cabinets and their objectives makes it difficult to make long-term policy changes. Each time officials change, their policy directives may also change and advocates have to start from scratch. Job turnover also affects advocacy at smaller scales when leadership changes within CHCs or hospitals. For instance, community liaisons referred to a management shift in some Toronto hospitals that had previously been run by religious orders. The shift from nuns to lay CEOs and management involved a conceptual shift from hospitals as sanctuary zones invested in religious ideas of charity to a framework of risk abatement and financial responsibility.

Relating Strategies for Access to Frameworks for Membership

While the strategies and limitations health care workers experience point to the opening and closing off of access for precarious status migrants in Toronto, they also point to contending ideas of membership. Put differently, at the same time that health care workers actively participate in drawing and redrawing the boundaries of access and quality of care, they reimagine the boundaries of who should receive care and thus be considered "a member." As stated earlier, while health care workers do not necessarily have the power or the objective to change citizenship law and its accompanying discourses, their role as gatekeepers does affect the boundaries of substantive citizenship. It is here where the boundaries between citizenship and non-citizenship as practiced through access to health care become more porous.

In interviews and focus groups, respondents discussed a range of often competing proposals and ways of talking about health and access to care for precarious status migrants. Sometimes variation was a function of a person's institutional location and experience working in health care. At other times it was their recounting of how they heard others in the sector talk about access to health care for migrants. At times, a person's interpretation of the issues and how to solve them shifted over the course of the conversation. These varying and often competing frameworks address formal or "legal" citizenship (having a Canadian passport or permanent residence versus more precarious forms of status), and also take into account other bases of membership, including participation in a community and length of residence.

Frontline workers and community liaisons articulate different understandings of access and the strategies to obtain it. Frontline workers identified legal status as a social determinant of health, where having precarious status also meant bad jobs, poor housing, and lack of access to a range of social services, all of which had negative and cumulative impacts on migrants' health and mental well-being. In this framework, access to health care becomes a fundamental human right that everyone has regardless of legal status. Furthermore, well-being encompasses a comprehensive idea of healthy bodies, the need for interpreter services for non-English speakers when they seek care, decent housing, legal aid, and a range of income security issues.

Frontline workers envisioned themselves as being more attuned to the needs of uninsured migrants and therefore had specific solutions to improve health disparities. One frontline worker proposed the following:

> Give everybody a bloody health card … if you can tell other groups that the more grassroots the organization … that the closer folks are to the situation the better the grasp and that's where the wisdom lies and where the solutions … they can see the solution … I think the answers would be to the people who are funding these things … think about how the social determinants of health play out for folks who do not have a health card … all of the other social determinants of health start to be affected.

In her comments, the frontline worker identifies the health card as a starting point for access, something she feels those who have the power to fund health care institutions do not see. Giving everyone a health card means no differential treatment in terms of legal status; if you live and work in Canada you should be issued a health card.

The frontline worker also referred to a common quandary in the sector: how to advocate for change. Although both frontline workers and community liaisons agreed that some type of change was necessary, there were differing opinions as to how to proceed. Frontline workers saw their work as grassroots advocacy. Seeing patients on a day-to-day basis, they feel, gives them inside information on how to improve the situation. A shared concern of frontline workers was that efforts to improve the policy and procedural landscapes through standardization of care for precarious status migrants would destroy the networks they had built up to secure care for migrants under the radar. They did not think that formalization of networks and partnerships would bring better or more inclusive care, but rather minor shifts in inclusion (e.g., ending the three-month wait for permanent residents) and more policing of their own activities. The formalization of partnerships would, they felt, make informal loopholes and attendant strategies for extending care beyond designated groups less viable.

Community liaison workers understood frontline workers' fear, though they also felt that the status quo was not the answer. They were more interested in thinking of ways to frame the issue to make it appealing for decision makers (CHC executive directors, hospital CEOs, policy makers, etc.). This means focusing on concrete and winnable policy directives. One example comes from an equity report prepared for the Toronto Central LHIN. Its author consulted with a local network of advocates for his recommendations on uninsured clients, which included the creation of "consistent policies and procedures" to ensure equitable treatment for all patients, as well as "systematizing and extending existing ad hoc arrangements" (Gardner, 2008, p. 22).

Still unclear in this advocacy work is the question of how health care professionals understand the relationship between access to health care and membership in Canadian society more broadly. What, if any, are the implications, for them, of securing health care for precarious status migrants and extending their rights of membership and perhaps citizenship? The answer is of course complex. While respondents embraced a "social determinants of health" approach, their understanding of membership and specifically of a nation state–bound version of citizenship generated restrictions in what legal status categories (of people) had a right to access health care. None of the respondents thought that health care should be limited to citizens and permanent residents, but that did not mean they all thought that everyone who is "here" (i.e., a resident) should have the right to health care.

At times some of the frontline workers in the focus group invoked a "no borders" framework for health care and membership. Later in the focus group, however, the range of access narrowed as they referred to health care providers who choose only to work with recently arrived permanent residents, uninsured for their first three months in Ontario, or refugee claimants covered under IFHP. Their rationale was that these populations were on a pathway to citizenship and therefore there should be no delays in their right to access the public goods associated with Canadian citizenship.

Focus group participants had more difficulty with the idea of extending health care coverage to precarious status migrants who were considered more transient or temporary. This is the limit or boundary for negotiated citizenship and where the "no borders" approach broke down. The visitor – tourists and international students – generated considerable ambiguities and anxieties among focus group participants. "Medical tourism" was part of the reason for this concern. One community liaison explained how medical tourists are imagined in the sector:

Well, visitors could include people who came without health insurance and medical tourists. Like at one meeting we were at ... they were talking about people arriving at the airport, jumping in a cab and driving straight to the emerg ... again I don't think these numbers are huge but because they become the typical threat when they are mentioned ... and then the arguments within government about the 45 million south of the border .without medical coverage ... it is a hard thing to respond to when you are challenged that way.

Although the respondent explains that the number of medical tourists coming to Canada is not large, he draws on discourses that depict Canada's southern neighbour (and potentially the whole world) as likely to infiltrate an already under attack universal health system.

Frontline workers voiced similar concerns about visitors. Some felt that visitors could be potential medical tourists, while others worked in institutions that refused to treat visitors. One frontline worker explained: "we do have a couple of policies, and that's no visitors and no students." The frontline worker went on to say that the process involved in negotiating care was very time consuming, having to call her organization's financial and social work departments to see what could be done, and often receiving negative responses. Absent from the discussion was the tourist visa overstayer who comes to Canada to work. Ironically, then, until their visa expires and they became unauthorized, health care professionals would not consider this population part of their target group.

The figure of the visitor encapsulates many fears. In a framework where citizenship is conceptualized as participation, obligations, and rights (as opposed to only status), temporariness can mean a person will not fulfil their obligations to the community. Thus visitors are imagined to produce a cost they may not be able to pay back. While frontline workers explained that they did not have many cases of medical tourists, the image and what it represents remained powerful. This was particularly the case for the pregnant medical tourist because the end result is a Canadian citizen who will not participate in Canadian citizenship practices if she/he lives abroad.

Conclusion

In order to analyse the practices, negotiations, and frameworks for access mobilized by Toronto health care workers, this paper makes four key points. First, while there are formal and substantive rules and structures that affect how access is understood, health care workers mobilize specific strategies to open up access for precarious status migrants. The process of negotiating access is time consuming and taxing, making health care workers rely on specific strategies like networking to provide care. Second, I propose that the process of negotiating access tells us something about how the boundaries of citizenship operate. Because access to health care is linked to citizenship, when workers negotiate access for their patients, they also negotiate understandings of citizenship. Third, there are limits to such negotiations, which tells us something about the boundaries that health care workers maintain in relation to immigration status and temporariness/permanence. They also reflect the limits to a notion of membership that does not draw on citizenship status. The concept of precarious immigration status can be a way to bridge our ideas regarding health care and well-being, on the one hand, and membership beyond citizenship status, on the other. Precarious immigration status, with its attention to the fluidity of status at one point in time (refugee claimants, denied claimants, visa overstayers, international students, etc.) as well as over time (the pathways each person encounters moving through different types of status), allow us to question our assumptions of who participates in society and how long one has to be in a place in order to belong.

NOTE

1 The project was entitled "Negotiating Access to Public Goods: Education and Healthcare for Toronto Immigrants with Precarious Status." Patricia Landolt was the principle investigator; it was funded by CERIS - The Ontario Metropolis Centre, 2009–2010.

12 "People's Priorities Change When Their Status Changes": Negotiating the Conditionality of Social Rights in Service Delivery to Migrant Women

RUPALEEM BHUYAN

Canada welcomes migrants for economic, family, and humanitarian reasons, but it is increasingly conferring temporary legal status on migrants, mitigating their full inclusion into society (see Valiani, this volume), a situation that Goldring, Berinstein, and Bernhard (2009) refer to as "precarious migratory status." Families with mixed or unclear statuses – including citizen children – may face deep social exclusion, which contributes to negative social and health outcomes (Bernhard et al., 2007; Fix & Laglagaron, 2002).

Drawing upon conceptualizations of citizenship as a "negotiated relationship" (Stasiulis & Bakan, 2005), this chapter examines how social service providers are involved in determining social membership and social rights for the people who come to them for help and support. The findings are based on empirical research, specifically interviews with service providers working in violence against women shelters in Toronto, Ontario. Exploring how social service providers work with women with precarious status who are subjected to violence can help clarify how service providers negotiate different dimensions of citizenship during times of crises, when their services are vital to personal safety.

This chapter was adapted from an earlier version of the paper (Bhuyan, 2012). The research was funded by CERIS - The Ontario Metropolis Centre. Special thanks go to Daphne Jeyapal, Tracy Smith-Carrier, and Helen Waigumo Gateri for their research assistance. I also thank the service providers, community members, and community organizers whose advocacy for women's rights inspired this work.

Toronto's diverse population and the concentration of poverty among immigrants pose challenges to the delivery of culturally – and linguistically – appropriate services. Toronto has a population of 2.48 million, with 5.5 million residents in the Greater Toronto Area (GTA). Half of Toronto's population was born outside of Canada, and half of all immigrants have resided in Canada for less than fifteen years (City of Toronto, 2006). The Social Planning Council of Toronto characterizes the diverse communities in Toronto as "representing more than 200 different ethno-cultural backgrounds ... diverse communities of colour, a strong Aboriginal community, a large lesbian, gay, bisexual, and transgender community, and an active community of people with disabilities. One in four Toronto residents lives below the poverty line; with poverty rates as high as 46% for recent immigrants, 33% for racialized populations and 32% for children below the age of 6" (Social Planning Toronto, 2010b, p. 2). The large proportion of residents with precarious immigration status, who are ineligible for many sources of provincial and federal funding, further compounds the challenges of providing social services in Toronto.

In this chapter, I begin with an analysis of citizenship as not merely a legal status, but also as a relationship or negotiated practice. I will then provide an overview of how feminism relates to the state in the context of neoliberal restructuring characterized by the devolution and privatization of social services. Finally, I will provide empirical examples to illustrate how service providers navigate different dimensions of citizenship for women with precarious immigration status in Toronto. This empirical analysis will focus on (1) the socio-political context of women's shelters in Toronto; (2) practices that define identity and membership in violence against women shelters; (3) strategies to negotiate rights for women relative to their immigration status; (4) advocacy with non-status women; and (5) efforts to deflect immigration enforcement practices within the space of the violence against women shelter.

Precarious Migratory Status in Canada

By conceptualizing precarious migratory status (or "precarious status") as a continuum, we can distinguish how the production of illegality and exclusion in Canada's immigration regime differs from the phenomena of *"sans papiers"* in France or "the undocumented" in the United States. Few studies have focused on non-status migrants in Canada, but shifts in Canadian immigration policy have resulted in new and longer episodes of temporary and precarious status through more restrictive refugee determination processes and marked growth in temporary foreign worker programs: in 2010 Citizenship and Immigration Canada (2011a) reported nearly one million new and continuing temporary residents. Considering that the total population in Canada is approximately thirty-four million, this represents a sizable flow of people entering and residing in Canada with a form of precarious migratory status – and these data do not include the unknown number of non-status people residing in Canada.

Emerging scholarship on precarious status has explored how national regimes of citizenship are inherently exclusionary and produce separate legal codes and practices to differentiate groups of people within the same country (Sharma, 2007). In her research with labour migrants in Canada, Basok (2004) argued for the need "to analyze citizenship not as a status but as a process which involves negotiation over access to and the exercise of rights" (p. 48). Both Isin (2000) and Basok (2008) placed less emphasis on legal rules and state membership and more emphasis on "norms, practices, meaning and identities" (Basok, 2008, p. 266, quoting Isin, 2000, p. 5). Bosniak (2000a) argued that citizenship is a signal of material and political consequence; "to describe a set of social practices in the language of citizenship serves to legitimize them and grant them recognition as politically consequential, while to refuse them the designation is to deny them that recognition" (pp. 452–3). She identified four different components of citizenship: a legal status, a system of rights, a form of political activity, and a form of identity and solidarity. Within each of these realms, new sites and scales form where citizenship, rights, and membership are negotiated, reinforcing that "struggles over belonging in real places are central to the daily practice of individuals as citizens" (Varsanyi, 2006, p. 253). The conditionality that accompanies precarious status not only signals the state-imposed conditions associated with one's legal status, but also shapes how non-state actors and institutions respond to state authority to define social membership and rights (see Goldring and Landolt, this volume).

The Battered Women's Movement and Women's Full Citizenship

The extension of social rights to vulnerable groups within a nation has always relied on grassroots mobilization. Social movements in North America throughout the twentieth century advocated for the extension of legal personhood and rights of citizenship to excluded groups such as women, African Americans, indigenous/Aboriginal people, and other racialized minorities. The battered women's movement played a key role in the broader women's movement for full citizenship. Violence against women shelters originated out of the need to provide refuge to women who otherwise would have been unable to leave abusive partners. Shelters provided a space for women to flee violence, but also developed social programs to support women's transition to independent lives, including access to welfare, affordable housing, criminal justice, and paid employment. As Nancy Janovicek (2007) writes of the women's shelter movement in Ontario, "Because they offered safety from abusive husbands, transition houses were also a profound critique of the assumption that the family offered protection to women and children, its more vulnerable members" (p. 3). The right to social welfare in order to establish independence from an abusive spouse required changes in the administration of welfare benefits to women and their children, who were previously considered dependents of their spouse/father. Thus violence against women programs have been, and continue to be, instrumental in advocating for women's claims to social rights.

The Paradox of State Power in Violence against Women Organizations

While the anti-violence against women political movement secured stable funding from the state for services to abused women, contractual agreements with the federal and provincial governments prohibited political activity that is critical of the state (Bonisteel & Green, 2005; Harvie, 2002). Reliance on state funding thus produced an "advocacy chill" within feminist anti-violence organizations, which is defined by DeSantis (2010) as "the inhibitory effect that government laws and funding regimes have had on NPOs [Not-for-Profit Organizations]" (p. 26). Feminist historian Cynthia Daniels (1997) refers to this dilemma as "the paradox of state power – a state which both promises state protection, but protects the interests of men" (p. 1). Daniels asserts that the state has failed to address the sources of socio-economic oppression and inequality that impede women's long-term empowerment (Daniels, 1997). While violence against women organizations have adopted anti-oppressive policies and practices to better respond to diverse women (Barnoff & Moffatt, 2007), there has been less attention to the ways in which service providers address oppressive barriers facing immigrants with precarious status.

Community reports and scholarship on non-status immigrants have identified that women living with precarious status in Canada face significant constraints on their social rights when responding to gender-based violence. This group is known to experience an increased risk of homelessness, fear of calling the police, fear of losing their children, and risk of detention and deportation when seeking professional support (Alaggia, Regehr, & Rishchynski, 2009; Menjivar & Salcido, 2002; Raj, Silverman, McCleary-Sills, & Liu, 2004; Sharma, 2001). Exploring how service providers manage the risks of deportation and negotiate rights to social and health services offers one entry point into understanding how service providers take part in producing the sites and scales where citizenship is practiced.

Data and Methods

This research draws from ethnographic participant observation and interviews conducted in the Greater Toronto Area with service providers and management personnel and their funding bodies. The study's aims were to explore: (1) how immigration status and citizenship influence everyday encounters with social service providers; (2) how providers manage the sensitive issue of identity information for service users; and (3) how documentation requirements can affect an organization's ability to provide comprehensive services to those in need.

Data collection took place between July 2009 and June 2010. Fifteen semi-structured interviews were conducted: five with front-line staff and seven with management personnel at violence against women shelters; and three with funding officers who administer provincial and/or municipal funds to violence against women programs in Toronto. The latter explored the relationship between government funders and these organizations. In addition to conducting interviews, I participated in a number of coalition meetings held at the Woman Abuse Council of Toronto and as part of the Shelter|Sanctuary|Status campaign since 2008. This engagement helped to contextualize the research findings within a broader political context of feminist anti-violence and immigrant rights work in Toronto. Quarterly meetings with a community advisory board comprised of service providers and users provided ongoing guidance to the research.

The analysis of citizenship as a "negotiated relationship" draws upon governmentality scholarship and the productive capacity of discourse (Foucault, 1979, 1980; Rabinow, 1984) to examine how social actors at all levels of society – including service providers – take part in the regulation of migrants and their participation in society (Grewal, 2005; Ong, 1996, 2003). This analytic framework focuses on how individuals self-govern as well as discipline others via market participation and (neo)liberal-democratic constructions of rights and freedoms. I employ Lipsky's (1980) conceptualization of street-level bureaucrats to examine encounters that individuals have with service providers as "a kind of policy delivery" (p. 3). The discretionary power that frontline workers exercise in these encounters enables workers to conform to or resist policy directives in their everyday decision making. Their high levels of discretion and relative autonomy from authority allow service providers to play a critical role in deciding who is included within the boundaries of citizenship and to what extent service providers facilitate the process of claiming social rights from the state.

The Setting: Advocating for Women's Safety and Full Citizenship in Ontario

The Ontario Ministry of Community and Social Services is the primary funder for thirteen violence against women (VAW) shelters in the Toronto region. VAW shelters are part of a range of shelter services provided to people who are vulnerable to homelessness and insecurity, including emergency shelters and family shelters. In addition to providing emergency housing, VAW shelters provide a range of services that may include childcare, counselling services, and advocacy and referral for housing, employment, immigration, health care, and social assistance. VAW shelters typically operate at maximum capacity, regularly turning away women and children seeking safety.

Women residing in VAW shelters in Toronto are linguistically, ethnically, and racially diverse, reflecting the diversity of people residing in Toronto and the socio-economic factors that lead women to seek emergency shelter. According to one shelter manager, "We often say they're a combination of mostly newcomers and oldcomers. We get a fair number, a disproportionate number of Aboriginal women to the population and lots of newcomer women ... Typically [we're] working with the women with the least safety nets under them." Service providers and managers with long histories in the violence against women movement talked about how broader social welfare reforms and the current economic downturn significantly affect the women they serve. One shelter manager recalls how social welfare reforms introduced in Ontario during the 1990s have contributed to fewer safety nets for women fleeing abuse:

> About five years ago we noticed that there was a trend in shelters, that we were serving about half of the women and kids that we had served probably 10 years ago ... We found that all of a sudden we had people staying four to six months, and sometimes up to a year. A lot of different reasons for that. Some of it is immigration. Some of it is lack of affordable housing. Some of it is the lack of ability to access any kind of private market on your social systems cheque. So all of those things combined meant that women were kind of stuck. So we couldn't get people out. So people couldn't come in.

Coulter (2009) characterizes the Ontario government in the 1990s, led by populist neoliberal Mike Harris, as "aggressive and unapologetic as they began their substantial restructuring of government" in accordance with neoliberal principles (p. 30). Feminist scholarship has documented the gendered impacts of "the Harris years" (Bezanson, 2006; Neysmith, Bezanson, & O'Connell, 2005), which made significant cutbacks to public services and contributed to criminalization based on poverty and race (Chan & Mirchandani, 2007). At this time, the provincial government tightened restrictions on charitable organizations, undermining anti-oppression advocacy (Bonisteel & Green, 2005). While the current government in Ontario, led by Premier Dalton McGuinty, has been more supportive of women's issues and instituted a Domestic Violence Action Plan for Ontario in 2004, violence against women programs in Ontario remain underfunded. Furthermore, current funding continues to prohibit anti-violence advocacy and community mobilization, strategies that are vital to the social movement that fought to raise public consciousness of violence against women as a social justice and women's rights issue.

Negotiating Social Membership in the VAW Shelter

VAW shelters in Toronto are open to all women fleeing abuse in addition to their accompanying children. The provincial Ministry of Community and Social Services, which funds all of the VAW shelters in Toronto, deliberately refrains from defining eligibility criteria. Although shelters in the area have adopted different criteria for the category of "woman" (i.e., some including transgender women and some not) and children (i.e., different age limits for male children residing in the shelter with their mother), provincial guidelines state that shelters funded by the ministry should be accessible to non-status women. While the ministry does not require organizations to report demographic information about women residing in ministry-funded shelters, they do expect organizations to maintain documentation for auditing purposes. Thus the prospect of being scrutinized for who they serve, while not currently exercised, is always a possibility for violence against women service providers.

With regard to inclusion in the shelter, service providers alluded to feminism as a guiding principle, stating that they "don't care" about women's status when providing services. Thus, with regard to social membership, entrance into the shelter is, in theory, open to all women who seek safety from abuse. The circumstances of women – and their children – who have precarious status while residing in VAW shelters include: women who no longer have status due to the expiration of a visitor visa; women in the midst of "sponsorship breakdown"; and women waiting for their refugee or humanitarian claim decision. In some cases, a woman may already have a warrant for her deportation, due to a failed refugee claim or denied application based on humanitarian and compassionate considerations.

While women with precarious status are using VAW shelters, status does play a role in interactions with service providers in the shelter. Through the course of conducting an "intake" and developing rapport with women, shelter staff ask questions about migratory status as a way to assist shelter residents with applying for public assistance and for general safety planning; "Immigration status is not something that we are looking at for a woman to be allowed to enter, to live in the house. However, we ask the question because that makes an impact on all the services" (shelter advocate). Status also determines what resources the shelter will need to support women and children residing in the shelter. Because women without status are ineligible for many forms of social entitlements and safety nets (e.g., social housing, rent supplement programs, provincial medical insurance, child care support, legal employment), non-status women are more likely to remain for longer and to require non-traditional sources of support.

The length of stay in a VAW shelter is one mechanism that illustrates how the tension between inclusion and limited resources pivots around a woman's immigration status. Shelters vary in their rules regarding length of residence. Some have no predetermined length of stay, while others limit stays to three months, with exceptions made for women in extraordinary circumstances. Both frontline staff and management emphasize that VAW shelters operate as emergency shelters. Providing support to women and helping them transition out of the shelter is considered critical to opening space for other women. There were many factors that contribute to decisions to limit length of stay, including lack of external funding; pressures to be able to demonstrate that shelter beds are used by a maximum number of people; internal assessment of who will most benefit from the shelter; and recognition that shelters are not the best environments for long-term residence. These contrasting views represent competing interests for service providers, who in principle support women's human rights, but work within organizations that have limited resources to carry out their work.

While none of the research participants talked about overt practices that excluded women from shelters based on status, decisions to limit stays for women with precarious status were discussed within an assessment of a woman's ability to demonstrate movement towards economic independence. Women who are ineligible for public housing or unable to pay for affordable private housing were sometimes characterized as "no better off" if they stayed three months versus a year in the shelter. Thus the "emergency" state of women's shelters characterizes not only the context in which a woman might seek temporary residence, but also speaks to the overall social and political context where many women fleeing abuse, especially those with children, have few opportunities to establish stable households. Considering the overarching neoliberal regulatory context that affects both service providers and service users, women with precarious status are constructed as a financial burden, relative to women who have status, because they are less able to perform up to the standards of neoliberal citizenship through paid work and self-sufficiency.

Negotiating Social Rights Relative to Immigration Status in Canada

The following shelter-based service provider's narrative illustrates the contrasting frameworks for defining rights as universal – invoking the

Canadian Charter of Rights and Freedoms or international conventions – versus a privilege of citizenship:

> Priorities change as soon as people's status changes as well. When you do not have status, any small thing is a big thing, is a big deal. If I get just a little appointment at the community health centre, it's a big achievement, when you do not have status. When you are a refugee claimant, you have access to medical attention, but you want to go to university. So that's your dilemma. When you're a [legal permanent] resident, you can now access medical attention, but you want to leave the country more frequently. You see, people's priorities change when their status changes ... Citizens have such high expectations in terms of what they want to achieve. So different from the person without status. It is heart breaking ... once you are in the ground level, anything would be a benefit. But it shouldn't be that way. Because medical attention for a pregnant woman, it shouldn't be a privilege, it should be a right.

Several participants in this study talked about rights that the women they work with *should* have, some even referencing the Canadian Charter of Rights and Responsibilities. However, eligibility and access to health and social services are legislated through a combination of federal, provincial, and municipal laws. In this context, non-governmental service providers play a critical role in supporting women's claims to social rights by linking women with community resources and helping them access resources that may protect them from their abusers without increasing their risk of deportation (Nankani, 2000).

Due to the large proportion of residents who are involved in the immigration process, shelter staff often function as immigration advocates. Basok illustrates how social exclusion of migrants is perpetuated through depriving migrants of "the *knowledge*, skills and support required to *negotiate* their rights effectively" (Basok, 2004, emphasis in original). Knowledge about immigration law similarly affects providers' ability to advocate for their clients' rights. Shelter staff and management staff report having varying levels of knowledge about immigration policy and thus employ different strategies to connect women with immigration advice and obtain public funds to pay for legal representation to support women's applications for social and health benefits. In one shelter, a frontline staff person was a former immigration paralegal who assisted women in making informed decisions about immigration options and in filling out immigration applications. Other service providers rely on pro bono immigration lawyers to consult with residents who might be interested in making a refugee or humanitarian claim. Access to and participation in the production of legal immigration knowledge is often a determining factor in whether women with precarious status make rights-based claims and if their claims-making activities are successful.

As part of their comprehensive advocacy, service providers in shelters typically assist women in applying for public benefits for themselves and their children. The standardized practice of shelter intake is to inquire about a woman's eligibility for social assistance, social or subsidized housing, and other supports. Invoking empowerment principles, shelter workers portray their role as presenting "options" to women who do not have status, which may include applying for a refugee or humanitarian claim in order to – at least temporarily – access social rights.

> We try to really leave it up to the client to decide what she wants to do. We want to present all the options and we're not trying to be unrealistic about what the possibilities are and what they are not. But you know, she may not know all of the possibilities, so we provide as much information as we can, but it's up to her to decide." (shelter-based service provider)

Within the process of facilitating women's decision making, service providers do encourage non-status women to apply for immigration status as a primary strategy to bring women into the boundaries of formal membership in Canada's welfare state. Advocates differ, however, in their assessment of the potential risks and benefits associated with this strategy. Applying for status can expose women to the potential risk of the denial of their application and their forced removal (i.e., deportation) from Canada. Despite the low odds of achieving status, some shelter workers talk about having "hope" when assisting a woman to apply for a refugee claim or humanitarian and compassionate considerations application. Others are more forthcoming about the low probability of a woman's successful application and discuss the potential dangers of encouraging migrant women to enter into the surveillance of the immigration regime.

Practices within the shelter that encourage women onto the legal path towards obtaining social rights could be interpreted as a form of disciplining in accordance with neoliberal values of citizenship as an earned right. Some service providers constructed women who had lived without status for long periods – ten to fifteen years – prior to coming to the shelter as survivors who might be better off not applying for status, which, if denied, would lead to a warrant for their arrest and deportation. The characterization of these women as able to survive on their own without government assistance may indirectly reinforce neo-liberal values of self-sufficiency. Alternatively, perceiving some women who remain without status and live under the radar as "better off" re-inforces tolerance for "illegality" and acceptance of the stark realities that women and their children endure without the rights of citizenship.

"I Know How to Pick My Battles": Advocating for Non-status Women

Advocacy for women without status represents the most challenging dimension of service delivery in the VAW shelter and often requires workers to challenge policies and practices across social and health ser-vice sectors. Service providers regularly utilize their personal contacts and networks to secure resources unique to a woman's case – asking a friend who is a dentist to provide free emergency dental care, work-ing with a landlord to allow a woman to rent an apartment without the first and last months' deposit. Some shelters help women pay for im-migration application fees, or in cases where a woman and her children are scheduled to be deported, raise basic funds to support the family's return to their country of origin. Service providers also advocate for in-dividual clients when brokering with immigration officials to delay the date of deportation, to allow a woman and her children to reside in the shelter up until a scheduled deportation date (rather than be detained in the detention centre), or to secure access to basic health insurance through the Interim Federal Health Program.

Proactively notifying immigration authorities that a woman is resid-ing in a shelter is a last-resort strategy for women who are vulnera-ble to deportation due to an abusive partner or other service providers who might divulge their whereabouts to immigration officials. In one case, a woman who was in her third term of pregnancy had arrived in the shelter with a deportation warrant. After consultation, the shel-ter worker used her contacts in the Canada Border Services Agency (CBSA) to alert them of the woman's presence in the shelter. Because the shelter worker was able to convince CBSA that this woman was not a flight risk, they authorized her access to the Interim Federal Health

Program (temporary health insurance for refugees, asylum seekers, and protected persons) and delayed her deportation date until after the birth of her child. Although deportation was imminent for this woman, access to health care at a critical time in her pregnancy and the extra time in Canada supported her and her child's health, while also buying her more time to complete an application for permanent residence on humanitarian and compassionate grounds.

The following excerpt highlights the calculations that inform the use of this potentially risky strategy:

> I hope that there is a certain level of humanity there, when they [immigration authorities] are receiving information because I'm not calling about any criminal, I'm calling about women who are having a difficult time. And I know how to pick my battles. I'm not gonna call if I feel it's not gonna fly. I know how to pick my battles. (shelter worker).

While these advocacy strategies for individual women can minimize the negative impact of a sudden deportation or connect a woman with vital resources (e.g., to complete a pregnancy in Canada), these advocacy strategies do not address broader structural issues of inequality and exclusion.

Navigating Different Levels of Government to Gain Access to Services

Structural or policy advocacy took form when shelter staff worked across the VAW sector to secure entitlements from different levels of government. Service providers expressed uncertainty over whose jurisdiction provided different types of funding and how identifying information was shared across different levels of government. Since the passage of the Canada Health and Social Transfer in 1995, the federal government transfers funds for social and health programs for provinces to administer while drastically cutting spending on these programs (Doherty, Friendly, & Oloman, 1998). The downloading of responsibility continues on from provincial to municipal governments. In this context, the City of Toronto is currently responsible for administering a range of programs (e.g., Ontario Works, the provincial welfare payment program), each with different sources of funding and agreements with regard to eligibility criteria and information sharing among different levels of government.

As compared to the federal and provincial governments, the City of Toronto has the broadest definition of inclusion; it states that city services are open to all residents of Toronto. In practice, however, inclusion pivots around the source of funding and related eligibility criteria that the City of Toronto must adhere to when administering a program. Universal social entitlements with the broadest eligibility are also the most stringently regulated by the federal or provincial government. For example, gaining access to the Ontario Health Insurance Plan, the universal health coverage for qualified residents of Ontario, requires multiple forms of identification to prove your citizenship/immigration status in Canada and verify your residence in Ontario. In contrast, for some programs intended as safety nets, the City of Toronto has maintained looser eligibility criteria (e.g., drop-in centres are open to anyone who crosses the threshold).

The process through which shelter residents apply for and access the Personal Needs Allowance (PNA), a basic cash supplement issued by the city to all shelter residents, exemplifies how service providers make the most of the city's policy of accessibility, while considering the potential risks of information sharing among different levels of government. VAW shelter workers regularly assist women to apply for PNA, which provides a nominal amount of cash (i.e., thirty-five dollars for a single person for one week) to purchase toiletries and other personal needs. Eligibility for the PNA is consistent with the province's welfare-assistance guidelines, making individuals who are receiving welfare payments ineligible for the PNA funds. The provincial eligibility for welfare is limited to citizens, residents, and refugee claimants. However, the City of Toronto leaves the method of distribution to the discretion of the shelter. The City of Toronto currently processes PNA applications that are missing some identity information, which allows people who seek shelter but do not have identity documents – for whatever reason – to receive cash assistance.

While service providers frame the PNA as an entitlement for shelter residents, the following except illustrates how service providers consider the risks associated when residents disclose identity information that could be shared among government agencies:

> If she wants to receive PNA, personal needs allowance, that is money coming from the City. Any woman living in a shelter is entitled to receive that money, however, women with nonstatus, especially women with the deportation orders or warrant for arrest need to be aware that if they were to

receive that money, it could happen that their name could be pulled out, because [of] the connection between Ontario Works and Immigration. It is clear that there is a connection. It is clear that they share information. It is absolutely clear that it is happening. (shelter service provider)

Service providers employed a range of tactics to minimize the potential risk of immigration surveillance by encouraging women to apply for the PNA but leave out their social insurance number, or in other cases by encouraging women to use a pseudonym in addition to omitting the social insurance number. Some service providers would also discourage non-status women from applying for the PNA altogether. The range of strategies to support women's claims to PNA reflected the general unease service providers expressed over bringing visibility to their work with women with precarious status, with many providers preferring to keep this work "under the radar." The administration of the PNA provides the City of Toronto with a mechanism to deliver on their promise that city services will be open to all residents of Toronto. The practice of information sharing between the federal and provincial governments, however, raises the risks for individuals seeking social assistance when residing in emergency shelters.

Deflecting Immigration Control in Violence against Women Spaces

Responding to more overt immigration enforcement practices represents one of the most divisive issues among shelters at the time of this study. Many VAW shelters are in the process of developing internal policies for responding when Canada Border Services Agency (CBSA) agents or the Toronto police appear at the shelter. The Toronto police continue to share information with CBSA despite community mobilization to encourage the police to ensure "access without fear" to all city residents (Nyers, Zerehi, & Wright, 2006). In November 2008, Toronto police chief Bill Blair publicly asserted that Toronto police are required to share information about non-status persons with immigration officials, in compliance with Canadian federal law (despite alternative interpretations of federal law offered by immigrant rights attorneys). The implications of information sharing between the police and immigration enforcement are particularly frightening for abused women, who may be wary of turning to the police for help in order to avoid being forcibly uprooted from Canada.

After learning about incidences of immigration officers appearing at VAW shelters, the grassroots organization No One Is Illegal – Toronto launched a campaign "to mobilize the anti-VAW sector to support the call for status for all women surviving violence" (Fariah Chowdhury, personal communication; see Fortier, in this volume, for more on No One is Illegal movements in Canada). In November 2008, the Shelter I Sanctuary I Status campaign initiated a collective stance among VAW service providers and service users to oppose CBSA agents appearing at violence against women organizations to arrest women on immigration charges. Service providers across Toronto expressed differing views, however, about the risks involved in overtly taking a stance in opposition to immigration enforcement. While several shelters and support services readily joined the campaign, some organizations expressed fear that by confronting CBSA, they would invite public scrutiny of their support for non-status women, which could jeopardize their funding. Organizations also expressed fear that such political activity would be detrimental to the safety of women in their shelters, by raising their visibility to CBSA and other immigration officials.

Service providers' varied response to the symbolic language used in the Shelter I Sanctuary I Status campaign exemplifies the conflicting political positions within the violence against women sector. Some service providers and organizations articulate support for the campaign and take part in community-organizing events. Others are cautious of being portrayed as a "sanctuary" for women without status. Still others are critical of community-organizing tactics that have brought media attention to women's shelters that house women without status.

Within this contentious political climate, one shelter administrator deploys the term "precarious status" to communicate to her board that the majority of shelter residents are "legal"; they have some sort of status and are somewhere in the process of seeking permanent residence through the legal immigration system:

> We've been using the term "precarious status" for women who are still involved with the immigration system in some way and haven't managed to attain their landed status or citizenship ... We found that most women are in fact somewhere in the legal process. You know they are either in the refugee process or they have applied and have been turned down and they're about to make an appeal. Or they've applied for an H&C or you know they're somewhere in that process ... But almost all of the women

that we serve are somewhere in that process which I think is a really important clarification which we wanted to bring to our board.

Goldring and Landolt's (2009a) conceptualization of "precarious status," invoking the uncertainty and potential deportability of migrants who are not permanent residents in Canada, is akin to Cecilia Menjívar's (2006) theorization of "liminal legality" experienced by undocumented immigrants from Central America residing in the United States. Yet the use of this term in the excerpt above illustrates how an administrator constructs women with precarious status as "legally present" to garner support from her board of directors (and ostensibly their funding support). By constructing some women as legal/legitimate, the byproduct of women who are "illegal" is left unchallenged, thus reinforcing lines of exclusion within anti-violence against women spaces. The above statement also exemplifies the political climate within non-profit organizations that may vocalize their broad support for women's rights, yet seek to preserve an image as law abiding in deference to their government funders.

In an unusual example of negotiations between community organizers, service providers, and the federal government, in July 2010 the Shelter | Sanctuary | Status campaign brokered a deal with the regional director of CBSA in Toronto to prohibit immigration enforcement in violence against women spaces. Previously, the Shelter | Sanctuary | Status campaign had engaged in popular education and community-organizing activities, including dozens of workshops with VAW service providers, teach-ins for VAW shelter residents, marches and demonstrations at the Bureau of Immigration Affairs offices in Toronto, a press conference highlighting immigration enforcement in VAW shelters, a letter-writing campaign demanding that border service agents cease attending women's shelters in Toronto, and a protest that led to the regional CBSA director's office. Following these actions, CBSA's Toronto regional director agreed to sit down to negotiations with members of the campaign, including several executive directors of violence against women service providers.

Unfortunately, despite the success of organizing against local officials within the bureaucracy of the CBSA, the mobilization of violence against women organizations to support women fleeing abuse, irrespective of their status, led CBSA to issue a national policy, authorizing CBSA officers to enter VAW shelters if they suspect a woman is a threat to national security. The national directive, issued 14 February 2011, was developed without any consultation with women's organizations and replaced the directive issued by the Toronto Regional Office of CBSA that had been endorsed by violence against women organizations. In response to the new CBSA policy, anti-violence organizations renewed their commitment to support women fleeing abuse, irrespective of their status. Eileen Morrow of the Ontario Association of Interval and Transition Houses states:

> Services that work with women and children who experience violence are dedicated to keeping women safe from violence and maintaining their confidentiality. That is our mandate and it is the mandate of all services that work to end violence against women. We'll continue to follow that mandate. If CBSA isn't prepared to comply with the Charter of Rights and Freedoms in Canada, we still are. Services will need to make decisions about how they can do that to protect women and their children from violence. (personal communication, 14 February 2011)

Through community organizing with the Shelter | Sanctuary | Status campaign, service providers are advocating for their right to provide services to women regardless of their status in Canada. Challenging immigration enforcement practices at the local level in Toronto is one strategy that service providers have employed to secure space within violence against women shelters for all women fleeing abuse. While the impact of CBSA's national directive for violence against women's shelters is yet unknown, the negotiation with CBSA's regional office provides an example of how violence against women service providers who take part in community organizing seek to influence local decision makers within the bureaucracies of Canadian immigration in support of women's rights to access services without fear of deportation.

Conclusion

In this chapter, I illustrated how violence against women service providers negotiate social rights and social membership in the process of their service delivery to women with precarious migratory status. Within the complex terrain of funding, access to social services, and securitization, shelter staff advocate to expand membership and secure social rights for shelter residents. The ability of service providers to deflect immigration enforcement or publicly challenge state regulation of migrants, however, operates in tension with deference to federal legal constructions of immigration status and neoliberal values of citizenship. The response to women who seek services also depends on staff members' level of knowledge, their confidence in navigating immigration policies, and their political commitment to critique the role that immigration policy plays in gender-based violence. These factors contribute to significant variability in service delivery to women with precarious status.

I show that VAW shelters employ their pre-existing principles grounded in feminism to extend belonging in the shelter to all women fleeing abuse (cf. Basok 2004). Service providers' efforts to expand membership beyond the shelter and to connect to a broader range of social and health services, however, is less than complete and is potentially vulnerable to surveillance from funders and from immigration enforcement agencies (Daniels 1997). I would add that the diverse social issues that accompany the women who seek shelter are insufficiently addressed within shelters, and, in the case of immigration, are perceived as too volatile for the VAW sector to incorporate into their political activities.

Violence against women organizations make a strategic choice to avoid direct conflict with the politics of immigration in order to maintain public support and funding. However, by aligning with the state, service providers fail to address how a major social institution – immigration – shapes the experiences of racialized women contending with domestic violence. Shelter staff do support women with precarious status who seek shelter, but they also maintain a certain "respect" for the law. They comply and cooperate with immigration enforcement practices and restrictions on access to service for non-status women. Service providers support women's rights to flee violence and call for broad changes in immigration policies that contribute to migrant women's vulnerability. Yet few are willing to directly challenge state practices that inflict structural violence on racialized migrant women. Community organizers active in the Shelter l Sanctuary l Status campaign viewed resistance from violence against women organizations as fundamentally racist.

Immigrant women and children with precarious status remain a vulnerable population with limited access to resources in times of crisis. While the exercise of discretionary powers in everyday interactions with immigrants provides social service providers with tangible opportunities to advance the human rights of individuals regardless of status, federal authority to manage the boundaries of citizenship continues to influence service delivery through both overt enforcement and bureaucratic management of identifying information. Service providers are uniquely positioned to develop individual, organizational, and policy alternatives to redress the current state of injustice facing migrants with precarious status in Canada and other immigrant receiving nations. They may face significant social costs in doing so, but the costs to those marginalized by exclusionary practices of citizenship in the process of service delivery is even greater.

13 Getting to "Don't Ask Don't Tell" at the Toronto District School Board: Mapping the Competing Discourses of Rights and Membership

FRANCISCO VILLEGAS

In 2007, the Toronto District School Board (TDSB) unanimously passed the "Students Without Legal Immigration Status Policy" (TDSB, 2007). This policy, also known as a "Don't Ask Don't Tell" (DADT) policy, stipulated that the board would "protect the rights of children and their families by not asking for, reporting or sharing information about any student's or a student's family's immigration status" (TDSB, 2007, p. 2). DADT came as a result of community pressure against the non-compliance of Ontario school districts with Section 49.1 of the Ontario Education Act, which already delineated the right of students to attend schools regardless of immigration status. While the passing of the DADT policy became a major victory for community organizers, it has yet to be fully implemented and students continue to be shut out of the schooling process. This chapter explores how discourses of membership affect how three groups of stakeholders engage with the inclusion of precarious status students in Toronto schools. I will argue that discursive understandings about this population, as well as the employment of specific discourses of membership, affect how stakeholders engage with this issue as well as the range of possibilities imagined or sought. As such, discourses of membership have material consequences for the daily lives of precarious status migrants.

Conceptual Framework

This chapter uses the concepts of discourse, counter-narratives, and precarious immigration status. I begin by defining the ways I employ these concepts, starting with "precarious immigration status.". I use this term because it allows for the possibility of fluctuations in immigration status across time and space, as well as varying "gradations" of status (Goldring et al., 2007; Goldring and Landolt, in this volume). I focus on those I believe live in the greatest state of precarity: people who no longer have the possibility of moving through the gradations of immigration status and are in constant jeopardy of being deported. This includes individuals who have had a refugee claim denied and have no other options in the immigration system, as well as those who have had a visa expire or entered the country without state-sanctioned documents and plan to remain in Canada. For those with no remaining options through the immigration system, the precarity of their status does not stem from the possibility of losing status, but rather, the permanence of being out of status.

In this chapter, "discourse" refers to "regulated practices that account for a number of statements, that is, the unwritten rules and structures which produce particular utterances and statements" (Mills, 2003, p. 53). Statements include both verbal and written expressions that come together around a particular theme. There is no singular discourse; rather, discourses are contentious and often vie for primacy. This primacy is based on power, as "discourse transmits and produces power; it reinforces it, but also undermines it and exposes it, renders it fragile and makes it possible to thwart it" (Mills, 2003, p. 54).

Because there is no singular discourse, the concept of counter-narratives can be used to clarify how contending discourses arise. Latina/o critical race theory (LatCrit) writers have used counter-narratives to explore the experiences within schooling institutions (Bernal, 2002; Fernandez, 2002; Solorzano & Bernal, 2001; Solorzano & Yosso, 2001). According to Fernandez (2002), a counter-narrative "subverts the dominant story or the reality that is socially constructed ... it places the truthfulness and 'objectivity' of the narrative in question" (p. 48). This is done in order to "challenge, displace, or mock ... pernicious narratives and beliefs" (Delgado & Stefancic, 2000, p. 43). This chapter focuses on counter-narratives that are developed by migrant rights organizations to counteract exclusionary discourses of membership. These contending discourses bring into question the boundaries drawn by institutional practices and laws. They place the affected individual at the centre of the analysis by exposing the inequities experienced by precarious status migrants in the context of schooling.

Discourses shape people's perception of the world and how they imagine possible solutions to social problems. In other words, they set the terms of reference as well as the boundaries of any given problem. A contending discourse can therefore offer alternative solutions not considered possible within other discourses. In the context of schooling, several discourses of membership arise. The most obvious is a dichotomy between access and exclusion, but others are also in play, and often include various understandings of what constitutes access as well as who is considered a legitimate recipient of this public good. These discursive formations become apparent in organizations' mission statements, directives, actions, and the literature they publish.

The ways in which an issue and its solutions are framed provide insight into how it is understood, as well as the interplay of race and class underpinning these understandings. Some discourses of membership simultaneously advocate for what is considered to be access to schools while positioning migrants in ways that rob them of agency or criminalize their presence. For example, strict legal frameworks may emphasize the Convention on the Rights of the Child as a reason to provide schooling opportunities to precarious status children while at the same time criminalizing their parents for transgressing the rule of law. Reliance on such non-critical discourses serves to de-emphasize the effects of race and other intersecting influences relevant to the lived experiences of the affected population. Such discourses are also based on ideals about the population that presuppose the innocence of children (permitting the request of access for those within a specific age) while criminalizing adults or those transitioning into adulthood.

Methods

This chapter applies three types of data: semi-structured interviews, grey literature, and experiential knowledge. In 2009, semi-structured interviews were conducted with five key social actors involved in the discussions and negotiations concerning access to schooling for precarious status migrants.[1] Interviewees included members of grass-roots organizations (the Education Rights Task Force and the Don't Ask Don't Tell coalition) and individuals at three levels of the TDSB bureaucracy (a senior executive official, a long-standing trustee, and a member of an advisory committee to the TDSB). All interviews were then transcribed and coded for themes.

Data also included "grey documents," limited-circulation material that includes memos from Citizenship and Immigration Canada, the Ministry of Education, and the TDSB to individuals within the board, as well as pamphlets and flyers created by activist organizations, including No One Is Illegal – Toronto, the Don't Ask Don't Tell coalition, and the Education Rights Task Force. These documents provide a historical context for how various institutional actors have understood membership and the actions and solutions they have imagined to be possible.

Finally, given my background as a member of the Don't Ask Don't Tell coalition and the Education Not Deportation campaign, my analysis applies some of my experiences as a coalition representative in various meetings with school board officials regarding ongoing concerns about student exclusion and DADT policy implementation. By attending such meetings and participating in the community organizing group, I have learned how the problem is understood by various actors and gained insight into the way the board operates.

Analysis

This analysis is organized into four sections. First, I identify the legal and institutional context within which the DADT policy emerged in Toronto. Second, I discuss three contending discourses of membership that different groups of stakeholders invoke to make sense of access to schooling for precarious status students. The third section focuses on the method employed by each group to discuss access to schooling. Finally, I analyse the solutions proposed by each group, as well as two different interpretations of a policy implementation plan.

Historical and Policy Context

Legal changes and policy shifts do not happen spontaneously. In the case of DADT at the Toronto District School Board, community mobilization and the eventual passage of the DADT policy involved a number of important changes. In 1989, the Convention on the Rights of the Child was adopted by the United Nations. Canada ratified the convention but to date has not fully implemented it in domestic law. However, ratification opened a way for children's rights to become a focus for policy and advocacy. In 1993, schooling advocates successfully lobbied the province to change the Ontario Education Act, allowing for the legal access of some precarious status migrants to the school system. According to the new Section 49.1, "A person who is otherwise entitled to be admitted to a school and who is less than eighteen years of age shall not be refused admission because the person or the person's parent or guardian is unlawfully in Canada." Before this change, the Education Act was more ambiguous as to who could be granted access, leading to case-by-case decisions. Advocates hoped that Section 49.1 would clear up any ambiguities.

However, ambiguities did arise. Those not "entitled to admission," according to Section 49.1, include individuals who hold a valid visa (visitor, study permit, etc.); this makes them liable for tuition fees. Therefore, "admission" in Section 49.1 refers to admission without a fee, which is available to citizens and permanent residents under the law. Study permits and visas are examples of where schooling and immigration policies converge to increase precarity. Every year students outside of Canada apply to the federal government for a study permit. To qualify, they must undergo a highly classist, racist, and ableist process that requires proof of sufficient funds to pay international tuition and live in Canada, as well as a health exam if applying from a list of non-Western countries. These individuals are highly sought after by school boards, as they become sources of revenue: the TDSB charges ten to twelve thousand dollars in tuition fees per student.

A second contextual element is the institutional restructuring that occurred in 1998/1999 in Toronto. At this time six municipalities were amalgamated into the new City of Toronto and seven different school boards were folded into the TDSB. This created the largest school board in the country, with roughly 30,000 employees, 265,000 students across 560 schools, and a budget of more than two billion dollars (Anderson & Jaafar, 2003; TDSB, 2010). The restructuring of the schooling system has been marked by budget cuts and considerable loss of school-level and classroom-level autonomy over budget planning and curriculum. The logic of fiscal responsibility and "risk management" has filtered into most arenas of decision making, including discussions about access to schooling for precarious status migrants.

A third contextual element is the Education Rights Task Force (ERT), which was established in 1999 and is primarily composed of members of the Toronto legal community. The ERT successfully lobbied for the inclusion of Section 49.1 as well as a change to Section 49.7 of the Ontario Education Act. Section 49.7 was changed because some school officials interpreted existing policy in a way that required precarious status students to apply for study permits in order to be enrolled. The danger for these students was that by applying for a study permit they would make themselves known to immigration authorities, something they may not want to do. The minister of education at the time, Eleanor Kaplan, clarified the policy at the ERT's behest.

The inclusion of Section 49.1 and the change to Section 49.7 of the Ontario Education Act were important. However, despite this legislation, access to public schooling for precarious status students remained informal and discretionary before the emergence of the DADT policy. Interviews with school board trustees, legal aid workers, and members of the ERT confirmed that people often encountered difficulties when enrolling, and obstacles to access were handled on a case-by-case basis. Furthermore, the changes to the Ontario Education Act did not protect students from immigration enforcement on school property.

In 2006, the issue of access to schooling for precarious status migrants caught the attention of the media and public when two Toronto Catholic School Board students, Kimberly and Gerald Lizano-Sossa, were apprehended by immigration authorities while at school. This highlighted the disparities between international and provincial law – specifically Sections 49.1 and 49.7 of the Ontario Education Act – and the school board's policy, establishing the need for schools as sanctuary zones in ensuring safe access to schooling. Following the detention and eventual deportation of the Lizano-Sossa family, groups of stakeholders weighed in on the issue, and after the mobilization of a campaign by the Don't Ask Don't Tell coalition, the TDSB passed a policy in 2007. Organizers believed that this policy eliminated the barriers to enrolment for precarious status students, a feat that had not been accomplished through provincial legislation. However, similar to the provincial ministry, the TDSB has been slow to ensure implementation of the policy, and students continue to be excluded from schooling.

Discourses

This section focuses on three contending discourses of membership. These emerged from organizations with very different backgrounds: the ERT, the TDSB, and the Don't Ask Don't Tell coalition.

As mentioned above, the ERT was established in 1999 primarily by members of the legal community. In an interview, a member of the task force stated that the ERT was "set up to act as an umbrella group for other groups: legal aid clinics, parents, children and educators to advocate for kids whose parents have ambiguous immigration status." According to the respondent, the group had a "very defined agenda." Relying on discourses of membership based on legal rights, including the UN Convention on the Rights of the Child, they focused their efforts exclusively on children, and more specifically on precarious status children. However, while their target population did not have full immigration status, the ERT worked solely on the right to schooling, not migrant rights. This is not to say that members were not involved in migrant rights struggles, but the ERT was conceptualized in a very specific manner so as to work only on issues regarding access to schooling. As such, a member of the task force explained that the group defined the agenda as "ensuring that schooling is a universal right" and "every child should go to school."

Prior to the time that the ERT was most active, there was little policy recourse at the provincial level regarding the enrolment of precarious status students. Because they worked under a juridical discursive framework where membership and access to school were based on legal rights, it was necessary for the ERT to attach themselves to discourses of membership that followed law, and specifically the UN Convention on the Rights of the Child. Under this convention and the discourse stemming from it, all children were understood as having full membership rights in the context of schooling. Membership, however, was not extended to adult learners or visa holders. Furthermore, as mentioned above, while immigration status was seen as an obstacle to the enrolment of children into schools, the ERT did not see itself as a migrant rights organization – they did not see their work as including broader immigration reform. This example demonstrates how law and policy can frame a discourse of membership that, while extending rights to an often-excluded group, can still reinforce or uphold the parameters by which "legitimate" membership is constructed.

The second discourse emerged from the TDSB's policies for enrolling precarious status students. Prior to the passage of the DADT policy, precarious status students were enrolled into TDSB schools on a case-by-case basis at the discretion of trustees and senior officials. The DADT policy was introduced to the board by two sympathetic trustees, who worked with community organizers to engage with the board strategically. However, many TDSB trustees disagreed with the DADT policy. Despite the Ontario Education Act, intended to ensure access to public schooling for precarious status migrants, during board discussions various trustees expressed concerns regarding the passing of this policy and the affected population.

These discussions resulted in a discourse of membership based on a tension between four concerns: legal rights as stipulated by the Ontario

Education Act; questions regarding the well-being of children; criminalizing ideas about precarious status migrants; and concerns over the board's potential loss of revenue. As will be discussed below, this discourse was superseded by a strategic counter-narrative created by the DADT coalition, whereby a decision against DADT was portrayed to the media as being in favour of "keeping children out of schools."

During committee meetings and at large board meetings, trustees voiced nativist as well as financial concerns. They raised questions about the overall eligibility of precarious status students to access public goods, the possibility of enrolling children with communicable diseases, and the loss of international tuition revenues, as well as concerns about possible abuse and fraud. Some trustees worried that current international visa students would decide to opt out of status to receive free schooling. Trustees were concerned that the policy would act as a "global beacon" to all migrants regarding free schooling in Toronto. These concerns revealed how institutional stakeholders within a purportedly liberal institution articulate notions of membership and draw the boundaries of membership in ways that exclude individuals constructed as non-citizens from public entitlements. Furthermore, suggestions that migrants would rush to give up their status to take advantage of free schooling reflects trustees' lack of understanding about the ramifications of being out of status in Canada, including the inability to procure health care and limited access to police services. They also reflect a long history of criminalizing tropes associated with border crossing, immigration, and precarious status migrants in particular.

The DADT policy was passed unanimously, but the policy has yet to be fully implemented despite the existence of an implementation plan voted on by trustees. This plan included training of all staff in new enrolment procedures, changing the enrolment form, and the creation of public information materials to publicize the policy. However, this plan has encountered a number of difficulties, including continued concerns that too much publicizing of the policy will have negative consequences including the possibility of abuse and fraud by individuals considered outside the boundaries of membership. The concerns voiced about pre- and post-DADT display a criminalizing and racist discursive construction of precarious status migrants. Thus, while on paper the policies have changed, the discourse and practice have remained the same.

The third discourse in this debate involved grass-roots activists. In 2006 when the Lizano-Sossas were apprehended on school grounds, the Don't Ask Don't Tell coalition was already mobilizing in Toronto. It demanded access to city services for precarious status migrants and an information wall between municipal service providers and immigration authorities. The DADT coalition was multisectoral and drew on a wide-ranging set of resources, ways of doing politics, political skill sets, and agendas: it included labour unions, individuals in the health sector, people from the legal community, and members of No One Is Illegal – Toronto.

No One Is Illegal set the discursive terms for the coalition, including a framework that decriminalized precarious status migrants and called for a stop to all deportations (see Fortier, this volume). In a way, the name of the group is as much a counter-narrative as a group philosophy. It sets out how precarious status migrants are conceptualized and counters the predominant perception of that population as "illegal."

By making various demands, No One Is Illegal created a contending discourse of membership based on residence rather than legal policies or immigration status. The fact that an individual currently resides in a particular community is the only prerequisite for membership and having the right to all social goods, including formal citizenship. No One Is Illegal sees its work on various campaigns around specific access issues (schooling, violence against women shelters, police services, etc.) as contributing to a wider agenda of redefining membership and mobilizing for comprehensive immigration reform. This counter-narrative is centred on the lives of precarious status migrants and is based on a contending discourse of membership whereby membership is not exclusive but rather must be readily available to all residents of the community (see P. Villegas, in this volume).

Method of Intervention

The discursive framework used by each group to mobilize their claims about membership also influenced their method(s) of intervention. Here, "method of intervention" refers to the practices and strategies used by stakeholders to advocate for extending access to schooling for precarious status students. This includes how the directly affected population is engaged or excluded from the process of intervention, as well as how the particular organization positions itself in relation to the problem. As discussed in the last section of this chapter, the choices made by stakeholders have long- and short-term ramifications for outcomes.

As noted, the ERT used the UN Convention on the Rights of the Child as the basis of their work. Given the particular expertise of its members, it sought to influence policy makers in order to generate legislative changes regarding how access to schooling is configured for precarious status migrants. ERT focused on highlighting the dissonance between international law (to which Canada is a signatory) and what was happening on the ground. Their primary method involved lobbying the government through formal channels. They also implemented letter-writing campaigns targeting ministers of education, as well as generating media interest . Through it all, the message centred upon the conflict between the exclusion of students on the basis of their immigration status and the rule of law.

The methods employed by the ERT reflected their perception of the situation. Given the discourse of law, membership in the context of schooling was understood as encompassing those with a legal right to it. Therefore, the ERT implemented strategies involving informing and pressuring legal and institutional bodies to enforce such policies. This process is severely limited given the ways in which the law defines certain individuals as "illegal" (Calavita, 1998; de Genova, 2005) and, as such, as non-members and illegitimate recipients of public social goods.

The TDSB created a number of limitations involving the proceduralized ways it engaged in the discussion of access to schooling for precarious status students. These acted as barriers for many wishing to communicate and engage in making change with the board, both at the time of the introduction of the DADT policy and currently with regard to its implementation. The TDSB is an immense bureaucracy, which makes change difficult and time consuming. While the DADT coalition was successful in navigating the bureaucracy of the TDSB, this bureaucratic process served to alienate many people. During committee hearings, only individuals who had formally requested time to make deputations were allowed to address committee members. All others, while allowed to witness the proceedings, were expected to remain quiet. Similarly, in the at-large meeting with all board trustees, only trustees and TDSB officers were allowed to speak – and the latter only when asked a question. This process of dialogue made for an intricate system, wherein only those familiar with it could participate and where interventions needed to be highly focused. Thus, in addition to the criminalizing and racist discourse expressed by decision makers within the TDSB, the bureaucracy that guides the board also creates a highly exclusionary system.

The bureaucracy of the TDSB affects not only community engagement but also how policy is implemented. In some ways, the methods of implementation employed by the board mirror the discourses exhibited during board meetings. Because trustees were fearful of potential abuse and questioned the legitimacy of receiving public goods like schooling, this discourse carried over to TDSB employees as they attempted to navigate a plan of implementation that could reach the targeted population without appearing to "encourage" migrants to opt out of status or to "set a global beacon" of free Canadian schooling.

Within the TDSB, the Student and Community Equity Office is formally responsible for implementing these changes. This office is quite small and is responsible for vetting and overseeing every equity agenda that comes to the board. Implementation requires the Equity Office to negotiate with different departments about a variety of issues related to the policy. In this case, this has included liaising with the Communications Office to develop dissemination materials and adhering to guidelines regarding the content, layout, and length of the enrolment form. Much of the implementation delay has to do with the criminalizing discourse regarding precarious status migrants, the belief that this population is quite small, and the fact that this office is constantly facing a variety of equity concerns. In this context, equity agendas can become zero-sum – attending to one agenda means not attending to another. Given this situation, the inner workings of the bureaucracy and the discursive understanding of the affected population hinder the possibilities for effective intervention and implementation.

The discursive understanding regarding the methods for enacting change is determined by a systematized process that includes very few people. There is also a disconnect between changing policy in writing and its materialization. Policies are passed down to offices within the bureaucracy, but implementation is hampered by the immensity and complexity of the board. Finally, with regard to addressing equity concerns through policy change, public intervention remains necessary even at the phase of policy implementation. In this way, the work of the board becomes downloaded to communities, who must ensure policies materialize before undertaking a different project.

In contrast to the ERT and TDSB, the methods, strategies, and practices of intervention employed by the DADT coalition and No One Is Illegal involved a higher degree of community consultation as well as the inclusion of individuals from diverse arenas (see Fortier, this volume).

Following the arrest and deportation of the Lizano-Sossa children, No One Is Illegal and the DADT coalition created a separate campaign on access to schooling. With this new focus, new voices and organizations began to participate, particularly those already involved with schooling advocacy. While some campaign participants played specific roles according to their profession and skill sets, many were engaged in a variety of facets of the campaign. Those from the legal community prepared a legal opinion explaining the autonomy of the schooling sector (outside the immigration system) and cleared up misinformation regarding the supposed responsibility of employees to report people to immigration authorities. Individuals from teachers' unions helped create spaces where the group could present its platform for a DADT policy. Members of non-school-related labour unions presented deputations at the TDSB explaining the need for their constituents' children to attend school.

Although the arrests of the Lizano-Sossas occurred at a Toronto Catholic District School Board school, one interviewee explained that the coalition "went to the TDSB because we thought if we won any sort of victory there it could set a precedent for other schools because they are the largest." However, this interviewee went on to say that "the response was grim. We were told by the lawyer at the TDSB that implementing such a policy would in fact be asking administrators to break the law, we were told by most trustees that this was not feasible and there wasn't a lot of interest." As a result, the coalition had to develop a strategy to create public pressure as well as dispel myths regarding migrants' inadmissibility. To this end, the coalition "got legal opinions drafted and lawyers to present on the ... Education Act and the section within that stipulates that non-status children should have access to schooling." This demonstrates that the coalition, similar to the ERT before it, also employed a legalistic method of intervention to legitimize their claims to the TDSB. However, to the coalition, the legal opinion did not create the frame of understanding regarding the problem; it became one strategic tool among many.

In addition to their legal opinion, the DADT coalition developed a media strategy to inform the public about the issue in a strategic manner that did not further criminalize or marginalize precarious status migrants. The coalition used the media and public demonstrations as a backdrop to its formal discussions with the school board. This was a learning process: members of the coalition had to learn how to engage the media in a way that reinforced their contending discourse of membership, while still being able to appeal to the public. This method yielded results. As one member of the coalition stated, "the Canada Border Services Agency issued a statement saying that they would not enter schools to do immigration enforcement and we believe that is because they were shamed in a very public way and so many organizations spoke out against it." In addition, the coalition had individuals from a number of sectors and organizations deliver deputations at TDSB board meetings linking this issue to their mission statements:

> youth organizations talk[ed] about community safety and youth being at further risk if not allowed access to school; we had trade unions like the CAW [Canadian Auto Workers] speak to the barriers that face workers who are contributing very significantly to this city's economy yet they are unable to access essential services for their kids such as education.

While the method of involvement for the DADT included a large number of voices, the bureaucratic processes of the TDSB only allowed for a few individuals to speak at committee meetings and none at all at board meetings. As a member of the coalition stated, "In larger board meetings, not the committee meetings, where we didn't have speaking right we went in wearing t-shirts, buttons, stickers and that kind of thing and the presence of the community was strongly felt in all of these meetings." This effort, as well as the legal opinion provided by the coalition, the presence of media, and the support provided through deputation by a myriad of organizations signalled to trustees (who are publically elected) that their decisions were being scrutinized and evaluated. In this way, the campaign was able to shift the predominant discourse to frame a negative decision to DADT as a decision "in favour of keeping children out of school" – a decision no politician considering a future in politics could make.

Range of Solutions

This section analyses the range of possible solutions to ensuring access to schooling for precarious status students considered by each of the three groups under analysis. These solutions are directly related to the discourses of membership employed by each group.

The actions undertaken by the ERT reflect a discursive understanding that the solution would come through governmental intervention and the implementation of existing legislation. Ministers of education were asked to inform school boards of their non-compliance with provincial and international law should they deny access to students with precarious status. This effort resulted in a number of memos explaining Section 49.1 of the Ontario Education Act and how it applied to precarious status migrants. One ERT member told me about a number of these memos from former ministers of education Gerard Kennedy and, later, Kathleen Wynne.

Because this group understood the situation in terms of legal discourse, the method of intervention as well as the solutions offered mirrored this approach. The particular discourse of membership employed in these instances required a legal body to award certain membership rights to the population in question – in this case, children with precarious immigration status and without a current visa. However this policy's definition of a legitimate or deserving member also served to construct or reinforce definitions of non-members and non-beneficiaries. These definitions further illegalized those outside the parameters, as they were further conceptualized as illegitimate or undeserving of public goods.

By the time the DADT policy passed at the TDSB, the ERT was less involved in advocating for access. However, the remaining parties, the TDSB and the DADT coalition, understood the plan for implementation – passed at the same time as the policy – in very different ways. These reveal underlying differences in the way each group conceptualizes membership and rights.

Given the bureaucracy in the TDSB, offices understood the process of policy implementation in terms of efficiency and impact, and gave it a low priority. The Equity Office considered sending out annual memos on the DADT policy as an effective mechanism of dissemination. That office also continues to adhere to the idea that a family having difficulties enrolling their children can simply contact it or ask a legal aid worker to act on their behalf. Similarly, trustees expect migrants to understand how schools are configured and to communicate with them if any problems occur. This creates a practice of downloading responsibility: the board passes a policy and places responsibility for implementation with the Equity Office, even though the Equity Office may not have sufficient resources to do so. In turn, the office downloads responsibility by sending memos to schools and making school administrators responsible. This approach does not take into account the large number of memos administrators receive at the beginning of each year and how overworked frontline staff are. It also presupposes that if at any time a mistake is made, it is the responsibility of the affected party to report it – despite the possible stress and fear associated with doing so. In this way, the board vacillates between a highly formalized system of policy adoption and implementation and a highly informal mechanism for addressing the gaps between policy and practice.

After the passage of the DADT policy at the TDSB, members were too quick to claim victory and the DADT coalition was largely disbanded. Given the lack of implementation of the policy and the continued rejection of students at the TDSB (Sidhu, 2008), No One Is Illegal has now taken the lead in pushing for implementation of the DADT policy. No One Is Illegal clearly has a different understanding of implementation than the TDSB. First, because migrants arrive in Toronto daily, they believe it is imperative that the TDSB advertise their policy on an ongoing basis, so that school staff and the public have a clearer sense of their rights and obligations. In addition, they believe that training and dissemination must go beyond the sending of memos, and developed a video describing the need for policy in all school boards and calling for its implementation at the TDSB (Education Not Deportation Committee, 2009). This video prompted a few meetings with the board to talk about steps to implement the policy.

No One Is Illegal also rejects making precarious status families responsible for their children's right to schooling. As mentioned above, the TDSB often assumes that, faced with obstacles, families will advocate for themselves – by contacting legal aid workers, school trustees, or the Equity Office, who can make a call or write a letter – but this reveals a profound unwillingness to recognize the fear and uncertainty associated with living without status. Faced with perhaps well-intentioned questions from frontline workers in a school, many precarious status migrants will walk away. Some students are even explicitly told that they will not be registered without immigration documents (Sidhu, 2008). All of this can create a pervasive barrier to the enrolment of precarious status students.

No One Is Illegal perceives the school board as an institution that must take a more active role in the well-being of their students. Therefore, they charge the board with the responsibility to advocate for increased access to social services and rights in addition to schooling. They are aware that Toronto schools are severely underfunded, and that the environment for racialized and poor students is violent and consistently pushes students out of the schooling process. Thus, they see the solution as improving social services for precarious status migrants and pushing for comprehensive immigration reform from a number of diverse arenas (health care, post-secondary schooling, shelters, food banks, etc.). This solution aims to improve the life of the migrant while maintaining the end goal of decriminalizing and de-illegalizing all migrants.

Conclusion

Although the DADT policy was passed in 2007, students are still being asked for immigration documents and families are required to advocate for themselves (see Young, in this volume). Through the interview data, I learned that in 2009 one community legal clinic was involved in enrolling more than sixty students. While presumably these students eventually were enrolled in school, it is difficult to know what strategies families without this institutional resource might have used. No information is available about the number of students who were ultimately not enrolled. In addition, students who still hold a valid visa but will remain in the country past its expiration are not eligible to enrol in the TDSB under its DADT policy while it is valid. This creates a lag for many students who cannot afford to pay TDSB rates and can lose a significant part of their schooling.

Both provincial legislation and the DADT policy make an explicit commitment to allow children access to schooling regardless of immigration status. In tracing the various moments in the passage and implementation of DADT at the TDSB, I have identified some of the organizational and discursive reasons for the gap between the law and practice of membership. The ERT, TDSB, and No One Is Illegal have from the start had very different ideas of who is responsible for ensuring precarious status children get to school, the intervention necessary to ensure it, and how precarious status is lived by children and families. The gap between law and practice reveals that citizenship is a practice, not merely a status, and that the boundaries of membership and rights are drawn in day-to-day and local-level negotiations between various individuals. This gap also displays the need for comprehensive immigration reform, as institutional bodies have found it easy to circumvent provincial and school board directives.

NOTE

1 This project, entitled "Negotiating Access to Public Goods: Education and Health Care for Toronto Immigrants with Precarious Status," was headed by Patricia Landolt, funded by CERIS - The Ontario Metropolis Center, and conducted during 2009–2010.

14 No One Is Illegal Movements and Anti-colonial Struggles from within the Nation-State

CRAIG FORTIER

Borders have been used as a colonial tool in North America to divide, to exclude, and to assert nation-state authority over the free movement of people. The Canada–United States border has divided indigenous territories like Awkwesasne in the east and the Coast Salish Territories in the west, just as the United States–Mexico border has divided numerous indigenous territories in the south. The border has been used to create a class of precarious migrant labour, from the Chinese workers who constructed the railroads in the nineteenth century to the Mexican and Caribbean farmworkers who pick fruit and tobacco today. The regulation and control of the supply of cheap exploitable labour is a pivotal feature of migration and border policy.

The modern exercise of state border and immigration policy increasingly extends far beyond the regulation, disciplining, and exclusion of foreign nationals at points of entry. People also *experience* and *resist* borders in a multitude of ways *inside* the nation-state. A high school student is called to the principal's office in the middle of class, where immigration enforcement officials await to take her to detention; a community radio programmer is arrested while at an International Women's Day bake sale at a local university because her exotic dancer visa has expired and she has failed her refugee claim; a gay Nicaraguan youth is forced into hiding because a refugee board member believes he does not look "gay enough" to be granted refugee status; a migrant woman avoids accessing a women's shelter after hearing that immigration enforcement has entered the shelter in her pursuit; a temporary foreign worker program is expanded in order to build sites for the 2010 Olympics in Vancouver on unceded indigenous land. Berinstein et al.

(2006) note that "for non-status immigrants the borderline is not just at physical entry points at ports, airports, or land crossings. Rather the border exists where and whenever they try to access social services" (p. 9). Thus, accessing vital services or simply going about one's daily life as a precarious status person is often a challenge to borders.

While migrant justice organizing has been a consistent part of social movements in Canada for decades, an organized movement challenging the legitimacy of borders and the nation-state is a shift away from traditional left nationalist politics (Sharma, 2003). Slogans these groups put forward such as "no one is illegal," "no borders, no nations, stop the deportations," and "we didn't cross the border, the border crossed us" problematize traditional discourse around citizenship rights and benevolent "host country" claims. Inspiring a variety of creative and complex strategies and tactics, the process of challenging the border has become both instrumental and contradictory in social struggles for migrant rights within nation-states. It has also provided the impetus for a reframing of migrant justice in relation to (and specifically referring to) indigenous sovereignty (Lawrence & Dua, 2005) and rights to the commons (Sharma, 2006). This, in turn, affects the goals, campaigns, tactics, and alliances that emerge within contemporary struggles for migrant justice.

Nationalist, Transnationalist, and Counter-nationalist Frameworks

This chapter looks specifically at movements that reconceptualize borders and, in doing so, rethink ways of removing them. More specifically, the network of No One Is Illegal groups in Toronto, Montreal, and Vancouver will serve as a case study in order to trace an important political shift within the struggle for migrant justice in Canada. While these groups are not fully representative of the diversity of migrant justice organizations adopting an anti-colonial analysis (many of which are directly led and populated by undocumented migrants), the network of No One Is Illegal groups has played a significant role in altering the discursive and political terrain with regard to migration and borders in Canada (see Wright, this volume; also Shantz, 2005; Wright, 2006). Fundamentally, these groups are engaged in negotiating an important shift in theory and political practice: the move from national and transnational frameworks for migrant rights towards anti-colonial/ counter-national frameworks for migrant justice.

What kind of impact does the reframing of these emerging migrant justice movements as anti-colonial, anti-capitalist, anti-imperialist, and/

or counter-nationalist[1] have on strategies and decision making within movements? How do these movements negotiate the contradictions inherent in fighting for regularization while advancing opposition to the legitimacy of borders? What are the implications with respect to the types of societies imagined by these movements?

Social movements focused on migrant rights in Canada within a nationalist or assimilationist theoretical framework have sought improvements in the lives of immigrants and refugees by resisting differentialization (Brubaker, 2001; Kurthen & Heisler, 2009), by promoting multiculturalism (Bloemraad, 2007; Gaonkar & Taylor, 2006; Winter, 2010), and by supporting the settlement needs of immigrant populations (Bai, 1991; Fontaine, 2005). These movements have often provided social services and resources to people who, through displacement and in search of better material conditions, have migrated to Canada.

Social organizing strategies around migrant rights within a nationalist framework have tended to include the formation of settlement houses, English as a second language programming, job search services, and the contradictory struggle between assimilationist and multicultural policies (Brubaker, 2001). Political organizing, however, has for the most part within this framework been centred on the rights of immigrants and refugees *within* the "host" nation-state and tends to be disconnected from movements that focus on displacement, illegalization, and globalization.

Scholars and activists engaged in organizing for migrant rights within a transnational framework have challenged the dominant nationalist discourse theoretically and in practice. They suggest that transnational migrant frameworks are helpful in problematizing the reasons why people migrate in the first place, which is largely left out of nationalist discourse. For instance, Portes et al. (1999) note that transnational migration "commonly developed in reaction to governmental policies and to the condition of dependent capitalism fostered on weaker countries, as immigrants and their families sought to circumvent the permanent subordination to which these conditions condemned them" (p.,220). In organizing within a transnational framework, migrants facing a context of social exclusion and exploitative work conditions in the "host" country develop interlocking systems of solidarity with struggles taking place in countries of origin (Landolt, 2007). Transnational political organizing has an impact on political strategy and culture. In their study of Chilean and Colombian activists in Toronto, Landolt and Goldring (2010), for instance, found that the transnational links between country of origin and the Canadian context produced very different fields of action, including types of campaign, strategies, and relationships with non-migrant organizers in the city. Moreover, the desire of migrants to effect political change in the country of origin often requires a contradictory relationship with the nation-state in which activists are lobbying for better living conditions in Canada while at the same time seeking the Canadian state's support in intervening in an international context (Karpathakis, 1999; Sundar, 2007).

Transnational frameworks also provide a context for resisting the illegalization of migrants. Significant academic work supporting transnational migrant rights organizing has focused on the social construction of "illegal" and/or "undocumented" people (de Genova, 2002, 2007; McNevin, 2006; Peutz, 2006). De Genova (2002) problematizes the construction of migrant "illegality" as deriving from "the law's seemingly uniform application among asymmetrically constituted migrations from distinct countries (p. 424)." Arguing that the immigration system is set up precisely in order to illegalize some migrants (racialized and poor migrants from the Global South) and to fast-track others (wealthy professionals and business people from both Global North and South countries), de Genova (2002) asserts that current immigration legislation in North America is set up to create precarity and uncertainty in the domestic labour market and to maintain an underclass of migrant labour with none of the corresponding rights of permanent residents or citizens.

In Toronto, migrant precarity and legality were addressed at the STATUS Conference in 2004 when community organizers, academics, migrant groups, labour, and allies came together to assert principles of organizing around migrant rights that included calls for the regularization of all undocumented people and the parameters of a national campaign for permanent immigration status. These principles formed part of the foundation of what was emerging as a radical shift in migrant justice organizing in Toronto, Montreal, and Vancouver that was calling for status for all while challenging the legitimacy of borders.

Researchers studying this emerging discourse within migrant justice movements in Canada highlight the greater emphasis on the right to free movement, an anti-capitalist orientation borrowed in part from the global justice movements and the radical anti-racist principles of groups like No One Is Illegal, as departing in some ways from traditional modes of organizing for migrant rights (Basok, 2009; Fortier, 2005; Khandor, McDonald, Nyers, & Wright, 2004; Lowry & Nyers,

2003; Nyers, 2006; Wright, 2006). Focusing specifically on the Canadian context, Wright (in this volume) characterizes movements that seek to legalize undocumented people, that oppose detentions and deportations, and that have no-border/anti-globalization orientations as being bolstered by an anti-imperial lens that also includes oppositions to wars, occupations, and economic devastations, all of which often cause conditions that force people to migrate.

This chapter looks more closely at the key issues that emerge in the shift towards anti-colonial and counter-nationalist migrant justice work in Canada. Moreover, I seek to historicize the emergence of No One Is Illegal groups in Canada and to characterize some of the major theoretical contradictions that these groups attempt to negotiate in practice.

No One Is Illegal and Counter-nationalism in Canada

In 2006, in both Canada and the United States, an organized public movement challenging the illegalization of migrants and the legitimacy of borders emerged in response to significant increases in repression throughout North America. Millions of migrants, people of colour, and allies took to the streets in urban centres throughout the United States in what was called "a day without migrants," a general strike and walk-out flexing the power of migrants in the face of serious racism, xenophobia, and repression. In Canada, the first National Day of Action for Status for All was organized in Montreal, Vancouver, Toronto, and other cities where thousands of people took to the streets in immigrant neighbourhoods in opposition to a repressive shift in immigration enforcement strategies following the election of the Conservative government in late 2005.

The origins of movements organized under the banner "No One Is Illegal" in Canada can be traced to a response to the increased border securitization, tightened immigration policy, and racial profiling that occurred in North America following the attacks of 11 September 2001 (Basok, 2009; Wright, 2006). Heightened anti-terrorism legislation was combined with existing immigration laws to create a state of continual uncertainty and legal precarity for many migrants in Canada. When the Canadian government ended the moratorium on deportations of Algerian refugees in April 2002, Algerian migrants in Montreal organized the Action Committee for Non-Status Algerians and began using increasingly confrontational tactics in order to fight deportations in their community (Lowry & Nyers, 2003). The newly formed No One Is Illegal group in Montreal became intimately involved in supporting the Algerian community in that city and developed a set of demands, including an end to detentions and deportations and immigration status for all, that would become foundational demands for No One Is Illegal groups organized in Toronto, Vancouver, and other cities. In conjunction with the campaign in support of non-status Algerians in Montreal, which included a No One Is Illegal contingent at G8 protests in Ottawa in 2002, organizers from Vancouver, Toronto, Ottawa, and Guelph met in Montreal in February 2003 to host a conference that helped to develop a basis of unity and core demands for the loose coalition of groups.

In Toronto, organizers had also become more invested in issues of borders and migration, particularly within the Ontario Coalition Against Poverty (OCAP), the Campaign to Stop the Secret Trials, and Project Threadbare. The Ontario Coalition Against Poverty, for instance, had adapted its style of direct action casework to support cases of people facing deportations (Shantz, 2005); similarly, organizers within Project Threadbare, including a significant number of newcomer and second-generation immigrant youth and youth of colour, mobilized against the arbitrary arrest, detention, and eventual deportation of twenty-three Pakistani men accused of having links to terrorism (Odartey-Wellington, 2009). The Campaign to Stop the Secret Trials emerged in opposition to the imprisonment of five Muslim men on unsubstantiated terrorism accusations under Canada's security certificate legislation and developed a strong analysis connecting the wars in Iraq and Afghanistan to the rise of Islamophobia, racism, and xenophobia in Canada.

The shift in discourse within these formations towards more anti-colonial and anti-imperial politics differed significantly from other mainstream advocacy efforts for immigration reform in Canada (Shakir, 2007). This, in turn, resulted in more aggressive political tactics that focused less on lobbying the state for immigration reform and more on building community power to openly defy immigration legislation. As one organizer interviewed by Lowry and Nyers in their 2003 study noted:

> The traditional tactics just aren't working. I mean they are actually an abject failure. They try to work within a system, to basically humanize a system that is essentially inhumane ... I think we need to talk and adopt various tactics to the broader strategy of making fundamental policy changes: the regularization of all, amnesties, the treatment of migrant workers. (p. 71).

It is within this context that a No One Is Illegal group premised on similar goals as those set out in Montreal formed in Toronto. Similarly, in Vancouver a No One Is Illegal collective emerged out of organizing taking place under the banner Open the Borders!, which coordinated militant campaigns opposed to deportation and detentions. No One Is Illegal – Vancouver based much of its initial work in building strong relations with Coast Salish indigenous communities in British Columbia (Wright, 2006). This relationship with indigenous sovereignty struggles influenced both the political goals and tactics of No One Is Illegal – Vancouver.

Differing from past national migrant rights networks, No One Is Illegal groups are not organized as a national network, nor are they organized as a coalition. Instead, they are organized as local expressions of a migrant justice framework that is expressly anti-capitalist, opposes borders, fights detentions and deportations, and works in solidarity with indigenous sovereignty struggles. This anti-colonial and counter-nationalist framework produces different discussions, strategies, and tactics in local contexts but is held together by a shared political ideal. Each No One Is Illegal group is organized autonomously from the others, makes its own decisions, decides on its own campaigns and actions, and develops its own relationships to allied groups and communities. This political organization significantly affects the differing campaigns and strategies and provides both a flexibility to adapt to local challenges and a malleability to respond to major shifts in national and international political climates. While maintaining strong allegiance to unifying principles that include an end to detentions and deportations, the implementation of a full and inclusive regularization program for all non-status people, the recognition of indigenous sovereignty, end to war and occupation, and an end to exploitative temporary work programs (No One Is Illegal – Toronto, 2010), each of the autonomous collectives has worked to negotiate these principles within their local context.

The following section seeks to analyse how No One Is Illegal groups negotiate and confront some of the contradictions inherent in engaging in anti-borders politics from *within* a colonial nation-state. Specifically, how do No One Is Illegal groups work in solidarity with indigenous sovereignty struggles while simultaneously calling for open border policies? How do No One Is Illegal groups build mass resistance to border policies while maintaining locally constituted political campaigns? How do migrant justice groups negotiate the contradictions in demanding that the Canadian government stop deportations and improve the day-to-day living conditions of migrants while at the same time questioning the legitimacy of the state to enforce immigration laws?

Anti-colonial Framework: Indigenous Sovereignty and Migrant Justice

In a 2005 article entitled "Decolonizing Antiracism," Lawrence and Dua argue that "antiracist and postcolonial theorists have not integrated an understanding of Canada as a colonialist state into their frameworks" (p. 123). Acknowledging the differences between much of the oppressive settlement of migrant workers, poor people, slaves, and refugees and that of the ruling European elite, the authors nonetheless seek to make critical interventions in anti-racist scholarship that seeks to place indigenous sovereignty and colonialism as central to any radical anti-oppression work. Similarly, they challenge migrant justice activists calling for "no borders" to "think through how their campaigns can preempt the ability of Aboriginal communities to establish title to their traditional lands" (p. 136). While somewhat controversial in their intervention, Lawrence and Dua pose important questions for theorists and activists engaged in emancipatory work for migrant justice.

In response to Lawrence and Dua (2005), Sharma and Wright (2009) argue in "Decolonizing Resistance, Challenging Colonial States" that "decolonization can be construed as a liberation of "nations" rather than as a liberation of people from social relations that are organized through their hierarchical placement within a ruthless, global competition for profits, whether private or public" (p. 128). Sharma and Wright (2009) critique Lawrence and Dua's calls for the support of indigenous national struggles, rejecting nationalisms of the dominant and the dominated as being equally dangerous to a liberatory praxis. They suggest instead a process for activists and academics to problematize the legitimacy of the Canadian state to determine who can migrate and who cannot as a major factor in decolonizing resistance. Moving away from a national liberation discourse, Sharma and Wright argue that "decolonization projects must challenge capitalist social relations and those organized through the nation state, such as sovereignty. Crucially, their goal must be the gaining of a global *commons*" (p. 131). Such a reframing of anti-colonial resistance is exemplified in the "free movement" and "no borders" movements in Europe.

No One Is Illegal groups, among other anti-capitalist and radical organizations in Canada, have undertaken the slow process of decolonizing resistance in practice. This has included acknowledging serious contradictions and missteps, engaging in critical internal discussions, approaching indigenous communities with humility, and attempting diverse yet imperfect models for indigenous solidarity. For groups like No One Is Illegal, an anti-colonial/counter-nationalist politics means understanding the risk of undermining significant struggle by indigenous communities for sovereignty and land by not attempting to problematize potentially serious contradictions of a no borders politics with a desire to make tangible contributions to indigenous sovereignty struggles. In other words, calls to stop deportations must inevitably engage with the immigration bureaucracy, the minister of citizenship and immigration, and the Canadian government in order to be effective. This in turn, without being openly discussed or problematized, legitimizes the Canadian state as the arbiter of who can and cannot enter and stay within the nation-state. This legitimization, then, plays a role in strengthening state claims to power and sovereignty *over* indigenous communities seeking sovereignty.

The act of engaging in solidarity with indigenous struggles for self-determination as a fundamental part of migrant justice organizing is best exemplified by the long-term and sustained work undertaken by No One Is Illegal – Vancouver with the indigenous nations of Coast Salish Territories. In its guiding principles, No One Is Illegal – Vancouver (2010) prioritizes building solidarity with indigenous sovereignty struggles, noting:

> As we struggle for the right for our communities to maintain their livelihoods, we prioritize building alliances and supporting indigenous sisters and brothers fighting displacement. We recognize that those colonial and capitalist forces that create war, poverty, and destruction throughout the global South are causing dispossession of indigenous peoples within the global North. Therefore our work must be carried out in solidarity with the struggles for the self-determination and justice of indigenous communities.

No One Is Illegal – Vancouver's sustained engagement with the struggle for self-determination among west coast indigenous nations on Turtle Island exemplifies its long-term commitment to making "the ongoing colonization of Indigenous peoples foundational" to its agenda for migrant justice as advocated by Lawrence and Dua (2005, p. 137). It has also resulted in important actions that both foreground indigenous sovereignty and challenge the use of border policy to regulate migrant labour. For instance, on 12 February 2010 protesters in East Vancouver successfully blocked and rerouted the Olympic Torch on the last leg of the corporate-sponsored torch run prior to the opening ceremonies of the Vancouver 2010 Olympics and then sustained a strong movement of resistance for the duration of the games (Dyck, 2010). Heeding the call from Coast Salish Territories, demonstrations and protests in dozens of cities across Canada united under the slogan "No Olympics on Stolen Native Land" in an effort to highlight the colonial legacy of theft of indigenous land and particularly the fact that the Province of British Columbia sits on unceded indigenous territory. The resistance to the Vancouver 2010 Olympics also highlighted the federal government's expansion of repressive temporary work programs in order to use migrant labour to build much of the Olympic village and stadiums. Integrating a migrant justice framework within the day-to-day anti-capitalist and anti-colonialist orientation of the No Olympics on Stolen Native Land campaign was an important element in No One Is Illegal – Vancouver's ongoing engagement with the struggle for self-determination of the Coast Salish indigenous nations.

No One Is Illegal groups in Toronto and Montreal have also started the process of relationship building with indigenous nations, particularly with the Haudenosaunee Confederacy at Six Nations and Mohawks at Tyendinaga. There has also been increased contact and relationship building with the Algonquins at Barriere Lake and with Grassy Narrows First Nation. This solidarity work has, however, often occurred in times of crisis, such as the 2006 standoff with RCMP at the Six Nations Reclamation site near Caledonia, Ontario, or support of the Mohawks at Tyendinaga during their struggle against the illegal dumping of hazardous waste at the Culbertson Tract. No One Is Illegal – Toronto, in particular, has struggled to develop a sustained form of indigenous solidarity work with the Haudenosaunee, Algonquin, and Anishnabeg nations struggling for sovereignty in Ontario and Quebec. While this has been a challenge, individual members of the group have consistently worked to maintain strong links to indigenous struggles for self-determination, which was best exemplified in Toronto-based demonstrations for indigenous sovereignty in support of Grassy Narrows, the Indigenous Day of Action in 2007, and most recently during the G20.

Taking leadership from indigenous communities and expressing demands for self-determination, rejecting Canada's legitimacy in setting immigration policy, and building internal knowledge of the histories of colonization have all increased No One Is Illegal – Toronto's ability to work more closely as allies with indigenous groups in struggle. It has also meant sustained work to educate the largely migrant and non-indigenous communities of the importance of engaging simultaneously in indigenous sovereignty and migrant justice struggles. Conversely, it has also forced the group to reframe their understanding of the reasons for migration as being part of a broader system of colonization that displaces indigenous peoples and forces them to seek refuge or economic opportunities in other territories that continue to be directly engaged in the colonial process.

In the recommendations that Sharma and Wright (2009) put forward in their response to Lawrence and Dua (2005), they suggest that migrant justice organizations' call for open borders or free movement can simultaneously be integrated with solidarity for indigenous sovereignty struggles through "a consideration of ways to undo the divide between 'indigenous' people and 'migrants' by working towards practices of decolonization that are fundamentally antiracist and toward an antiracist politics fully cognizant of the necessity of anti-capitalist decolonization" (p. 122). While this has played a role in building the relationship between migrant justice groups and indigenous communities struggling for sovereignty, in practice No One Is Illegal groups have been faced with trying to negotiate both the legitimate critiques by Lawrence and Dua (2005) and the suggested ways forward of Sharma and Wright (20009). In particular, groups have tried to address the need to re-envision a call for "no borders" as being in line with the rejection of Canada's colonial authority to "control who comes in and who comes out" while maintaining respect for indigenous peoples' right to self-determination. This is partly the result of ongoing analysis of an anti-colonial political frame that takes into account indigenous sovereignty as being integral to any process of liberation of migrants. It is also based on the understanding that colonial practices in the Global South that continue to displace people are inherently linked to the dispossession of indigenous land in the Global North (No One Is Illegal – Vancouver, 2010).

Counter-national Framework: Organizing to Resist Local Borders and Boundaries

A frequent criticism of migrant justice organizing in Canada is that it lacks national coordination (Wright, 2006). In comparison to the United

States, which relies heavily on national networks (particularly within the Mexican and Latin American communities) to coordinate mass mobilizations and work stoppages in an effort to gain legislative reforms such as the DREAM act (see Barreto et al., 2008), No One Is Illegal groups in Canada tend to be more locally based and to blur the lines between national and local organizing (Shantz, 2005). While there have been nationally coordinated days of action called by No One Is Illegal groups in Canada (notably in 2006–2008) that have been expressly aligned with political actions for migrant justice in the United States, the day-to-day campaigns for migrant justice within a counter-national framework in Toronto, Montreal, and Vancouver have been highly decentralized and locally oriented.

In Toronto, the best example of this localized work is the emergence of the Access Not Fear and Shelter, Sanctuary, Status (SSS) campaign (Bhuyan, in this volume; F. Villegas, in this volume). This kind of campaign is often described by No One Is Illegal – Toronto as a form of "regularization from the ground up" (Mishra & Kamal, 2007). More specifically, the campaign seeks to empower migrant communities, community workers, shelter workers, civil sector employees, local shopkeepers, and other migrant organizations to create policies and develop action protocols that would bar immigration enforcement from entering into their spaces. It also advocates for the right of undocumented migrants to access basic services (health, housing, women's shelters, emergency services, food banks) without the fear of being detained or deported (P. Villegas, in this volume). This strategy is not unique and has been effectively used within migrant justice struggles in the United States (Wright, 2006). What is interesting about this particular local strategy is that by seeking to engage community workers to redefine the way borders regulate people's lives at a local level, it oscillates between calls to expand the welfare state (through provisions of services to undocumented people) and simultaneously to reject the nation-state as a legitimate migrant regulatory body. In other words, the campaign breaks from traditional nationalist and transnationalist migrant rights frameworks by seeking to push community workers to intervene directly against immigration enforcement in the city.

While, in practice, these campaigns offer the potential for a fundamental shift in how community activism around migrant justice occurs within institutional spaces such as community centres and women's shelters, it also produces a significant tension with traditional social service providers who are oriented towards expanding access to services but less comfortable with defying federal immigration laws. Thus, throughout the various campaigns, including working with schools, community centres, and women's shelters, staff and local officials working with No One Is Illegal – Toronto have engaged, to varying degrees, in both expanding access and shutting out immigration enforcement. No One Is Illegal – Toronto's SSS campaign, a coalition of migrant justice organizers, women's shelters, and violence against women activists, have challenged how women's organizations have traditionally thought of how borders affect the lives of women experiencing violence (Bhuyan, in this volume). They have also engaged in a reframing of detentions and deportations of migrant women as part of the ongoing perpetuation of state violence against women.

In March 2010, immigration enforcement entered a women's shelter in Toronto in search of a woman who had fled abuse in Ghana, in order to deport her. Seeing this as a violation of sanctuary provided to women fleeing violence, women's organizations and shelters from across the city held a press conference to denounce the incursion and proclaimed their goal of resisting immigration enforcement within the shelter system (Bonnar, 2010). Contextualizing deportations as violence against women, the groups mobilizing around SSS have highlighted the high-profile case of the murder of a young Mexican woman who sought refuge in Canada twice (and was deported both times), showing how the state violence of immigration policy directly contributes to violence against women (see Keung, 2009b). This political stand makes a traditional call for the expansion of the welfare state to meet the needs of undocumented migrant women fleeing physical violence, while at the same time pushing a radical agenda of delegitimizing the state violence of immigration enforcement, detention, and deportations. Similar experiences have been developing within the school system through the Education Not Deportation campaigns that have pushed for the implementation of school policies preventing immigration enforcement from entering schools (F. Villegas, in this volume).

While the autonomous and localized organizing structure of No One Is Illegal groups does not currently have the highly coordinated national mass base similar to movements in Britain and the United States, the flexibility and versatility with which groups organize locally allow for a counter-nationalist orientation that differs from nationalist and transnationalist migrant rights frameworks. No One Is Illegal – Toronto seeks to use the need undocumented people have for basic services as a means to start a discussion and dialogue with social service providers and other community workers about how borders can be challenged directly in a local context. Attempting to disrupt the day-to-day operations of the enforcement arm of Citizenship and Immigration Canada is part of a broader counter-nationalist strategy of challenging the border and the legitimacy of the Canadian state to determine who should be provided with basic services. It seeks to put the power to shift state immigration policy into the hands of the community, without lobbying for national immigration reforms. It provides the potential for transformative and long-term change and recentres the power for those changes towards the local community and away from the federal government. However, as with all campaigns that attempt to integrate organizations funded by federal, provincial, and municipal grants and with a radical anti-state agenda, it remains to be seen whether or not local community service organizations can harness the leverage building through the Access Not Fear campaigns and effectively move towards an interventionist approach in state immigration policy.

Anti-imperialist and Anti-capitalist Frameworks: Status for All versus No One Is Illegal

The overarching demand made by No One Is Illegal groups across Canada has been for a full and inclusive regularization program that would ensure that all people living in Canada would acquire full and permanent status. While this demand is critical to the movement's analysis, it is not clearly a call for open borders or for free movement; rather, it is an explicit negotiation with the Canadian state to reform immigration legislation in order to remove the conditions that produce illegality and precarity among migrants (de Genova, 2002; Goldring, Berinstein, & Bernhard, 2009). While this is seemingly contradictory to the counter-nationalist stance advocated by No One Is Illegal groups, a fuller analysis of strategy, tactics, and goals is warranted.

Rooted in much of the anti-globalization and anti-war struggles that have emerged since the late 1990s in North America, No One Is Illegal groups seek to negotiate their demand for status for all within the context of anti-capitalist and anti-imperialist struggles. Supporting the resistance to Canada's occupation of Afghanistan, its economic support for the war in Iraq, and its role in the Haitian coup, No One Is Illegal groups make the links between Canada's role in displacing people and its regressive immigration policies. Similarly, No One Is Illegal groups have supported campaigns against global mining companies like Barrick Gold, whose operations have displaced people through-out the Global South. The groups have also engaged in the support of numerous Mexican migrants displaced and dispossessed of land due to free trade agreements like NAFTA that included the elimination of Article 27 of the Mexican constitution, which guaranteed land rights to indigenous people in Mexico.

The anti-imperialist framework expands the transnational frame-work by implicating the Canadian state and Canadian companies in the displacement of people. A good example of the expansion of this framework is the group's solidarity with the Palestinian liberation struggle. Significant to this struggle is the call for a right of return for Palestinians displaced by the Israeli state. In a 2006 statement released by No One Is Illegal – Toronto in support of Palestinian refugees, the group asserts the demand for

> the right of displaced Palestinian refugees and their descendants to return to the Occupied Territories and that complete compensation is required for lost property and other assets for all refugees, regard-less of their willingness to return, by the responsible governmental authorities.

This statement also recognizes the right of Palestinians to self-deter-mination and gives support for the liberation struggles of the people of Palestine. Support for national liberation struggles remains a point of contention within organizing strategies, however, as there is significant slippage between calls for the end to occupations and the reaffirmation of nationalism as a political practice. These tensions exist within a num-ber of contexts in which No One Is Illegal seeks to assert the right to free movement but also the right to stay without being displaced, which is exemplified by the support of Tamil liberation demonstrations, Haitian anti-occupation struggles, and anti-war demonstrations opposing Can-ada's role in Iraq and Afghanistan. Such solidarity links the politics of justice for migrants with a politics of the right not to be displaced and sees Canada's imperial, environmental, and corporate policies as being intimately linked with displacement globally. Differing from a domi-nant strain of left nationalism in Canada (particularly within the labour and environmental movements), these anti-imperial movements seek to problematize Canada's colonial legacy as intricately embedded in capitalist globalization.

Conclusion

This chapter attempts to articulate an emergent shift in migrant justice organizing in Canada. It uses the network of No One Is Illegal groups in Canada to analyse how these groups work within anti-colonial, counter-nationalist, anti-imperialist, and anti-capitalist frameworks that differ substantively from traditional nationalist and transnationalist movements for migrant rights.

I argue that the emergence of movements that challenge borders within the Canadian political landscape has significantly altered how migrant justice activism is framed. These movements have had an impact on official discourse by challenging the legitimacy of the colonial Canadian state's right to determine immigration policy by supporting calls for indigenous sovereignty. The movements have dislocated activism in support of those without documentation by empowering people in the local context to directly intervene in immigration enforcement. They have also mobilized to demand status and rights for unauthorized migrants by working to expose and resist Canadian state and corporate complicity in global displacement. Starr and Adams (2003) suggest that groups that organize within an "autonomous" framework such as the No One Is Illegal collectives are more likely to "assert the legitimacy of autonomous community authority in diverse local political systems" (p. 20). Such local autonomy allows for the diversity and creativity that emerges within the context of collective principles and demands for migrant justice. While no cohesive decision-making structure within the network exists, an attempt to build respect, solidarity, and creativity among the various No One Is Illegal collectives has allowed for flexible tactics and strategies that incorporate a process of decolonization within each groups' local political context.

In framing their movements as part of anti-colonial and anti-imperial struggles, No One Is Illegal groups have broadened the strategic focus of "no-borders" politics to include a greater emphasis on indigenous solidarity, a firm commitment to challenging Canadian and US imperialism abroad – while maintaining concentration on building community power and a specific call for immigration legislation reforms. While contradictions remain pervasive with respect to an acknowledged desire to both oppose the legitimacy of Canadian immigration legislation and seek redress from such policies, organizing within an anti-colonial and counter-nationalist framework allows the groups to negotiate such contradictions strategically. This requires building more long-term and consistent solidarity with indigenous communities fighting for sovereignty as well as recentring the power structure towards the local rather than national. Inherent in such struggles is the shift in slogans and language within the migrant justice movement that challenges the legitimacy of borders as a colonial project, exclaiming emphatically that "We didn't cross the borders, the borders cross us!" Such framing suggests a desire to grapple with the complexities of colonialism and to assert the rights of individuals to stay in their lands unhindered by colonial incursions, in a sense articulating a free movement of people by asserting that "no one is illegal."

NOTE

1 I use the terms "anti-colonial," "anti-imperialist," and "counter-nationalist" to describe aspects of a framework underlying a particular segment of migrant justice organizing in Canada that is represented in part by the autonomous network of No One Is Illegal groups.

15 From Access to Empowerment: The Committee for Accessible AIDS Treatment and Its Work with People Living with HIV-AIDS and Precarious Status

ALAN LI

Immigrants, refugees, and those who lack full legal status in Canada with HIV/AIDS (IRN-PHAs) face barriers in accessing health, legal, and support services. In addition to settlement stress and the marginalization that results from systemic and institutionalized racism, IRN-PHAs also face the stigma of having HIV/AIDS (Lawson et al., 2006). The fear of rejection by their own ethno-racial community compounds their lack of support and heightens their social exclusion (Li et al., 2008). This has a profound impact on their physical health and mental well-being. Their precarious status in Canada and the fear of deportation drive them underground, effectively preventing them from advocating for their needs. While the health of many people with HIV/AIDS is improving as a result of better treatment, IRN-PHAs are an underclass suffering from delayed diagnoses, suboptimal treatment, and tragic health outcomes (Mitra, Jacobsen, O'Connor, Pottie, & Tugwell, 2006; Worthington and Myers, 2003). Addressing the complex barriers to treatment requires the committed collaboration of all stakeholders.

This chapter documents the experience of the Committee for Accessible AIDS Treatment (CAAT) in mobilizing a multisector response to improve treatment access for IRN-PHAs through a community-based participatory action research project from 2000 to 2001. It describes how we engaged a marginalized, hidden, and vulnerable population; how

Special thanks to Derek Thaczuk and Josephine P. Wong for their input and assistance in the preparation of this chapter.

we built equitable collaborative partnerships with different community, institutional, government, and corporate stakeholders; and how we translated research into concrete and innovative actions. Inclusive, equitable, and accountable community-based research processes enabled transformative changes that led to long-term community empowerment.

Precarious Status Migrants and HIV/AIDS

The burden of HIV/AIDS is disproportionate among immigrants, refugees, and non-status people, especially those from countries with high HIV rates. Since mandatory HIV testing was implemented for all newcomer applicants to Canada in June 2002, epidemiological data from the Public Health Agency of Canada (2006) have consistently shown that immigrants and refugees made up 15–20 per cent of all new HIV cases each year in Canada, while comprising only one per cent of the total population. In addition, racialized communities continue to experience a high level of vulnerability to HIV infection even after their migration to Canada; a research study at the University of Toronto demonstrated that about 40 per cent of infections among African and Caribbean communities in Ontario occurred after migration and settlement (Remis, Swantee, Schiedel, Merid, & Liu, 2006).

Who Are IRN-PHAs?

Immigrant, refugee, and non-status people living with HIV/AIDS are an especially vulnerable population. They have diverse backgrounds including regular individual immigrant and refugee applicants whose applications failed after their entry to Canada; long-term residents from countries that are part of the British Commonwealth (and hence, till recently, have not required a visa to enter Canada); migrant workers and students whose visas have expired; sponsored family class applicants who have experienced sponsorship breakdowns; and people who entered with a tourist visa and overstayed. Most have made Canada their home and contribute to the social, economic, and cultural landscapes of their communities (Li, 2003). The conditionality of immigration status and citizenship rights poses many challenges common to most racialized newcomer communities: losses and adaptation stressors of settlement in a new country, and barriers to employment, housing, and access to services. IRN-PHAs suffer additional challenges as a result of their HIV status.

IRN-PHAs: Multilayered Vulnerability and Barriers Affecting Health

IRN-PHAs face alienation and exclusion from mainstream Canadian society, the mainstream HIV community, and their own ethno-racial communities as a result of profound and compounding systemic racism, AIDS phobia, and xenophobia. The prevalent stigmatization of and discrimination against HIV prevents most IRN-PHAs from disclosing their status and accessing many of the resources available to newcomer and racialized communities, including faith-based organizations, settlement service agencies, and ethno-linguistic-specific health and social support groups. These individuals are also marginalized from mainstream HIV/AIDS health and social services due to language barriers, lack of cultural sensitivity and competencies, and discriminatory attitudes among service providers. However, the most urgent issue facing IRN-PHAs is the difficulty they have accessing anti-HIV medications because of their precarious status; in many cases, this means the difference between life and death.

Due to their immigration status, IRN-PHAs without health insurance are often also ineligible for medication coverage such as provincial drug benefits for people on social assistance and the Trillium Drug Program, which helps individuals with limited incomes to cover the costs of catastrophic illnesses. In Ontario, it is difficult for those who do not possess immigration documents to access health care, despite the national universal health care system. The current health care system does not address fluctuations from one type of precarious status to another (P. Villegas, this volume). Uninsured IRN-PHAs cope with the treatment gaps using a variety of strategies, including postponing treatments, sharing medications within their peer networks, or by recycling unused "leftover" medications from others who have died or changed their medication regimens. These strategies act as urgently needed lifelines for some, but compiling and maintaining a continuous supply of HIV "cocktails" that involve three or more drugs is difficult. As a result, many IRN-PHAs only take medications when they are available; this greatly increases their risk of developing viral resistance to available medications. Some health care providers collect and recycle unused medications to help these suffering individuals, but this work is stressful and frustrating, and may even pose legal and professional risks as their professional colleges or institutions may not sanction such practices.

Frontline clinical service providers in the community health centre sector first identified the specific needs of IRN-PHAs. Community health centres (CHCs) are publicly funded, community-run health service organizations traditionally set up in high-need locales to serve diverse inner-city populations. They serve new immigrants, refugees, and other individuals lacking full health coverage. CHCs are often the first place precarious status IRN-PHAs turn when in need of care, yet they do not necessarily possess the equipment or facilities required to treat those with more complex needs (P. Villegas, in this volume).

In late 1999, physicians from several downtown Toronto CHCs met to discuss a major challenge they were encountering in the HIV community: the growing number of IRN-PHAs without health coverage. Most uninsured PHAs were in the process of applying for immigration or refugee status and faced gaps in their health care and medication coverage. Many had been forced underground and struggled to remain invisible to their communities or government authorities due to stigma and/or fear of deportation. Many were unaware of what health coverage they had; many of those who were eligible were reluctant to access health care for fear of their immigration or refugee application being rejected.

IRN-PHAs were often referred to CHCs after arriving at hospital emergency departments with advanced AIDS-related complications. Most had no ongoing health care and had never been on HIV medications; some had only taken medications sporadically due to lack of access; many were afraid to follow up with authorities or health providers after testing positive for HIV. A significant portion had not even been tested and only became aware of their HIV status upon developing severe AIDS-related opportunistic infections. They faced the added challenges of dealing with the shock of the HIV diagnosis and with disclosure – often unplanned – to their families. Some sought care too late and were too sick to recover from a life-threatening situation.

Service Providers: Shared Frustration and Helplessness

Health service providers working with these IRN-PHA populations faced the complex task of trying to provide care to a patient population

Figure 15.1. Key Challenges Affecting IRN-PHAs

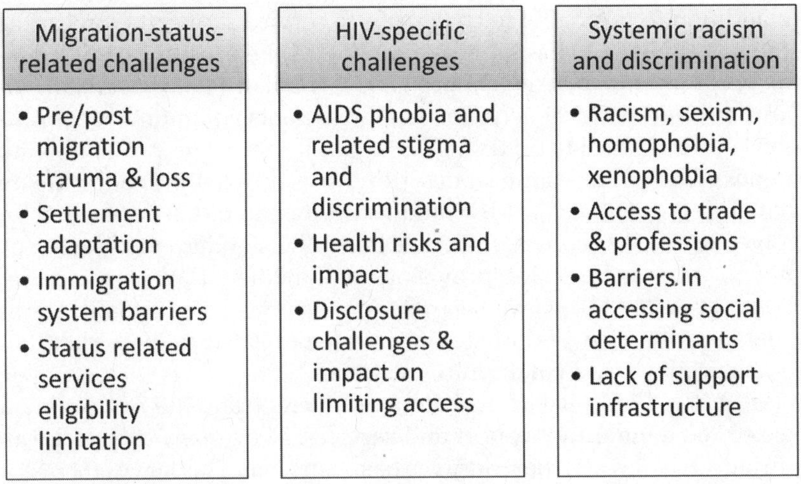

Migration-status-related challenges	HIV-specific challenges	Systemic racism and discrimination
• Pre/post migration trauma & loss • Settlement adaptation • Immigration system barriers • Status related services eligibility limitation	• AIDS phobia and related stigma and discrimination • Health risks and impact • Disclosure challenges & impact on limiting access	• Racism, sexism, homophobia, xenophobia • Access to trade & professions • Barriers in accessing social determinants • Lack of support infrastructure

Source: Figure 15.1 was made by the author.

with limited or no coverage to access medication, monitoring tests, or specialist care. They often felt they were providing suboptimal care to their clients but could not effectively address or advocate for their needs.

Clinicians working with these IRN-PHAs were frustrated with the inordinate amount of paperwork and pre-approval required to get services for their patients, even refugee claimants who had interim federal health coverage. They were also frustrated by poor health outcomes resulting from delayed treatment and service gaps that complicated follow-up care. A common scenario was the suboptimal way many IRN-PHAs shared medications or took whatever medications were available through peer-based recycling or sharing. As a result, the HIV virus became resistant to the medications, limiting subsequent treatment options, complicating treatment and care, and often requiring more costly medications. Overall, clinicians were frustrated and saddened by the human tragedy and injustice they were witnessing and their inability to effect systemic changes in immigration and health care policies.

Barriers to Systemic Advocacy

In addition to posing huge challenges to service access, the precarious status of IRN-PHAs has greatly complicated the process of advocating for program and policy changes. The Canadian HIV movement was built through political activism and grass-roots community mobilization in the 1980s, when HIV/AIDS began to devastate predominantly homosexual white communities (Roy & Cain, 2001). Leadership by people living with HIV/AIDS and the principle of GIPA (Greater Involvement of People with HIV/AIDS) set the standard for grass-roots mobilization and service provision in Canadian HIV communities. However, IRN-PHAs have been hindered from adopting similar strategies because of several unique phenomena related to their identities, social locations, and community dynamics.

Most IRN-PHAs live in isolation and secrecy and are not well connected to community support and services. They often only seek care during a crisis, when the priority is basic survival. This leaves them and their health care providers with little time and few resources for work at a systemic level. Jurisdictional differences act as another unique barrier. Immigration and citizenship issues fall under federal jurisdiction while health care provision is primarily a provincial mandate, so IRN-PHAs are caught between the various levels of government, all of which seem unable or unwilling to take ownership of the problem.

A Call to Action: Formation of the Committee for Accessible AIDS Treatment

When we (CHC health service providers) met to explore strategies to address the barriers facing IRN-PHAs, we identified the need for broader-sector allies who had experience and insight in working with the affected communities. We invited other health sectors, AIDS service organizations, and the HIV & AIDS Legal Clinic (Ontario) to attend follow-up meetings, and encouraged IRN-PHAs to work with us. The coalition rapidly grew to more than twenty partners from the health, legal, settlement, and HIV/AIDS service sectors. In January 2000, we formed the Committee for Accessible AIDS Treatment (CAAT) to facilitate collaborative strategies to address the multiple barriers faced by IRN-PHAs.

In the early days of CAAT, research was not yet a realistic option due to lack of motivation, difficulties in engaging target communities, and lack of resources. Many community members were also discouraged by their previous experiences with traditional academic and institutionally based research. Some felt they had been treated as "token" partners with limited opportunity to contribute meaningful input, and felt that there was a lack of accountability and relevance of results to the target communities being researched. Although there has been a recent increase in community-based research in the Toronto area, our particular partners had little experience with such research, which can facilitate community engagement and participatory action.

In addition, many of us felt that we understood the nature of the problems faced by our populations: there were no obvious knowledge gaps, and we had no specific hypothesis to prove. None of the network members belonged to research institutions, nor did they have the knowledge and expertise to access research funding. Finally, the urgent needs of our IRN-PHAs meant that at first sight we needed to focus on treatment, rather than research.

CAAT members began by learning from each other about the interplay of legal, settlement, and health service barriers affecting IRN-PHAs. We created new partnerships and streamlined referrals between service providers. Later, we engaged pharmaceutical companies and government partners to advocate for compassionate health care and treatment. As these discussions continued, we found that gaps in information and evidence were a key barrier to our advocacy.

Moreover, after a preliminary assessment, we realized that we had not fully assessed the needs of our populations or the options for addressing them. IRN-PHAs worked to stay invisible and were reluctant to share their experiences. This made it difficult to understand the exact nature of the barriers they faced and to develop effective strategies. The lack of evidence and personal testimonials also weakened the power of our humanitarian efforts. This invisibility and the consequent evidence gaps also disenfranchised us from stakeholders who needed to be part of the solution: government, hospitals, and pharmaceutical partners. Research became an important and necessary tool.

CAAT Improving HIV Treatment Access Study: A Community's Collective Learning Journey

Developing a Principled Research-Guiding Framework

After assessing our research options, we eventually adopted a community-based participatory action framework (Koch & Kralik, 2006;

Minkler & Wallerstein, 2008). We based our study on the principles of accountability to the affected communities, respect for their lived experiences, maximal community involvement, equity in partnerships, and community empowerment by ensuring concrete responsive strategies.

The study, "Improving Treatment Access to Marginalized (Immigrant, Refugee and Non-status) PHAs," was funded by the Ontario HIV Treatment Network under their Community Priority Initiative funding. Its goals were to document barriers to treatment and health care and their effects on IRN-PHAs, to document existing strategies used by IRN-PHA s and their providers to ensure some level of health care for themselves and their families, to explore solutions to barriers, and to increase dialogue and action among stakeholders.

Most network members had collaborated on research studies and had some knowledge about research methodologies but had not led any formal research project. We decided to reach out to potential academic collaborating partners. We were fortunate to have the support of Dr Greg Robinson, an HIV physician with a long history of community activism and rich research experience. Dr Robinson connected us with the Community Linked Evaluation AIDS Resource at McMaster University in Hamilton and worked with us to develop innovative strategies to address the ethical and methodological challenges involved in our research. Finally, we gathered information from thirty-eight IRN-PHAs, twenty-eight community and health service providers, and ten physicians who were active in HIV care and treated uninsured IRN-PHAs.

Because of the vulnerable social position of IRN-PHAs and the distinct relationship we had with them as service providers, we faced several ethical concerns. The first challenge was developing an effective recruitment strategy for our IRN-PHA populations without compromising the integrity of our existing provider-client relationships. We did not want to add to the risk already faced by those who chose to participate (also see Young and Bernhard, in this volume), and we needed to maintain trust and confidentiality.

Recruitment was hampered by the fact that many of the most vulnerable IRN-PHAs were not well connected to community service agencies or peer networks. Contact had to be done primarily through clinical service providers and caseworkers. Potential participants were concerned that service providers directly involved in the research could access more information than participants were willing to disclose. To address these concerns, we developed clear recruitment flyers for health care providers and scripts to guide their conversations with potential participants about the research, specifically stressing confidentiality and that their decision about participation would not affect their treatment.

A second challenge was balancing the target community's expectations with the scope of the research; we anticipated identifying numerous unmet needs and challenging situations. The research project was not set up as a service, but CAAT was committed to a long-term role in engaging the affected communities. Providing some level of support was necessary to help build trust and avoid retraumatizing participants by reinforcing their helplessness and disillusionment with the service system. Support was also necessary from a humanitarian and compassionate perspective. We asked our community, legal, and health service partners to commit to respond to urgent needs that might surface during the research process. We compiled an urgent referral list for distribution to participants, and research staff members were trained in basic counselling and referral skills.

Another challenge was the confidentiality concerns of health care providers. In 2000, few clinicians were active in HIV care: about forty primary care physicians, fewer than ten infectious disease specialists, and only five HIV clinics in the entire Toronto area. Physicians were concerned that they might be identified if they participated in the research, especially if they described providing what they considered suboptimal care, thereby exposing themselves to potential liability suits and/or peer criticism. Nurses and other professional staff were concerned about jeopardizing their employment because they were engaged in unsanctioned activities such as recycling unused medications, writing off service charges, and so on. To alleviate these confidentiality concerns, we engaged three HIV primary care physicians on our research advisory team and trained them as peer research interviewers. We also stressed total anonymity in reporting information and promised to double-check details with participants before publication. These measures were effective, and we gathered substantive and candid data about the experiences of health care providers.

Methodological Innovation to Sort through Intersecting Challenges

Methodologically, a key challenge was finding a way to effectively describe and analyse the complexity and scope of the problems faced by our target population, given our limited resources and sample size. Canadian immigration and refugee policies affect service eligibility and health care coverage; health care providers were not trained in these areas and IRN-PHAs were confused about how they fit in. Staff from the HIV & AIDS Legal Clinic (Ontario) and one lawyer who was knowledgeable about HIV and immigration issues trained the research team and collaborated in the development of a questionnaire. This improved the rigour of the data collection process and contributed to the eventual development of solutions. In addition, our experiences as we developed the urgent resource list and learned about migration and service eligibility helped us set up long-term community empowerment strategies at the end of the project.

We devised a three-stage mixed-method data-gathering process. We started by identifying key informants in the health care and community service sectors and engaging them as project advisory team members. We conducted training sessions on the Canadian immigration system and related policies and trained several key informants as peer researchers. The advisory group also helped to identify the recruitment targets, sites, and methods.

The first stage of the data collection involved brief semi-structured interviews with community and health service providers and physicians. Respondents were asked about issues such as how many of their HIV-positive clients had experienced barriers in accessing health care or treatment, what kind of barriers they faced, what strategies had been used to address these barriers, what resources have been helpful, what changes in public policies and procedures would be helpful to improve access, and what suggestions they had for reaching and engaging uninsured IRN-PHAs in our study.

The responses provided a knowledge base to improve IRN-PHA engagement and interviewing processes. The interviews helped elucidate the complex continuum of status changes that could affect IRN-PHA eligibility for health care and drug coverage. They also helped identify service partners that could recruit IRN-PHAs and alerted us to the need to involve peer/community interviewers to reach different target populations.

The second stage involved a brief semi-structured survey with thirty-eight target-group IRN-PHAs who had experienced gaps or barriers to their health care or treatment coverage. Interviews were conducted by eight community-based AIDS service agency workers whom we had trained as peer researchers. The survey gathered information about demographics, legal status in Canada, health care and treatment insurance coverage, difficulties and barriers faced in accessing health care and treatment, related factors that pose additional challenges to their health (e.g., stigma, confidentiality concerns, legal assistance), and ways they have coped with all these challenges.

Based on the responses, we identified cases that represented a range of unique scenarios: rejected refugee claimants, failed family sponsorship, cases involving domestic violence, students and workers with permits who tested positive during their stay, humanitarian and compassionate cases that never got resolved, IRN-PHAs who were refused care, and IRN-PHAs who had suffered major health consequences due to access problems. The scenarios also represented the various types of barriers experienced at different points of the immigration/refugee status continuum: differences in access to health care coverage, social assistance, and drug plans; and a range of legal statuses such as visitors, short-term resident/workers, refugee claimants, sponsored family members, independent immigrants, and people who have no legal status in Canada.

We approached these individuals and invited them to participate in in-depth interviews. These interviews included questions about testing HIV-positive, getting connected to services and health care, the kinds of difficulties they experienced, the support they had and the strategies they used, and their suggestions for changes in health care organizations and government policies that would improve access and the health of IRN-PHAs.

We extracted key themes from the preliminary data, which included limited eligibility and entitlement to health care and treatment coverage for many newcomer applicants; the complexity of the immigration refugee system, causing much fear and confusion; undue delay and economic burden in the immigration application process, rendering people's status in limbo; shortage of culturally competent health care, legal, and social service providers who are knowledgeable in both HIV and immigration issues; and the profound impact of the compounded fear of deportation, HIV stigma, and discrimination in worsening isolation and preventing access to services. Coping strategies included informal peer networks that recycled and shared medications; community health centres that serve uninsured clients; getting treatment through clinical trials; and a small number of legal and health providers who have expertise in both HIV and immigration. Recommendations included developing improved mechanisms for monitoring and accessing compassionate and recycled drugs; having designated hospitals and increasing funding to community health centres to serve uninsured IRN-PHAs; and developing accessible legal information and support systems to assist IRN-PHAs in immigration-related issues and to strengthen resources to build a more supportive environment.

The draft report was circulated to engage stakeholders with relevant experience in a series of advocacy think tanks; long-time activists and experienced advocates from the LGBT, HIV/AIDS, immigrant and refugee rights, social justice, and legal sectors provided feedback about our preliminary recommendations and proposed strategies. This engagement was extremely helpful in a number of ways: it enriched and broadened our alliances with stakeholders who were not already engaged in the research process, and it also acted as a peer review process, helping us to critically examine the feasibility of our proposals.

More than We Expected: New Knowledge and Pivotal Findings

We had begun the study under the impression that we already had fairly good insights into the existing problems, but we were surprised by what we learned. Much of the findings confirmed what we already knew (the gaps in health care coverage, the barriers to accessing treatment and hospital and subspecialty care, and the compromising ways people shared and recycled medications). Two pieces of new information became pivotal in designing strategic solutions.

One surprising finding was the existence of a little-known compassionate drug access mechanism available through several pharmaceutical companies that manufacture HIV medications. Through this system, physicians can apply to pharmaceutical manufacturers for short-term compassionate access to medication for their HIV patients. Only three of our HIV specialists had ever accessed these mechanisms. The paperwork was quite complicated and the system differed with each drug company; a month's supply of a full HIV treatment regimen would typically require writing to three different drug companies. Most HIV physicians were either unaware of this program or did not have the time and resources to handle the paperwork needed to negotiate through the systems. Despite these practical barriers, learning about this mechanism was an important step from which we could build a systemic response to the problem.

The second critical finding was how strongly legal service barriers affected all other health care access problems. We found a huge gap in legal service access literacy not only among our target group IRN-PHAs (58 per cent reported gaps in their legal information and support) but also among service providers. Most IRN-PHAs were unaware of how to access legal aid and often paid thousands of dollars for legal services, but of the hundreds of practising lawyers in the Greater Toronto Area, only a handful had specialized knowledge and expertise in HIV and immigration issues. Most of the HIV/AIDS service providers were unaware of immigration-related issues and lacked knowledge of proper referrals for legal support. No legal clinics provided individual case representation for IRN-PHAs on immigration-related issues, and at the time, the HIV & AIDS Legal Clinic (Ontario) only provided information and referral services on immigration-related matters.

IRN-PHAs reported being given inaccurate, misleading, or incomplete information about the immigration system and its processes, resulting in untimely delays, complications in the application processes, the need to resubmit applications and documents, and sometimes failed applications. Some IRN-PHAs said that unregulated immigration consultants had mishandled their cases. Because of homophobia and AIDS phobia, some IRN-PHAs were afraid to disclose details of their sexual orientation or HIV status to their lawyers; ultimately this denied them potentially valid grounds for application and jeopardized their cases.

Significantly, our analysis revealed that, despite their fears, 75 per cent of our IRN-PHA population had valid grounds for application for some type of long-term status in Canada. Moreover, the gap in legal support had a ripple affect throughout their lives and created a whole new series of problems. Our outreach processes and surveys of our hospital and clinical partners revealed that the uninsured IRN-PHA population was likely several hundreds, rather than thousands, as originally feared by many stakeholders.

These two pieces of information were critical in alleviating the cost-related concerns of government stakeholders and helped convince our pharmaceutical partners that a short-term investment in our population would generate more healthy long-term users for their products. Their support permitted a multisectoral and sustainable response to the problem of access.

Conclusion

Our community-based research process strengthened community partnerships, facilitated new referral networks development, and connected target IRN-PHAs to services. Knowledge generated by the research was translated into concrete program development to improve treatment and service access. Changes include the new HIV and Immigration Service Access Training Program (housed at Regent Park Community Health Centre) and the incorporation of immigration-related services at the HIV & AIDS Legal Clinic (Ontario). The results inspired broader community mobilization and catalysed more collaborative strategies for systemic changes. One particularly effective strategy was the multisectoral invested HIV Treatment Access Program (now housed at the Toronto People With AIDS Foundation) to facilitate coordinated compassionate access to anti-HIV medications. Others include a research study that is analysing the effects and gaps of existing government policies on newcomer populations living with HIV/AIDS, and a study that is challenging the medical exclusion threshold that the Canadian government uses to exclude immigrants. In the long term, our commitment to capacity building and equitable partnerships has fostered a new generation of leaders and activists working to improve the health of diverse communities, and CAAT has matured into a vibrant and sustainable network – a leader in meaningful target-community involvement and accountability in the community-based research field.

16 Confidentiality and "Risky" Research: Negotiating Competing Notions of Risk in a Canadian University Context

JULIE YOUNG AND JUDITH K. BERNHARD

Researchers face many institutional obstacles and methodological challenges when conducting research on vulnerable populations such as precarious status migrants. In our negotiations with the ethics review board at our institution, we were faced with a system of ethical governance adapted from medical models, which was inappropriate for research with people whose legal status was precarious. This chapter discusses how the various interpretations of risk and confidentiality among different stakeholders – university ethics review boards, academic researchers, and research participants – led us to make ethical, legal, and methodological decisions that shaped the outcomes of the research. Following a brief review of the need for research about this population and our proposed research contributions, we elaborate on how the concepts of risk and vulnerability were negotiated in the context of academic research.

Research about the lives of Canadian residents without full legal status has sparked considerable interest over the last decade. Some of the simplest questions – such as "how many are there?" – have not been answered. Estimates ranging from 40,000 to 600,000 individuals (Jiménez, 2003; Robertson, 2005) are based on newspaper articles and have no documented basis. Almost no data are available about many aspects of this population, especially their daily, lived experiences of precarious status. In addition, much of the research that has been conducted to date is comprised of small-scale needs assessments by and for service providers.

We envisioned our research, entitled "Living with Less than Full Status: Impacts on Families, Livelihoods, and Access to Services," as a large-scale survey to be followed up by interviews with a sample of participants over several years. Longitudinal, qualitative interviews were an essential component of the proposed project. This kind of approach allows researchers to establish trust with participants over time so that they feel comfortable disclosing their experiences. Longitudinal interviewing would have allowed us to capture the strategies of people with precarious status as they negotiated their lives in various areas, such as workplaces and neighbourhoods.

The longitudinal interview strategy raised concerns for the ethics review board. Carrying out multiple interviews with participants over a period of time would require us to collect and store their contact information. The ethics review board stated that filing this personal information risked drawing the interest of immigration enforcement officers, who might subpoena our documents, placing research participants at risk of detention and deportation and placing us, the researchers, at risk of litigation and even jail. It was difficult to assess the extent of these risks. On one hand, we knew it was unlikely that immigration authorities would subpoena our files, but on the other hand, the political climate in Toronto gave board members and researchers pause, as there had been some high-profile immigration raids and arrests throughout the city that year.

Our project was the first of its kind at our university and, as a result, the first to raise these issues with the ethics review board (ERB). We were negotiating the notion of risk and the boundaries of confidentiality along with the board, because the potential risks facing our participants were of concern to all of us. The ethical issues related to our research were complicated by the fact that the research population we wanted to engage was not homogeneous: we wanted to gain the trust of people whose situations ranged from hidden (e.g., entered Canada undetected) to hyper-visible (e.g., rejected refugee claimants). Confidentiality is crucial in many research contexts but especially for this population; we did not want to subject our participants to more risk than they already faced in their daily lives. Throughout the ethics review process we had to balance different perspectives of risk held by the ERB, the potential participants, and the research team, which included academic and community-based researchers.

As researchers, our understanding of the risks faced by potential research participants and ourselves as academics at the time of the project was situated within a very tense political moment. In the spring of 2005, there was an active campaign to implement a city-wide "Don't

Ask Don't Tell" policy that argued that local service providers, including police officers, should not be enforcing federal immigration policies, either by requiring people to disclose their immigration status to access programs and services or by reporting people with precarious legal status to authorities.[1] According to local advocates, these sorts of practices had been happening throughout the city. Most dramatically, on 5 March 2005 a non-status woman who had been volunteering at an International Women's Day event at our university was detained by campus security and later arrested by Toronto police (Rebick, 2005); she was deported from Canada a week after her arrest. Thus, immigration enforcement practices were not a distant possibility but a local, albeit unpredictable, reality. We were therefore making decisions about the research process in the context of a heightened focus on immigration enforcement.

The Ethics Review Board and the Negotiation of Risk

Our university, like those in the rest of Canada, was required to implement an ethics review process in compliance with a statement developed by the federal government (for the UK situation, see Dyer & Demeritt, 2009; for the United States, see Bledsoe et al., 2007). In Canada, the Tri-Council Policy Statement[2] sets out the protocols and requirements for evaluating proposed research projects involving human subjects. The ethics review board has the authority to alter projects or even prevent them altogether to protect participants. In most cases, however, projects are approved, often with some adjustments to the wording of informed consent documents or recruiting procedures. In our case, the key issues that arose during the ethics review process were related to the evaluation and mitigation of potential risks to individuals who agreed to participate in the research and the extent to which we could promise to maintain their confidentiality. Before reviewing in detail our ethics review process, we will explain the function and role of ethics review boards in Canada.

Ethics review boards were institutionalized as a result of highly unethical practices of researchers in various settings, especially medical and psychological research.[3] In Canada, ethical guidelines were systematized in 1976 (Fitzgerald, 2005) and the Tri-Council Policy Statement was adopted in 1998. Ethics review boards hold researchers accountable for the content of their research and their treatment of participants. The ethics review board serves a dual role that complicates its relationship with researchers: it is charged with protecting the rights of "human subjects" involved in research projects and it is subject to state control because the state establishes the board's terms of reference and standards of practice.

The ethics review process is based on a scientific (medical) model of research in which procedures and protocols are much more standardized than they need to be in social science research. It uses a standard application form, modelled after biomedical research designs, to evaluate all projects. A number of researchers have argued that some assumptions underlying the ethics review process pose an epistemological challenge to qualitative research, especially projects in which it is necessary to build trust with participants, and have suggested that the ethics review process is unwieldy and poorly suited to social sciences and humanities research (Bledsoe et al., 2007; Dyer & Demeritt, 2009; Grayson & Myles, 2005; Sikes & Piper, 2008; Stark, 2006). Grayson and Myles (2005) argued that the formal written consent requirement immediately formalizes an interaction, making it more threatening to participants.

Many researchers consider the ethics review board to act as a regulatory system to monitor the work of researchers. Koro-Ljungberg et al. (2007) argued that in obtaining approval from the ethics board, "researchers are constrained and continuously 'produced' though normalization" (p. 1076). Haggerty (2004) argued that ethics review boards have expanded their purview and demanded more detailed regulations in all areas, calling this trend "ethics creep." Board requirements structure all interactions with participants, precluding unplanned interactions and formalizing others (Alcadipani & Hodgson, 2009; Haggerty, 2004).

Other authors have suggested that seemingly inflexible ethics protocols might lead researchers simply to fill out the required forms and get through the ethics review process without sufficiently engaging with difficult ethical questions that are not addressed in the formal review process (Allen, 2008; Halse & Honey, 2005; Koro-Ljungberg et al., 2007). Moreover, researchers might not actually follow their stated protocols. According to Dyer and Demeritt (2009), "ethical frameworks applied by formal ethical review processes ignore ... wider normative and political concerns at best, and at worst actively subvert ongoing efforts to infuse [research] practice with an ethical sensibility" (p. 48).

Haggerty (2004) claimed that ethics review boards focus on risk without evaluating the actual likelihood that these risks will materialize;

board members "generally do not know the empirical likelihood of the potential untoward outcomes that they try to regulate" (p. 402; see also Lowman & Palys, 2007). Haggerty extensively investigated the area of risk to participants and suggested that "the range of potential research related harms envisioned by ERBs at times seems to be limited only by the imagination of the reviewers" (p. 400). By focusing on worst-case scenarios in proposed research projects, the ethics review board determines the topics and questions on which researchers are able to focus; Bledsoe et al. (2007) argued that the ethics review system "regulates creativity":

> Facing demands that spiral to the level of sheer impracticality, faculty and students at many institutions face a stark choice: to conduct innovative research in their fields or to meet the requirements of their institutions' IRBs [Institutional Review Boards] ... This strikes to the core of the research enterprise. (pp. 594–6)

Haggerty (2004) referenced the case of an American researcher named Wax who was unable to carry out a study about teenagers who sniffed glue. The ethics review board denied Wax's application because he did not include "provisions for securing parental consent – an impracticality given the nature of the topic being studied. Enforcing this rule for such research bears little relationship to the aim of protecting research subjects from harm" (p. 410). He cited another ethics review board that would not allow a research project involving children's teeth, because they faced the risk of finding out that the tooth fairy might not exist.

Lowman and Palys (2000, 2007) examined the fallout from a case at Simon Fraser University in Vancouver, challenging ethics review boards that place a priori limits on participant confidentiality. In 1994, Russel Ogden, a master's student in criminology at Simon Fraser University, was subpoenaed by the Vancouver Coroner and asked to reveal two of his confidential sources. Part of Ogden's research had focused on people who had witnessed an assisted suicide within the HIV/AIDS community. Ogden invoked the Wigmore criteria (discussed in further detail below), arguing that public interest in the research outweighed the court's desire to know the identity of his participants. This argument was accepted by the coroner, but despite Ogden's vindication and the upholding of participant confidentiality in this case, Simon Fraser University's vice president of research quickly put limitations to confidentiality on the agenda of the ethics review board: "It was agreed that in cases where it can be foreseen that the researchers may not legally be in a position to ensure confidentiality to their subjects, these researchers must be required to provide only limited confidentiality in the wording of the consent form" (p. 250).

Most ethics review boards in Canada require researchers to provide informed consent documents that assure the protection of participants' confidentiality to the extent permitted by law, effectively limiting confidentiality before research has even begun. Lowman and Palys (2007) argued that this *a priori* limitation of confidentiality amounts to a "buyer-beware" approach to ethics, absolving "researchers and universities of the responsibility of spending the time and resources necessary to even assert research-participant privilege" (p. 173). Limiting confidentiality removes the responsibility from researchers to protect participants and "is likely to facilitate 'liability management' by universities: 'we warned you that confidentiality is limited, so do not complain to us if the information you gave us falls into the hands of the courts or police'" (p. 171). Lowman and Palys asked, "Is this how universities should 'respect' the 'human dignity' of research participants?" (p. 171), and argued that research that aims to protect "health, safety and human life" and advance the public interest requires confidentiality (p. 169).

The so-called "Wigmore criteria" are especially important in this kind of balancing act between participant confidentiality and the public interest. The Wigmore test was developed in the United States to address this kind of decision (Lempert & Saltzburg, 1982; Lindgreen, 2002; Lowman & Palys, 2001). This procedure, now also followed in Canadian courts, allows researchers to protect the confidentiality of their sources (Wigmore, 1905). The researcher must be able to demonstrate that the results of the research and the interests of the participants are of greater importance than resolving a legal matter. The Wigmore test does not contest the law, but claims that the litigant's research would benefit the community to the extent that it ought to be made an exception. To meet the conditions of the Wigmore test, researchers must show that the community can benefit from the research *only* if researchers are able to protect the confidentiality of participants.

The decision by Simon Fraser University officials to mandate "limited confidentiality" in cases where the ethics review board feels there is potential risk of subpoena affected subsequent research at the university. According to the Research Ethics Policy Revision Task Force, implemented at the school in 1998, "sociologists, criminologists, and others – particularly graduate students working with time restrictions

– began to avoid field and interview research" (Lowman & Palys, 2000, p. 253). We felt that limited promises of confidentiality would negatively affect our ability to conduct our research about people living in Toronto with precarious status.

Negotiating "Risk" through the Ethics Review Process

In our proposed research, the key issues related to the ethics review process were risk and confidentiality; confidentiality was especially important but it was inseparable from risk, in that our participants faced risk in their everyday lives.[4] Our proposal highlighted the importance of studying precarious status and called for a large-scale, longitudinal, mixed-methods study. The study was to include 1,700 surveys and 250 in-depth interviews with both individuals living with precarious status and the "institutional actors" – such as service providers, religious leaders, union organizers, and teachers – with whom they came into contact, in four southwestern Ontario cities. Before carrying out this large-scale, multi-year project, we received funding to conduct a pilot study in which we would interview people living with precarious status in Toronto. At the same time, a master's student who became affiliated with the research team developed a project that would use semi-structured, open-ended interviews to focus on the experiences of youth living with precarious status in Toronto (Young, 2005; see Young, in this volume).

We were not aware of the Ogden case when we began our discussions with the ethics review board, but concerns about potential risks facing participants and about protecting participant confidentiality became central to our negotiations. The main issue revolved around our plan to conduct multiple interviews with people living with precarious status. In the first two interviews we would ask participants about their migration and settlement experiences. In the third and fourth interviews we planned to ask research subjects about their strategies for living and working with precarious legal status.

In order to do multiple interviews, we would need to collect and retain participants' contact information. The board worried that our files might be subpoenaed by immigration enforcement officials and recommended two possible options: (1) we were not to pursue more than one interview with each participant; or (2) we were to indicate clearly in the informed consent documents that we could only promise confidentiality "to the extent permitted by law." Both options presented serious limitations to our methods and our proposed research. A longitudinal study comprised of multiple interviews over time would allow us to establish trust with participants before delving into their experiences of living with precarious status.

The main concern of board members was that if we possessed participants' contact information, there was a risk their information could be traced back to their identities. Even if we used pseudonyms and code numbers, having a list of their phone numbers put them at risk if records were subpoenaed and we were ordered to disclose contact information to the Canada Border Services Agency (CBSA). This risk was seen as so dangerous that we were directed not to pursue any follow-up interviews. We learned that a number of researchers in the United States had been subpoenaed to produce their field notes to identify participants. In 1971, a researcher was subpoenaed for his study about whether participants had collected welfare while receiving income maintenance in the United States. In 1972, Samuel Popkin, a Harvard professor, was jailed for eight days for refusing to reveal the identities of the people he interviewed for a secret war study (Lowman & Palys 2001). In 1973, the US Federal Bureau of Investigation threatened to subpoena the Kinsey Institute for its work on human sexuality. In some cases, after failing to produce field notes, researchers were jailed for several months at a time (Caroll & Knerr, 1975; Lowman & Palys, 2001). In many cases, universities had not supported their researchers, allowing them to be sued and even to go to jail despite the fact that the research was conducted as part of the terms of their employment. Although only one Canadian researcher (Ogden, as discussed above) had been asked – unsuccessfully – to hand over files, we felt the risk of having our files subpoenaed was plausible.

The ethics review board and our group discussed options such as keeping the contact information in a separate location from the surveys or converting it into digital data. Because of the sensitive nature of our topic, no one disputed that confidentiality was essential or that it was our duty to assure participants of confidentiality. The board insisted that we could not promise complete confidentiality, only confidentiality permitted by law. We felt that the coy assurance "Confidentiality will be provided to the fullest extent possible by law" would mislead study participants into a false sense of security.

Finally, we approached a Toronto law firm for advice. The lawyers said we should anticipate a Wigmore defence from the beginning of the research process and that the research should not go ahead unless we were able to promise complete confidentiality. They suggested that when starting an interview, the researcher should discuss confidentiality with the participant, and specifically ask, "If there was no promise of confidentiality, would you be willing to talk to me about this matter?" They said that recording the promise of confidentiality in field notes would be absolutely essential to meet the conditions of the Wigmore test.

We sought further advice from Ted Palys, a colleague who has written extensively about the Wigmore defence. In response to our question about how to conduct research with participants whose legal status makes them vulnerable to detention and deportation, he agreed with the lawyers that we should be "anticipating Wigmore from the start" and that taking actions like meeting with the full ethics review board, obtaining legal counsel, and consulting with him would be well regarded by a court as it showed that we had always acted as though confidentiality was essential:

> Basically you should be thinking of "evidence" and the creation of a record showing how much you are concerned about your participants, which you obviously are, and of the steps you are taking to ensure that your interactions with them are as bulletproof as you can make them. This interchange between you and I [the email exchange] is similarly important insofar as it shows you are going as far as seeking expert advice on what to do. You should also make it clear in your interactions with the ERBs. Bottom line here is that it is pretty clear that everyone you are contacting recognizes that confidentiality is essential to gathering valid data and protecting the research participants, and that the project cannot happen, and the data will not exist for anyone's use (i.e., yours OR the court's) without it. (Palys, e-mail message to authors, 29 June 2005)

As a last step before finalizing our ethics protocols, and at the suggestion of a former immigration minister who was a visiting scholar at our institution at the time, we contacted CBSA asking for a letter promising to respect the confidentiality of our participants. We explained that our research was for the public good, but the response was that the agency was "mandated to remove inadmissible persons from Canada as soon as is practical." Therefore, it would be contrary to the legislative obligations of CBSA to agree not to pursue enforcement action regarding the study participants (Doiron, 2005). This meant it was even more important for us to ensure participant confidentiality.

We decided to reconsider our plan to conduct multiple interviews, and instead to carry out a single interview. This would mean that we did not need to collect any contact information. We scaled back our research plans and, in 2005, surveyed eighteen individuals living with precarious status whom we recruited through ten entry points. The survey consisted of short-answer, closed questions and was administered by the research team in the language in which the participant was most comfortable. The interview protocol concluded with four open-ended questions to draw out further details. The youth study, which had a shorter time frame for completion, involved open-ended, semi-structured interviews with six participants recruited through four entry points. We still felt that the research would provide invaluable insights into what it is like to live in Canada with precarious status, but we felt that a door had been shut. The obstacles we faced during the ethics review process prevented us from carrying out what would have been an innovative study.

The inability to conduct a follow-up interview is one of our major concerns with the legal restrictions on being able to promise complete confidentiality to participants. Data about precarious situations are incomplete and superficial unless participants are willing to tell their stories and share troubling personal experiences, and people are not willing to share this kind of personal information unless trust is established in a normative manner over the course of multiple meetings. Our inability to engage in multiple meetings was a limitation to both projects, but it was a decision we needed to make to protect our participants.

Conclusion

While the obstacles raised by our institution's ethics review board affected our subsequent decisions about the project, we do not want to overstate the role of the board in policing knowledge production in our case. We agreed with board members that the risks of detection, detention, and deportation are and were real for our participants. The board's response to our application and its cautious approach to the issues of risk and confidentiality contributed to our methodological decisions that were perhaps overly cautious; we erred on the side of caution at the expense of conducting a comprehensive study. Haggerty (2004) and Lowman and Palys (2007) have noted that research can be limited and compromised when ethics review boards focus on risk without evaluating the likelihood that potential risks might materialize. In our case, local context was an important factor in our decisions, because we faced a very real risk of being subpoenaed given the heightened focus on immigration enforcement in the city. Haggerty (2004) noted, "While academics have only rarely been asked to reveal their sources, because research is not a statutorily protected form of communication researchers can be faced with difficult decisions about whether they are willing to go to jail rather than reveal their sources" (p. 407).

Academic researchers facing such options are in an untenable position. On one hand, they face the threat of being served with a subpoena to disclose the names and phone numbers of participants and possibly being responsible for a person's life falling apart due to detention or deportation. On the other hand, they face the moral, academic, and professional dilemmas inherent in being unable to capture an individual's full experience because she or he may be safely interviewed once and only once. According to the Tri-Council Policy Statement, "Researchers should avoid being put in a position of becoming informants for authorities" (Lowman & Palys, 2007, p.170). Our research engaged two faces of the state: its research arm through the main research funding agency, the Social Science and Humanities Research Council (SSHRC), which funded our pilot study, and the Tri-Council Policy Statement, which governs the ethics review process; and its immigration enforcement arm, the Canada Border Services Agency, which polices immigration violations and which we did not want to assist. The Canadian government oversees both SSHRC and CBSA; although they are separate departments, they function within the same broad context of governance and oversight.

In this chapter we have illustrated how the ethics review board at one university tried to support what it categorized as "risky" research while prioritizing the protection of participants who are in a vulnerable position in relation to the state and whose whereabouts are of interest to particular authorities. Because of concerns about potential risks to participants and researchers, as well as different perspectives with regard to the limits of confidentiality, the voices of those who are marginalized due to their immigration status were not adequately heard. New paradigms and protocols are required so that this and other vital areas of research with marginalized populations may flourish.

NOTES

1 The local DADT campaign was launched in 2004. See http://Toronto.noo-neisillegal.org/dadt for more details.

2 The Tri-Council consists of the Social Sciences and Humanities Research Council (SSHRC), the Natural Sciences and Engineering Research Council (NSERC), and the Canadian Institutes of Health Research (CIHR), which are the three major funding bodies for research in Canada.
3 For a history of the development of institutional ERBs see Alcadipani and Hodgson (2009).
4 A more detailed account of our experiences with the ethics review process is recorded in Bernhard and Young (2009).

Bibliography

Abella, I., & Troper, H. (1982). *None Is Too Many: Canada and the Jews of Europe.* Toronto: Lester and Orpen Dennys.

Abu-Laban, Y., & Gabriel, C. (2002). *Selling Diversity: Immigration, Multiculturalism, Employment Equity and Globalization.* Peterborough: Broadview.

Access Alliance Multicultural Community Health Centre (AAMCHC). (2005). *Racialised Groups and Health Status: A Literature Review Exploring Poverty, Housing, Race-Based Discrimination and Access to Health Care as Determinants of Health for Racialised Groups.* Toronto: AAMCHC.

Adepoju, A. (2007). Creating a Borderless West Africa: Constraints and Prospects for Intra-regional Migration. In A. Pecoud & P. de Guchteneire (Eds.), *Migration without Borders: Essays on the Free Movement of People* (pp. 161–74). New York: Berghahn.

Alaggia, R., Regehr, C., & Rishchynski, G. (2009, Nov.–Dec.). Intimate Partner Violence and Immigration Laws in Canada: How Far Have We Come? *International Journal of Psychiatry and the Law, 32*(6), 335–41. http://dx.doi.org/10.1016/j.ijlp.2009.09.001. Medline:19804906.

Alba, R. (2005). Bright vs. Blurred Boundaries: Second Generation Assimilation and Exclusion in France, Germany and the United States. *Ethnic and Racial Studies, 28*(1), 20–49. http://dx.doi.org/10.1080/0141987042000280003.

Alboim, N. (2009). *Adjusting the Balance: Fixing Canada's Economic Immigration Policies.* Toronto: Maytree Foundation.

Alcadipani, R., & Hodgson, D. (2009). By Any Means Necessary? Ethnographic Access, Ethics and the Critical Researcher. *Tamara Journal, 7*(4), 127–46.

Aleinikoff, T.A., & Klusmeyer, D.B. (2001). *Citizenship Today: Global Perspectives and Practices.* Washington, DC: Carnegie Endowment for International Peace.

Alfred, A. (2002). *It's Too Expensive and Too Small: Research Findings on the Housing Conditions of Newcomers.* Toronto: St. Stephen's Community House Language Training and Newcomers Services.

Allen, G. (2008). Getting beyond Form Filling: The Role of Institutional Governance in Human Research Ethics. *Journal of Academic Ethics, 6*(2), 105–16. http://dx.doi.org/10.1007/s10805-008-9057-9.

Ang, I. (2000). Beyond Transnational Nationalism: Questioning Chinese Diasporas in the Global City. Paper presented at the International Conference on Transnational Communities in the Asia-Pacific Region, Singapore. Cited in S. Castles, Migration and Community Formation under Conditions of Globalisation, paper presented at the conference Reinventing Society in the New Economy, Toronto, 9–10 March 2001.

Anderson, B., Sharma, N., & Wright, C. (2009). Why No Borders? *Refuge: Canada's Periodical on Refugees, 26*(2), 5–17.

Anderson, K. (1991). *Vancouver's Chinatown: Racial Discourse in Canada, 1875–1980.* Montreal/Kingston: McGill-Queen's University Press.

Anderson, S.E., & Jaafar, S.B. (2003). *Policy Trends in Ontario Education 1990–2003.* International Centre for Educational Change Working Paper no. 1.

Andrijasevic, R. (2010). From Exception to Excess: Detention and Deportations across the Mediterranean Space. In N. de Genova & N. Peutz (Eds.), *The Deportation Regime: Sovereignty, Space, and the Freedom of Movement* (pp. 147–65). Durham, NC: Duke University Press.

—. (2010). Searching for Belonging – An Analytical Framework. *Geography Compass, 4*(6), 644–59. http://dx.doi.org/10.1111/j.1749-8198.2009.00317.x.

Arat-Koc, S. (1992). Immigration Policies, Migrant Domestic Workers and the Definition of Citizenship in Canada. In V. Satzewich (Ed.), *Deconstructing a Nation: Immigration, Multiculturalism and Racism in '90's Canada* (pp. 229–42). Halifax: Fernwood.

—. (2001). *Caregivers Break the Silence.* Toronto: INTERCEDE.

Atungo, S., Edwards, R., Gardner, L., Hobbs, S., Mohamed, A., & Robertson, A. (2010). Connecting Services to the Uninsured: Collaboration between CHCs and Hospitals. Paper presented at the AOHC 2010 Conference, Niagara Falls, Ontario, 10–11 June.

Audette, T. (2010). Foreign Worker Program Reassessed. *Edmonton Journal.* Retrieved 28 July 2010 from http://www2.canada.com/edmontonjournal/news/cityplus/story.html?id=b61c8005-c01b-4fc9-b613-5849500e3b9b.

Austin, D. (2007). All Roads Led to Montreal: Black Power, the Caribbean, and the Black Radical Tradition in Canada. *Journal of African American History, 92,* 516–39.

Avery, D. (1979). *"Dangerous Foreigners": European Immigrant Workers and Labour Radicalism in Canada, 1896–1932*. Toronto: McClelland and Stewart.

Bacon, D. (2008). *Illegal People: How Globalization Creates Migration and Criminalizes Immigrants*. Boston: Beacon.

Bai, D.H. (1991). Canadian Immigration Policy: Twentieth-Century Initiatives in Admission and Settlement. *Migration World Magazine, 19*(3), 9–13. Medline:12284787.

Bailey, A.J., Wright, R.A., Mountz, A., & Miyares, I.M. (2002). (Re)producing Salvadoran Transnational Geographies. *Annals of the Association of American Geographers, 92*(1), 125–44. http://dx.doi.org/10.1111/1467-8306.00283.

Bakan, A., & Stasiulis, D. (Eds.). (1997). *Not One of the Family: Foreign Domestic Workers in Canada*. Toronto: University of Toronto Press.

Bakker, M. (2011). Mexican Migration, Transnationalism, and the Re-scaling of Citizenship in North America. *Ethnic and Racial Studies, 34*(1), 1–19. http://dx.doi.org/10.1080/01419870.2010.482159.

Balibar, E. (2004). *We, the People of Europe? Reflections on Transnational Citizenship*. Princeton: Princeton University Press.

Bangarth, S.D. (2003). "We Are Not Asking You to Open the Gates for Chinese Immigration": The Committee for the Repeal of the Chinese Immigration Act and Early Human Rights Activism in Canada. *Canadian Historical Review, 84*(3), 395–422. http://dx.doi.org/10.3138/CHR.84.3.395.

Bannerman, M., Hoa, P., & Male, R. (2003). *South Riverdale Community Health Centre's Exploration of Services for Non-insured People in East Toronto*. Toronto: South Riverdale Community Health Centre.

Barbosa-Nunes, R. (2002). Brazilian Emigration: A Late 20th Century Phenomenon. Paper presented at the Congress of the Canadian Association for Latin American and Caribbean Studies, Universié du Quèbec à Montréal, 24–26 October.

Barnoff, L., & Moffatt, K. (2007). Contradictory Tensions in Anti-oppression Practice in Feminist Social Services. *Affilia, 22*(1), 56–70. Retrieved from http://aff.sagepub.com. http://dx.doi.org/10.1177/0886109906295772.

Barreto, M.A., Manzano, S., Ramirez, R., & Rim, K. (2008). Mobilization, Participation, and *Solidaridad*: Latino Participation in the 2006 Immigration Protest Rallies. *Urban Affairs Review, 44*(5), 736–64. http://dx.doi.org/10.1177/1078087409332925.

Basok, T. (2002). *Tortillas and Tomatoes: Transmigrant Mexican Harvesters in Canada*. Montreal/Kingston: McGill-Queen's University Press.

—. (2004). Post-national Citizenship, Social Exclusion and Migrants Rights: Mexican Seasonal Workers in Canada. *Citizenship Studies, 8*(1), 47–64. http://dx.doi.org/10.1080/1362102042000178409.

—. (2008). Constructing Grassroots Citizenship for Non-citizens. *Peace Review: A Journal of Social Justice, 20,* 265–72.

—. (2009). Counter-hegemonic Human Rights Discourses and Migrant Rights Activism in the U.S. and Canada. *International Journal of Comparative Sociology, 50*(2), 183–205. http://dx.doi.org/10.1177/0020715208100970.

Basok, T., Ilcan, S., & Noonan, J. (2006). Citizenship, Human Rights, and Social Justice. *Citizenship Studies, 10*(3), 267–73. http://dx.doi.org/10.1080/13621020600772040.

Basu, R. (2004). The Rationalization of Neoliberalism in Ontario's Public Education System, 1995–2000. *Geoforum, 35*(5), 621–34. http://dx.doi.org/10.1016/j.geoforum.2004.03.003.

—. (2007). Negotiating Acts of Citizenship in an Era of Neoliberal Reform: The Game of School Closures. *International Journal of Urban and Regional Research, 31*(1), 109–27. http://dx.doi.org/10.1111/j.1468-2427.2007.00709.x.

Bauder, H. (2006). *Labor Movement: How Migration Regulates Labor Markets.* New York: Oxford University Press.

Becerril Quintana, O. (2007). Transnational Work and the Gendered Politics of Labour: A Study of Male and Female Mexican Migrant Farm Workers in Canada. In L. Goldring & S. Krishnamurti (Eds.), *Organizing the Transnational: Labour, Politics, and Social Change* (pp. 157–72). Vancouver: UBC Press.

Bejan, R., & Sidhu, N. (2010). *Policy without Practice: Barriers to Enrolment for Non-Status Immigrant Students in Toronto's Catholic schools.* Toronto: Social Planning Toronto.

Benhabib, S. (2002). *The Claims of Culture: Equality and Diversity in the Global Era.* Princeton: Princeton University Press.

—. (2007). Twilight of Sovereignty or the Emergence of Cosmopolitan Norms? Rethinking Citizenship in Volatile Times. *Citizenship Studies, 11*(1), 19–36. http://dx.doi.org/10.1080/13621020601099807.

Berinstein, C., McDonald, J., Nyers, P., Wright, C., & Zerehi, S. (2006). *"Access Not Fear": Non-Status Immigrants and City Services.*

Berk, M.L., & Schur, C.L. (2001, July). The Effect of Fear on Access to Care among Undocumented Latino Immigrants. *Journal of Immigrant Health, 3*(3), 151–6. http://dx.doi.org/10.1023/A:1011389105821. Medline:16228780.

Bernal, D.D. (2002). Critical Race Theory, Latino Critical Theory, and Critical Raced-Epistemologies: Recognizing Students of Color as Holders and Creators of Knowledge. *Qualitative Inquiry, 8*(1), 105–26.

Bernhard, J.K., & Freire, M. (1997). Caring for and Teaching Children of Refugee Families. In K.M. Kilbride (Ed.), *Include Me Too: Human Diversity in Early Childhood* (pp. 177–96). Toronto: Harcourt Brace.

Bernhard, J.K., Goldring, L., Young, J., Berinstein, C., & Wilson, B. (2007). Living with Precarious Legal Status in Canada: Implications for the Well-Being of Children and Families. *Refuge: Canada's Periodical on Refugees, 24*(2), 101–14.

Bernhard, J.K., Landolt, P., & Goldring, L. (2005). *Transnational, Multi-local Motherhood: Experiences of Separation and Reunification among Latin 'American Families in Canada.* CERIS Working Paper no. 40. Toronto: CERIS.

Bernhard, J.K., & Young, J.E.E. (2009). Gaining Institutional Permission: Researching Precarious Legal Status in Canada. *Journal of Academic Ethics, 7*(3), 175–91. http://dx.doi.org/10.1007/s10805-009-9097-9.

Bernhardt, A.D., Boushey, H., Dresser, L., & Tilly, C. (2008). *The Gloves-Off Economy: Workplace Standards at the Bottom of America's Labor Market.* Champaign, IL: Labor and Employment Relations Association.

Bezanson, K. (2006). *Gender, the State and Social Reproduction.* Toronto: University of Toronto Press.

Bhuyan, R. (2012). Negotiating Citizenship on the Frontlines: How the Devolution of Canadian Immigration Policy Shapes Services Delivery to Women Fleeing Abuse. *Law & Policy, 34*(2), 211–36. http://dx.doi.org/10.1111/j.1467-9930.2011.00361.x.

Binford, L., Carrasco Rivas, G., Arana Hernandez, S., & Santillana de Rojas, S. (2004). *Rumbo a Canadá: La Migración Canadiense de Trabajadores Agrícolas Tlaxcaltecas.* Mexico City: Ediciones Taller Abierto.

Black, R., Collyer, M., Skeldon, R., & Waddington, C. (2006). Routes to Illegal Residence: A Case Study of Immigration Detainees in the United Kingdom. *Geoforum, 37*(4), 552–64. http://dx.doi.org/10.1016/j.geoforum.2005.09.009.

Bledsoe, C.H., Sherin, B., Galinsky, A.G., Headley, N.M., Heimer, C.A., Kjeldgaard, E., et al. (2007). Regulating Creativity: Research and Survival in the ERB Iron Cage. *Northwestern University Law Review, 101*(2), 593–642.

Bloch, A. (2010). The Right to Rights?: Undocumented Migrants from Zimbabwe Living in South Africa. *Sociology, 44*(2), 233–50. http://dx.doi.org/10.1177/0038038509357209.

Bloch, A., & Schuster, L. (2005). At the Extremes of Exclusion: Deportation, Detention and Dispersal. *Ethnic and Racial Studies, 28*(3), 491–512. http://dx.doi.org/10.1080/0141987042000337858.

Bloemraad, I. (2006). *Becoming a Citizen: Incorporating Immigrants and Refugees in the United States and Canada.* Berkeley: University of California Press.

—. (2007). Unity in Diversity? Bridging Models of Multiculturalism and Immigrant Integration. *Du Bois Review, 4*(2), 317–36.

Bloom, T., & Feldman, R. (2011). Migration and Citizenship: Rights and Exclusions. In R. Sabates-Wheeler & R. Feldman (Eds.), *Migration and Social*

Protection: Vulnerability, Mobility and Access (pp. 36–60). Houndmills, Basingstoke, UK: Palgrave Macmillan.

Bohaker, H., & Iacovetta, F. (2009). Making Aboriginal People "Immigrants Too": A Comparison of Citizenship Programs for Newcomers and Indigenous Peoples in Postwar Canada, 1940s–1960s. *Canadian Historical Review, 90*(3), 427–62. http://dx.doi.org/10.3138/chr.90.3.427.

Bombardier, C.A. (2007). The Lived Realities of Less than Full Immigration Status Women Navigating "The System." Major research paper, Ryerson University. http://catalogue.library.ryerson.ca/.

Bonacich, E. (1979). The Past, Present, and Future of Split Labour Market Theory. In C.B. Marrett & C. Legon (Eds.), *Research in Race and Ethnic Relations,* vol. 1 (pp. 17–64). Greenwich, Ct: JAI Press.

Bonisteel, M., & Green, L. (2005). *Implications of the Shrinking Space for Feminist Anti-Violence Advocacy.* Paper presented at the Canadian Social Welfare Policy Conference, Fredericton, New Brunswick, 16–18 June.

Bonnar, J. (2010, 10 March). Community Groups Demand an End to Immigration Enforcement Entering Women's Shelters. *Rabble.* Retrieved 29 March 2010 from http://rabble.ca/blogs/bloggers/johnbon/2010/03/community-groups-demand-end-immigration-enforcement-entering-women%E2%80%99s-.

Bose, P. (2007). Development and Diasporic Capital: Nonresident Indians and the State. In L. Goldring & S. Krishnamurti (Eds.), *Organizing the Transnational: Labour, Politics and Social Change* (pp. 173–87). Vancouver: University of British Columbia Press.

Bosniak, L. (1994). Membership, Equality, and the Difference That Alienage Makes. *New York University Law Review, 69*(6), 1047–1149.

—. (2000a). Citizenship Denationalized. *Indiana Journal of Global Legal Studies, 7*(2), 447–510.

—. (2000b). Universal Citizenship and the Problem of Alienage. *Northwestern Law Review, 94,* 963–84.

—. (2006). *The Citizen and the Alien: Dilemmas of Contemporary Membership.* Princeton: Princeton University Press.

—. (2009). Citizenship, Noncitizenship, and the Transnationalization of Domestic Work. In S. Benhabib & J. Resnik (Eds.), *Migrations and Mobilities: Citizenship, Borders, and Gender* (pp. 127–56). New York: New York University Press.

Bourdieu, P. (1979). *Distinction: A Social Critique of the Judgement of Taste.* Cambridge, MA: Harvard University Press.

Boyd, M., & Grieco, E. (2003). *Women and Migration: Incorporating Gender into International Migration Theory.* Washington, DC: Migration Policy Institute.

Retrieved from Migration Information Source, http://www.migrationinformation.org/Feature/display.cfm?ID=106..

Brennan, R. (2012, 31 May). Refugees Will Die If Health Care Cuts Go Ahead Ontario Nurses Say. *Toronto Star*. Retrieved 5 June 2012 from http://www.thestar.com/news/canada/politics/article/1202871--refugees-will-die-if-health-care-cuts-go-ahead-ontario-nurses-say.

Brennan, R., & Wong, T. (2006, 22 March). Don't Deport Honest Workers: Builder Skills Are Critical for Construction. *Toronto Star*, p. A1.

Brettell, C.B. (2005). Voluntary Organizations, Social Capital, and the Social Incorporation of Asian Indian Immigrants in the Dallas–Fort Worth Metroplex. *Anthropological Quarterly*, 78(4), 853–82. http://dx.doi.org/10.1353/anq.2005.0052.

Briere, J., & Scott, C. (2006). *Principles of Trauma Therapy: A Guide to Symptoms, Evaluation, and Treatment*. London: Sage.

Brubaker, R. (2001). The Return of Assimilation? Changing Perspectives on Immigration and Its Sequels in France, Germany, and the United States. *Ethnic and Racial Studies*, 24(4), 531–48. http://dx.doi.org/10.1080/01419870120049770.

Burawoy, M. (1976). The Functions and Reproduction of Migrant Labor: Comparative Material from Southern Africa and the United States. *American Journal of Sociology*, 81(5), 1050–87. http://dx.doi.org/10.1086/226185.

Burgers, J. (1998). In the Margin of the Welfare State: Labour Position and Housing Conditions of Undocumented Immigrants in Rotterdam. *Urban Studies (Edinburgh, Scotland)*, 35(10), 1855–68. http://dx.doi.org/10.1080/0042098984187.

Burridge, A. (2009). Differential Criminalization under Operation Streamline: Challenges to Freedom of Movement and Humanitarian Aid Provision in the U.S.–Mexico Borderlands. *Refuge: Canada's Periodical on Refugees*, 26(2), 78–91.

Cahill, C. (2010). "Why Do *They* Hate *Us*?" Reframing Immigration through Participatory Action Research. *Area*, 42(2), 152–61. http://dx.doi.org/10.1111/j.1475-4762.2009.00929.x.

Calavita, K. (1998). Immigration, Law, and Marginalization in a Global Economy: Notes from Spain. *Law & Society Review*, 32(3), 529–66. http://dx.doi.org/10.2307/827756.

Camiscioli, E. (2009). *Reproducing the French Race: Immigration, Intimacy, and Embodiment in the Early Twentieth Century*. Durham: Duke University Press.

Campion-Smith, B. (2006, 23 March). No Hike in Deportations, Solberg Says. *Toronto Star*, pp. A1, A6.

Canada Mortgage and Housing Corporation. (2006). *Canadian Housing Observer 2006*. Ottawa: Canada Mortgage and Housing Corporation.

Canadian Association of Refugee Lawyers. (2012, 8 March). Highlights – Bill C-31. Retrieved 10 April 2012 from http://www.cdp-jrc/uottawa.ca/projects/refugee-forum/documents/CARLC-31HIGHLIGHTSENGLISH.pdf.

Canadian Bar Association. (2006). Low Skilled Worker Pilot Project. Ottawa. Retrieved 5 May 2010 from http://www.cba.org/CBA/submissions/pdf/06-24-eng.pdf.

Canadian Centre for Victims of Torture (CCVT). (2010). http://ccvt.org/2010/02/children-youth-program/. Accessed 19 July 2010.

Canadian Council for Refugees (CCR). (1999). Proposed Changes to the Immigration Act: Gender Analysis. Retrieved 29 November 2005 from http://www.web.net/%7Eccr/whitegen.htm#N_1_.

—. (2006). Refugee Appeal Division Backgrounder. Retrieved 30 November 2010 from http://www.ccrweb.ca/RADbackgrounder.pdf.

—. (2007, 25 September). Canadian Refugee System Made Vulnerable by Government Inaction. Press release. http://www.ccrweb.ca/eng/media/pressreleases/25sept07.htm. Accessed 28 December, 2008.

—. (2009a). Comments on Proposed Changes to the Temporary Foreign Workers Program. Retrieved 4 December 2009 from http://www.ccrweb.ca/documents/TMWregulationscomments.pdf.

—. (2009b). The Challenges of Fair and Effective Refugee Determination. Retrieved 10 June 2010 from http://www.ccrweb.ca/documents/fairdetermination.pdf.

—. (2009c). Grant Rates by Country of Origin. Retrieved 22 November 2010 from http://www.ccrweb.ca/documents/rehaag/2009/Table%206.xls.

—. (2010). Proposed Refugee Reform Undermines Fairness to Refugees. Retrieved 31 March 2010 from http://ccrweb.ca/en/bulletin/10/03/30.

Canadian Labour Congress. (2006). Submission by the Canadian Labour Congress to the House of Commons Standing Committee on Human Resources, Social Development and the Status of Persons with Disabilities, 28 November 28. Ottawa: Canadian Labour Congress. http://www.canadianlabour.ca/sites/default/files/pdfs/HUMA-Brief-FINAL-E.pdf.

Capps, R., Fix, M.E., Passel, J.S., Ost, J., & Perez-Lopez, D. (2003). A Profile of the Low-Wage Immigrant Workforce. Washington, DC: Urban Institute.

Caroll, J., & Knerr, C. (1975). Confidentiality and Social Science Research Sources and Data: The Popkin Case. Political Science Quarterly, 6, 268–80.

Castañeda, H. (2010). Deportation Deferred: "Illegality," Visibility, and Recognition in Contemporary Germany. In N. de Genova & N. Peutz (Eds.), The Deportation Regime: Sovereignty, Space, and Freedom of Movement (pp. 245–61). Durham: Duke University Press.

Carter, T. (2008). *The Housing Circumstances of Recently Arrived Refugees: The Winnipeg Experience*. Winnipeg: Prairie Metropolis Centre.

Castles, S., & Kosak, G. (1973). *Immigrant Workers and Class Structure in Western Europe*. London: Oxford University Press.

Castles, S., & Miller, M.J. (1998). *The Age of Migration: International Population Movements in the Modern World*. 2nd ed. New York: Guilford.

—. (2009). *The Age of Migration*. 4th ed. New York: Guilford.

Caulford, P., & Vali, Y. (2006, 25 April). Providing Health Care to Medically Uninsured Immigrants and Refugees. *CMAJ (Canadian Medical Association Journal)*, 174(9), 1253–54. http://dx.doi.org/10.1503/cmaj.051206. Medline:16636321.

Cavazos-Rehg, P.A., Zayas, L.H., & Spitznagel, E.L. (2007, Oct.). Legal Status, Emotional Well-Being and Subjective Health Status of Latino Immigrants. *Journal of the National Medical Association*, 99(10), 1126–31. Medline:17987916.

Chakkalakal, E.J., & Neve, A. (1998). Living without Status in Canada: Human Rights Underground. Paper presented at the Inter-American Human Rights Commission, Toronto, 22 October.

Chan, W., & Mirchandani, K. (2007). *Criminalizing Race, Criminalizing Poverty: Welfare Fraud Enforcement in Canada*. Black Point, NS: Fernwood.

Chavez, L.R. (1991). Outside the Imagined Community: Undocumented Settlers and Experiences of Incorporation. *American Ethnologist*, 18(2), 257–78. http://dx.doi.org/10.1525/ae.1991.18.2.02a00040.

Cheran, R. (2007). Transnationalism, Development and Social Capital: Tamil Community Networks in Canada. In L. Goldring & S. Krishnamurti (Eds.), *Organizing the Transnational: Labour, Politics and Social Change* (pp. 129–44). Vancouver: University of British Columbia Press.

Chun, J. (2009). *Organizing at the Margins: The Symbolic Politics of Labor in South Korea and the United States*. Ithaca, NY: Cornell University Press.

Cholewinski, R. (2004). *The Legal Status of Migrants Admitted for Employment*. Strasbourg: Council of Europe.

Citizenship and Immigration Canada. (2008a). Canada's Government to Help Temporary Foreign Workers and Foreign Student Graduates Become Permanent Residents. Press release. Ottawa, 12 August.

—. (2008b, November). Facts and Figures 2007 – Immigration Overview: Permanent and Temporary Residents. Retrieved 21 December 2008 from www.cic.gc.ca/english/pdf/pub/facts2007.pdf.

—. (2008c). Operational Bulletin 087 – Separation of Processing Streams at CPC-V, New vs. Existing Employer Applications, Applications Processed in Canada. Ottawa, 14 November. http://www.cic.gc.ca/english/resources/manuals/bulletins/2008/ob087.asp.

—. (2009a). *Annual Report to Parliament on Immigration*. Ottawa: CIC.

—. (2009b). *Facts and Figures 2008 – Immigration Overview; Permanent and Temporary Residents, Canada, Temporary Residents by Yearly Status, 1984 to 2008*. Ottawa: CIC.

—. (2009c). Formative Evaluation of the Pre-Removal Risk Assessment Program. Ottawa: CIC. Retrieved 13 June2010 from http://www.cic.gc.ca/english/resources/evaluation/prra/section4.asp.

—. (2009d). Minister Kenney Proposes Significant Improvements to the Live-in Caregiver Program. Press release. http://www.cic.gc.ca/english/department/media/releases/2009/2009-12-12.asp. Accessed 19 August 2010.

—. (2009f). Operational Bulletin 092 – New Directives on Implied Status. 15 January. Ottawa: CIC.

—. (2010a). Applying to Change Conditions or Extend Your Stay in Canada – Worker. IMM 5553E (02–2010). February. Ottawa: CIC.

—. (2010b). Changes at the Immigration and Refugee Board of Canada (IRB). Ottawa: CIC. Retrieved 13 May2011 from http://www.cic.gc.ca/english/refugees/reform-irb.asp.

—. (2010d). *Facts and Figures 2009*. Ottawa: Minister of Public Works and Government Services. http://www.cic.gc.ca/english/resources/statistics/facts2009/temporary/01.asp. Accessed 16 August 2010.

—. (2010e). FW 1: Temporary Foreign Worker Guidelines. Ottawa: CIC.

—. (2011a). Facts and Figures 2010 – Immigration Overview: Permanent and Temporary Residents. Updated 30 August 2011. Retrieved various dates, most recently 17 December 2011, from http://www.cic.gc.ca/english/resources/statistics/facts2010/index.asp.

—. (2011b). Regulatory Changes to the Temporary Foreign Worker Program Take Effect April 1st, 2011. Updated 31 March 2011. http://www.cic.gc.ca/english/work/changes.asp.

—. (n.d.). Skilled Workers and Professionals: Who Can Apply – Six Selection Factors and Pass Mark. Retrieved 11 July 2007 from http://www.cic.gc.ca/english/immigrate/skilled/apply-factors.asp.

City of Toronto. (1999). *Taking Responsibility for Homelessness: An Action Plan for Toronto*. Toronto: Mayor's Homelessness Action Task Force. http://www.toronto.ca/pdf/homeless_action.pdf.

—. (2006). *Toronto's Racial Diversity*. Retrieved 5 November 2010 from http://www.toronto.ca/toronto_facts/diversity.htm.

Clandestino Project. (2009). Size and Development of Irregular Migration to the EU. Comparative policy brief. Retrieved 13 January 2012 from http://clandestino.eliamep.gr.

Clapham, D. (2002). Housing Pathways: A Post Modern Analytical Framework. *Housing Theory and Society, 19*, 57–68.

Cobb-Clark, D.A., & Kossoudji, S.A. (1999). Did Legalization Matter for Women? Amnesty and the Wage Determinants of Formerly Unauthorized Latina Workers. *Gender Issues, 17*(4), 3–14. http://dx.doi.org/10.1007/s12147-998-0001-5.

Collacott, M. (2010). Reforming the Canadian Refugee Determination System. *Refuge: Canada's Periodical on Refugees, 27*(1), 110–18.

Committee for Accessible AIDS Treatment (CAAT). (2001). *Improving Access to Legal Services and Health Care for People Living with HIV/AIDS Who Are Immigrants, Refugees or without Status.* Action research report. Toronto: Regent Park Community Health Centre. http://www.regentparkchc.org/CAAT%20com%20Final%20report.PDF. Accessed 23 October 2009.

—. (2006). Status, Access & Health Disparities: A Literature Review Report on Relevant Policies and Programs Affecting People Living with HIV/AIDS Who Are Immigrants, Refugees or without Status in Canada. Toronto: CAAT.

Community Health Centres of Greater Toronto. (2008, September). *Community Health Centres, Hospitals and People without Health Insurance.* Toronto: CHCGT. Cook, C. (2009, 4 April). Immigration Raids and Mass Detentions Come to Canada. Online. http://www.pacificfreepress.com/news/1/3971-immigration-raids-and-mass-detentions-come-to-canada.html.

Cook, M.L. (2009). The New Normal: Illegality, Detention, Exclusion. Paper presented at the conference Migration, Work and Citizenship: Toward Decent Work and Secure Citzenship, Toronto, 1–3 October.

—. (2010). The Advocate's Dilemma: Framing Migrant Rights in National Settings. *Studies in Social Justice, 4*(2), 145–64.

Cornelius, W. (1982). *Interviewing Undocumented Immigrants: Methodological Reflections Based on Fieldwork in Mexico and the U.S.* San Diego: University of California.

Coulter, K. (2009). Women, Poverty Policy, and the Production of Neoliberal Politics in Ontario, Canada. *Journal of Women, Politics & Policy, 30*(1), 23–45. http://dx.doi.org/10.1080/15544770802367788.

Coutin, S.B. (1998). From Refugees to Immigrants: The Legalization Strategies of Salvadoran Immigrants and Activists. *International Migration Review, 32*(4), 901–25. http://dx.doi.org/10.2307/2547665. Medline:12294301.

—. (2000). *Legalizing Moves: Salvadoran Immigrants' Struggle for U.S. Residency.* Ann Arbor, MI: University of Michigan Press.

—. (2005). Contesting Criminality: Illegal Immigration and the Spatialization of Legality. *Theoretical Criminology, 9*(1), 5–33. http://dx.doi.org/10.1177/1362480605046658.

Crépeau, F., & Nakache, D. (2006). Controlling Irregular Migration in Canada: Reconciling Security Concerns with Human Rights Protection. *IRPP Choices, 12*(1), 1–44.

Cross, J. (2010). Neoliberalism as Unexceptional: Economic Zones and the Everyday Precariousness of Working Life in South India. *Critique of Anthropology, 30*(4), 355–73. http://dx.doi.org/10.1177/0308275X10372467.

Daly, G. (1996). *Homeless*. London: Routledge.

Daniels, C. (1997). The Paradoxes of State Power. In C. Daniels et al. (Eds.), *Feminists Negotiate the State: The Politics of Domestic Violence* (pp. 1–4). Lanham, MD: University Press of America.

Dauvergne, C. (2008). *Making People Illegal: What Globalization Means for Migration and Law*. New York: Cambridge University Press.

de Genova, N. (2002). Migrant "Illegality" and Deportability in Everyday Life. *Annual Review of Anthropology, 31*(1), 419–47. http://dx.doi.org/10.1146/annurev.anthro.31.040402.085432.

—. (2005). *Working the Boundaries: Race, Space and "Illegality" in Mexican Chicago*. Durham: Duke University Press.

—. (2007). The Production of Culprits: From Deportability to Detainability in the Aftermath of "Homeland Security." *Citizenship Studies, 11*(5), 421–48. http://dx.doi.org/10.1080/13621020701605735.

de Genova, N. & Peutz, N. (Eds.). (2010). *The Deportation Regime: Sovereignty, Space, and Freedom of Movement*. Durham: Duke University Press.

Decter, A. (2007). *Lost in the Shuffle: The Impact of Homelessness on Children's Education in Toronto: Phase 3 of the Kid Builders Research Project*. Toronto: Community Social Planning Council of Toronto.

Delgado, H.L. (1993). *New Immigrants, Old Unions: Organizing Undocumented Workers in Los Angeles*. Philadelphia: Temple University Press.

Delgado, R., & Stefancic, J. (2000). *Critical Race Theory: The Cutting Edge*. 2nd ed. Philadelphia: Temple University Press.

Dennis, J. (2002). *A Case for Change: How Refugee Children in England Are Missing Out*. London: Refugee Children's Consortium.

Denton, F., Feaver, C., & Spencer, B. (1997). *Immigration, Labour Force, and the Age Structure of the Population*. Quantitative Studies in Economics and Population Research Reports. Hamilton: McMaster University.

Derrida, J. (1968). "La Différance." In Tel Quel, *Théorie d'ensemble* (pp. 41–66). Paris: Seuil.

—. (1992). *The Other Heading: Reflections on Today's Europe*. Bloomington: Indiana University Press.

—. (2002, August/September). "What Is Owed to the Stranger?" 60 *Arena Magazine* 5. Available from http://www.thefreelibrary.com/Arena+Magazine/2002/August/1-p5699.

Department of Finance Canada. (2007). A Stronger Canada through a Stronger Economy. In Department of Finance Canada, *Budget Plan* (pp. 147–248). Ottawa: Department of Finance.

Department of Manpower and Immigration Canada. (1975). *Canadian Immigration and Population Study: Green Paper on Immigration and Population*. Ottawa: Information Canada.

—. (2005). *1966–1976 Immigration Statistics*. Ottawa: Canada Immigration Division. http://epe.lac-bac.gc.ca/100/202/301/immigration_statistics-ef/index.html. Accessed 16 August 2010.

DeSantis, G. (2010). Voices from the Margins: Policy Advocacy and Marginalized Communities. *Canadian Journal of Nonprofit and Social Economy Research*, 1(1), 23–45.

Dion, K. (2001). Immigrants' Perceptions of Housing Discrimination in Toronto: The Housing New Canadians Project. *Journal of Social Issues*, 57(3), 523–39.

Doherty, G., Friendly, M., & Oloman, M. (1998). Women's Support, Women's Work: Childcare in an Era of Deficit Reduction, Devolution, Downsizing and Deregulation. Vol. Cat. no. SW21–28/1998. Ottawa: Status of Women Canada.

Doiron, M. (2005). Email message to authors, 16 September.

Doolittle, R. (2008, 21 November). Board Rejects "Don't Tell" Policy: Police Service's Decision to Stick to Rules on Illegal Immigrants Puts Women at Risk, Advocates Say. *Toronto Star*. Retrieved 9 January 2009 from http://www.thestar.com/article/540891.

Dua, E. (2000). The Hindu Woman's Question. *Canadian Woman Studies*, 20(2), 108–16.

—. (2003). Towards Theorizing the Connections between Governmentality, Imperialism, Race, and Citizenship: Indian Migrants and Racialisation of Canadian Citizenship. In D. Brock (Ed.), *Making Normal: Social Regulation in Canada* (pp. 40–62). Scarborough: Nelson.

Dyck, D. (2010). Olympic Torch's Long Journey at Emotional End. *Canadian Press*. Retrieved 25 March 2010 from http://www.cbc.ca/news/canada/british-columbia/story/2010/02/12/bc-olympic-relay-final-day.html.

Dyer, S., & Demeritt, D. (2009). Un-ethical Review? Why It Is Wrong to Apply the Medical Model of Research Governance to Human

Geography. *Progress in Human Geography, 33*(1), 46–64. http://dx.doi.
org/10.1177/0309132508090475.

Ebaugh, H.R., & Curry, M. (2000). Fictive Kin as Social Capital. *Sociological Perspectives, 43*(2), 189–209.

Edoney, H.T. (1979). *Cry of the Illegal Immigrants*. Republished as J.C. Fraser (1980), *Cry of the Illegal Immigrant*. Toronto: Williams-Wallace.

Education Not Deportation Committee. (2009). Education Not Deportation: Access without Fear. http://toronto.nooneisillegal.org/node/235.

Edwards, R. (2009). Creating Health Equity in the Toronto Central LHIN. http://www.stjoe.on.ca/community/pdf/health_equity_report.pdf. Accessed 1 December 2010.

Elgersma, S. (2008). *Immigration Status and Legal Entitlement to Insured Health Services*. PRB 08–28e. Pp. 1–11. Ottawa: Library of Parliament, Political and Social Affairs Division.

Ellermann, A. (2005). Coercive Capacity and the Politics of Implementation: Deportation in Germany and the United States. *Comparative Political Studies, 38*(10), 1219–44. http://dx.doi.org/10.1177/0010414005279117.

Employment and Immigration Canada . (2005). *1977–1987 Immigration Statistics*. Ottawa: Minister of Supply and Services. http://epe.lac-bac.gc.ca/100/202/301/immigration_statistics-ef/index.html. Accessed 16 August 2010.

Enns, R. (2005). Immigrant Households and Homelessness. *Canadian Issues*, Spring: 127–30. http://canada.metropolis.net/pdfs/CITC_Spring_05_EN.pdf.

Faist, T. (2000). Transnationalization in International Migration: Implications for the Study of Citizenship and Culture. *Ethnic and Racial Studies, 23*(2), 189–222. http://dx.doi.org/10.1080/014198700329024.

Fanon, F. (1963). *The Wretched of the Earth*. New York: Grove.

Fantino, A.M., & Colak, A. (2001). Refugee Children in Canada: Searching for Identity. *Child Welfare, 80*(5), 587–96. Medline:11678416.

Federal Court, Canada. (2006). Judicial Review (Immigration). Practice guide. Retrieved 13 June 2010 from http://casncrnter03.cassatj.gc.ca/portal/page/portal/fc_cf_en/Practice_Guide_Immigration/Practice_Guide_Immigration2.

Feldman, D. (2007). Global Movements, Internal Migration, and the Importance of Institutions. *International Journal of Social History, 52*, 105–9.

Fernandez, L. (2002). Telling Stories about School: Using Critical Race and Latino Critical Theories to Document Latina/Latino Education and Resistance. *Qualitative Inquiry, 8*(1), 45–65.

Fiedler, R.N., Schuurman, N., & Hyndman, J. (2006). Hidden Homelessness in Greater Vancouver. *Cities, 23*(3), 205–16. http://dx.doi.org/10.1016/j.cities.2006.03.004.

Fitzgerald, D. (2006). Inside the Sending State: The Politics of Mexican Emigration Control. *International Migration Review, 40*(2), 259–93. http://dx.doi.org/10.1111/j.1747-7379.2006.00017.x.

Fitzgerald, M. (2005). Punctuated Equilibrium, Moral Panics and the Ethics Review Process. *Journal of Academic Ethics, 2*(4), 315–38. http://dx.doi.org/10.1007/s10805-005-9004-y.

Fitzpatrick, P. (2001). *Modernism and the Grounds of Law*. Cambridge: Cambridge University Press.

—. (1995). *Nationalism, Racism, and the Rule of Law*. Aldershot, UK: Dartmouth.

Fix, M., & Laglagaron, L. (2002). *Social Rights and Citizenship: An International Comparison*. Washington, DC: The Urban Institute.

Fix, M.E., & Zimmermann, W. (1999). *All under One Roof: Mixed-Status Families in an Era of Reform*. Washington, DC: Urban Institute.

Fontaine, L. (2005). Processus d'établissement, nouvel arrivant et structure d'accueil a Halifax (Nouvelle-Ecosse): Une exploration de quelques actions concrètes. *Canadian Ethnic Studies, 38*(3), 136–49.

Fortier, C. (2005). Regent Park Is Our Fallujah: Constructing an Activist Praxis within Local Contestations of War & Globalization in Toronto. Master's thesis, University of Toronto.

Foucault, M. (1979). *Discipline and Punish: The Birth of the Prison*. Trans. A.M. Sheridan. New York: Vintage.

—. (1980). *Power/Knowledge: Selected Interviews and Other Writings, 1972–1977*. Trans. C.Gordon, L. Marshall, J. Mepham, & K. Soper. New York: Pantheon.

Fox, J. (2005). Unpacking "Transnational Citizenship." *Annual Review of Political Science, 8*(1), 171–201. http://dx.doi.org/10.1146/annurev.polisci.7.012003.104851.

Francis, J. (2009). *"You Cannot Settle like This": The Housing Situation of African Refugees in Metro Vancouver*. Working Paper Series no. 09-02, Metropolis British Columbia, Vancouver.

—. (2010). Poor Housing Outcomes among African Refugees in Metro Vancouver. *Canadian Issues,* Fall, 59–63. http://canada.metropolis.net/publications/aec_citc_fall2010_e.pdf.

Fudge, J., & MacPhail, F. (2009). The Temporary Foreign Worker Program in Canada: Low-Skilled Workers as an Extreme Form of Flexible Labour. *Comparative Labor Law & Policy Journal, 31*, 5–45.

Gabaccia, D. (1997). The "Yellow Peril" and the "Chinese of Europe": Global Perspectives on Race and Labor, 1815–1930. In J. Lucassen & L. Lucassen (Eds.), *Migration, Migration History, History* (pp. 177–96). Bern: Peter Lang.

Gabaccia, D., & Iacovetta, F. (2002). *Women, Gender, and Transnational Lives: Italian Workers of the World*. Toronto: University of Toronto Press.

Galabuzi, G.E. (2004). Social Exclusion. In D. Raphael (Ed.), *Social Determinants of Health: Canadian Perspective* (pp. 235–51). Toronto: Canadian Scholars' Press.

Gaonkar, D., & Taylor, C. (2006). Block Thinking and Internal Criticism. *Public Culture, 18*(3), 453–55. http://dx.doi.org/10.1215/08992363-2006-014.

Gardner, B. (2008). *Health Equity Discussion Paper.* Toronto: Toronto Central LHIN.

Giddens, A. (1984). *The Constitution of Society: Outline of a Theory of Structuration.* Berkeley: University of California Press.

Gill, N. (2009). Whose "No Borders"? Achieving Border Liberalization for the Right Reasons. *Refuge: Canada's Periodical on Refugees, 26*(2), 107–20.

Girzu, A. (2010, 21 April). Fewer Refugees Allowed in Under Conservative Rule, Figures Show. *Embassy.* Retrieved 14 June2010 from http://www.embassymag.ca/page/view/refugees-04-21-2010.

Gluszyski, T., & Dhawan-Biswal, U. (2008). *Reading Skills of Young Immigrants in Canada: The Effects of Duration of Residency, Home Language Exposure and Schools.* Learning Policy Directorate, Strategic Policy and Research, Human Resources and Social Development Canada. http://www.hrsdc.gc.ca/eng/publications_resources/learning_policy/sp_849_06_08/page01.shtml. Accessed 18 August 2010.

Go, A. (2002, March). The Broken Dream of an Immigrant without Status. *OCASI* (Ontario Council of Agencies Serving Immigrants) *Monthly Report,* p. 5.

Goldring, L. (2010). The Conditionality of Precarious Legal Status. Paper presented at the Workshop on Liberating Temporariness: Imagining Alternatives to Permanence as a Pathway to Social Inclusion, Toronto, 10–11 December.

Goldring, L., & Berinstein, C. (2003). More and Less Legal: Bringing Legal Status and Rights into the Open in Canada. Paper presented at Migration and Integration in the Americas, Annual Conference of the Center for Research on Latin America and the Caribbean, Toronto, 19–20 September.

Goldring, L., Berinstein, C., & Bernhard, J.K. (2007). *Institutionalizing Precarious Immigration Status in Canada.* CERIS Working paper no. 61. Toronto: CERIS.

—. (2009). Institutionalizing Precarious Migratory Status in Canada. *Citizenship Studies, 13*(3), 239–65. http://dx.doi.org/10.1080/13621020902850643.

Goldring, L., Hennebry, J., & Preibisch, K. (2009). Temporary Worker Programs: North America's Second-Class Citizens. *Canada Watch,* Summer.

Goldring, L., & Landolt, P. (2009a). Immigrants and Precarious Employment. Research brief. Retrieved 14 August 2009 from http://www.arts.yorku.ca/research/ine/research/publications.html.

—. (2009b). *Research Brief 1 – The Index of Precarious Work (IPW): A Measure to Track Progress towards Decent Work*. Toronto: Cities Centre, CERIS, York University.

—. (2009c). *Research Brief 2 – Immigrants and Precarious Work*. Toronto: Cities Centre, CERIS, York University.

—. (2009d). *Research Brief 3 – Immigrant Strategies to Improve Work and Achieve Income Security*. Toronto: Cities Centre, CERIS, York University.

—. (2011). Caught in the Work-Citizenship Matrix: The Lasting Effects of Precarious Legal Status on Work for Toronto Immigrants. *Globalizations, 8*(3), 325–41. http://dx.doi.org/10.1080/14747731.2011.576850.

Gonzáles, R.G. (2008). Left Out but Not Shut Down: Political Activism and the Undocumented Student Movement. *Northwestern Journal of Law and Social Policy, 3*, 219–39.

Goutor, D. (2007). *Guarding the Gates: The Canadian Labour Movement and Immigration, 1872–1934*. Vancouver: University of British Columbia Press.

Government of Alberta. (2009). Filing a Complaint with Employment Standards. Retrieved 1 November 2009 from http://www.employment.alberta.ca/SFW/1697.html.

Government of Canada. (1976). Immigration Act. SC 176-77, c. 52. Ottawa: Supply and Services.

—. (1996). Employment Insurance Act. S.C. 1996, c. 23. Ottawa: Supply and Services.

—. (2008, November). Ministerial Instructions. *Canada Gazette, 142*(48).

—. (2009, 10 October). Regulations Amending the Immigration and Refugee Protection Regulations (Temporary Foreign Workers) – Statutory Authority: Immigration and Refugee Protection Act, Sponsoring Department: Department of Citizenship and Immigration. *Canada Gazette, 143*(41).

Goza, F. (1994). Brazilian Immigration to North America. *International Migration Review, 28*(1), 136–52. http://dx.doi.org/10.2307/2547029. Medline:12287274.

—. (2003). Redes sociais e a integraçao de brasileiros no Canadá e nos Estados Unidos. In A.C.B. Martes & S. Fleischer (Eds.), *Fronteiras cruzadas: Etnicidade, gênero e redes sociais* (pp. 263–88). São Paulo, Brazil: Paz e Terra.

Granovetter, M.S. (1973). The Strength of Weak Ties. *American Journal of Sociology, 78*(6), 1360–80. http://dx.doi.org/10.1086/225469.

Grayson, J.P., & Myles, R. (2005). How Research Ethics Boards Are Undermining Survey Research on Canadian University Students. *Journal of Academic Ethics, 2*(4), 293–314.

Grewal, I. (2005). *Transnational America: Feminisms, Diasporas, Neoliberalisms.* Durham: Duke University Press.

Grimson, A. (2011). *Los límites de la cultura: Crítica de las teorías de la identidad.* Buenos Aires: Siglo Veintiuno.

Grunert, J., & Adomatis, M.B. (2008, 7 July). Family Stress Adaptation Theory. Retrieved 18 August2010 from http://stress.lovetoknow.com/Family_Stress_Adaptation_Theory.

Gutiérrez, D. G. (2007). The Politics of the Interstices: Reflections on Citizenship and Non-citizenship at the Turn of the Twentieth Century. *Race/Ethnicity, 1*(1), 89–120.

Hagan, J.M. (1994). *Deciding to Be Legal: A Maya Community in Houston.* Philadelphia: Temple University Press.

Hage, G. (1998). *White Nation: Fantasies of White Supremacy in a Multicultural Nation.* Annadale, NSW: Pluto.

Hagen. (2005, 28 June). Precarious, Precarization, Precariat? http://reinventinglabour.wordpress.com/2010/06/05/precarious-precarization-precariat/.

Haggerty, K.D. (2004). Ethics Creep: Governing Social Science Research in the Name of Ethics. *Qualitative Sociology, 27*(4), 391–414. http://dx.doi.org/10.1023/B:QUAS.0000049239.15922.a3.

Halse, C., & Honey, A. (2005). Unraveling Ethics: Illuminating the Moral Dilemmas of Research Ethics. *Signs: Journal of Women in Culture and Society, 30*(4), 2141–62. http://dx.doi.org/10.1086/428419.

Hanes, A. (2008, 20 November). Policy Chief Kills "Don't Tell" Immigration Policy. *National Post.* Retrieved 21 November 2008 from http://www.canada.com/montrealgazette/story.html?id=e060308a-5681-4cc6-89a3-9fbb55a7e18f.

Hannerz, U. (1996). *Transnational Connections: Culture, People, Places.* New York: Routledge.

Harding, K., & Walton, D. (2007, 24 Feb.). Canada's Hottest New Import? Employees. *Globe and Mail,* p. A 14.

Harvie, B.A. (2002). Regulation of Advocacy in the Voluntary Sector: Current Challenges and Some Responses. Ottawa: Voluntary Sector Secretariat, Government of Canada.

Hawkins, F. (1989). *Critical Years in Immigration: Canada and Australia Compared.* Montreal/Kingston: McGill-Queen's University Press.

Health Canada (2002). *What Is the Population Health Approach?* Ottawa: Health Canada.

—. (2003). *What Determines Health?* Ottawa: Public Health Agency of Canada.

Hennebry, J.L. (2006). Globalization and the Mexican-Canadian Seasonal Agricultural Worker Program: Power, Racialization & Transnationalism in Temporary Migration. Doctoral diss., University of Western Ontario.

—. (2008). *Bienvenidos a Canadá?* Globalization and the Migration Industry Surrounding Temporary Agricultural Migration in Canada. *Canadian Studies in Population, 35*(2), 339–56.

—. (2010a). Not Just a Few Bad Apples: Structural Vulnerability, Health Risks and Temporary Migration in Canada. *Canadian Issues / Thèmes Canadiens*, March, 73–9.

—. (2010b). Who Has Their Eye on the Ball?: Jurisdictional *Fútbol* and Canada's Temporary Foreign Worker Program. *Policy Options, 63*, 62–8.

Hennebry, J.L., & Preibisch, K. (2010a, February). A Model for Managed Migration? Re-examining Best Practices in Canada's Seasonal Agricultural Worker Program. *International Migration, 50*, s.1, e19–e40. http://onlinelibrary.wiley.com/doi/10.1111/j.1468-2435.2009.00598.x/abstract.

—. (2010b). Permanently Temporary: The Second Generation of Temporary Migration – Canada in the World. Paper presented at the community forum Permanently Temporary: Temporary Foreign Workers and Canada's Changing Attitude to Citizenship and Immigration, Toronto, February.

Hennebry, J.L., Preibisch, K., & McLaughlin, J. (2010). *Health across Borders – Health Status, Risks and Care among Transnational Migrant Farm Workers in Ontario.* Toronto: CERIS Ontario Metropolis Centre.

Hernández, E., & Coutin, S.B. (2006). Remitting Subjects: Migrants, Money and States. *Economy and Society, 35*(2), 185–208. http://dx.doi.org/10.1080/03085140600635698.

Heyman, J.M., & Cunningham, H. (2004). Introduction: Mobilities and Enclosures at Borders. *Identities (Yverdon), 11*(3), 289–302. http://dx.doi.org/10.1080/10702890490493509

Hiebert, D. (1999). Local Geographies of Labor Market Segmentation: Montréal, Toronto, and Vancouver, 1991. *Economic Geography, 75*(4), 339–69. http://dx.doi.org/10.2307/144476.

Hiebert, D., D'Addario, S., & Sherrell, K. (2005). *The Profile of Absolute and Relative Homelessness among Immigrants, Refugees, and Refugee Claimants in the GVRD: Final Report.* Vancouver: MOSAIC.

Hiebert, D., & Mendez, P. (2008). *Settling In: Newcomers in the Canadian Housing Market.* Metropolis British Columbia, Working Paper no. 2008–04.

Hill, S. (2009, 29 May). Immigration Raids Firm, 8 Detained Mexican Greenhouse Workers in Custody. *Windsor Star.* http://www2.canada.com/windsorstar/news/story.html?id=accae204-960f-40ba-b0b7-7c8cb0333a23.

Holston, J. (1998). Spaces of Insurgent Citizenship. In L. Sandercock (Ed.), *Making the Invisible Visible: A Multicultural Planning History* (pp. 37–56). Berkeley: University of California Press.

Hondagneu-Sotelo, P. (1994). *Gendered Transitions: Mexican Experiences of Immigration*. Berkeley: University of California Press.

Honig, B. (2001). *Democracy and the Foreigner*. Princeton: Princeton University Press.

House of Commons, Canada. (2009). *Temporary Foreign Workers and Non-status Workers*. Ottawa: Standing Committee on Citizenship and Immigration.

Hulchanski, J.D. (2004). What Factors Shape Canadian Housing Policy? The Intergovernmental Role in Canada's Housing System. In R. Young & C. Leuprecht (Eds.), *Canada, State of the Federation, 2004: Municipal, Federal, Provincial Relations in Canada* (pp. 221–47). Montreal/Kingston: McGill-Queen's University Press.

Human Resources and Skills Development Canada (HRSDC). (2009a). Digest of Benefit Entitlement Principles – Chapter 10. Ottawa. Modified 10 July. http://www.servicecanada.gc.ca/eng/ei/digest/10_10_0.shtml#a10_10_8.

—. (2009b). Eligibility for Canadian Employment Insurance. Ottawa. Modified 20 February. http://www.hrsdc.gc.ca/eng/workplaceskills/foreign_workers/ei_tfw/ceie_tfw.shtml.

—. (2009c). Temporary Foreign Worker Program: Labour Market Opinion (LMO) Statistics, Annual Statistics 2005–2008. Ottawa. Modified 1 October. http://www.hrsdc.gc.ca/eng/workplaceskills/foreign_workers/stats_annual2008/annual_stats_list.shtml.

—. (2009d). Temporary Foreign Worker Program: Monitoring Initiative Fact Sheet. Ottawa. Modified 22 April. http://www.hrsdc.gc.ca/eng/workplaceskills/foreign_workers/ercompreview/factsheet.shtml.

—. (2009e). Temporary Foreign Worker Program. Ottawa: Modified 15 October. http://www.hrsdc.gc.ca/eng/workplaceskills/foreign_workers/index.shtml.

Iacovetta, F. (2006). *Gatekeepers: Reshaping Immigrant Lives in Cold War Canada*. Toronto: Between The Lines.

Ilcan, S., Oliver, M., & O'Connor, D. (2007). Spaces of Governance: Gender and Public Sector Restructuring in Canada. *Gender, Place and Culture, 14*(1), 75–92. http://dx.doi.org/10.1080/09663690601122333.

International Organization for Migration (IOM). (2008). *Evaluación Programa Trabajadores(as) Agrícolas Temporales a Canadá*. Cuadernos de Trabajo Sobre Migración, no. 25. Guatemala City: IOM.

Isin, E.F. (2000). Introduction: Democracy, Citizenship and the City. In E. Isin (Ed.), *Democracy, Citizenship and the Global City* (pp. 1–22). Innis Centenary Series. London: Routledge.

—. (2002). *Being Political: Genealogies of Citizenship*. Minneapolis: University of Minnesota Press.

Isin, E., & Wood, P.K. (1999). *Citizenship and Identity*. London: Sage.

Itzigsohn, J. (2000). Immigration and the Boundaries of Citizenship: The Institutions of Immigrants' Political Transnationalism. *International Migration Review, 34*(4), 1126–54. http://dx.doi.org/10.2307/2675977.

Janovicek, N. (2007). *No Place to Go: Local Histories of the Battered Women's Shelter Movement*. Vancouver: University of British Columbia.

Jiménez, M. (2003, 15 Nov.). 200,000 Illegal Immigrants Toiling in Canada's Underground Economy. *Globe and Mail*.

Jiménez, M., & Alphonso, C. (2006, 2 May). Pupils Held in Asylum Case Spark Review. *Globe and Mail*, p. A1.

Jiménez, M. (2006, 27 Oct.). Ottawa Rules Out Amnesty for 200,000 Illegal Workers. *Globe and Mail*.

Joppke, C. (2007). Transformation of Citizenship: Status, Rights, Identity. *Citizenship Studies, 11*(1), 37–48. http://dx.doi.org/10.1080/13621020601099831.

Junaid, B. (2002). *First Contact: The Arrival Needs of Refugee Claimants*. Toronto: Canadian Red Cross, Toronto Region.

Kalleberg, A.L. (2008). Precarious Work, Insecure Workers: Employment Relations in Transition. *American Sociological Review, 74*(February), 1–22.

Karpathakis, A. (1999). Home Society Politics and Immigrant Political Incorporation: The Case of Greek Immigrants in New York City. *International Migration Review, 33*(1), 55–78. http://dx.doi.org/10.2307/2547322.

Kazimi, A. (Director). (2004). *Continuous Journey* (film). Produced in association with TVOntario.

Kelley, N., & Trebilcock, M. (1998). *The Making of the Mosaic: A History of Canadian Immigration Policy*. Toronto: University of Toronto Press.

Kempadoo, K., Sanghera, J., & Pattanaik, B. (Eds.). (2011). *Trafficking and Prostitution Reconsidered: New Perspectives on Migration, Sex Work, and Human Rights*. 2nd ed. Boulder: Paradigm.

Keung, N. (2002, 11 March). Final Dignity for a Homeless Man. *Toronto Star*.

—. (2006, 8 May). MPs Offer to Pay Bail for Mother: Want to See Illegal Immigrant Family Back Together: Costa Rican's Kids Were Arrested at Their School. *Toronto Star*, p. A9.

—. (2008a, 5 April). Refugees May Lose Last Hope. *Toronto Star*. http://www.thestar.com/article/410527. Accessed 27 April 2011.

—. (2008b, 29 August). Compassion Lacking Lawyers Say. *Toronto Star*. http://www.thestar.com/article/487469. Accessed 27 April 2011.

—. (2009a, 22 October). Clerk Fired after Boy, 7, Sent from ER. *Toronto Star*. http://www.thestar.com/article/714042. Accessed 5 August 2010.

—. (2009b, 26 October). Canada Deported Mexican Woman to Her Death. *Toronto Star*. Retrieved 29 March 2010 from Factiva database.

Khan, M., Lalani, N., Plamadeala, C., Sun, E., & Gardner, B. (2010). *Highlights: February 12, 2010 Research Conference on Healthcare for the Uninsured and Undocumented*. Toronto: Wellesley Institute.

Khandor, E., McDonald, J., Nyers, P., & Wright, C. (2004). *The Regularization of Non-Status Immigrants in Canada 1960–2004: Past Policies, Current Perspectives, Active Campaigns*. Toronto: Status Campaign, Access Alliance, and OCASI.

Khanlou, N., Gonsalves, T., & Mill, C. (2010). Women without Legal Immigration Status: Health Consequences and Barriers to Healthcare. Paper presented at the Conference on Research on Healthcare for the Undocumented and Uninsured: Systems, Policies, Practices and Their Consequences, Toronto, 12 February.

Kilbride, K., Anisef, P., Baichman-Anisef, E., & Khattar, R. (2000). *Between Two Worlds: The Experiences and Concerns of Immigrant Youth in Ontario*. Toronto: CERIS.

Kilbride, K.M., & Webber, S. (2006). *Plug Them In and Turn Them On: Homelessness, Immigrants, and Social Capital*. Report submitted to the Housing and Homelessness Branch of the Department of Human Resources and Social Development Canada.

Kissoon, P. (2010a). An Uncertain Home: Refugee Protection, Illegal Immigration Status, and Their Effects on Migrants' Housing Stability in Vancouver and Toronto. *Canadian Issues/Thèmes Canadiens*, Fall, 64–7.

—. (2010b). From Persecution to Destitution: A Snapshot of Asylum Seekers' Housing and Settlement Experiences in Canada and the United Kingdom. *Journal of Immigrant & Refugee Studies, 8*(1), 4–31. http://dx.doi.org/10.1080/15562940903575020.

Kivisto, P., & Faist, T. (2007). *Citizenship: Discourse, Theory, and Transnational Prospects*. Malden, MA: Blackwell.

Klodawsky, F., Aubry, T., Behnia, B., Nicholson, C., & Young, M. (2005). *Comparing Foreign Born and Canadian Born Respondents to the Panel Study on Homelessness (Phase 1)*. Ottawa: National Secretariat on Homelessness.

Koch, T., & Kralik, D. (2006). *Participatory Action Research in Health Care*. Oxford: Blackwell.

Koro-Ljungberg, M., Gemignani, M., Brodeur, C.W., & Kmiec, C. (2007). The Technologies of Normalization and Self: Thinking about IRBs and Extrinsic Research Ethics with Foucault. *Qualitative Inquiry, 13*(8), 1075–94. http://dx.doi.org/10.1177/1077800407308822.

Kossoudji, S.A., & Cobb-Clark, D.A. (2000). IRCA's Impact on the Occupational Concentration and Mobility of Newly-Legalized Mexican Men.

Journal of Population Economics, 13(1), 81–98. http://dx.doi.org/10.1007/s001480050124.

—. (2002). Coming Out of the Shadows: Learning about Legal Status and Wages from the Legalized Population. *Journal of Labor Economics, 20*(3), 598–628. http://dx.doi.org/10.1086/339611.

Kurthen, H., & Heisler, B. (2009). Immigrant Integration: Comparative Evidence from the United States and Germany. *Ethnic and Racial Studies, 32*(1), 139–70. http://dx.doi.org/10.1080/01419870802298439.

Kyambi, S. (2004). National Identity and Refugee Law. In P. Fitzpatrick & P. Tuitt (Eds.), *Critical Beings: Law, Nation and the Global Subject* (19–36). Burlington: Ashgate.

Kymlicka, W. (1995). *Multicultural Citizenship: A Liberal Theory of Minority Rights.* Oxford: Clarendon.

Lambertson, R. (2001). The Dresden Story: Racism, Human Rights, and the Jewish Labour Committee of Canada. *Labour/Le Travail, 47,* 43–82.

Lamont, M., & Molnár, V. (2002). The Study of Boundaries in the Social Sciences. *Annual Review of Sociology, 28*(1), 167–95. http://dx.doi.org/10.1146/annurev.soc.28.110601.141107.

Landolt, P. (2007). The Institutional Landscapes of Salvadoran Refugee Migration: Transnational and Local Views from Los Angeles. In L. Goldring & S. Krishnamurti (Eds.), *Organizing the Transnational: Labour, Politics, and Social Change* (pp. 191–205). Vancouver: UBC Press.

Landolt, P., & Goldring, L. (2010). Political Cultures and Transnational Social Fields: Chileans, Colombians and Canadian activists in Toronto. *Global Networks, 10*(4), 443–66. http://dx.doi.org/10.1111/j.1471-0374.2010.00290.x.

Langevin, L., & Belleau, M. (2000). *Trafficking in Women in Canada: A Critical Analysis of the Legal Framework Governing Immigrant Live-in Caregivers and Mail-Order Brides.* Ottawa: Status of Women Canada.

Law Union of Ontario. (1981). *The Immigrant's Handbook.* Montreal: Black Rose.

Lawrence, B., & Dua, E. (2005). Decolonizing Antiracism. *Social Justice, 32*(4), 120–43.

Lawson, E., Gardezi, F., Calzavara, L., Husbands, W., Myers, T., & Tharao, W.E. (2006). *HIV/AIDS Stigma, Denial, Fear and Discrimination: Experiences and Responses of People from African and Caribbean Communities in Toronto.* Toronto: ACCHO and the HIV Social, Behavioural and Epidemiological Studies Unit, University of Toronto.

Le Page, K. (2010, 26 May). How Do People React to Trauma. Retrieved 15 August 2010 from http://post-traumatic-stress-disorder.suite101.com/article.cfm/how-do-people-react-to-trauma.

Lempert, R.O., & Saltzburg, S.A. (1982). *A Modern Approach to Evidence: Text, Problems, Transcripts, and Cases.* 2nd ed. St. Paul, MN: West.

Lentin, A. (2004). *Racism and Anti-racism in Europe.* London: Pluto.

Levitt, P., & Glick Schiller, N. (2004). Conceptualizing Simultaneity: A Transnational Social Field Perspective on Society. *International Migration Review, 30*(3), 1002–39.

Lewchuk, W., Clarke, M., & de Wolff, A. (2008). Working without Commitments: Precarious Employment and Health. *Work, Employment and Society, 22*(3), 387–406. http://dx.doi.org/10.1177/0950017008093477.

Li, A., Cain, R., Cedano, J., Chen, Y.-Y., Fung, K., Kafele, K., & Wong, J.P. (2008). *Transformation through Collective Action: Best Practices in Migration, HIV and Mental Health.* Toronto: Committee for Accessible AIDS Treatment.

Li, P.S. (2003). *Destination Canada: Immigration Debates and Issues.* Don Mills, ON: Oxford University Press.

—. (2008). World Migration in the Age of Globalization: Policy Implications and Challenges. *New Zealand Population Review, 33*(34), 1–22.

Lindgreen, J. (2002). Discussion: Anticipating Problems: Doing Social Science Research in the Shadow of the Law. *Sociological Methodology, 32*(1), 29–32. http://dx.doi.org/10.1111/1467-9531.00109.

Lipsky, M. (1980). *Street-Level Bureaucracy: Dilemmas of the Individual in Public Services.* New York: Russell Sage Foundation.

Lister, R. (1997). Citizenship: Towards a Feminist Synthesis. *Feminist Review, 57* (Autumn), 28–48. http://dx.doi.org/10.1080/014177897339641.

Longhurst, R. (2010). Semi-structured Interviews and Focus Groups. In N. Clifford, S. French, & G. Valentine (Eds.), *Key Methods in Geography* (pp. 103–15). London: Sage.

Lowman, J., & Palys, T. (2000). Ethics and Institutional Conflict of Interest: The Research Confidentiality Controversy at Simon Fraser University. *Sociological Practice: A Journal of Clinical and Applied Sociology, 2*(4), 245–64. http://dx.doi.org/10.1023/A:1026589415488.

—. (2001). The Ethics and Law of Confidentiality in Criminal Justice Research: A Comparison of Canada and the United States. *International Criminal Justice Review, 11*(1), 1–33. http://dx.doi.org/10.1177/105756770101100101.

—. (2007). Strict Confidentiality: An Alternative to PRE's "Limited Confidentiality" Doctrine. *Journal of Academic Ethics, 5*(2–4), 163–77. http://dx.doi.org/10.1007/s10805-007-9035-7.

Lowry, M., & Nyers, P. (2003). "No One Is Illegal": The Fight for Refugee and Migrant Rights in Canada. *Refuge: Canada's Periodical on Refugees, 21*(3), 66–72.

Lucassen, J. & Lucassen, L. (Eds.). (1997). *Migration, Migration History, History.* Bern: Peter Lang.

Lucassen, L. (2007). Migration and World History: Reaching a New Frontier. *International Review of Social History, 52*(01), 89–96. http://dx.doi.org/10.1017/S0020859006002793.

Macklin, A. (2005). Disappearing Refugees: Reflections on the Canada-US Safe Third Country Agreement. *Columbia Human Rights Law Review, 36,* 365–426.

—. (2009). Refugee Roulette in the Canadian Casino. In J. Ramji-Nogales, A. Schoenholtz, & P. Schrag (Eds.), *Refugee Roulette: Disparities in Asylum Adjudication and Proposals for Reform* (pp. 135–63). New York: New York University Press.

—. (2011). Historicizing Narratives of Arrival: The Other Indian Other. In H. Lessard, R. Johnson, & J. Webber (Eds.), *Storied Communities: Narratives of Contact and Arrival in Constituting Political Community* (pp. 40–67). Vancouver: University of British Columbia Press.

MacLaren, B., & Lapointe, L. (2010). Employment Insurance: How Canada Can Remain Competitive and Be Fair to Migrant Workers. *Policy Options,* February, 73–6.

Magalhaes, L., Carrasco, C., & Gastaldo, D. (2010, February). Undocumented Migrants in Canada: A Scope Literature Review on Health, Access to Services, and Working Conditions. *Journal of Immigrant and Minority Health, 12*(1), 132–51. http://dx.doi.org/10.1007/s10903-009-9280-5. Medline:19657739.

Mamann, G. (2010, 15 March). The Incredible Shrinking of the Canadian Experience Class. *Metro Canada.*

Mar, L.R. (2010). *Brokering Belonging: Chinese in Canada's Exclusion Era, 1885–1945.* Oxford: Oxford University Press.

Martin, P. (2006). Managing Labor Migration: Temporary Worker Programs for the 21st Century. Paper presented at the International Symposium on International Migration and Development, Turin, Italy, 28–30 June.

Martínez Veiga, U. (2007). Irregular Migration, Informal Labour and Poverty in the Agricultural Sector in Spain. In E. Berggren, B. Likic-Brboric, G. Toköz, & N. Trimikliniotis (Eds.), *Irregular Migration, Informal Labour and Community: A Challenge for Europe* (pp. 199–214). Maastrich: Shaker.

Mattu, P. (2002). *A Survey on the Extent of Substandard Housing Problems Faced by Immigrants and Refugees in the Lower Mainland of British Columbia.* Multilingual Orientation Service Association for Immigrant Communities (MOSAIC), BC. http://www.mosaicbc.com/sites/all/.../SCPI%20Summary%20Report_0.pdf.

Mazumdar, S. (2007). Localities of the Global: Asian Migrations between Slavery and Citizenship. *International Review of Social History, 52*(01), 124–33. http://dx.doi.org/10.1017/S0020859006002847.

McBride, S., & Shields, J. (1997). *Dismantling a Nation: The Transition to Corporate Rule in Canada.* Halifax: Fernwood.

McDonald, J. (2009). Migrant Illegality, Nation-Building and the Politics of Regularization in Canada. *Refuge: Canada's Periodical on Refugees, 26*(2), 65–77.

McDonald, L. (n.d.). Hill's Theory of Family Stress and Buffer Factors: Build the Protective Factors of Social Relations and Positive Perception with Multi-Family Groups. Retrieved 10 August2010 from http://cecp.air.org/vc/presentations/2selective/3lmcdon/HILL%27S_FAMILY_STRESS_THEORY_AND_FAST.htm.

McKay, I. (2008). *Reasoning Otherwise: Leftists and the People's Enlightenment in Canada, 1890–1920.* Toronto: Between the Lines.

McKay, S., Markova, E., Paraskevopoulou, A., & Wright, T. (2009). *The Relationship between Migration Status and Employment Outcomes (Final Report).* London: Working Lives Research Institute, London Metropolitan University.

McLaughlin, J. (2007). Falling through the Cracks: Seasonal Foreign Farm Workers' Health and Compensation across Borders. *IAVGO Reporting Service, 21*(1), 20–33.

—. (2008). Gender, Health and Mobility: Health Concerns of Women Migrant Farm Workers in Canada. *FOCALPoint: Canada's Spotlight on the Americas,* 7(9).

—. (2009a, October). *Migration and Health: Implications for Development.* Policy Paper no. 2. Ottawa:The Canadian Foundation for the Americas Labour Mobility and Development Project.

—. (2009b). Trouble in Our Fields: Health and Human Rights among Mexican and Caribbean Migrant Farm Workers in Canada. Doctoral diss., University of Toronto.

—. (2010). Classifying the "Ideal Migrant Worker": Mexican and Jamaican Transnational Farmworkers in Canada." *Focaal: Journal of Global and Historical Anthropology, 57,* 79–94.

—. (2011). Research Spotlight: Health of Migrant Farm Workers in Canada. *Health Policy Research Bulletin, 17* (January).

McNevin, A. (2006). Political Belonging in a Neoliberal Era: The Struggle of the Sans-Papiers. *Citizenship Studies, 10*(2), 135–51. http://dx.doi.org/10.1080/13621020600633051.

Menjívar, C. (2000). *Fragmented Ties: Salvadoran Immigrant Networks in America.* Berkeley: University of California Press.

—. (2006). Liminal Legality: Salvadoran and Guatemalan Immigrants' Lives in the United States. *American Journal of Sociology, 111*(4), 999–1037. http://dx.doi.org/10.1086/499509.

Menjívar, C., & Salcido, O. (2002). Immigrant Women and Domestic Violence: Common Experiences in Different Countries. *Gender & Society, 16*(6), 898–920. http://dx.doi.org/10.1177/089124302237894.

Mezzadra, S. (2010). Anti-racist Research and Practice in Italy. *Darkmatter,*
6. Retrieved on 10 December 2010 from http://www.darkmatter101.org/
site/2010/10/10/anti-racist-research-and-practice-in-italy/.

Miki, R. (2004). *Redress: Inside the Japanese-Canadian Call for Justice.* Vancouver:
Raincoast.

Mills, S. (2003). *Michel Foucault.* London: Routledge. http://dx.doi.
org/10.4324/9780203380437.

—. (2010). *The Empire Within: Postcolonial Thought and Political Activism in Sixties
Montreal.* Montreal/Kingston: McGill-Queen's University Press.

—. (2011). Quebec, Haiti, and Echoes of Empire: The Deportation Crisis of 1974.
Unpublished manuscript. University of Toronto, Department of History.

Minkler, M., & Wallerstein, N. (2008). Introduction to Community-Based
Participatory Research: New Issues and Emphases. In M. Minkler & N.
Wallerstein (Eds.), *Community-Based Participatory Research for Health: From
Process to Outcomes,* 2nd ed. (pp. 5–23). San Francisco: Jossey-Bass.

Miraftab, F. (2000). Sheltering Refugees: The Housing Experience of Refugees
in Metropolitan Vancouver, Canada. *Canadian Journal of Urban Research,*
9(1), 42–57.

Mishra, M., & Kamal, F. (2007). Regularization from the Ground Up: The
Don't Ask, Don't Tell Campaign. Toronto: No One Is Illegal – Toronto. Retrieved 30 March 2010 from http://noiireference.wordpress.com/resources/
regularization-from-the-ground-up/.

Mitra, D., Jacobsen, M.J., O'Connor, A., Pottie, K., & Tugwell, P. (2006, Nov).
Assessment of the Decision Support Needs of Women from HIV Endemic
Countries regarding Voluntary HIV Testing in Canada. *Patient Education
and Counseling, 63*(3), 292–300. http://dx.doi.org/10.1016/j.pec.2006.04.005.
Medline:16876376.

Molinaro, D.G. (2010). A Species of Treason? Deportation and Nation-Building
in the Case of Tomo Čačić, 1931–1934. *Canadian Historical Review, 91*(1), 61–85.
http://dx.doi.org/10.3138/chr.91.1.61.

Mongia, R. (1999). Race, Nationality, Mobility: A History of the Passport. *Public
Culture, 11*(3), 527–55. http://dx.doi.org/10.1215/08992363-11-3-527.

Mongia, R.V. (2003). Race, Nationality, Mobility: A History of the Passport. In A. Burton (Ed.), *After the Imperial Turn: Thinking with and through
the Nation* (pp. 196–214). Durham: Duke University Press. http://dx.doi.
org/10.1215/08992363-11-3-527.

Montgomery, C. (2002). The "Brown Paper Syndrome": Unaccompanied Minors
and Questions of Status. *Refuge: Canada's Periodical on Refugees, 20*(2), 56–67.

Morris, C. (2009). Your Money or Your Life. *This Magazine.* http://www.this-
magazine.ca/issues/2009/03/immigrant_health_money_life.php. Accessed 12
June 2009.

Moulin, C. (2009). Border of Solidarity: Life in Displacement in the Amazon Tri-Border Region. *Refuge: Canada's Periodical on Refugees, 26*(2): 41–54.

Mountz, A. (2003). Human Smuggling, the Transnational Imaginary, and Everyday Geographies of the Nation-State. *Antipode, 35*(3), 622–44. http://dx.doi.org/10.1111/1467-8330.00342.

Mountz, A., Wright, R., Miyares, I., & Bailey, A.J. (2002). Lives in Limbo: Temporary Protected Status and Immigrant Identities. *Global Networks, 2*(4), 335–56. http://dx.doi.org/10.1111/1471-0374.00044.

Mountz, A. (2009). The Enforcement Archipelago: Haunting and Asylum on Islands. Paper presented at the CRS - CERIS Autumn Seminar Series. Toronto: York University.

Munck, R. (2008). Globalisation, Governance and Migration: An Introduction. *Third World Quarterly, 29*(7), 1227–46. http://dx.doi.org/10.1080/01436590802386252.

Murdie, R., Chambon, A., Hulchanski, J.D., & Teixeira, C. (1996). Housing Issues Facing Immigrants and Refugees in Greater Toronto: Initial Findings from the Jamaican, Polish and Somali Communities. In E.M. Komut (Ed.), *Housing Question of the "Others"* (pp.179–90). Ankara: Chamber of Architects of Turkey.

Murdie, R.A. (2003). Housing Affordability and Toronto's Rental Market: Perspectives from the Housing Careers of Jamaican, Polish and Somali Newcomers. *Housing, Theory and Society, 20*(4), 183–96.

—. (2005). Pathways to Housing: The Experiences of Sponsored Refugees and Refugee Claimants in Accessing Permanent Housing in Toronto, Canada. Paper presented at the European Network for Housing Research Conference, Reykjavik, Iceland, 29 June–3 July.

—. (2008). Pathways to Housing: The Experiences of Sponsored Refugees and Refugee Claimants in Accessing Permanent Housing in Toronto. *Journal of International Migration and Integration, 9*(1), 81–101. http://dx.doi.org/10.1007/s12134-008-0045-0.

Nakache, D. (2010). The Canadian Temporary Foreign Worker Program: Regulations, Practices, and Protection Gaps. Presented at the Workshop on Producing and Negotiating Precarious Migratory Status in Canada, York University, Toronto, 16 September. http://www.yorku.ca/raps1/.

Nakache, D., & D'Aoust, S. (2012). Provincial and Territorial Nominee Programs: An Avenue to Permanent Residency for Low-Skilled Migrant Workers in Canada? In C. Straehle & P. Tamara Lenard (Eds.), *Partial Members: Low-Skilled Temporary Labour Migrants in Canada*. Montreal/Kingston: McGill-Queens University Press.

Nakache, D., & Kinoshita, P.J. (2010). *The Canadian Temporary Foreign Worker Program: Do Short-Term Economic Needs Prevail over Human Rights Concerns?* IRPP Study no. 5. Ottawa: IRPP.

Nakano Glenn, E. (2002). *Unequal Freedom: How Race and Gender Shaped American Citizenship and Labor.* Cambridge: Harvard University Press.

Nankani, S. (Ed.). (2000). *Breaking the Silence: Domestic Violence in South Asian-American Community.* Philadelphia: Xlibris Corporation.

Neocosmos, M. (2010). *From "Foreign Natives" to "Native Foreigners": Explaining Xenophobia in Post-Apartheid South Afric,. Citizenship and Nationalism, Identity and Politics.* Dakar, Senegal: CODESRIA.

Newman, K.S. (2006). Chutes and Ladders: Navigating the Low-Wage Labor Market. New York/Cambridge, MA: Russell Sage Foundation/Harvard University Press.

Neysmith, S., Bezanson, K., & O'Connell, A. (2005). *Telling Tales: Living the Effects of Public Policy.* Black Point, NS: Fernwood.

Ngai, M. (2002). *Impossible Subjects: Illegal Aliens and the Making of Modern America.* Princeton: Princeton University Press.

—. (2004). *Impossible Subjects: Illegal Aliens and the Making of Modern America.* Princeton: Princeton University Press.

No One Is Illegal – Toronto. (2006). No One Is Illegal Statement on 1948 and 1967 Palestinian Refugees and Right of Return. Pamphlet. Toronto: No One Is Illegal - Toronto.

—. (2010). Our Demands. Retrieved 25 March 2010 from http://toronto.nooneisillegal.org/demands.

No One Is Illegal – Vancouver. (2010). Our Principles. Retrieved 26 March2010 from http://noii-van.resist.ca/?page_id=17.

Novac, S. (1996). *A Place to Call One's Own: New Voices of Dislocation and Dispossession.* Ottawa: Status of Women Canada.

Nyers, P. (2003). Abject Cosmopolitanism: The Politics of Protection in the Anti-deportation Movement. *Third World Quarterly, 24*(6), 1069–93. http://dx.doi.org/10.1080/01436590310001630071.

—. (2006). The Accidental Citizen: Acts of Sovereignty and (Un)making Citizenship. *Economy and Society, 35*(1), 22–41. http://dx.doi.org/10.1080/03085140500465824.

Nyers, P., Zerehi, S.S., & Wright, C. (2006). *"Access Not Fear": Non-Status Immigrants and City Services.* Toronto: CERIS.

Odartey-Wellington, F. (2009). Racial Profiling and Moral Panic: Operation Thread and the al Qaeda Sleeper Cell That Never Was. *Global Media Journal - Canadian Edition, 2*(2), 25–40.

Office of the Auditor General of Canada. (2009). *Report of the Auditor General of Canada to the House of Commons.* Ottawa: Office of the Auditor General of Canada.

Ong, A. (1996). Cultural Citizenship as Subject-Making: Immigrants Negotiate Racial and Cultural Boundaries in the United States. *Current Anthropology, 37*(5), 737–62. http://dx.doi.org/10.1086/204560.

—. (1999). *Flexible Citizenship: The Cultural Logics of Transnationality.* Durham: Duke University Press.

—. (2003). *Buddha Is Hiding: Refugees, Citizenship, the New America.* Berkeley: University of California Press.

Oxman-Martinez, J., Hanley, J., Lach, L., Khanlou, N., Weerasinghe, S., & Agnew, V. (2005, Oct). Intersection of Canadian Policy Parameters Affecting Women with Precarious Immigration Status: A Baseline for Understanding Barriers to Health. *Journal of Immigrant Health, 7*(4), 247–58. http://dx.doi.org/10.1007/s10903-005-5122-2. Medline:19813291.

Painter, J., & Philo, C. (1995). Spaces of Citizenship: An Introduction. *Political Geography, 14*(2), 107–20. http://dx.doi.org/10.1016/0962-6298(95)91659-R.

Papademetriou, D.G., & O'Neil, K. (2004). *Efficient Practices for the Selection of Economic Migrants.* Washington, DC: Migration Policy Institute.

Papadopoulos, D., Stephenson, N., & Tsianos, V. (2008). *Escape Routes: Control and Subversion in the Twenty-First Century.* London: Pluto Press.

Paradis, E., Hulchanski, J.D., Novac, S., & Murdie, R. (2008). Immigrants, Discrimination, and Homelessness: A Longitudinal Study of Homeless Immigrant Families in Toronto. Presentation to the Rights of Non-Status Women Network, Toronto, 11 June.

Paradis, E., Novac, S., Sarty, M., & Hulchanski, J.D. (2008). *Better Off in a Shelter? A Year of Homelessness & Housing among Status Immigrant, Non-Status Migrant, & Canadian-Born Families.* Research Paper no. 213, Centre for Urban and Community Studies, Cities Centre, University of Toronto, July.

Parnaby, A., & Kealey, G.S. (2003). The Origins of Political Policing in Canada: Class, Law, and the Burden of Empire. *Osgoode Hall Law Journal, 41*, 211–39.

Parreñas, R.S. (2001). Transgressing the Nation-State: The Partial Citizenship and "Imagined (Global) Community" of Migrant Filipina Domestic Workers. *Signs, 26*(4), 1129–54. http://dx.doi.org/10.1086/495650. Medline:17607870.

Pashang, S. (2008). The Impact of Immigration Status on the Health and Well-being of Non-status Children in Canada. *The Newsletter of Infant Mental Health Promotion,* no. 50 (Spring).

Passel, J.S., & Cohn, D.V. (2011). *Unauthorized Immigrant Population: National and State Trends, 2010.* Washington, DC: Pew Research Center.

Patarra, N.L., & Baeninger, R. (1996). Migrações internacionais recentes: O caso do Brasil. In N. Patarra (Coordinator), *Emigração e imigração internacionais no Brasil contemporâneo*, vol. 1. (pp. 78–88). Campinas, São Paulo, Brazil: Programa Interinstitucional de Avaliação e Acompanhamento das Migrações Internacionais no Brasil.

Patrias, C., & Frager, R. (2001). "This Is Our Country, These Are Our Rights": Minorities and the Origins of Ontario's Human Rights Campaigns. *Canadian Historical Review, 82*(1), 1–35. http://dx.doi.org/10.3138/CHR.82.1.1.

Pendakur, R. (2000). *Immigrants and the Labour Force: Policy, Regulation, and Impact*. Montreal/Kingston: McGill-Queen's University Press.

Peutz, N. (2006). Embarking on an Anthropology of Removal. *Current Anthropology, 47*(2), 217–41. http://dx.doi.org/10.1086/498949.

Peutz, N., & de Genova, N. (2010). Introduction. In N. de Genova & N. Peutz (Eds.), *The Deportation Regime: Sovereignty, Space, and the Freedom of Movement*. Durham, NC: Duke University Press.

Phillips, J.A., & Massey, D.S. (1999). The New Labor Market: Immigrants and Wages after IRCA. *Demography, 36*(2), 233–46. http://dx.doi.org/10.2307/2648111. Medline:10332614.

Picchio, A. (1992). *Social Reproduction: The Political Economy of the Labour Market*. Cambridge: Cambridge University Press.

Piliavin, I., Entner Wright, B.R., Mare, R.D., & Westerfelt, A.H. (1996). Exits From and Returns to Homelessness. *Social Service Review, 70*, 33–57.

Piliavin, I., Sosin, M., Westerfelt, A.H., & Matsueda, R.L. (1993). The Duration of Homeless Careers: An Exploratory Study. *Social Service Review, 67*, 576–98.

Piore, M.J. (1979). *Birds of Passage: Migrant Labor in Industrial Societies*. New York: Cambridge University Press. http://dx.doi.org/10.1017/CBO9780511572210.

Portes, A. (1978). Introduction: Toward a Structural Analysis of Illegal (Undocumented) Immigration. *International Migration Review, 12*(4), 469–84. http://dx.doi.org/10.2307/2545446. Medline:12310695.

Portes, A., Guarnizo, L.E., & Landolt, P. (1999). The Study of Transnationalism: Pitfalls and Promise of an Emergent Research Field. *Ethnic and Racial Studies, 22*(2), 217–37. http://dx.doi.org/10.1080/014198799329468.

Pratt, A. (2005). *Securing Borders: Detention and Deportation in Canada*. Vancouver: UBC Press.

Pratt, G. (1999). Is This Canada? Domestic Workers' Experiences in Vancouver, BC. In J. Momsen (Ed.), *Gender, Migration and Domestic Service* (pp. 23–42). London: Routledge.

—. (2005). Abandoned Women and Spaces of Exception. *Antipode, 37*(5), 1052–78. http://dx.doi.org/10.1111/j.0066-4812.2005.00556.x.

Preibisch, K. (2004). Migrant Agricultural Workers and Processes of Social Inclusion in Rural Canada: *Encuentros* and *Desencuentros*. *Canadian Journal of
Latin American and Caribbean Studies, 29*(57/8), 203.

—. (2007). Local Produce, Foreign Labor: Labor Mobility Programs and Global
Trade Competitiveness in Canada. *Rural Sociology, 72*(3), 418–49. http://dx.doi.
org/10.1526/003601107781799308.

—. (2010). Pick-Your-Own Labor: Migrant Workers and Flexibility in Canadian Agriculture. *International Migration Review, 44*(2), 404–41. http://dx.doi.
org/10.1111/j.1747-7379.2010.00811.x

Preibisch, K., & Binford, L. (2007). Interrogating Racialized Global Labour Supply: An Exploration of the Racial/National Replacement of Foreign Agricultural Workers in Canada. *Canadian Review of Sociology and Anthropology.
La Revue Canadienne de Sociologie et d'Anthropologie, 44*(1), 5–36. http://dx.doi.
org/10.1111/j.1755-618X.2007.tb01146.x.

Preibisch, K.L., & Encalada Grez, E. (2010). The Other Side of *el Otro Lado:*
Mexican Migrant Women and Labor Flexibility in Canadian Agriculture.
Signs: Journal of Women in Culture and Society, 35(2), 289–316. http://dx.doi.
org/10.1086/605483.

Preibisch, K., & Hennebry, J. (2011). Temporary Migration, Chronic Impacts: International Migrant Worker Health in Canada. *CMAJ (Canadian Medical Association Journal)*, first published 18 April, http://dx.doi.org/10.1503/cmaj.090736.

Public Health Agency of Canada. (2006). HIV/AIDS Epi Updates, August 2006.
Surveillance and Risk Assessment Division, Centre for Infectious Disease
Prevention and Control, Public Health Agency of Canada.

Pulido, L. (2007). A Day without Immigrants: The Racial and Class Politics of
Immigrant Exclusion. *Antipode, 39*(1), 1–7.

Pullenayegem, C. (2007, 13 December). Dismantling the Safe Third Country
Agreement. *Citizens for Public Justice*. Retrieved 14 June 2010 from http://
www.cpj.ca/en/content/dismantling-safe-third-country-agreement.

Pysklywec, M., McLaughlin, J., Tew, M., & Haines, T. (2011). Doctors within Borders: Meeting the Health Care Needs of Migrant Farm Workers in Canada.
CMAJ (Canadian Medical Association Journal), 183(9), 1039–43.

Rabinow, P. (Ed.). (1984). *The Foucault Reader*. New York: Penguin.

Raj, A., Silverman, J.G., McCleary-Sills, J., & Liu, R. (2004). Immigration Policies
Increase South Asian Immigrant Women's Vulnerability to Intimate Part-
ner Violence. *Journal of the American Medical Women's Association, 60*(1), 26–32.
Medline:16845767.

Rajaram, P.K., & Grundy-Warr, C. (2004). The Irregular Migrant as *Homo Sacer:*
Migration and Detention in Australia, Malaysia, and Thailand. *International
Migration, 42*(1), 33–64. http://dx.doi.org/10.1111/j.0020-7985.2004.00273.x.

Ramos-Zayas, A.Y. (2004). Delinquent Citizenship, National Performances: Racialization, Surveillance and the Politics of "Worthiness" in Puerto Rican Chicago. *Latino Studies, 2*(1), 26–44. http://dx.doi.org/10.1057/palgrave. lst.8600059.

Raphael, D. (2009). Social Determinants of Health: An Overview of Key Issues and Themes. In D. Raphael (Ed.), *Social Determinants of Health: Canadian Perspective,* 2nd ed. (pp. 2–19). Toronto: Canadian Scholars' Press.

Rebick, J. (2005). Stop the Deportation of Wendy Maxwell. *Rabble,* 8 March. http://rabble.ca/news/stop-deportation-wendy-maxwell. Accessed 17 August 2010.

Reddy, C. (2005). Asian Diasporas, Neoliberalism, and Family: Reviewing the Case for Homosexual Asylum in the Context of Family Rights. *Social Text, 23*(3–4 84–5), 101–19. http://dx.doi.org/10.1215/01642472-23-3-4_84-85-101.

Reinharz, S. (1992). Feminist Interview Research. In S. Reinharz & L. Davidman (Eds.), *Feminist Methods in Social Research* (pp. 18–45). London: Oxford University Press.

Remis, R.S., Swantee, C., Schiedel, L., Merid, M.F., & Liu, J. (2006). *Report on HIV/AIDS in Ontario 2004.* Toronto: Ontario Ministry of Health and Long-Term Care.

Rivera-Batiz, F.L. (1999). Undocumented Workers in the Labor Market: An Analysis of the Earnings of Legal and Illegal Mexican Immigrants in the United States. *Journal of Population Economics, 12*(1), 91–116. http://dx.doi. org/10.1007/s001480050092. Medline:12295042.

Roberts, B. (1988). *Whence They Came: Deportation from Canada 1900–1935.* Ottawa: University of Ottawa Press.

—. (1994). Shovelling Out the "Mutinous": Political Deportation from Canada before 1936. In G. Tulchinksy (Ed.), *Immigration in Canada: Historical Perspectives* (pp. 265–96). Toronto: Copp Clark.

Robertson, G. (2005, 30 May). Canada Has No Handle on Illegal Immigrant Workers. *Edmonton Journal,* p. A5.

Rodgers, G. (1989). Precarious Employment in Western Europe: The State of the Debate. In G. Rodgers & J. Rodgers (Eds.), *Precarious Jobs in Labour Market Regulation: The Growth of Atypical Employment in Western Europe* (1–16). Belgium: International Institute for Labour Studies.

Rose, D., & Ray, B. (2001). The Housing Situation of Refugees in Montreal Three Years after Arrival: The Case of Asylum Seekers Who Obtained Permanent Residence. *Journal of International Migration and Integration, 2*(4), 493–529.

Rosenberg, C. (2006). *Policing Paris: The Origins of Modern Immigration Control between the Wars.* Ithaca: Cornell University Press.

Rousseau, C., ter Kuile, S., Muñoz, M., Nadeau, L., Ouimet, M.-J., Kirmayer, L., & Crépeau, F. (2008, July–Aug.). Health Care Access for Refugees and Immigrants with Precarious Status: Public Health and Human Right Challenges. *Canadian Journal of Public Health, 99*(4), 290–92. Medline:18767273. ·

Roy, C.M., & Cain, R. (2001, Aug.). The Involvement of People Living with HIV/AIDS in Community-Based Organizations: Contributions and Constraints. *AIDS Care, 13*(4), 421–32. http://dx.doi.org/10.1080/09540120120057950. Medline:11454263.

Ruhs, M. (2006). The Potential of Temporary Migration Programs in Future International Migration Policy. *International Labour Review, 145*(1–2), 7–36. http://dx.doi.org/10.1111/j.1564-913X.2006.tb00008.x.

Ryan, L. & Woodill, J. (2000). *A Search for Home: Refugee Voices in the Romero House Community.* Toronto: Maytree Foundation.

Saad, S. (2011). *A Secret Life: The Psychosocial Impact of Falling Out of Status.* Master's thesis, York University.

Saint-Cyr, Y. (2010, 10 June). Regulating Immigration Consultants and Cracking Down on Ghost Consultants. Retrieved 30 July 2010 from http://www.slaw.ca/2010/06/10/regulating-immigration-consultants-and-cracking-down-on-ghost-consultants/.

Sales, T. (1999). Identidade étnica entre imigrantes brasileiros na regiao de Boston, EUA. In R.R. Reis & T. Sales (Eds.), *Cenas do Brasil Migrante* (pp. 17–44). São Paulo, Brazil: Boitempo.

Sandborn, T. (2009). Setback for Historic Effort to Unionize Guest Farm Workers. Shuffled Work Force Votes to Decertify UFCW. *The Tyee,* 29 June.

San Pedro, N. (2001). Improving Housing Outcomes for Refugees. *Parity, 14*(4), 4.

Sassen, S. (2004). The Repositioning of Citizenship. In A. Brysk & G. Shafir (Eds.), *People Out of Place* (pp. 191–208). New York: Routledge.

—. (2006). *Territory, Authority, Rights: From Medieval to Global Assemblages.* Princeton: Princeton University Press.

Schierup, C.-U. (2007). "Bloody Subcontracting" in the Network Society: Migration and Post-Fordist Restructuring across the European Union. In E. Berggren, B. Likic-Brboric, G. Toköz, & N. Trimikliniotis (Eds.), *Irregular Migration, Informal Labour and Community: A Challenge for Europe* (pp. 150–64). Maastrich: Shaker. http://dx.doi.org/10.1093/0198280521.003.0009.

Scott, D. (2004). *Conscripts of Modernity: The Tragedy of Colonial Enlightenment.* Durham: Duke University Press.

Scott, M. (2010). Immigration Information Forum. Presented at The Lighthouse, Toronto, 20 February.

Secor, A. (2004). "There Is an Istanbul That Belongs to Me": Citizenship, Space, and Identity in the City. *Annals of the Association of American Geographers. Association of American Geographers, 94*(2), 352–68. http://dx.doi.org/10.1111/j.1467-8306.2004.09402012.x.

Shafir, G. (Ed.). (1998). *The Citizenship Debates*. Minneapolis: University of Minnesota Press.

Shakir, U. (2007). Demystifying Transnationalism: Canadian Immigration Policy and the Promise of Nation Building. In L. Goldring & S. Krishnamurti (Eds.), *Organizing the Transnational: Labour, Politics, and Social Change* (pp. 67–82). Vancouver: UBC Press.

Shantz, J.A. (2005). No One Is Illegal: Organizing beyond Left Nationalism in Fortress North America. *Socialism and Democracy, 19*(2), 179–85. http://dx.doi.org/10.1080/08854300500122449.

Sharma, A. (2001). Healing the Wounds of Domestic Abuse: Improving the Effectiveness Of Feminist Therapeutic Interventions with Immigrant and Racially Visible Women Who Have Been Abused. *Violence Against Women, 7*(12), 1405–28. http://dx.doi.org/10.1177/10778010122183928.

Sharma, N. (2003). No Borders Movements and the Rejection of Left Nationalism. *Canadian Dimension, 37*(3), 37–9.

—. (2006). *Home Economics: Nationalism and the Making of "Migrant Workers" in Canada*. Toronto: University of Toronto Press.

—. (2007). Global Apartheid and Nation-Statehood: Instituting Border Regimes. In J. Goodman & P. James (Eds.), *Nationalism and Global Solidarities* (pp. 92–109). London: Routledge.

Sharma, N., & Wright, C. (2009). Decolonizing Resistance: Challenging Colonial States. *Social Justice), 35*(3), 120–38.

Sherrell, K., & Hyndman, J. (2006). Global Minds, Local Bodies: Kosovar Transnational Connections beyond British Columbia. *Refuge: Canada's Periodical on Refugees, 23*(1), 16–26.

Sherrell, K., & Immigrant Services Society of BC. (2009). *At Home in Surrey? The Housing Experiences of Refugees in Surrey, B.C.: Final Report*. Surrey: City of Surrey.

Shields, J., & Russell, B. (1994). Part-Time Workers, the Welfare State, and Labour Market Relations. In A. Johnson, S. McBride, & P. Smith (Eds.), *Continuities and Discontinuities: The Political Economy of Social Welfare and Labour Market Policy in Canada* (pp. 327–49). Toronto: University of Toronto Press.

Sidhu, N. (2008). *The Right to Learn: Access to Public Education for Non-status Immigrants*. Toronto: Community Social Planning Council of Toronto.

Sikes, P., & Piper, H. (2008). Risky Research or Researching Risk: The Role of Ethics Review. In J. Satterthwaite, M. Watts, & H. Piper (Eds.), *Talking Truth, Confronting Power*. Stoke on Trent, UK: Trentham.

Simich, L., Wu, F., & Nerad, S. (2007, Sept.–Oct.). Status and Health Security: An Exploratory Study of Irregular Immigrants in Toronto. *Canadian Journal of Public Health, 98*(5), 369–73. Medline:17985677

Smith, M.P., & Bakker, M. (2008). *Citizenship across Borders: The Political Transnationalism of* el migrante. Ithaca: Cornell University Press.

Smith, M., & Segal, J. (2008, Nov.). Healing Emotional and Psychological Trauma: Symptoms, Treatment, and Recovery. Retrieved 15 August 2010 from http://helpguide.org/mental/emotional_psychological_trauma.htm..

Stobart, L. (2009). Borders, Labour Impacts, and Union Responses: Case of Spain. *Refuge: Canada's Periodical on Refugees, 26*(2), 29–40.

Social Planning Toronto. (2010a). Toronto Community Services Resource Guide. Retrieved 24 October 2010 from http://socialplanningtoronto.org/wp-content/uploads/2010/10/Toronto_Community_Services_Resource_Guide_2010.pdf.

—. (2010b). Toronto's Social Landscape: 10-Year Trends, 1996–2006. Retrieved 3 February 2011 from http://socialplanningtoronto.org/reports/torontos-social-landscape/.

Solorzano, D.G., & Bernal, D.D. (2001). Examining Transformational Resistance through a Critical Race and Latcrit Theory Framework: Chicana and Chicano Students in an Urban Context. *Urban Education, 36*(3), 308–42. http://dx.doi.org/10.1177/0042085901363002.

Solorzano, D.G., & Yosso, T.J. (2001). Critical Race and Latrcit Theory and Method: Counter-Storytelling. *International Journal of Qualitative Studies in Education, 14*(4), 471–95. http://dx.doi.org/10.1080/09518390110063365.

Soysal, Y. (1994). *Limits of Citizenship: Migrants and Postnational Membership in Europe*. Chicago: University of Chicago Press.

Stark, L.J.M. (2006). Morality in Science: How Research Is Evaluated in the Age of Human Subjects Regulation. Doctoral diss., Princeton University.

Starr, A., & Adams, J. (2003). Anti-globalization: The Global Fight for Local Autonomy. *New Political Science, 25*(1), 19–42. http://dx.doi.org/10.1080/0739314032000071217.

Stasiulis, D., & Bakan, A. (1997). Negotiating Citizenship: The Case of Foreign Domestic Workers in Canada. *Feminist Review, 57*(1), 112–39. http://dx.doi.org/10.1080/014177897339687.

Stasiulis, D., & Bakan, A.B. (2005). *Negotiating Citizenship: Migrant Women in Canada and the Global System*. Toronto: University of Toronto Press.

Statistics Canada. (2010, 28 April). Canada's Population Estimates. *The Daily*. http://www.statcan.gc.ca/daily-quotidien/100628/dq100628a-eng.htm.

Stoffman, D. (2002). *Who Gets In: What's Wrong with Canada's Immigration Program – And How to Fix It.* Toronto: Macfarlane Walter & Ross.

Stothers, S. (2010). Immigration Information Forum. Panel presentation at The Lighthouse, Toronto, 17 April.

Stueck, W. (2008, 16 Sept.). Migrant Workers Fired from B.C. Greenhouse as Union Vote Neared. *Globe and Mail.* http://m.theglobeandmail.com/news/national/migrant-workers-fired-from-bc-greenhouse-as-union-vote-neared/article4179523/?service=mobile.

Suarez-Orozco, C., & Suarez-Orozco, M. (2001). *Children of Immigration.* Cambridge, MA: Harvard University Press.

Sundar, A. (2007). The South Asian Left Democratic Alliance: The Dilemmas of a Transnational Left. In L. Goldring & S. Krishnamurti (Eds.), *Organizing the Transnational: Labour, Politics, and Social Change* (pp. 206–14). Vancouver: UBC Press.

Sylvan, D., & Chetail, V. (2007–2011). Global Detention Project. Retrieved 19 September 2010 from http://www.globaldetentionproject.org.

Tambar, J. (2008, 7 Dec.). Foreign Farm Workers Fired and Evicted. *Toronto Star.* http://www.thestar.com/News/Ontario/article/549805.

Taylor, S. (1994). "Darkening the Complexion of Canadian Society": Black Activism, Policy-Making and Black Immigrants from the Caribbean to Canada, 1940s to 1960s. Doctoral diss., University of Toronto.

Thobani, S. (2007). *Exalted Subjects: Studies in the Making of Race and Nation in Canada.* Toronto: University of Toronto Press.

Thomas, D. (2010). Foreign Nationals Working Temporarily in Canada. In *Canadian Social Trends* (pp. 34–50). Ottawa: Statistics Canada. http://www.statcan.gc.ca/pub/11-008-x/11-008-x2010002-eng.htm.

Thomas, R.J. (1981). The Social Organization of Industrial Agriculture. *Insurgent Sociologist, 10,* 5–20.

—. (1992). *Citizenship, Gender and Work: Social Organization of Industrial Agriculture.* Los Angeles: University of California Press.

Toronto District School Board. (2007, 16 May). Summary of Decisions, Regular Meeting. Retrieved 1 July 2009 from http://www.tdsb.on.ca/wwwdocuments/students/pathways_for_success/docs/70516%20summ.pdf.

—. (2010). About the TDSB. Retrieved 20 August 2010 from http://www.tdsb.on.ca/aboutUs/.

Toronto Police Services. (2007). Victims and Witnesses without Legal Status. Retrieved 16 November 2010 from http://www.torontopolice.on.ca/publications/files/victims_and_witnesses_wthout_legal_status.pdf.

Toronto Refugee Affairs Council. (2005, Summer). Statistics: Refugee Claims, 2005. Retrieved 14 June 2010 from http://www.cleonet.ca/resource_files/TR-ACNewsletter.doc.

Torpey, J. (2000). *The Invention of the Passport: Surveillance, Citizenship and the State*. Cambridge: Cambridge University Press.

Tucker, E. (2006). Will the Vicious Circle of Precariousness Be Unbroken? The Exclusion of Ontario Farm Workers from the Occupational Health and Safety Act. In L.F. Vosko (Ed.), *Precarious Employment: Understanding Labour Market Insecurity in Canada* (pp. 256–76). Montreal/Kingston: McGill-Queen's University Press.

Tulchinsky, G. (Ed.). (1994). *Immigration in Canada: Historical Perspectives*. Toronto: Copp Clark Longman.

Turner, B.S. (2006). Citizenship and the Crisis of Multiculturalism. *Citizenship Studies, 10*(5), 607–18. http://dx.doi.org/10.1080/13621020600955041.

UNESCO. (2009). *Global Education Digest 2009, Comparing Education Statistics across the World*. Montreal: UNESCO Institute for Statistics.

UNHCR. (2011a). Canada: 2011 Regional Operations Profile – North America and the Caribbean. Retrieved 18 February 2011 from http://www.unhcr.org/cgi-bin/texis/vtx/page?page=49e491336.

—. (2011b). United Nations High Commissioner for Refugee's UNHCR Global Trends 2010 (cited 10 January 2012). Available from http://www.unhcr.org/pages/49c3646c4d6.html.

United Nations. (2008). International Migration Stock: The 2008 Revision. Retrieved 14 October 2010 from http://esa.un.org/migration/index.asp.

Valiani, S. (2007a). *Analysis, Solidarity, Action: A Worker's Perspective on the Growing Use of Migrant Labour in Canada*. Ottawa: Canadian Labour Congress.

—. (2007b). *The Temporary Foreign Worker Program and Its Intersection with Canadian Immigration Policy*. Ottawa: Canadian Labour Congress.

—. (2009). The Shift in Canadian Immigration Policy and Unheeded Lessons of the Live-in Caregiver Program. Retrieved on 7 December 2010 from http://mrzine.monthlyreview.org/2009/valiani030309.html.

Varela, A. (2009). Residency Documents for All! Notes to Understand the Movement of Migrants in Barcelona. *Refuge: Canada's Periodical on Refugees, 26*(2), 121–32.

Varsanyi, M.W. (2006). Interrogating "Urban Citizenship" vis-à-vis Undocumented Migrants. *Citizenship Studies, 10*(2), 229–49. http://dx.doi.org/10.1080/13621020600633168.

Vasta, E. (2011). Immigrants and the Paper Market: Borrowing, Renting and Buying Identities. *Ethnic and Racial Studies, 34*(2), 187–206. http://dx.doi.org/10.1080/01419870.2010.509443.

Veronis, L. (2006). *Rethinking Transnationalism: Latin Americans' Experiences of Migration and Participation in Toronto.* CERIS Working Paper no. 51. Toronto: CERIS.

Vicente, T.L. (2000). Irregular Immigrants to Spain. *Research on Immigration and Integration in the Metropolis: Working Paper Series* (Special Edition). Vol. 00–S2. Vancouver: Vancouver Centre of Excellence.

Vidal, S.M.S. (2000). *Brasileiros no Canadá: A descoberta de novos caminhos.* Master's thesis, Pontifícia Universidade Católica de São Paulo, Brazil.

Villegas, F. (2010). Strategic in/Visibility and Undocumented Migrants. In G.J.S. Dei & M. Simmons (Eds.), *Fanon & Education: Thinking through Pedagogical Possibilities* (pp. 147–70). New York: Peter Lang.

Villegas, P.E. (2012). Assembling and Re(marking) Migrant Illegalization: Mexican Migrants with Precarious Status in Toronto. Doctoral thesis, OISE/University of Toronto.

Villegas, P.E., & Landolt, P. (2010). Negotiating Access to Public Goods: Providing Healthcare to Toronto Immigrants with Precarious Status. Paper presented at the conference Healthcare for the Undocumented and Uninsured, Toronto, 12 February.

Vosko, L.F. (Ed.). (2006). *Precarious Employment: Understanding Labour Market Insecurity in Canada.* Montreal/Kingston: McGill-Queen's University Press.

Vosko, L. (2010). *Managing the Margins: Gender, Citizenship, and the International Regulation of Precarious Employment.* Oxford: Oxford University Press.

Vosko, L.F., Zukewich, N., & Cranford, C. (2003). *Precarious Jobs: A New Typology of Employment. Perspectives on Labour and Income.* Statistics Canada, Catalogue no. 75–001-XIE.

Walker, J.W.S.G. (1997). *"Race," Rights and the Law in the Supreme Court of Canada.* Waterloo: Osgoode Society for Canadian Legal History/Wilfrid Laurier University Press.

Walters, W. (2010). Deportation, Expulsion, and the International Police of Aliens. In N. de Genova & N. Peutz (Eds.), *The Deportation Regime: Sovereignty, Space, and Freedom of Movement* (pp. 69–100). Durham: Duke University Press. http://dx.doi.org/10.1080/1362102022000011612.

Watt, S. (2006). *Formal and Practiced Citizenships: "Non Status" Algerians and Montreal, Canada.* Master's thesis, York University, Toronto.

Weissbrodt, D., & Meili, S. (2009). Human Rights and Protection of Non-Citizens: Whither Universality and Indivisibility of Rights? *Refugee Survey Quarterly, 28*(4), 34–58. http://dx.doi.org/10.1093/rsq/hdq020.

Wellesley Institute. (2010). *Precarious Housing in Canada.*Toronto: Wellesley Institute. Available at http://www.wellesleyinstitute.com/publication/new-report-precarious-housing-in-canada-2010.

Wheeler, M. (2009, 13 July). Children of Undocumented Parents May Be at Higher Developmental Risk. Retrieved 15 May2011 from http://www.ucla-health.org/body.cfm?xyzpdqabc=0&id=403&action=detail&ref=1242.

Wicker, H.-R. (2010). Deportation at the Limits of "Tolerance": The Juridical, Institutional, and Social Construction of "Illegality" in Switzerland. In N. de Genova and N. Peutz (Eds.), *The Deportation Regime: Sovereignty, Space, and Freedom of Movement* (pp. 224–44). Durham: Duke University Press.

Wigmore, J.H. (1905). *A Treatise on the System of Evidence in Trials at Common Law, Including the Statuses and Judicial Decisions of All Jurisdictions of the United States, England and Canada.* Boston: Little, Brown.

Winter, E. (2010). Trajectories of Multiculturalism in Germany, the Netherlands and Canada: In Search of Common Patterns. *Government and Opposition,* 45(2), 166–86. http://dx.doi.org/10.1111/j.1477-7053.2009.01309.x.

Women's College Hospital. (2009). Women's College Hospital Health Equity Plan. http://www.womenscollegehospital.ca/pdfs/Health_Equity_Plan(February262009).pdf. Accessed 1 December 2010.

—. (2010). Women's College Hospital Network on Uninsured Clients. http://www.womenscollegehospital.ca/programs/network-on-uninsured-clients.html. Accessed 5 August 2010.

Workers' Compensation Board – Alberta. (2004a). Principles of Alberta Workers' Compensation. In *WCB Policies and Information Manual.* Retrieved 3 November 2009 from http://www.wcb.ab.ca/pdfs/public/policy/manual/printable_pdfs/0405_2_app2.pdf.

—. (2004b). Return-to-Work Services. In *WCB Policies and Information Manual.* Retrieved 3 November 2009 from http://www.wcb.ab.ca/pdfs/public/policy/manual/printable_pdfs/0405_2_app2.pdf.

—. (2008). 2008 Annual Report. Retrieved 3 November 2009 from http://www.wcb.ab.ca/pdfs/public/annual_report_2008.pdf.

World Health Organization. (2003). *International Migration, Health and Human Rights.* Retrieved 7 March 2010 from http://www.who.int/hhr/activities/en/FINAL-Migrants-English-June04.pdf.

—. (2010). *Health of Migrants – The Way Forward: Report of a Global Consultation, Madrid, Spain, 3–5 March 2010.* Geneva: WHO.

Worthington, C., & Myers, T. (2003, May). Factors Underlying Anxiety in HIV Testing: Risk Perceptions, Stigma, and the Patient-Provider Power Dynamic. *Qualitative Health Research,* 13(5), 636–55. http://dx.doi.org/10.1177/1049732303013005004. Medline:12756685.

Wright, C. (2000). Nowhere at Home: Gender, Race and the Making of Anti-immigrant Discourse in Canada. *Atlantis,* 24(2), 38–48.

—.. (2003). Moments of Emergence: Organizing by and with Undocumented and Non-citizen People in Canada after September 11. *Refuge: Canada's Periodical on Refugees, 21*(3), 5–15.

—. (2006). Against Illegality: New Directions in Organizing by and with Non-status People in Canada. In C. Frampton, G. Kinsman, A.K. Thompson, & K. Tilleczek (Eds.), *Sociology for Changing the World: Social Movements/Social Research* (pp. 189–208). Halifax: Fernwood.

Yau, M. (1995). *Refugee Students in Toronto Schools: An Exploratory Study.* Toronto: Toronto Board of Education, Research Services.

Young, J.E.E. (2007). "I've Been Illegal My Whole Life": Spatial Performances of Uncertain Legal Status. Paper presented at Redefining Borders: Dialogues of Displacement, Identity, and Community Conference, Toronto, 3 May.

—. (2005). "This Is My Life": Questions of Agency and Belonging among Youth Living with Less Than Full Status. Master's major research paper, Ryerson University.

—. (2011). "A New Politics of the City": Locating the Limits of Hospitality and Practicing the City-as-Refuge. *ACME: An International E-Journal for Critical Geographies, 10*(3), 534–63.

Zentella, A.C. (1997). *Growing Up Bilingual: Puerto Rican Children in New York.* Malden, MA: Blackwell.

Zine, J. (2002). *Living on the Ragged Edges: Absolute and Hidden Homelessness among Latin Americans and Muslims in West Central Toronto.* Equinox Research and Consulting Services.

Zlolniski, C. (2006). *Janitors, Street Vendors, and Activists: The Lives of Mexican Immigrants in Silicon Valley.* Berkeley: University of California.

—. (2008). Political Mobilization and Activism among Latinos/as in the United States. In H. Rodríguez, R. Sáenz, & C. Menjívar (Eds.), *Latinas/os in the United States: Changing the Face of América* (pp. 352–68). New York: Springer. http://dx.doi.org/10.1007/978-0-387-71943-6_23.

Zolberg, A., & Woon, L.L. (1999). Why Islam Is Like Spanish: Cultural Incorporation in Europe and the United States. *Politics & Society, 27*(1), 5–38. http://dx.doi.org/10.1177/0032329299027001002.

Index

The letter t *following a page number denotes a table; the letter* f *following a page number denotes a figure.*